Also by Anna Thomas

The Vegetarian Epicure
The Vegetarian Epicure, Book Two

The New Vegetarian Epicure

The New Vegetarian Epicure

Menus for family and friends

By ANNA THOMAS

Illustrations by RODICA PRATO

ALFRED A. KNOPF New York 1996

This Is a Borzoi Book
Published by Alfred A. Knopf, Inc.

Copyright © 1996 by Anna Thomas
Illustrations copyright © 1996 by Rodica Prato

All rights reserved under International and Pan-American Copyright
Conventions. Published in the United States by Alfred A. Knopf, Inc.,
New York, and simultaneously in Canada by Random House of Canada
Limited, Toronto. Distributed by Random House, Inc., New York.

Library of Congress Cataloging-in-Publication Data

Thomas, Anna.
The new vegetarian epicure :
menus for family and friends / by Anna Thomas
p.   cm.
Includes index.
ISBN 0-679-42714-7
0-679-76588-3 (pbk.)
1. Vegetarian cookery.   I. Title.
TX837.T463   1996
641.5'636—dc20   95-25656
CIP

Manufactured in the United States of America

First Edition

For Christopher and Teddy—eat your vegetables!

Acknowledgments

I'd like to express my gratitude to the many people who helped me make this book—my family, who were the first to try everything; Guillermina Alonzo, who taught me so much about chiles and nopalitos; Liz Gardner, who helped me tame the manuscript in the computer; Judith Jones, my extraordinary editor; and all my wonderful friends who pour through the kitchen in waves whenever I'm cooking for a big event, chopping and slicing and stirring and laughing, doing all the hard work and making me look good.

Contents

Little Dinner Parties for
Fall and Winter   187

Recipes

Salads

A Big Tossed Salad

A Relish Plate

Beet Salad in Raspberry Vinaigrette

Fresh Herb Salad

Minted Tomato Salad with Feta Cheese

Panzanella

Revised Caesar Salad

Rice and Corn Salad

Roasted Beet, Asparagus, and Garlic Salad

Roasted Green Bean Salad

Salad of Arugula and Persimmons

Salad of Arugula and Radicchio

Salad of Bitter Greens

Salad of Endive, Avocado, Grapefruit, and Fennel

Salad of Endive, Fennel, Roquefort, and Celery

Salad of Peppery Greens

Salad of Radicchio, Fuji Apples, and Pistachio Nuts

Spa Salad with Bitter Greens, Asparagus, and Mint

Summer Tomato Salad

Teddy's Fruit Salad

Tri-Color Salad

Tuscan Salad

Watercress and Curly Endive Salad

Watercress and Radicchio Salad

Yogurt with Cucumber, Mint, Raisins, and Nuts

HEARTY SALADS

Haricots Verts, Red Potato, and Cucumber Salad

Lentil Salad

Mixed Greek Salad

Nopalito Salad

Salad with Sautéed Mushrooms

Salad with Wheat Pilaf and Red Grapes

Stuffed Artichokes

White Bean and Tomato Salad

White Bean Salad

Wild Rice Salad

Appetizers, Pestos, and Spreads

Baba Ganouj

Bruschetta with Caramelized Fennel and Onion

Charred Tomatoes with Garlic and Olives

Cheddar Cheese Straws

Dolmades (Stuffed Vine Leaves)

Eggplant and Olive Relish

Fresh Cheese with Basil Pesto

Fresh-Chopped Tomatoes with Basil

Breads

Pasta and Polenta

PASTA

POLENTA

Savory Tarts, Frittatas, and Other Substantial Dishes

Crepes and Griddlecakes

Vegetable Dishes

Roasted Fennel and Red Onions

Roasted Green Beans with Garlic

Roasted Kabocha Squash and Green Tomatoes

Roasted Pearl Onions and Green Beans

Roasted Potatoes and Fennel

Roasted Radicchio and Endive

Roasted Summer Vegetables

Roasted Whole Garlic

Roasted Winter Squash and Apples

Roasted Yams with Green Tomatoes

Sautéed Spinach and Garlic

Sautéed Winter Greens

Stewed Green Tomatoes with Red Jalapeños

Stuffed Artichokes

Timbales of Tahitian Squash and Pears

Winter Vegetable Stew

Yogurt and Potatoes with Mint

Legumes

Black Bean Chili

Black Bean Tacos

Black Bean Tostadas

Boiled Pinto Beans

Everyday Black Beans

Hummous

Lentil Salad

Lima Bean Purée

Refried Pinto Beans

Stewed Garbanzo Beans and Potatoes in Indian Spices

Tuscan White Beans

Tuscan White Beans with Chard

White Bean and Tomato Salad

White Bean Salad

White Beans with Baby Potatoes and Herbs

Risotto, Pilaf, and Couscous

Brown and Wild Rice Pilaf

Bulgur Pilaf

Couscous with Moroccan Spices

Cranberry Couscous

Fragrant Rice Pilaf with Currants and Almonds

Fresh Tomato Risotto

Garlic and Cumin Rice

Rice and Corn Salad

Rice Pilaf

Risotto di Zucca

Risotto with Zucchini Flowers

Simple Couscous

Sweet Corn Risotto

Wheat and Lentil Pilaf

Wild Mushroom Risotto

Wild Rice Pilaf Frittata

Wild Rice Salad

Salsas, Relishes, and Salad Dressings

Chile Ancho Salsa

Chunky Tomato Sauce

Cranberry Chutney

Cranberry Sauce

Cranberry, Orange, and
Red Wine Sauce

Cranberry-Jalapeño Sauce

Ginger-Sesame Dressing

Green Chile and Mint
Chutney

Guacamole

Guajillo Chile Salsa

Hot Chipotle Salsa

Mole Poblano

Roasted Tomato Sauce

Salsa Cruda

Sesame Oil Dressing

Simple Chipotle Sauce

Summer Tomato Sauce

Sweet Chipotle Sauce

Sweet Red Pepper Purée

Tomato and Garlic
Fondue

Tomato Sauce for the
Winter

Snacks and Sandwiches

Avocado Sandwiches

Cheese Toasts

Chopped Egg and Dill
Sandwiches

Garlic Bread

Molletes

Pan Bagnia

Parmesan Cheese Toasts

Pumpernickel Parmesan
Toasts

Quesadillas

Toasts with Grilled
Chèvre

Tomato Sandwiches for
a Summertime Tea

Watercress Sandwiches

Miscellaneous

Bread Stuffing with
Apples and Walnuts

Cabbage Filling for
Pierogi

Cafe de Olla

Fruit Smoothie

Herbed Croutons

Mimosas

Potato Filling for Pierogi

Pumpkin Butter

Toasted Walnuts with
Rosemary and Sage

Yogurt Cheese

Cookies, Pastries, and Cakes

Anise Cookies

Apple and Pear Crumble

Apple Crisp

Apple Pie

Basque Cake

Biscotti

Brownies

Buttermilk Coffee Cake

Chocolate and Chile Torte

Chocolate Caramel Nut Tart

Chocolate-Dipped Macaroons

Chocolate Spongecake

Cranberry Tart

Easter Baba

Gypsy Mazurek

Honey Pie

Pineapple Meringue Torte

Plum and Walnut Galette

Pumpkin Cheesecake

Russian Tea Cakes

Rustic Plum Pie

Walnut Tart

Warm Chocolate Cakes

Puddings and Desserts

Apple Pudding

Applesauce

Baked Pears in Caramel Syrup

Berry Cobbler

Chilled Orange Slices in Grand Marnier and Cognac

Chunky Applesauce

Clafouti with Apricots

Coffee Flan

Flan with Caramel and Pineapple

Parfaits of Fruit and Mascarpone

Pumpkin Flan

White Peach Mousse

White Peach Mousse in Chocolate Collars

Winter Fruit Compote

Yogurt Cheese with Honey and Fresh Figs

SWEET SAUCES

Caramelized Walnut and Ginger Sauce

Crème Anglaise

Raspberry Coulis

Sweetened Yogurt Cream

Sorbets and Ice Creams

Cafe de Olla Sorbet

Cardamom Ice Cream

Cassis Sorbet

Cinnamon Custard Ice Cream

Coffee Granita

Fresh Peach Ice Cream

Green Apple Sorbet

Lemon Cheesecake Ice Cream

Mango Sorbet

Orange and Mango Sorbet

Pear Sorbet

Pink Grapefruit Sorbet

Strawberry Ice Cream with Triple Sec

Rosemary Sorbet

Introduction

I wrote the original *Vegetarian Epicure* when I was barely out of my teens, in a rush of enthusiasm for the great-tasting food I wanted to enjoy but could not find in the cookbooks I saw then. In the late sixties and early seventies, when I was a college student, vegetarianism was a popular idea, but most vegetarian food was pretty awful. I wanted food made from fresh ingredients, not a substitute for anything but true to its own bright flavors and, above all, delicious to eat. I wanted to enjoy myself, not deny myself. The book I wrote seemed to fill that need for me and, to my great delight, for a great many others. That first *Vegetarian Epicure*, and its sequel, *The Vegetarian Epicure, Book Two*, captured the *geist* of a certain time—it was a guilt-free era, when butter and cream were used without a care and when cheese ruled. Today, of course, our attitudes are different. And while some may say, "Alas, things are so different now," I say thank goodness they are. We are all finding healthier ways to eat and enjoying lighter food, and I, for one, have never enjoyed it more. But this is not the only change that inspired me to work on a new book.　The years roll by, crowded with living, and so many things have changed since then. I have lived and cooked in many different situations. I have traveled and worked. I've started raising two wonderful children. I've grown older. My food now is a product of those years. It's full of souvenirs of life abroad and things learned from friends.　As a country, too, we've grown more sophisticated about cooking. Ethnic and cultural influences keep surfacing, and the availability of good raw materials continues to expand. Ingredients that were unheard of twenty years ago are now common on supermarket shelves, and farmers' markets are sprouting up everywhere, providing the freshest seasonal produce in greater abundance than ever. American food is not just healthier but infinitely more interesting and varied than it was when I first started to cook.　Still, above all, this is a personal book, about the flavors I love, the places I've been, and the way I cook now.　Because I adore Italy and Provence, because I've spent time in many Mediterranean regions and live in a similar climate, virgin olive oil, sweet basil, ripe tomatoes, and peppery green leaves are essential to me. Because I live in southern California and I'm crazy about chiles, the flavors of Mexican and southwestern foods have become a part of me, too. And because I'm Polish, I learned to make Easter Baba from my mother, and the taste of wild forest mushrooms runs in my veins.　I decided to organize this book around menus for two reasons. First, because I so much enjoy putting things together in interesting ways and also because I like planning a menu to suit the season and the moment. For me, it's another recipe—the big recipe for the whole experience of the meal. But I've also found that many people who want to eat well in new ways are baffled when it comes to devising a menu without meat as a main course. I hope that these menus, arranged loosely according to seasons, will be used as guides and will give rise to many creative variations.   Some of what I cook now is fancier, like the big multicourse dinners I've done for events and celebrations. A lot of it is simpler than ever: the plain, rustic foods that kids love, and I do too. And, of course, my cooking is lighter and leaner now than it once was—with a few indulgent exceptions.   And yet, the really important things don't change. Food is part of our lives every day. We eat to live, and why not live well? Fresh food, prepared with pleasure, is a wonderful thing—whether it is a piece of home-baked country bread with a thick slice of ripe tomato from the garden eaten at the kitchen table or a dinner party served with crystal and silver, with guests in their elegant clothes. Good food brings sustenance and joy. Friendships are formed over it, wounds are healed, milestones are celebrated, and children raised on it. Good food is more than a recipe; it's part of everything else.   I'm flattered when people tell me they've used one of my recipes—and what a delicious dish it made. And then I'm amused when they add, apologetically, "But I changed it a little—I didn't do it exactly the way it's written . . ." Well, of course not. Why should you? You're cooking, not slavishly following a formula. You're participating in something that's part of nature, and nature is always alive, always changing. Moreover, cooking is a fusion of nature with culture. Food binds us to our roots as strongly as any song or poem. Many of us have learned more about our ancestors in the kitchen than we ever will from a book. The mother who stirs the soup and says to her children "Eat your vegetables" might also say "Eat your history." And no recipe from a book will ever have the meaning of the food we learn to make at someone's side, hands in the dough together, watching, kneading, tasting, smelling, learning, and holding dear. Early on in my cooking days, I realized that I have as much fun preparing food as I do eating it. I know we live in an age of fast food, but I admit to a strong bias for slow food. I talk frequently about the importance of using good ingredients, but the truly essential ingredient of all my food is the pleasure I take in preparing it. Yes, there are times when the various demands of life collide, and food must be prepared and eaten on the run. I have children who have soccer schedules, play rehearsals, piano recitals, and important dates with friends. I have jobs, meetings, and deadlines. I know that life cannot always be an ideal of relaxed gourmet cooking in a sunlit kitchen, wine with dinner, dishes washed by helpful children, and no weight gain from dessert. I live with reality like everyone else, and there are times when I will gladly settle just for the sight of my kids eating a green vegetable. I myself have eaten a fast sandwich for lunch. I've eaten it in the car, on my way to work, between phone calls.　　　It's too easy to get caught up in the rush of things and lose the enjoyment of them. For me, a day spent at the farmers' market, in the kitchen, and at the table with my family is a beautiful day well spent. I love to choose the nicest produce, see the changes of the season in the market stalls, take my time preparing food, and enjoy it at leisure with congenial company. Now I have a new enjoyment: a few days ago, my eleven-year-old son, Christopher, said to me, "Mom, tonight I want to fix dinner." He measured my curious stare for a moment and then added, "And I want you to show me how." What a real source of pleasure we lose when we think of cooking as a mere chore!　　　Food is not a chore; it's a gift. Food shared with others repays you many times over.　　　And cooking is mythology—a story told over and over, passed on again and again, always with the same meaning but expressed in endlessly different ways.　　　Perhaps I love cooking even more because it has never been my profession. I am a dedicated and ardent amateur. I was not trained for restaurant cooking, and the foods in this book are all things I've cooked at home and eaten with my family or friends. They are the foods I love. Their tastes, their vivid colors, and fragrant aromas are part of my life. This is my telling of the story, and I hope you like it, change it, and make it part of yours.

The New
Vegetarian
Epicure

Spring

and

Summer

AN EARLY SPRING DINNER

*Spa Salad with Bitter Greens,
Asparagus, and Mint*

Risotto di Zucca

*Strawberries
with Honey-Sweetened Yogurt Cheese*

This is a delightful meal for early spring or even late
winter, when you can still find good winter squashes and when
asparagus is arriving in the markets.

If it's too early to find slender, crunchy asparagus
to slice raw into the salad, something else could be sneaked in—
sugar peas, or even the tender stalks of broccoli, peeled and thinly
sliced. The important thing is the sparkling combination of
tastes in the salad, followed by the richness of the risotto, which
is so satisfying, yet amazingly low in fat.

Bright-red juicy strawberries for dessert, with a dollop of
Honey-Sweetened Yogurt Cheese, are perfect for the season and
in keeping with the very low-fat style of this meal. If you are
watching your fat intake diligently, use yogurt cheese made from
non-fat yogurt. And if you don't care, a wedge of Gorgonzola
cheese and a ripe pear would also make a fabulous ending.

SPA SALAD WITH BITTER GREENS, ASPARAGUS, AND MINT

I made up this salad once when I gave a talk about "spa cuisine," of all things. I wanted to give an example of why good salads did not need much oil or heavy dressing. If the salad is made of good things to begin with, things that are full of intense flavor, it stands to reason that you don't have to douse them with a lot of sauce. This combination of green, red, white, and gold tastes as explosively bright as it looks—it is tart and sweet, pungent and mild, and a teaspoon of good olive oil per serving feels like plenty to me.

½ lb. fresh young arugula (1 quart torn pieces)	¾ cup cooked adzuki beans
3–4 heads Belgian endive	½ cup thinly sliced green onions
¼ cup mint leaves	2–3 Tbs. golden raisins
1 large red bell pepper	2 Tbs. fruity green olive oil
½ lb. slender green asparagus	a splash of balsamic vinegar
4 oz. inoki mushrooms	a few drops soy sauce
	fresh-ground pepper to taste

Wash the arugula and spin it dry, then tear it into manageable pieces, discarding any heavy stems. You should have a full quart of torn greens. Wash and slice crosswise the Belgian endive, discarding the woody core in the center. Slice the clean mint leaves into strips if they are large, or just cut them in half if they are smaller.

Quarter the red bell pepper lengthwise, core it, and slice the quarters crosswise very thinly. Slice off the asparagus tips, then continue slicing thinly on a slant, using only the tender part of the stalk, and put the tips and slices into a large, shallow bowl. Raw asparagus is delightful in a salad, but you must stop short of the tough, fibrous bottom.

Trim off the bottoms of the inoki mushrooms above the point where their stems join together. Wash them, and dry them gently on a tea towel. Rinse and drain the cooked adzuki beans.

Toss the prepared ingredients together in the bowl with the asparagus, adding the oil, vinegar, soy sauce, and pepper at the end, just before serving.

This serves 6–8 people generously as a first-course salad. It is also interesting enough to be the centerpiece of a spring lunch for 4; just add a soup and some good bread.

Substitutions: This salad is wonderful because of the particular contrasts of flavor and texture, so substitute if you must, but with care. If you can't find good arugula, watercress could be used, or a combination of watercress and radicchio, but you need something with that peppery zing. The inoki mushrooms are pretty much available in supermarkets now, but they could be replaced with fresh white champignons, cleaned and very thinly sliced. I buy adzuki beans in the Asian section of a local health food store, but small black beans or cooked lentils could be used instead.

RISOTTO DI ZUCCA

My version of this Italian winter classic is a Kabocha squash risotto in which some of the dense golden squash falls apart into a sauce, and some stays in chunks amongst the rice. The nutty taste of Marsala and the caramelized onions support the sweet flavor of the squash. A touch of balsamic vinegar offsets it. The result is a rich and beautiful flavor with a hint of acid to enliven it.

2–3 medium-sized yellow onions
   (3 cups sliced)
1 medium-sized Kabocha squash*
   (2¼ lbs., about 3–4 cups cubed)
1½ Tbs. olive oil
1 Tbs. butter
1 clove garlic, chopped
1 tsp. salt
1 tsp. crumbled dried sage leaves

about 5 cups Basic Light Vegetable
   Broth (page 412, or canned
   broth)
1½ cups Arborio rice
¼ cup Marsala
¾ cup white wine
1 Tbs. balsamic vinegar
fresh-ground black pepper

garnishes: fresh-grated Parmesan cheese
           basil leaves, cut in thin slivers

Peel the onions and cut them in quarters, then slice them crosswise. Peel the Kabocha squash, cutting away any dark-green parts, seed it, and cut the firm yellow flesh into ½-inch cubes.

Heat the oil and butter in a large, preferably non-stick sauté pan. Add the onions and chopped garlic and stir over high heat for 3–4 minutes, then add the cubed squash, salt, and crumbled sage. Continue cooking on medium-high heat, stirring often, until the vegetables are spotted with golden brown and the

---

If Kabocha squash is unavailable, you can use buttercup squash, one of the Hubbards, or a couple of acorn squashes. Avoid the blander varieties such as butternut and banana squashes—you want rich, sweet flavor for this.

squash is becoming tender—about 15 minutes. Meanwhile, heat the vegetable broth to a simmer.

Add the rice to the squash mixture and stir constantly for 2 minutes. Add the Marsala, stir quickly as it cooks away, then add the white wine.

When the wine has all been absorbed, add about a cup of the hot broth, along with the balsamic vinegar. Lower the heat to a simmer and stir the risotto gently with a wooden spoon. As the broth is absorbed, add another ladle, and then another, always keeping the rice moist, and stirring constantly or at least very often. Some of the squash will fall apart into a purée.

Use as much broth as you need to achieve rice that is *al dente,* tender but firm, with a creamy sauce around it. It will take about 30 minutes, but start tasting after 20 minutes.

At that point, correct the seasoning with a touch more salt and some pepper if needed, and stir in about ¼ cup of grated Parmesan cheese. Add another ½ ladle of broth, stir well, and serve at once in warmed, shallow bowls. Garnish each serving with slivers of fresh basil, and pass more Parmesan cheese separately.

Serves 6.

STRAWBERRIES WITH HONEY-SWEETENED YOGURT CHEESE

2 cups Yogurt Cheese (page 77)　　**6 cups sliced ripe strawberries**
6–8 Tbs. honey　　**1–3 tsp. balsamic vinegar**

optional garnish: mint sprigs

Combine the Yogurt Cheese with 5 tablespoons of honey and whisk together until smooth. In a separate bowl, sprinkle the strawberries with a little balsamic vinegar, then drizzle them with 1–3 tablespoons of honey. How much vinegar and how much honey you use will be determined by how sweet or tart the berries are. Stir the berries gently with a large spoon, making sure not to bruise them.

Spoon the berries and their juice into 8 sorbet glasses, and top each serving with about ¼ cup of the sweetened Yogurt Cheese. Garnish with mint sprigs if desired.

Serves 8.

A MEXICAN DINNER

Fresh Corn Tamales with queso fresco and salsa
Black Bean Chili
Mango Sorbet

Here are the principal foods of pre-Columbian America: corn, beans, chiles, fruit. The flavors are straightforward and delicious, and the other beauty of this meal is that everything can be prepared ahead, so it works for the family or for a big group.

The tamales are the essence of corn—these are the simple tamales, with no filling. Tamales are actually not very hard to make, and you can prepare enough for six or eight people in less than an hour, but it's really a lot of fun to make tamales for a crowd. You do it with a circle of friends, and it becomes a social event of its own. Once we made about four hundred tamales for a school rummage sale—it was a blast.

Serve the tamales hot from the steamer, with your favorite fresh white cheese and a good salsa. The Black Bean Chili that follows is a hearty dish, and not terribly hot, but you could certainly crank up the volume on the chiles in it if you wish. After that, Mango Sorbet is just the clean, sweet, tropical taste you want.

If this is a party, and not just a Tuesday night dinner, you could add guacamole and fresh tortilla chips with margaritas at the start, or a ceviche if you eat fish. Then decorate the sorbet with bittersweet chocolate bark for a fancy dessert.

Variation: For an easier dinner, save the tamales for another time and serve the Black Bean Chili with cornbread (see Honey-Sweetened Buttermilk Cornbread, page 111). Cornbread can be made any time of the year, and does not require fresh corn or dried husks, so an hour of preparation time goes down to ten minutes for mixing up the batter. Add a salad if you like. For dessert, serve warm applesauce with cool cream, or a good store-bought ice cream.

FRESH CORN TAMALES

When I want a plain tamale, buttery and full of the taste of fresh corn, this is it. It can be served with a raw or cooked salsa, some queso fresco or any soft white cheese, and some sliced fruit—a combination that works for breakfast, lunch, or dinner.

3 cups roasted or steamed fresh corn kernels (about 4 large ears of corn)*
30–40 large dried corn husks (to yield 16–20)
1½ cups milk, or slightly more if needed

2 cups masa harina (page 34)
2 tsp. baking powder
1 tsp. salt
1 cup + 2 Tbs. butter, softened

To roast corn: Put the ears of corn, still in their husks, on a cookie sheet, and roast them in a 400° oven for about 40 minutes. Your kitchen will smell great. Allow them to cool a bit, then husk them and clean off the silk. Discard the husks; these are not the ones you will use to wrap the tamales.

To prepare the dried corn husks: Start with at least twice as many dried corn husks as you will need (they usually come in packages of a few dozen). Soak them in hot water for about 30 minutes. When they're soft, rinse them under running water as you separate them, discarding the very small or torn ones. Lay them flat on a plate and keep them covered with a damp tea towel until you need them. The longer torn ones can be torn further, into ½-inch strips, and used for ties.

To prepare the masa: Slice the kernels off of the roasted or steamed corn and scrape the cobs well. Simmer the corn in the milk for about 10 minutes, or until it's quite soft. Purée the mixture in a blender. Sometimes at this point I reserve a few spoonfuls of the corn kernels, and then stir them into the finished masa for more texture.

Sift together the dry masa, baking powder, and salt. In a large bowl, whip the softened butter with an electric mixer until it is fluffy. Alternately add spoonfuls of the corn purée and the dry mixture, beating each time, until everything is well combined. The masa should be light and fluffy, but firm enough to hold a stiff shape. Fold in the whole corn kernels if you have reserved them.

---

*Frozen corn kernels can be substituted in the winter. Spread them on a cookie sheet and roast in a 400° oven for about 10–15 minutes.

To form the tamales: Lay a prepared corn husk flat on your work surface. Put about ¼ cup of masa in the center of it and spread it slightly. Be sure to leave at least a 1½-inch border on each side and a couple of inches at each end.

Fold one side of the husk gently over the masa, then fold the narrow, pointy end in, and then finish rolling up the whole husk, loosely. If you have extra-long husks, you can fold the wide end in as well, envelope style, before you finish rolling, but this is not absolutely necessary.

Tie a thin strip of corn husk around the middle to hold everything together, but not too tightly, as the tamale will expand in cooking. If you have trouble tying strips of corn husk, use plain brown twine, or any other kind of tie that won't react with the food in steaming.

Forming tamales is tricky the first time, but soon gets much easier, and then becomes a lot of fun.

To steam the tamales: Arrange them loosely in a roomy vegetable steamer. If you left the wide end unfolded, be sure to handle them carefully and fit them into the steamer with the open end up. Steam the tamales for 35–45 minutes, then serve.

Tamales can be prepared a few hours ahead of time and held in the refrigerator, covered, until it's time to steam them—just add a few minutes to the cooking time to take the chill off. They can also be resteamed briefly a day or two later.

This makes 16 fairly large tamales.

BLACK BEAN CHILI

1 lb. dried black beans
pinch of baking soda
1 whole onion, peeled
2 whole cloves garlic
5–6 branches cilantro
1 tsp. salt, more to taste
    (3 lbs. canned black beans
    could be used in place of the
    first five ingredients)
5 ancho chiles (whole pods, dried)
2 chipotle chiles (whole pods, dried)
4 tsp. cumin seeds

4 tsp. dried oregano leaves
4 tsp. paprika
2–3 Tbs. corn oil, or olive oil
3 yellow onions, chopped
5 cloves garlic, minced
1 bay leaf
1 15-oz. can chopped tomatoes
½–1 tsp. salt
1–2 Tbs. wine vinegar
2–3 Tbs. chopped roasted green
   chiles (Ortega is OK)
½ cup chopped cilantro leaves

garnishes: sour cream
          additional green chiles
          shredded cheddar cheese
          cilantro leaves

If you're starting with dried beans, soak them overnight in cool water to cover with a pinch of baking soda, then change the water and simmer them with the whole onion, whole garlic cloves, and cilantro branches until almost tender. Cooking time will vary with the age of the beans, and could be anywhere from 1 hour to 3–4 hours. Stir in the salt and continue simmering until the beans are perfectly tender, adding water if needed to keep them covered with liquid. Discard the onion, garlic, and cilantro when the beans are done.

Meanwhile, soak the dried ancho and chipotle chiles in hot water to cover for about 20 minutes. When they are soft and pliable, take them out, remove the stems and as many seeds as come away easily, and then purée them with the soaking water in a blender or food processor.* Press the purée through a medium strainer and discard the skins.

Toast the cumin seeds in a small skillet until they begin to release their aroma. Add the dried oregano and the paprika, remove from the heat, and stir together in the hot pan for about a minute. Then pour the spice mixture into a stone mortar and grind it to a coarse powder. Add the spices to the chile purée.

See note about working with chiles on page 365.

Heat the oil in a large sauté pan and sauté the onions and minced garlic in it, with a bay leaf, until they just begin to color. Stir in the chile purée, the chopped tomatoes with their juices, the salt, the vinegar, and the chopped green chiles. Add the beans, with their liquid, and simmer the mixture over low heat, stirring occasionally, until it has the consistency you like. Stir in the ½ cup of chopped cilantro leaves.

Serve hot, with any or all of the garnishes, accompanied by cornbread, tamales, or any good bread.

Serves 8–10 generously.

MANGO SORBET

Treat yourself to this exceptional sorbet if you can get some ripe mangoes.

2 cups water	½–¾ cup fresh lemon juice
1 cup sugar	1 tsp. lemon zest, finely grated
2 cups mango pieces (2–3 ripe mangoes)	2 Tbs. Triple Sec

Put the water and sugar in an enameled pot and heat gently, stirring occasionally, until the sugar is completely dissolved. Wash down any sugar crystals from the sides with a brush or by swirling the liquid. Simmer the syrup for a few minutes, then allow it to cool completely.

Add the peeled, sliced mango to the syrup, along with ½ cup of lemon juice, the lemon zest, and the Triple Sec. Purée it all in a blender until perfectly smooth. Taste, and add more lemon juice as needed to balance the sweetness of the mangoes and achieve the greatest intensity of flavor.

Freeze in an ice cream freezer, according to manufacturer's instructions.

Makes a little more than 1 quart.

A PICNIC

Pan Bagnia
Artichoke Frittata
Lentil Salad
Gorgonzola cheese
baguettes
honeydew melon, cantaloupe, fresh berries
Chocolate-Dipped Macaroons

These are foods that travel well. All of them can be packed up in a cooler and taken somewhere beautiful without suffering. All taste wonderful in the open air with a fresh, light-hearted wine.

Pan Bagnia is the definition of picnic food—a tasty salad packed within a loaf of French bread. It's hard to explain how great this can taste after some walking or rowing. Artichoke Frittata and Lentil Salad are both substantial dishes, ready to satisfy hearty appetites, because we always eat more in the open air than we do at home. Together, these make a sumptuous plate.

A good piece of cheese is simply a requirement on a picnic, so I've included Gorgonzola, one of my personal favorites, but take any cheese you like. Bring along fresh baguettes to go with it.

The best fruits to take on a picnic are whole melons, which are ideally protected for travel by their own skins—cut them up on the spot. A basket of berries is also great, as long as you take care not to let anything land on top of it.

For a sweet, take along a tin of Chocolate-Dipped Macaroons. They're not likely to crumble or flatten or break—I still remember the time my two-year-old son sat on the birthday cake at a picnic— and they can be grabbed and eaten on the run, which makes them popular with children. And they're delicious.

Don't forget the sharp knife and the corkscrew.

PAN BAGNIA

This is a Provençal sandwich, of which there are many variations. The basic idea is to cut a long crusty loaf of French bread in half lengthwise, fill it with a terrific Mediterranean salad, drizzle oil and vinegar on it, then let it cure for a few hours in the refrigerator. It is one of the best picnic foods ever invented. Here is my variation:

1 long loaf French bread (1 lb.)
1 clove garlic
2–3 Tbs. olive oil, more to taste
10 black olives, pitted and chopped
3 ripe tomatoes, sliced
about 3 Tbs. basil leaves, coarsely chopped
about 3 Tbs. parsley leaves, coarsely chopped

½ onion, thinly sliced
1 small bunch arugula or watercress
2–3 red bell peppers, roasted (procedure follows), peeled, and sliced (1 cup slices; roasted peppers from a jar are also fine)
a few drops wine vinegar (optional)
salt and pepper

optional: sliced fresh mozzarella
thin-sliced Parmesan
or other cheese of choice

Split the bread in half lengthwise. Rub both halves very lightly with a cut clove of garlic and brush with a little olive oil. Spread most of the chopped black olives evenly over the bottom half, then layer on the sliced tomatoes, overlapping them. Salt the tomatoes delicately, sprinkle them with basil and parsley, then spread across them a few slices of onion—more or less, depending on the sharpness of the onion. On top of that, lay the arugula leaves, and then big strips of roasted red pepper. Drizzle a little more olive oil and, if desired, a few drops of wine vinegar, over the vegetables. Scatter on the remaining chopped olives. Add a few grinds of black pepper and cover with the top of the loaf.

Press down hard on the loaf to squash everything together somewhat. Wrap it tightly and refrigerate, preferably with a weight on top of it, for at least 30 minutes.

Other ingredients can be added to this, of course. Capers, grilled vegetables, slices of soft mozzarella cheese or thin slivers of Parmesan, anchovies or tuna, thin slices of radish . . .

Slice the loaf in 2-inch sections to serve. This is fabulous with a glass of cold, fruity wine.

To roast peppers: Arrange the whole peppers on a baking sheet and put them under a hot broiler or put them on a grill. Check them every few minutes and turn them from time to time as they blister and char. When they are soft and blistered all over, remove them and put them in a paper bag or wrap them in a kitchen towel for 3 or 4 minutes to sweat. Then slip off the charred skins, core the peppers, and cut them in strips.

Serves 6–8.

ARTICHOKE FRITTATA

A frittata is a flat, round omelet, in which herbs, vegetables, or other flavorings are mixed with beaten eggs and cooked into them. It is finished to a golden brown on both sides and cut into wedges to serve. Frittatas can be eaten hot, warm, or cool, and are sturdy enough to travel well.

I make this with marinated artichoke hearts, which are easily available in jars, and just drain them well to make sure they're not too oily. I like the slightly tart, lemony taste mixed with eggs—it reminds me a little of *avgolemono.* However, if you have an abundance of steamed artichokes and want to trim out the hearts and use those, by all means do.

2 medium onions	10 eggs
1 lb. small red-skinned potatoes	¼ cup chopped flat-leaf parsley
2 Tbs. olive oil	⅓ cup grated Parmesan cheese
1 large clove garlic, finely chopped	black pepper to taste
1 tsp. salt, more to taste	
1½ cups marinated artichoke hearts, well drained	

Peel, quarter, and slice the onions. Scrub the potatoes, and if they are very small, cut in ¼-inch slices; if they're larger, quarter them lengthwise, then slice them.

Heat 1½ tablespoons olive oil in a large non-stick sauté pan. Cook the onions, potatoes, and garlic in the oil, with a little salt, stirring them often until they are tender.

Drain the marinated artichoke hearts well and trim off any tough, fibrous leaves. Quarter the artichoke hearts and add them to the potatoes and onions in the pan; stir everything together, then remove the pan from the heat.

Beat the eggs in a large bowl with ½ teaspoon of salt, the chopped parsley, grated Parmesan cheese, and black pepper to taste. Add all the vegetables in the pan to the eggs, and stir it all together.

Clean the sauté pan to remove the starchy residue from the potatoes, wipe it dry, and then heat the remaining ½ tablespoon of olive oil in it. Pour in the egg and vegetable mixture, spreading it evenly, lower the heat to a very small flame, and cover the pan. Cook the frittata for 8–10 minutes, or until the eggs at the top are almost set.

Put the pan under a hot broiler for a few minutes to finish the frittata. It should be just slightly golden brown on top. Loosen the frittata gently with a knife or spatula until it moves freely in the pan, then slide it out onto a platter or place a platter over the pan and invert. Cut the frittata in wedges to serve.

This is best eaten warm or at room temperature, so, if you are taking it to a picnic, pack it into the hamper rather than the cooler. If you must keep it longer than a few hours, refrigerate it but allow it to come to room temperature before serving for best flavor.

Serves 6–8.

LENTIL SALAD

1 lb. lentils
3–4 cloves garlic
salt to taste
12 oz. white-skinned potatoes
1 large bunch spinach (4 cups
   chopped leaves)

4 Tbs. olive oil
3 Tbs. fruity wine vinegar
¾ cup thin-sliced green onions
½ cup chopped flat-leaf parsley
½ tsp. hot red pepper flakes
fresh-ground black pepper to taste

Pour boiling water over the lentils, covering them by at least 2 inches, and leave them to soak for ½ hour. Drain them, and put them in a pot with well-salted water to cover, and 2 whole cloves of peeled garlic. Bring the water to a boil, turn down the heat, and simmer the lentils for about 15 minutes, or until they are tender but not mushy. Drain them again, discarding the garlic cloves.

Meanwhile, boil the potatoes in their skins in salted water until they are tender. Drain them and allow them to cool completely, then peel them and cut them in ½-inch dice.

Wash the spinach thoroughly, and discard the tough stems. Chop the spinach leaves coarsely, or cut them in thin strips. Chop the remaining garlic. Heat 1 tablespoon of olive oil in a sauté pan, stir the chopped garlic in it for a minute or two, then add the spinach. Toss the spinach over high heat until it wilts and all the excess liquid cooks away. Sprinkle it with a tablespoon of the vinegar and toss again.

In a large, wide bowl, combine the drained lentils with the diced potatoes, sautéed spinach and garlic, green onions, parsley, and red pepper flakes. Drizzle the remaining 3 tablespoons of oil and 2 tablespoons of vinegar over it, add a little salt and pepper, and toss gently until everything is well mixed. Taste, and add more salt if needed. Let the salad sit for 30 minutes, then taste it again, and correct the seasoning.

This makes about 8 cups of salad, enough to serve 8–10 generously and still have leftovers for the next day's lunch.

CHOCOLATE-DIPPED
MACAROONS

5 large egg whites
pinch of cream of tartar
1½ cups powdered sugar
½ tsp. almond extract
2¼ cups ground blanched almonds
    (about 12 oz., or 2 cups whole
    almonds)

2½ cups shredded, sweetened
    coconut
grated zest of 1 lemon
6–7 oz. bittersweet or sweet
    chocolate

Allow the egg whites to come to room temperature, then beat them with the cream of tartar until they just begin to hold a stiff shape. Add the powdered sugar and the almond extract, and beat again until smooth. Mix in the ground almonds, the coconut, and the lemon zest. You'll have a thick, sticky batter.

Line 2 baking sheets with parchment. Drop heaping teaspoons of the batter onto the parchment, nudging it into a nice shape with the tip of the spoon. Bake the macaroons in a preheated 300° oven for about 40 minutes, or until the cookies are golden brown. Allow them to cool on wire racks.

Melt 6–7 ounces of best-quality sweet or bittersweet chocolate. As it begins to cool, dip macaroons into it, coating one half and leaving the other half plain. Lay them on wax paper to allow the chocolate to harden.

Apricot Variation: Add ½ cup of chopped dried apricots to the batter. When shaping the macaroons, if pieces of apricot are sticking out on top, poke them in with a toothpick so that they are not so exposed. Apricots left on the surface will turn quite dark during baking, but still taste great. Dried cherries could be used the same way.

This recipe makes about 3 dozen exquisite macaroons

RASPBERRY BORSCHT AND STUFFED CREPES

Raspberry Borscht

Pumpernickel Parmesan Toasts

Crepes with Swiss Chard

cantaloupe and honeydew slices

Walnut Tart

The foods in this meal are part of my culinary
history. Borscht, pumpernickel, crepes, fresh white cheese, a sweet
made with walnuts—my taste for these things is genetically
imprinted in my Polish blood. I was weaned on borscht, and cut
my teeth on pumpernickel.

But some of these familiar tastes have new little twists.
The beets are blended with raspberries in a cold, intensely flavorful
soup that is the reddest red you'll ever see. The pumpernickel
is made into Parmesan toasts. Crepes stuffed with chard and cheese,
on the other hand, are a nice, traditional dish, and the
Walnut Tart, which reminds me of walnut tortes I ate as a child, is
actually a variation on American pecan pie. It adds up to
a great-tasting dinner, just different enough to be interesting, yet
old-fashioned in the best sort of way.

RASPBERRY BORSCHT

The idea for this came from a recipe in *Eating Well* magazine, and whoever thought of pairing raspberries with beets is a genius. My version has quite a bit more lemon juice, enhancing the sweet-sour character, and an almost traditional spoonful of sour cream on top. It's an intensely flavored soup with an amazing color (don't wear white).

2 bunches beets (at least 2 lbs.)
spring water
pinch of salt
1 pint raspberries
¼ cup minced red onion

½ cup + 2 Tbs. fresh-squeezed
    lemon juice, strained
3 Tbs. balsamic vinegar
¼ cup sugar

garnish: reduced-fat sour cream (or the real thing if you like)

Cut the tops off the beets, scrub them thoroughly, and put them in a saucepan with enough spring water to cover them by an inch and a little pinch of salt. Simmer the beets, covered, for 30 minutes if they're small, closer to 45 minutes if large. They must be tender.

Drain the beets, reserving the cooking liquid, and allow them to cool. When you can handle them, peel them and cut them into quarters or eighths.

Combine the beets, raspberries, red onion, and 2 cups of the reserved cooking liquid, and purée it all in batches in a blender. Strain the purée through a sieve to remove the raspberry seeds. Stir in ½ cup of lemon juice, the balsamic vinegar, and 3 tablespoons of sugar. Stir until the sugar is dissolved, and taste. Add more lemon juice and more sugar only if needed, until the right sweet-sour balance is achieved. You might need a teensy pinch of salt, but be careful.

Chill the soup in the refrigerator, and when it is completely cold, taste it again. Correct the seasoning if necessary. Serve in chilled bowls, with a spoonful of sour cream in the center of each one.

Serves 8.

PUMPERNICKEL PARMESAN TOASTS

For these you need the dense square pumpernickel bread that is cut in very thin slices.

2½ Tbs. butter, softened
½ cup Parmesan cheese

8 thin square slices pumpernickel
bread (dense square type)

optional: finely chopped parsley

Mash the softened butter in a bowl with the Parmesan cheese, and a little chopped parsley if you like, until you have a thick, well-blended mass. Spread a rounded teaspoonful evenly over each slice of bread, taking it right out to the edges.

Cut the slices in half diagonally to make triangles, and arrange them on a baking sheet. Toast them under a hot broiler for a couple of minutes, watching them all the time, until they are turning golden brown in spots. Serve at once.

Makes 8 servings.

CREPES WITH SWISS CHARD

for the crepes:
3 large eggs
⅔ cup milk
⅓ cup light cream
½ cup water

½ tsp. salt
1 cup flour
1 Tbs. butter, melted
1 Tbs. sugar

butter for greasing baking sheet and
    for sautéing

for the filling:
1¼ lbs. fresh ricotta cheese, drained
2 eggs, lightly beaten
½ cup grated Parmesan cheese
1 large bunch dark-green chard
    (1½ lbs. untrimmed, or 4 cups
    chopped, packed)

1 large yellow onion
1–2 cloves garlic
2 Tbs. olive oil
2–3 tsp. red wine vinegar
¼ cup chopped fresh basil leaves
salt and pepper to taste

optional: 2 Tbs. cognac

garnishes: about 20–24 cantaloupe or honeydew slices
    sour cream or crème fraîche (see page 324)

To make the crepe batter: Beat the eggs, then beat in the milk, cream, water, and salt. When the mixture is well blended, add the flour gradually, whisking it in until the batter is perfectly smooth. Or combine all these things in a blender. Stir in the melted butter, sugar, and cognac, if using, and leave the batter to rest for at least 2 hours.

To make the filling: Allow the ricotta cheese to drain in a colander lined with cheesecloth until it is quite solid and dense. Then whisk it together with the beaten eggs and the Parmesan cheese.

Wash the chard, remove the stems and tough inner ribs, and chop it coarsely. Chop the onion and garlic and sauté them in the olive oil until the onion begins to color. Add the chopped chard and keep cooking over medium heat, stirring often, until the mixture is quite dry. Sprinkle it with the wine vinegar and toss over heat for another minute.

Combine the chard and onion mixture with the ricotta cheese mixture, stir in the chopped basil, and season to taste with salt and pepper.

To make the crepes: Heat a medium-sized (7–8-inch bottom) non-stick skillet and melt a small piece of butter in it. As soon as the foam subsides, pour a scant ¼ cup of batter into the pan, then quickly but gently tilt it around so that the batter spreads evenly over the bottom of the pan.

Cook the crepe over medium heat for about a minute. Loosen the edge by running a knife or thin spatula under it, turn the crepe over, and cook the other side for just under a minute. The crepe should be light golden, with golden-brown spots here and there. Brush the pan lightly with butter between crepes. Stack the crepes and keep them covered with a slightly damp towel as you work. They can be made ahead and stored, tightly covered, in the refrigerator up to a day. If you do refrigerate crepes, allow them to return to room temperature before filling or rolling them. This amount of batter makes 15 to 18 7-inch crepes, or a dozen larger ones.

To assemble and serve the crepes: Lightly butter a large baking sheet. Take 1 pliable crepe at a time and mound 2 rounded tablespoons of filling down the center of it, leaving plenty of room all around. Roll the crepe over the filling, folding in the sides envelope style as you finish rolling it up. Fill and fold all the crepes this way. Arrange the crepes, seam side down, close together on the prepared baking sheet. Brush their tops lightly with softened or melted butter. Bake the crepes for about 25 minutes at 350°—they will puff up like golden pillows.

Put 2 crepes on each plate, and garnish with sliced fruit. A spoonful of sour cream or crème fraîche (see page 324) could be added if you like.

Serves 6–7.

WALNUT TART

for the pastry:
1½ cups white flour
2 Tbs. sugar
pinch of salt
½ tsp. baking powder

4 oz. butter (1 stick), cold
¼ cup Yogurt Cheese (page 77),
    or cream cheese
1 egg
½ tsp. vanilla

for the filling:
3 eggs
pinch of salt
½ cup packed dark-brown sugar
1 cup light corn syrup
2 Tbs. melted butter

½ tsp. cinnamon
½ tsp. vanilla
grated zest of 1 large orange
1¼ cups coarsely chopped walnuts

Combine the flour, sugar, salt, and baking powder in the container of a food processor. Add the cold butter, cut up in pieces, and process until the mixture resembles coarse meal. Add the Yogurt Cheese and process again for a few seconds. Beat the egg with the vanilla, add it to the flour mixture, and process in several short pulses just until the pastry pulls itself together into a solid mass.

Remove the pastry from the processor and form it into a ball. Handling it as little as possible, lay the pastry on a well-floured board and roll it out into a circle about 14 inches across. Roll the circle of pastry loosely over the rolling pin, then unroll it over an 11-inch false-bottom tart pan. Fit the pastry into the pan, and trim the edges with a sharp knife, about ½ inch above the rim. Press the edges down slightly, making sure they are evenly thick and extended above the rim of the pan. Chill the prepared tart shell while making the filling.

Beat the eggs with a pinch of salt, the brown sugar, and corn syrup. Let the melted butter cool slightly, then beat it into the egg mixture. Add the cinnamon, vanilla, grated orange zest (orange only, no white), and chopped walnuts, and stir everything together well.

Pour the filling into the tart shell, spreading the walnuts evenly. Bake the tart in the lower part of a preheated 350° oven for 50 minutes. The filling should tremble only slightly or not at all when the tart is moved.

Allow the tart to cool on a wire rack before serving.

Serves 8–10.

A PASTA DINNER FROM THE SUMMER GARDEN

mixed salad of baby lettuces

Summer Vegetable Pasta

Fresh Peach Ice Cream

The menu is utter simplicity, formed around one fabulous pasta dish that combines the harvest of your garden (or the farmers' market)—eggplants, peppers, onions, basil, tomatoes, all full of the voluptuous flavors of midsummer.

A salad of your favorite greens can be served as a first course; add a good chewy country loaf, and that's all that is needed of food. Open a bottle of Chianti or a spicy-fruity California Zinfandel, and relax with this simple meal in the lingering twilight of a hot summer day.

Finish with Fresh Peach Ice Cream, a taste straight from heaven. If you're watching your fat or cholesterol, serve a plate of ripe peaches instead, big and sweet, the kind you want to eat out of hand with the juice running down between your fingers—a taste straight from low-fat heaven.

SUMMER VEGETABLE PASTA

The delicious taste of this vegetable-rich dish comes from cooking the onions forever, the eggplant and peppers a few minutes, and the tomatoes not at all—they're barely heated. Pungent olives and spicy red pepper flakes add a kick, and the result is just what you want on a summer evening with a bottle of red wine and a country loaf.

2 firm young eggplants
   (about 1½ lbs.)
salt
2 large yellow onions
2 Tbs. olive oil
4–6 Italian red and green peppers
   (1 lb.)
6 cloves garlic

12 Kalamata olives
6–8 ripest red tomatoes (2 lbs.)
2–3 Tbs. coarsely chopped fresh
   basil
black pepper
½ tsp. hot red chile pepper flakes
1 lb. penne or ziti noodles

optional: big shavings of Parmesan cheese

Wash, trim, and cut the eggplant in ½-inch cubes. Sprinkle it with salt and leave it in a colander to drain for about ½ hour as you proceed with the rest.

Roughly chop the onions and cook them slowly in 1 tablespoon of the olive oil, with a dash of salt, stirring occasionally, until they are melted into a caramel-colored marmalade.

Meanwhile, trim and seed the peppers and cut them into thin, inch-long strips. Chop the garlic, and slice the olives off their pits. Cut the tomatoes into chunks, keeping all their juice.

Press the eggplant gently to release excess water. Then heat the remaining olive oil in your largest non-stick skillet and sauté the peppers, eggplant, and garlic in it, stirring frequently over high heat until the vegetables are just tender and beginning to spot, about 5–7 minutes. Add the caramelized onions and cook everything together for a couple more minutes. Stir in the olives, basil, additional salt if you need it, a few grinds of black pepper, and the chile flakes. Now remove the mixture from the heat.

Cook the pasta in several quarts of boiling salted water until it is *al dente*. About 2 minutes before the pasta is ready to drain, replace the skillet of vegetables on a high flame and stir in the chopped tomatoes and their juice. Stir over maximum heat just until everything is thoroughly hot. Drain the pasta, add it to the skillet, toss everything together, and serve at once.

Big shavings of Parmesan cheese could be passed at the table, but aren't absolutely necessary. I love the taste of this just as it is—pure summer garden.

Serves 4–6. If you are serving appetizers, or a substantial salad, you will probably have 6–8 servings.

Variation: If you do not add the juicy tomatoes, the eggplant mixture could be cooled to room temperature and tossed with greens in a salad, or served as part of an antipasto.

FRESH PEACH ICE CREAM

The taste of fresh fruit ice creams made at home in the summer, when fruits are at the peak of ripeness, is incomparable. The fruit is never heated, and retains an orchard flavor and intensity that you can't get at the store.

For this ice cream, use juicy, heavy, fully ripe peaches.

½ cup heavy cream
1½ cups low-fat milk
1 cup sugar
1 tsp. pure vanilla extract

dash of nutmeg
6 medium peaches (about 2 cups chopped)
2 Tbs. fresh-squeezed lemon juice

Combine the cream, milk, ¾ cup sugar, vanilla, and nutmeg in a heavy saucepan, and heat, stirring gently, until all the sugar is dissolved and the liquid is near boiling. Cover and allow the mixture to cool, then chill it in the refrigerator for about an hour.

Peel the peaches and cut away any bruised or soft spots. Slice them off their stones, chop them roughly, and make sure you have at least 2 cups. Stir in the remaining sugar and the lemon juice. Leave them for a few minutes to let the sugar dissolve, then process them briefly in a food processor or blender to make a rough purée.

Strain the chilled cream mixture through a sieve into the peach purée, stir together well, and freeze according to manufacturer's instructions in an ice cream freezer.

Makes a little over a quart of ice cream.

ABOUT NOPALITOS

In the spring, we eat cactus. While folks in the East are hunting for fiddleheads, we in the Southwest are watching our enormous nopal cacti with greedy eyes. Dry and sagging at the end of the long summer, they puff up firm and juicy with the winter rains. Then, in the sunny days of early spring, they sprout their new little paddles, bright green and tender—nopalitos.

Within a few weeks those little "leaves" become big, thick gray-green paddles, destined to sprout their own nopalitos in another season, and no longer good to eat. They must be picked while still thin, and a bright, tropical green.

Around Easter, they turn up in the Mexican markets, at the farmers' markets, and in all the Mexican restaurants, because traditional Mexican Easter dishes are made with them. Nopalitos are sold in jars as well, all year round in the supermarket, but I don't think those are worth buying.

The important thing about nopalitos, my friend Guillermina always tells me, is to pick them in the afternoon on a sunny day, because that is when they are sweetest. On a foggy morning they are still sour.

Well, sweet or sour, I've personally found that the important thing about nopalitos is getting all the needles off without getting them under your skin. The thinnest ones, the ones you almost can't see, are the worst.

To be perfectly honest, my most successful approach to this task is to ask Guillermina for help. However, I like nopalitos enough to do it myself if need be, and this is how: Wear a rubber glove on one hand, or hold the nopalito with a folded tea towel or a pot holder. Take your sharpest, thinnest knife in your other hand and slice flat against the side of the nopalito, shaving away every last needle. Hold the nopalitos so that the spines point away from you, and slice in the same direction that the spines are pointing—away from you. Try not to cut too deeply into the paddle, but above all—get rid of all the needles! Then rinse the paddles well under running water. Now the work is done—the rest is nothing.

6 cups trimmed, sliced nopalitos	**4–5 large cilantro branches**
½ medium onion	**salt to taste**

Cut the trimmed nopalitos crosswise in ¼-inch strips. Put them in a non-reactive pot (i.e., stainless steel, enamel, Calphalon, etc.) with enough water to cover by 2 inches. Add half a peeled onion, several branches of cilantro, and some salt. Simmer for 20 minutes, or until the nopalitos are crunchy-tender. Cool and drain, discarding the onion and cilantro. The water you drain away will have a viscous quality, as it might from okra. This is normal.

The nopalitos are now ready to use in salads, soups, tacos, tostadas, or as a garnish for Cornmeal Griddlecakes (see page 325).

Makes approximately 6 cups.

Variation: for another way to cook them, see page 31.

If You Can't Find Nopalitos

In warm southern places, where the nopal cactus grows, nopalitos are free. They sprout, and you pick them, in your own yard or in someone else's, or along the roadside. But if in the north, look for a Hispanic market, and around Eastertime, you may find some fresh nopalitos.

Another idea is to find a Mexican or southwestern restaurant that serves nopalitos, and ask the chef who the supplier is. Many foods are delivered to restaurants that are never seen in markets, but wholesalers may be willing to deal with you if you can get to them. That's how I get fresh morels, for example.

Substitutions

If worse comes to worst and you find yourself looking at nopalitos in a jar on a supermarket shelf, my advice is to walk away and cook something else instead. If you were going to make Nopalito Salad, make green bean salad instead, using lightly steamed, tender, fresh green beans cut in 1-inch lengths. For Black Bean Tostadas, try zucchini cut in short "sticks" and quickly sautéed, with a squeeze of lemon. For Cornmeal Griddlecakes, do your best to find nopalitos, and if it just can't be done, retreat again to the tenderest, slenderest green beans or use strips of red and green bell peppers, lightly sautéed. (When I made that corncake dish—with nopalitos—for a fancy dinner at a fund-raiser, one lady ate it with relish, not having a clue what she was eating, then said, "These are the *best* green beans I've ever tasted!")

FIRST NOPALITOS
OF THE SPRING

Pan-Roasted Nopalitos

Guajillo Chile Salsa

Refried Pinto Beans

Hot Corn Tortillas

sliced fruit

coffee

It was still February, but the sun had blazed hot for a week after torrential winter rains. I had been working in my study, and wandered into the kitchen, hungry for lunch. At that moment, Guillermina came in the back door, carefully holding a big brown paper bag, and shimmering with excitement.

"Your nopalitos aren't coming up yet, but I found these in another place!" She dumped the contents of the bag onto the kitchen counter—there they were, the season's first bright-green little cactus paddles, bristling with needle-sharp spines. My mouth watered. Fleetingly I hoped that she hadn't invaded anyone's property too deeply to find them. . . .

"We need guajillo salsa," she said firmly. Who was I to argue?
Guajillo chiles were soon in the iron skillet, blistering and smoking. As
she tended the sauce, and the tantalizing aroma of charred chiles and
tomatillos filled the room, she quickly began slicing away the cactus
spines. I watched, rapt, coffee cup in hand. Once I blinked, and when
I looked again, the nopalitos were clean and sliced into thin strips.

As she ground the salsa in the big stone mortar, I was at her side,
dipping into it with a spoon, eating it even before it was finished, even
before the pungent cilantro leaves and sharp green onions were stirred in.

I wondered how she would cook the nopalitos. Here's how:
she threw them in a very hot skillet and turned them a few times
as they sizzled and spit, until they were tender. That's it. No oil,
no water, no anything—just nopalitos seared on hot metal.
It keeps the juices in, she explained.

A few minutes later, the rich red-brown salsa and deep-green
nopalitos were on the table, Guillermina was at the stove patting
out tortillas and laying them on the griddle, and I was on the phone,
calling a friend who lived almost next door. "Come at once," I said.
"Don't ask questions. Drop what you're doing."

The three of us spooned nopalitos and salsa into fresh, warm
tortillas, and devoured them in a trance of pure pleasure. We ate
them plain, and with refried beans. We washed them down with
cold beer, suddenly not caring about the afternoon's work. We ate
every last one of them and we ate all the salsa. Then we sighed
with contentment, and I put on a fresh pot of coffee.

We had eaten the first nopalitos. A rite of spring had been celebrated.

That was one of the best lunches I ever had, perfect in its freshness
and simplicity, one of those peasant meals that are as good as anything
you can get in a starred restaurant. Part of what made it so fabulous
was the unexpectedness of it. I can't give you the element of surprise,
but here is the exact menu that we ate that day, prepared just this way.
If you can get fresh nopalitos, treat yourself to this combination.

PAN-ROASTED NOPALITOS

This is a staggeringly simple dish—with one ingredient (unless you're picky, and count salt).

nopalitos—as many as you want   salt
    (about 4 oz. per person)

Take fresh nopalitos and trim away the sharp spines, using a thin, sharp knife and handling with care. Once they are entirely free of even the tiniest needles, rinse them and slice them crosswise into strips about the thickness of green beans.

Heat a seasoned cast-iron or non-stick pan for several minutes on a high flame. Throw the nopalitos into the hot pan with a good sprinkling of salt—they should sizzle at once. Be sure not to overload the pan, putting no more than 3 or 4 cups of sliced nopalitos into one large sauté pan, as you want to sear them, not steam them.

Turn the nopalitos frequently for about 8 or 10 minutes, keeping the flame hot. They'll spit and hiss and start to blister and release some juice. When the juice has cooked away, and the nopalitos are tender and beginning to color, they're ready.

Sprinkle on a little more salt, and serve the nopalitos at once, with lots of good home-made chile salsa—guajillo salsa is perfect—and fresh, warm corn tortillas. Refried pinto beans or black beans go well with these, also some crumbly, dry white cheese.

GUAJILLO CHILE SALSA

2 oz. dried guajillo chile pods
    (about 6–8 pods)
1 lb. fresh tomatillos
2 cloves garlic

1 tsp. salt, more to taste
½ cup thinly sliced green onions
½ cup chopped cilantro leaves

Toast the chile pods in a very hot cast-iron skillet, pressing them down with a spatula so that they make good contact with the hot pan. In a few minutes, they will release the exquisite perfume of roasting chiles, and dark-brown or blackish spots will develop on their red-brown skins. Put them in a dish with enough water just to cover, and let them soak for about 10 minutes.

Peel the dry husks off the tomatillos and put them in the hot iron pan or on the grill. Turn them occasionally for about 15–20 minutes as they sizzle and spit, until they are soft, and well charred in most places. Under cool running water, peel away the skins where they are black and blistered.

Pull the stems out of the soaked chiles, and grind the pods in a *molcajete* (see page 81) until you have a rough-looking purée with ragged bits of chile skin in it. Pull out as many of the skins as you can, squeezing the juice back into the sauce. Add the tomatillos, and grind them as well. Mix them with the ground chiles. Grind the garlic cloves into a paste, and mix it into the sauce.

Alternatively, combine the soaked chile pods, the charred, peeled tomatillos, and the garlic clove in the container of a food processor or blender, and process in brief bursts, scraping down as necessary, until you have a rough purée. Push it through a coarse sieve, and discard the pulp of skins that remain.

Stir in the salt, green onions, and cilantro. Taste, and add more salt to taste.

This makes about 2½ cups of salsa.

REFRIED PINTO BEANS

I like refried beans, but don't want to eat a lot of fat, so I've worked out my own way with them, not too heavy, but still very flavorful.

1½ Tbs. olive oil
1 large onion, minced
5 cups Boiled Pinto Beans, approx.
   (recipe follows)

salt if needed
1½–2 cups liquid from cooking
   beans

optional: chopped cilantro
        minced hot green chiles, or
        chopped mild green chiles

Heat the oil in a large non-stick sauté pan and stir the minced onion in it, over medium heat, until it colors. Add the beans in their liquid, and a little salt if it's needed, and let them simmer gently for a while, until the liquid is somewhat reduced and the beans are getting mushy. If you want drier beans, cook them longer. You can add some chopped cilantro at this point, or any kind of chiles, but these are extras, and not required.

Now take a potato masher and mash the beans with the remaining liquid. You can mash as few or as many as you like. I usually mash about half and leave the rest whole.

This makes about 5 cups of refried beans, 8–10 servings.

Suggestions: Scoop them up into a tortilla for a taco, add them to quesadillas, or serve them alongside Huevos Mexicanos. If you purée them with some broth and a chile salsa, you have a simple soup. Roll them up with anything you want in a big flour tortilla and you have a burrito.

Leftovers: I use refried beans to make one of my favorite breakfasts, Molletes (page 302).

BOILED PINTO BEANS

1 lb. dried pinto beans	5–6 cloves garlic
pinch of baking soda	several branches cilantro
1 onion	1½ tsp. salt, more as needed

Rinse the beans and put them in a pot with enough water to cover by a couple of inches, and the baking soda. Bring the water to a boil, let it boil for 5 minutes, then turn off the heat, cover the pot, and let the beans soak for an hour.

Add a peeled onion, cut in half, the whole, peeled garlic cloves, and the cilantro, and simmer the beans for at least an hour, or until they are completely tender. Cooking time will vary with the age of the beans. Add more water if needed to keep the beans covered. Near the end of the cooking time, add the salt.

When the beans are done, remove and discard the onion and cilantro. The cooked garlic, now very soft, can be left to become part of the broth.

This yields about 5 cups of cooked beans in a savory broth.

HOT CORN TORTILLAS

I am repeating here the technique for making fresh tortillas at home, which I gave in *The Vegetarian Epicure, Book Two*, because tortillas are so basic to all the foods of Mexico. If you're going to eat fresh nopalitos, you shouldn't miss the experience of eating them with fresh tortillas.

Furthermore, they're incredibly easy to make, and I want to encourage everyone to try it. I saw my 11-year-old son come home from school one day, hungry for a snack. He mixed up some masa, rolled it into balls, pressed them, put them on a hot skillet, and five minutes later he was having fresh, buttered tortillas, hot off the stove.

So here's how.

First, it helps to have a tortilla press. This simple and inexpensive gadget is available wherever Mexican products are sold, as well as in some stores which carry Indian foods. Practiced tortilla makers slap out perfectly round, thin tortillas between their hands in seconds, but trust me on this one—get the tortilla press.

2 cups masa harina*   **1 cup water, more as needed**

Put the dry masa in a mixing bowl and stir in a cup of water. Mix with a spoon, then knead for a few moments with your hand, until it comes together into a smooth, putty-like dough, stiff but moist. If it feels dry and crumbly, add a bit more water.

Heat a griddle or a couple of good, big sauté pans, non-stick or seasoned cast iron. Pinch off pieces of masa and roll them into balls a little bigger than walnuts. Put the thin plastic liner on the bottom of the tortilla press, place a ball of masa in the middle of it, and fold the plastic over it, leaving room all around for the tortilla to spread. Now fold the top of the press over it and bring the handle down. Open the press and there you are—a tortilla. Peel back the plastic liner from the top, turn the tortilla over

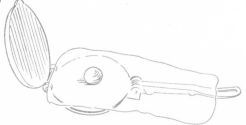

---

*Masa harina is a finely ground meal from corn that has been treated with lime water. It is available at most supermarkets. Do not confuse it with cornmeal, which is an entirely different thing, or cornstarch, which is another thing again.

onto the flat of your hand, and gently peel back the plastic from the bottom. Drop the tortilla onto the hot griddle.

(If you don't have a tortilla press and just can't wait until you do, put the ball of dough on your counter between two sheets of wax paper, then place the flat bottom of a heavy skillet on top of it and press down hard. It won't give you quite as thin a tortilla as the press, but it works pretty well.)

Remember, all this takes much longer to explain than to do.

Cook the tortilla on the hot griddle for about 40 seconds, then slide a spatula under it and turn it. Cook it another 40 to 50 seconds on the other side. If it starts to puff up, just press it down gently with the flat spatula to keep the bubbles even. For a thicker tortilla, you may want to give it another turn, and another ½ minute. The total cooking time will be about 1½ to 2 minutes, depending on thickness and the heat of the griddle.

The tortilla is done when it is pale gold all over and freckled here and there with dark spots. Brush it with a little butter and eat it. Or put it in a basket lined with a thick, folded kitchen towel. Stack all the tortillas there, and keep them well covered to preserve their heat. Serve them as quickly as possible. If you need to keep them for a while, let them cool slightly, then put them in a plastic bag. Reheat them by throwing them on a very hot griddle for a few seconds on each side, or heat them in the oven in packets of 6 or 8, tightly wrapped in aluminum foil.

This makes 12–18 tortillas, depending on size.

ARTICHOKES AND POLENTA DINNER

Stuffed Artichokes

Polenta with Leeks and Gorgonzola
Garnished with Caramelized Fennel and Onions

Coffee Flan

This strikes me as a restrained but sophisticated meal,
with flavors that are pleasantly familiar yet surprising in their
combinations. If you were to poll the next 20 people you see, I'll bet
that most of them would not have eaten Polenta with Leeks and
Gorgonzola in the last week or so, if you see what I mean.
Yet none of these are new tastes.

The artichokes are an extravagant creation, only because of the
way artichokes look. These are opened up to be the flowers they really
are, and spill over with a garlicky filling that tastes like your favorite
tomato bruschetta. If you have really giant artichokes, consider letting
people share, or there won't be room for polenta.

In this polenta, the taste of melted leeks and Gorgonzola is
subtle and seductive. Garnished with caramelized fennel and onions,
it becomes truly great. The whole combination cries out for a
big, marvelous Italian red wine, like a Barolo.

Having started with a flamboyant gesture, we can end with
the most elegant simplicity. The flan, with a suggestion of coffee
beans in the cream, is silky and beautiful.

There is no ingredient or technique in any of this that is strange or
difficult, but the way it all comes together is exceptionally good.

STUFFED ARTICHOKES

Giant artichokes are cooked, opened up into great blossoms and filled with tomatoes, garlic, olive oil, and Parmesan cheese. It's a spectacular first course or light lunch salad.

6 large artichokes	salt to taste
5–6 cloves garlic	2–2½ cups coarse breadcrumbs
2–3 Tbs. olive oil	from a good country loaf
3 lbs. tomatoes	¾ cup fresh-grated Parmesan
3 Tbs. chopped fresh basil	cheese
3 Tbs. chopped flat-leaf parsley	

optional: ½ Tbs. vinegar or lemon juice

Trim off and discard the stems of the artichokes, leaving about ½ inch. Scrub the artichokes clean under running water. Using sharp scissors, cut ½ inch off the top of each leaf, and with a very sharp knife slice about 1 inch off the top of the artichoke.

To a large kettle of boiling salted water, add 2 or 3 whole garlic cloves and a tablespoon of olive oil. Cook the artichokes, covered, for 45–55 minutes, or until tender. Remove them carefully with tongs or a big slotted spoon, and place them upside-down on a rack to drain as they cool.

To make the filling, cut the tomatoes into ¼-inch dice and chop the remaining garlic. Mix the tomatoes and garlic with the chopped herbs, ½ teaspoon of salt, 1½ tablespoons of olive oil, and a touch of vinegar or lemon juice if you want it. Stir in most of the breadcrumbs, check the consistency, then stir in more as needed to make a fairly thick mixture. Finally, add the Parmesan cheese.

When the artichokes are cool enough to handle, turn them right side up and gently pull open the leaves from the center of each one. Pull out the thin leaves from the very center and then scrape out the fibrous choke with a teaspoon.

Spoon some of the filling into the center cavity of each artichoke, then spoon a bit more here and there between the leaves. Distribute it evenly between the 6 artichokes, using about ⅔ cup for each. A little bit more olive oil can be drizzled over the artichokes just before serving.

Serve these at room temperature or chilled, and don't hold them longer than 3 or 4 hours.

Serves 6.

POLENTA WITH LEEKS AND GORGONZOLA

Garnished with Caramelized Fennel and Onions

2 large white fennel bulbs
3 large yellow onions
5 Tbs. fruity green olive oil
salt and pepper to taste
⅔ cup dry red wine
2 very large leeks, white only (about
    1½ cups, sliced)

1 tsp. butter
6–7 cups any low-salt vegetable
    broth
1 cup coarse or regular polenta
    (yellow cornmeal, page 230)
3 oz. Gorgonzola cheese
chopped flat-leaf parsley

Trim the fennel bulbs, wash them well, cut them in half lengthwise, and then slice them about ¼ inch thick. Peel the onions and slice them the same way.

Heat 3 tablespoons of the olive oil in a large non-stick pan and cook the fennel and onions in it slowly, stirring often, adding a little salt and pepper to taste, until they are completely soft and golden brown. Stir in the wine, and continue cooking until it almost all simmers away, then set the pan aside.

Clean the leeks thoroughly, cut them in half lengthwise, then slice them quite thinly crosswise. Heat the remaining olive oil and the butter in a non-stick pan and sauté the leeks in it, stirring them often, until they are soft and beginning to color. Add a little sprinkle of salt—but not too much.

Heat 6 cups of broth in a medium-sized saucepan and whisk in the polenta. Lower the heat and simmer the polenta, stirring with a wooden spoon constantly, or at least very often, until it is thick and smooth, about 30 minutes. Stir in the sautéed leeks; break the Gorgonzola into chunks and stir it in. Keep stirring until the cheese is all melted into the cornmeal. The polenta should be thick and smooth, but not stiff. If it is holding a shape as you stir it, gradually mix in a bit more vegetable broth.

Meanwhile, warm up the caramelized fennel and onion mixture. This too could be moistened with a bit of vegetable broth if needed.

Ladle the polenta into warm, shallow bowls or onto warm plates, and spoon some of the fennel and onion mixture around the polenta. Scatter some fresh flat-leaf parsley across the top and serve at once with a good red wine.

Serves 6.

COFFEE FLAN

The subtle, alluring flavor of this flan is created by steeping whole coffee beans and cinnamon sticks in the scalded milk and cream. It creates a flan that seems bigger, richer, and more complete, somehow. The actual taste of the coffee only becomes apparent when you're told about it.

2½ cups milk	1 cup sugar
½ cup cream	4 eggs
1 3-inch stick cinnamon	2 egg yolks
¼ cup whole coffee beans	½ tsp. vanilla

Heat the milk and the cream with the cinnamon stick and coffee beans until the milk barely begins to simmer. Turn off the heat and leave it to steep for at least an hour, longer if possible. Bring it to a simmer again, then let it cool down just a little.

Select a 6-cup baking dish, perhaps a soufflé dish or a casserole. Heat the dish in a 400° oven while you melt ½ cup of the sugar in a heavy-bottomed skillet over a medium flame. When the sugar is entirely melted and a rich golden caramel color, put on your thickest pot-holder gloves, take out the heated baking dish, and carefully pour the caramel into it, immediately tilting the dish around so that the caramel coats both the bottom and the sides. Set the prepared dish aside.

Beat the eggs and egg yolks with the remaining sugar and the vanilla until they are thick and smooth. Strain the milk, discarding the cinnamon and the coffee beans, and gradually beat the warm milk into the egg mixture.

Pour the custard into the caramelized baking dish, and place it in a larger baking pan in which there is at least an inch of hot water. Bake the flan, in its water bath, at 325° for about 50 minutes to an hour. The center should tremble just a little when moved, and a thin knife inserted in the center should come out clean.

Chill the flan for several hours, then invert it onto a large, deep platter just before serving, letting the caramel sauce pool around it. Cut in wedges to serve, spooning some of the caramel over each serving.

Serves 6–8.

A MIDSUMMER DINNER

Red Pepper Pesto

crostini

Salad of Arugula and Radicchio

Sweet Corn Risotto

Cassis Sorbet

Anise Cookies

This is summer food at its most vibrant, full of color
and brilliant flavors.

The Red Pepper Pesto is rich-tasting without being heavy,
with the sweetness of peppers and the pungency of olives and garlic.
Serve it with a cool apéritif—a simple kir or one of the lovely
champagne-based drinks.

The salad, dark green and red, is full of bite, preparing the way
for a Sweet Corn Risotto, creamy and pale gold.

After that, an intense concentration of blackberries and crème de
cassis in an icy purple sorbet, with delicate Anise Cookies.

RED PEPPER PESTO

This is a pesto made of sweet red peppers—the garlic is the only thing that has any bite. You can roast fresh red pimiento peppers over hot coals and peel them, for superb results, or use the roasted and peeled red peppers that are available in cans or jars in good Italian delis and some supermarkets. Just don't buy the pickled ones.

This spread is fabulous on crostini, served with a sweet, fruity apéritif. It's great with fresh white goat cheese.

3 oz. sun-dried tomatoes
1⅓ cups chopped roasted sweet red peppers
½ cup Kalamata olives, pitted and finely chopped
⅓ cup finely chopped flat-leaf parsley

⅓ cup finely chopped fresh basil
3–4 cloves garlic, minced
3 Tbs. olive oil
1 tsp. balsamic vinegar
fresh-ground black pepper to taste
salt if needed

Put the sun-dried tomatoes into a bowl and pour boiling water over them just to cover. Leave them to soak for 20–30 minutes.

If using canned peppers, rinse and drain them well, and blot them on paper towels, then chop them pretty finely. Combine them with the chopped Kalamata olives, the chopped fresh herbs, and the minced garlic.

Drain the sun-dried tomatoes, reserving the water, and press them gently in a colander. Pulse them in a food processor until they are finely chopped. (I don't use the food processor for the other ingredients, as it can too easily turn them into mush, and you want to keep a little texture in this spread.) Add the olive oil and vinegar, pulse again, scraping down as needed, until no large chunks of tomato are left.

If you do not have a food processor, just finely chop the soaked sun-dried tomatoes as you do all the other ingredients. It will only take a little longer.

Combine the tomato mixture with the other ingredients, mix well, and taste. Grind in some black pepper if you like, and add some salt if needed, though probably the olives provide enough. If the pesto is too thick for your taste, moisten it with a few drops of the reserved tomato water until it has the consistency you like. The texture should be somewhere between thick pesto and soft pâté.

Makes about 1 pint of intensely flavored spread.

SALAD OF ARUGULA AND RADICCHIO

This is a lively salad. The arugula or watercress gives it bite, the radicchio gives depth, peppers and raisins add sweetness, and altogether it's delicious.

8 oz. radicchio (about 5 cups torn pieces)
8 oz. arugula or watercress (about 5 cups torn pieces)
handful of fresh basil leaves
small handful of fresh mint leaves
1 large red bell pepper

½ cup plump raisins
4–6 oz. crumbled goat cheese or blue cheese
2 Tbs. walnut oil
2 Tbs. raspberry vinegar
salt and pepper to taste

Wash the radicchio and the arugula or watercress and spin it dry in a salad spinner. Trim off tough stems and tear everything into manageable pieces.

Cut the basil and mint leaves into thin slivers. Trim and core the bell pepper, quarter it lengthwise, and cut into very thin slices. If your raisins are not absolutely plump and soft, soak them briefly in a cup of scalding water with a dash of wine vinegar in it. Drain them well before adding them to the salad.

Toss everything together in a large mixing bowl, dress lightly with the walnut oil and raspberry vinegar, add a little salt and pepper if you like, and serve. A good olive oil can be used instead of walnut oil, and any vinegar with a slightly sweet overtone would be good with the sharp taste of arugula or watercress.

Serves 6–8.

SWEET CORN RISOTTO

If you haven't picked the corn yourself, it's a good idea to taste a bit of each ear and make sure it's fresh, sweet, and tender. Old corn tastes like wood, and if you ever chewed a pencil at school you know you wouldn't want to make a risotto with it. But with good, sweet corn, this is an ambrosial dish.

4 ears fresh-picked sweet corn
1½ cups chopped onion
1 Tbs. olive oil
½ Tbs. butter
salt
6–8 cups any delicate vegetable broth

2 cups Arborio rice
¾ cup dry white wine
¾ cup grated Parmesan cheese
2 Tbs. chopped flat-leaf parsley
additional Parmesan cheese and parsley for the table

Husk and wash the corn and peel away all the silk, then slice the kernels off the cobs with a sharp knife. You should have about 2½ cups of corn kernels. Spin about a cup of the kernels in a food processor until they are roughly chopped and milky. Scrape out the chopped corn and return it to the remaining whole kernels.

In a large non-stick sauté pan, sauté the onion in the olive oil and butter with a pinch of salt until it is translucent and tender. Meanwhile, heat the vegetable broth and regulate the flame to keep it just below a simmer. Add the Arborio rice to the onions and stir it gently in the pan for about 2 minutes. Pour in the wine and stir until it is absorbed.

Add a soup ladle of the heated broth and all the corn kernels to the rice and stir, keeping it just at a simmer. Keep stirring until the broth is nearly all absorbed into the rice, then add another ladle. Continue this way, adding a little broth at a time and stirring constantly, or at least very frequently, with a wooden spoon for about 25 minutes, or until the rice is *al dente*. It should form a creamy sauce around grains that are no longer crunchy, but still firm.

When the rice is just achieving this perfection of tender-firmness, stir in a last ladle of broth, the grated Parmesan cheese, and 2 tablespoons of chopped parsley. Serve the risotto at once in warm, shallow bowls of generous size, and pass additional parsley and grated Parmesan cheese.

Serves 6–8.

CASSIS SORBET

This is simple, elegant, and divine. Perhaps the only drawback is that you want to make it in that season when you might be wearing white linen, so be very careful handling those blackberries.

1 cup sugar   ¼ cup crème de cassis
1 cup water
5 cups blackberries or marionberries
   (approx. 1½ lbs.)

Stir the sugar and water together in a heavy-bottomed saucepan over low heat until the sugar is completely dissolved. Boil the syrup gently for 6–7 minutes, washing down the sides of the pan with a brush dipped in water to avoid forming crystals. Allow the syrup to cool.

Combine the syrup and the blackberries in a blender and purée. Force the purée through a sieve and discard the seeds. Stir in the crème de cassis, then chill the mixture well. Freeze according to manufacturer's instructions in an ice cream freezer.

Makes about 2 pints of intensely flavored sorbet.

ANISE COOKIES

6 oz. lightly salted butter (1½ sticks)   ½ tsp. ground ginger
1 cup packed light-brown sugar   2 tsp. anise seed, partly crushed
1 egg   2 cups flour + flour for rolling out

Cream the butter in a bowl with the brown sugar until it is fluffy and light. Beat in the egg, ginger, and lightly crushed anise seed. Stir in the flour, form the dough into a ball, wrap it in wax paper or plastic wrap, and chill it for at least an hour, longer if possible.

On a floured board, roll out half the dough to a thickness of about ¼ inch. Cut it with a sharp knife into 1½-inch squares or diamonds or cut out shapes with a cookie cutter. If you have a butter-decorating press, you can press in little designs in the center of each cookie.

Arrange the cookies on a buttered baking sheet and bake them in a 350° oven for 12–15 minutes, or until they are just becoming golden.

Makes about 4 dozen cookies.

TOMATOES

Tomatoes are the elixir of summer. I love them, red and heavy, warm in my hand from the sun that ripened them. I never tire of them. I eat them in salads and pastas, soups and sandwiches, salsas and risottos. And the best way of all—standing in the garden, biting into a sun-baked tomato that I have just picked, letting the juice run between my fingers.

So, even when I don't have time for a true garden, and happily buy my vegetables at the farmers' market, I always feel I must at least put in a few tomato plants.

I really have no excuse not to, because I'm blessed with the benign climate of southern California and I have a plot of land. But even if you only have a patio or a sunlit balcony in a city apartment, try growing some well-fertilized plants in tubs. If you have a windowbox, toss the geraniums one summer and put in a few tomato vines instead. Add a small pot of basil at either end, and see how your summer meals improve.

Luckily, tomatoes are hardy. Mine seem to thrive on neglect. I start by putting them in too late. I mean to put them in in February or early March, because we have such mild and sunny winters when we're not having floods, yet they sometimes don't go in until Mother's Day. But finally a fever takes me over. I drop everything and rush off to do what must be done.

I dig the soil, haul compost, clean out the tomato cages from last year, and buy new rolls of that green stuff to tie them up. I untangle the drip lines. Finally, I plant the baby plants, give them a good drink of water and tomato food.

After that, I forget them for a while, and by the time I check they are beginning to sprawl, and it's a big chore to get them into their cages. Over the next month or two, I go out occasionally, tie up branches, break off some suckers, and pull a thousand weeds. My hands turn black, but they smell like tomatoes.

If a plant gets sick, I yank it out. My method is to put in about three times as many plants as I really need. Then I can afford to lose a few. And I only water my tomatoes once every few weeks, letting the water drip into the beds for twenty-four hours. The plants grow deep roots, and the flavor of the tomatoes is better if they are not overwatered.

In July, when the sun burns and everyone is complaining, I secretly rejoice. My tomatoes are ripening.

For the next several months, I revel. I pick baskets of tomatoes. I eat them for breakfast on toast. I have tomato salad for lunch. Tomato bruschetta for dinner.

In late August or maybe in September, we have a heat wave. The temperature hits 100 degrees, then 105, and one day a hundred pounds of tomatoes are ripe at the same time. That is when I make sauce for the winter, and if you have such an opportunity, do not resist the call.

And even if you haven't grown a single plant, you might drive out to the nearest farm stand, buy a crate of the reddest tomatoes you can find, and indulge in this essential summer ritual, which will reward you all year long.

Tomato Sauce for the Winter

Like many other things, this is much more fun if you do it with a friend.

For **a hundred pounds of tomatoes,** you will want **four or five heads of garlic, several big bunches of fresh basil,** some **salt,** and only about **a quart of good olive oil.**

First the tomatoes must be peeled and cored and cut up, and that is the tedious part. Keep a large pot of water simmering. Cut crosses in the bottoms of all the tomatoes with a sharp knife. Put them into the hot water, ten or twelve at a time, and leave them in it for less than a minute, then fish them out and drop them into a bowl of cool water. Now you can easily slip off their skins.

Next, trim out the stem ends, and any hard cores. Cut larger tomatoes into quarters or halves. I usually run the tomatoes through the blender to make a rough purée, but you can leave them in big pieces if you prefer.

While you prepare the tomatoes, your friend peels and chops the garlic, rinses the basil and shakes it dry, and takes the leaves off the stems.

Canning jars, rings, and lids (always get new lids) should be sterilized or at least run through the dishwasher and dried, then lined upside-down on clean kitchen towels, ready for action. Have extra lids on hand, as some may be duds and then you have to reseal a jar with a fresh lid.

When your enormous piles of tomatoes have been tamed into several big bowls of purée or chunks, take out your biggest pots and sauté pans. Use only non-reactive pots. I personally like to use very large sauté pans, because they are so wide, and the sauce can cook down faster with greater air contact.

With the first batch of sauce, you will probably want to measure. For each quart or so of prepared tomatoes, heat a tablespoon of oil, add two cloves of chopped garlic, and stir for a minute, then pour in the tomatoes. Add half a teaspoon of salt or a little more, to your taste, and some basil, chopped or whole leaf. Let this simmer until it feels thick enough to be sauce and turns a dark-red color.

You will soon adjust your quantities to get the maximum use of your pots. Just remember, a gallon of tomatoes simmering in a giant pot will take longer to cook down to the right consistency than a quart, so be patient, watch, and stir. It's done when it looks and feels done.

At the end, you can combine all the finished batches of sauce in one very large kettle, stir it up, and adjust the salt if you need to.

Now you are ready to ladle hot tomato sauce into clean, dry jars, and to seal them according to the instructions that come with the canning jars. Here are my tips: Remember to leave at least half an inch of air space at the top of the jar. Wipe the rims of the jars until they are absolutely clean and dry. Check each lid to be sure that the little rubberized circle which forms the seal has no flaws in it. If you are using a boiling water bath, keep the jars completely submerged in boiling water for at least twenty minutes.

When you take your jars out of the boiling water, line them up on the counter to cool, and listen for the satisfying little "ping" of each lid as the vacuum seal is formed. If a lid does not seal properly, you must take it off, wipe the rim of the jar again, put on a fresh lid, and reprocess. Or put that jar in the refrigerator for more immediate use.

Let the jars cool, then label them with a date. You think you will never forget when you did this, but you will. And it's fun to see that date, later. I've kept tomato sauce in jars for up to two years with no problems.

When you have a cool, dark pantry shelf lined with shiny jars full of sweet red sauce, you will be able to face the winter. Every time you open a jar, the concentrated flavor of summer is there. You can whip together a great-tasting dish in no time, and you do not have to wait eight months for the wonderful, wonderful taste of tomatoes.

But never will the sauce taste as good as it will that evening, when you enjoy your well-earned Tomato Harvest Dinner.

The next four menus feature tomatoes in pasta, in soup, in risotto, and in salad. This is a little sampler of the bounty of summer tomatoes.

TOMATO HARVEST DINNER

Cream of Sweet Corn Soup

Fresh Pasta
with
Summer Tomato Sauce

sliced peaches, raspberries,
with sweetened crème fraîche

One day in August, when tomatoes all ripen at once,
I make my tomato sauce for the winter. As I stand over a hot stove on
a hot day, tomato-mania gets hold of me, and I want to eat
some of that sauce right away, with a good plate of pasta. This
might be my favorite summer meal.

Greg makes the fresh pasta—or we open a package of
good dried pasta if time is short. We save some of the last batch
of tomato sauce. We call a few friends, open a good Italian
wine, and set the table outside.

A fresh soup made of sweet corn from the same garden
is a very nice start, although a salad would do as well. Afterwards,
nothing could be better than summer fruits, with crème fraîche
(see page 324), slightly sweetened.

CREAM OF SWEET CORN SOUP

This is one of the simplest soups, and one of the best, and it has no cream in it.

9–10 freshly picked ears sweet corn (7 cups kernels)	3 Tbs. butter
	4 cups milk
1 large sweet onion	1 tsp. salt, more to taste
1 large clove garlic	

garnish: chopped chives or cilantro leaves

Husk and clean the corn, and slice the kernels off into a big bowl with a sharp knife. Scrape the cobs to release as much juice as you can. You need at least 7 cups of corn kernels.

Chop the onion and garlic and cook them in 2 tablespoons of the butter until they are soft and golden, about 10 minutes. Combine the corn kernels, the onions and garlic, and about a cup of the milk, and purée in a blender in batches.

Combine the purée with the rest of the milk in a soup pot, add the salt and the remaining butter, and simmer for 15–20 minutes. Taste and correct the seasoning if needed.

The soup can be run through the blender again at this point if the texture feels too rough for you. For an absolutely silky texture you can go a step farther and press it all through a sieve, which will reduce the quantity a bit.

Serve the soup hot and sprinkle each serving with chopped chives or cilantro.

Serves 6–8.

FRESH PASTA

We've used this recipe many, many times in the years since we've owned an electric pasta-cutting machine. It's been a foolproof formula. It makes the equivalent of about a pound of dried pasta, enough for 4–5 generous servings (people always want to eat more when it's home-made pasta).

1 lb. semolina flour*	½ cup water
1 tsp. salt	additional semolina for kneading
2 eggs	

Mix the semolina and salt together in a large mixing bowl. In a small bowl, lightly whisk together the eggs and water. Make a well in the center of the semolina, pour in the egg and water mixture, and gradually stir in the flour until it is all absorbed into a dough.

Turn the dough out onto a board lightly sprinkled with a little more semolina, and knead it with your hands until it begins to spring back quickly.

Finish kneading the dough by passing it repeatedly between the rollers of a pasta machine, until it is absolutely smooth and very elastic. You can also complete the kneading process by hand, but be ready for a workout.

Divide the dough into 2 or 3 parts, and keep the others covered with plastic wrap as you begin rolling out the first.

Roll out long sheets of pasta by adjusting the rollers on the machine progressively closer together until you achieve the thinness you want, probably about ¹⁄₁₆ inch or less.

Cut the pasta manually for ravioli, manicotti, lasagne, papardelle, or wide fettucine. Cut it with the blades of the machine for tagliatelle, linguine, or fettucine.

The pasta can be cooked immediately, or you can drape it over something or lay it on towels to dry until you need it. I have found the backs of my kitchen chairs ideal for this. I put a kitchen towel over the back of each chair and I'm ready to hang enough pasta for ten people. In fact, I got so used to doing this that it became a unit of measure for me. "How much pasta should I make?"—"Oh, about eight chairs."

When you're ready to eat, bring a very large pot of water to a rolling boil, salt it well, add a drop of olive oil (not absolutely required, but I like it), and cook the pasta in it for moments only, until it is *al dente*. I've found that about 30 seconds or a minute after the water returns to a boil is usually enough.

Drain the pasta at once and toss it with the sauce in a large, warm bowl. Serve immediately.

Serves 4–5.

Semolina is a pale-gold hard-wheat flour, more coarsely ground than bread flour. It is the preferred flour for making pasta, and is becoming much more commonly available in stores here. Look for it in health food stores, gourmet markets, Italian markets, and even in some supermarkets. It is usually labeled "semolina," but I have also seen it called "pasta flour."

SUMMER TOMATO SAUCE

This is the formula I use when I prepare tomatoes to put up in jars for the winter, but reduced to an amount that is right for one dinner—in case this *isn't* the day you cook 100 pounds of tomatoes. The important thing is to use absolutely vine-ripe tomatoes. It is the pure taste of the tomato that is wonderful. However, this sauce can be varied endlessly with the addition of herbs, scented vinegars, a bit of wine.

3 lbs. ripe tomatoes (at least a quart when chopped)
1 Tbs. fruity green olive oil
2–3 cloves garlic, minced

2 Tbs. finely chopped fresh basil leaves
salt and pepper to taste

Scald the tomatoes in boiling water for about 45 seconds and slip off their skins. Trim their stems and process briefly to a somewhat rough texture in a blender or food processor.

Heat the olive oil in a saucepan and add the garlic. Stir it for about a minute, then pour in the tomatoes. Add the basil and a little salt and pepper, and cook the sauce on a medium flame for about half an hour, or a little longer if the tomatoes were very juicy, until reduced by about a third.

You can use the sauce at once or keep it in the refrigerator, covered, for several days. You can also double or triple or quadruple the recipe, just remembering that if you are cooking down a huge pan-full of sauce it will take longer. And you can vary the proportions; it's pretty foolproof if the tomatoes are good.

This makes about 2½–3 cups of sauce.

TOMATO SOUP
AND PASTA

Summer Tomato Soup

*Penne with Goat Cheese
and Ruby Chard*

fresh fruit

You can just as easily make this dinner in the winter if
you have put some garden tomatoes into jars. Then it's even easier,
because the tomatoes are already peeled, and to have that true
tomato flavor in a steaming bowl when it's cold and gray outside
is a wonderful thing.

After the slight acidity of tomatoes, green or ruby chard in
a sauce of creamy, melted goat cheese is very pleasant. Because the
cheese adds an element of richness to the pasta dish, ripe,
fresh fruit of the season is the ideal dessert. In summer, serve
berries or melons or ripe peaches. In winter, pears or Fuyu
persimmons cut in thin slices.

SUMMER TOMATO SOUP

4 lbs. ripe, red tomatoes
2 Tbs. virgin olive oil
½ onion, finely chopped
3–4 cloves garlic, finely chopped
1 tsp. salt, more to taste

handful of fresh basil leaves,
  chopped
2 cups vegetable broth
2 cups cooked rice (white or brown)
fresh-ground pepper to taste

Scald and peel the tomatoes, and trim off their stem ends. Cut them in halves or in quarters, and then process them briefly in a blender; they should be somewhere between chopped and puréed.

Heat the olive oil in a large, non-stick sauté pan and stir the chopped onion in it over a medium flame for about 3 minutes. Add the garlic and sauté another 2–3 minutes.

Add the puréed tomatoes, a teaspoon of salt, and the basil. Simmer for about ½ hour, until the tomatoes are reduced to a sauce and dark red. Add the vegetable broth and the rice, and bring back to a simmer. Taste, and correct the seasoning if necessary with a touch more salt or a little fresh-ground pepper.

Serves 6–8.

PENNE WITH GOAT CHEESE AND RUBY CHARD

Chard and goat cheese always go well together. In this dish, the slightly bitter taste of chard and the creamy goat cheese melting into it make a superb pasta sauce. The pine nuts add an essential crunch to the texture.

The more commonly found dark-green Swiss chard can be substituted if ruby chard is unavailable.

1 large bunch ruby chard (about 1 lb.)	1–2 Tbs. balsamic vinegar (or 2 tsp. red wine vinegar)
2 large yellow onions, chopped	5 oz. creamy white goat cheese
2 Tbs. olive oil	¾ cup pine nuts
1 tsp. butter	1 lb. penne noodles
salt to taste	½ cup white wine

Wash the chard thoroughly, cut off and discard the thick stems, and chop the leaves and thin inner stems coarsely.

Sauté the chopped onions in the olive oil and butter until they are soft and beginning to color. Add the chard and toss it together with the onions until it wilts. Continue cooking, stirring occasionally, for a few more minutes, until the chard is tender. Toss the chard with a tiny bit of salt and the vinegar. Crumble the goat cheese and set aside. Lightly toast the pine nuts, stirring them in a small skillet over medium heat until they begin to turn golden and fill the air with fragrance. (At this point, you could set everything aside and hold it for a few hours if necessary.)

Boil the penne in several quarts of salted water until it is *al dente*. Just before it's ready, bring the chard back to high heat and add the white wine. Drain the pasta. Add the crumbled cheese to the hot chard mixture, along with the pasta, and mix it all together well. Serve at once on warmed plates, and sprinkle each serving with toasted pine nuts.

Serves 6–8.

TOMATO RISOTTO
FOR THE FAMILY

Fresh Tomato Risotto

Roasted Summer Vegetables

Parmesan Cheese Toasts

fresh fruit plate

This was a dinner I never planned. I just looked in the larder at the end of the day, saw what's always there all summer—zucchini, tomatoes, basil, peppers—and put together something easy. You can do the same.

Walk into the kitchen about an hour before dinner and put a nice bottle of white wine in to chill, and it will be ready to drink just a little while before the food is ready to eat.

Start by cutting up the vegetables and putting them into the oven. While they roast, prepare the risotto, and then put your children to the task of stirring it while you make the Parmesan Cheese Toasts and open the wine. Life does not have to be too complicated.

FRESH TOMATO RISOTTO

I make this easy risotto in the summer, when tomatoes are abundant and sweet, or in the winter with tomatoes I've put up in jars.

1 medium onion, chopped
1 Tbs. olive oil
1 tsp. butter
salt to taste
6 cups vegetable broth
2 cups Summer Tomato Sauce
    (page 51), or
        2 lbs. ripe tomatoes

1 additional Tbs. olive oil
2–3 cloves garlic, chopped
2 cups Arborio rice
¾ cup dry white wine
1–2 Tbs. chopped fresh parsley
1–2 Tbs. chopped fresh basil
½ cup grated Parmesan cheese

garnishes: additional Parmesan cheese
          slivered fresh basil
          toasted pine nuts

In a large non-stick sauté pan, sauté the onion in the olive oil and butter, with a dash of salt, until it begins to turn golden. In separate skillets, heat the vegetable broth and the tomato sauce, and keep them both just below a simmer.

If you are starting with fresh tomatoes: Scald and peel them, and chop them or process them in a blender for a few seconds. Heat a tablespoon of olive oil in a non-stick pan, sauté the chopped garlic in it for about 2 minutes, then add the tomatoes and cook them down for about 15 minutes.

Add the rice to the sautéed onion and stir it gently in the pan for about 2 minutes. Pour in the white wine and stir as it is absorbed.

Add a soup ladle of the heated broth and stir, keeping the mixture just at a simmer. Keep stirring until the broth is nearly all absorbed into the rice, then add a ladle of tomato sauce and the chopped herbs, and stir until that is nearly absorbed. Continue this way, alternating broth and sauce until the sauce is used up, then carry on with the broth until the rice is *al dente*. This process will take about 25 minutes, and at the end a creamy sauce will form around rice grains that are tender but firm.

At the moment the rice is no longer crunchy, stir in a last ladle of hot broth and the grated Parmesan cheese, and serve the risotto at once. Scatter slivered basil and toasted pine nuts over each serving, and pass additional Parmesan.

Serves 6–8.

ROASTED SUMMER VEGETABLES

Beginning in late summer, we get beautiful, huge squashes, and the little bit of sweet Tahitian squash added to the zucchini and peppers is so good in this. All the flavors sing when combined with the bright, fresh taste of tomatoes in a risotto (or in anything).

6 medium zucchini (about 1¼ lbs.)
1 large red bell pepper
1 large green bell pepper
1 large onion
2 cups cubed Tahitian squash (or
    other sweet squash, such as
    Kabocha, buttercup, or acorn)

4 garlic cloves, chopped
2 Tbs. olive oil
salt and pepper to taste

Trim the zucchini and slice them into ½-inch rounds. Trim and core the peppers and cut them in pieces about 1 inch square. Cut the onion into large chunks. Cut enough Tahitian squash into ½-inch cubes to fill about 2 cups.

In a large bowl, mix all these vegetables together with the chopped garlic, olive oil, and a liberal sprinkling of salt and pepper.

Spread the vegetables on 2 baking sheets and roast them in a 425° oven for 50 minutes to an hour, or until tender and spotted with dark golden brown here and there. You should turn the vegetables once or twice during the roasting time.

Serves 6.

Kabocha

PARMESAN CHEESE TOASTS

I have to ration these to my boys at dinner, or they simply will not eat anything else. They learned to make them perfectly, without my help, at an early age. Of course, you must use real aged Parmigiano from Parma.

12 thick slices excellent country bread, French bread, or sourdough bread	3½ Tbs. butter, softened ⅔ cup fresh-grated Parmesan

Be sure to use a good fresh bread with some texture to it. Warm the butter gently until it is as soft as it can be without being completely melted—and even if a bit of it melts, no matter.

Stir the grated cheese into the butter to form a thick, soft paste. Spread this mixture evenly over the slices of bread, all the way out to the crusts to prevent burnt edges.

Arrange the slices on a baking sheet and put them under a hot broiler for 2 minutes, moving their position once during that time if needed, until the cheese is golden brown and bubbling. Remove at once! It's a matter of seconds from perfectly browned to burnt, so watch them. Serve hot.

Serves 6.

A FRITTATA
SUPPER

Summer Tomato Salad

Garlic Bread

Green Herb Frittata

Berry Cobbler

Every part of this simple meal is saturated with flavor
and color: bright-red salad, dark-green frittata, and purple berries
bubbling under a golden crust.

The salad and Garlic Bread take only a few minutes.
Put the garlic into the oil to steep before you start doing other
things. You can prepare the cobbler early in the day, or just a while
before dinner—it's delicious hot or warm. Once the frittata is in the
pan, the rest of the meal can be made while it is cooking.

If you need to keep your preparation time really short,
replace the cobbler with berries and ice cream (but the delicious
cobbler only takes about fifteen minutes to prepare).

SUMMER TOMATO SALAD

In August, when you're carrying in those dark-red beefsteak tomatoes weighing 1½ pounds each, it's time for this salad.

This is one of those simple things—not really a recipe, just great food. I can eat a whole platter by myself for lunch and be ready for another by dinnertime.

3 or 4 big, juicy vine-ripened tomatoes (3–4 lbs.)	2 Tbs. fruity green olive oil
½ medium red onion	a few drops vinegar
1 cup flat-leaf parsley leaves	salt and fresh-ground pepper to taste

Wash the tomatoes and slice them thickly crosswise. Arrange them in a single layer on a large platter. Slice the onion crosswise, thinly but not paper thin. Scatter the onion rings over the tomatoes.

Wash the parsley leaves and spin them in a salad spinner. Arrange them in a wreath around the tomatoes. Drizzle the tomatoes with the olive oil and sprinkle them with a few drops of your favorite vinegar. Add salt to your taste, and grind on some black pepper. Serve within the hour, accompanied by some crusty, chewy bread. Do not refrigerate!

This makes enough for 6–8 normal salad servings. Or add a wedge of pungent hard cheese, some olives, and a good loaf of bread and it's a meal for a couple of voracious tomato-eaters.

GARLIC BREAD

garlic	coarse-textured country bread
fruity green olive oil	salt

Slice or coarsely chop a few cloves of garlic and combine it in a bowl with a few tablespoons of olive oil. I usually use 3 or 4 tablespoons of oil for an average loaf of French bread—but you might like a bit more. Crush the garlic into the oil a little and leave it to steep for at least 30 minutes, longer if you like.

Thickly slice as much bread as you think you'll need. Brush the bread slices lightly with the garlic-infused oil, and sprinkle them with a tiny bit of salt.

Toast the prepared bread slices on a rack under a hot broiler or on a grill over hot coals for a minute or two, watching them like a hawk, and remove them when they start to turn golden brown.

That method makes a nice, subtle garlic bread. If you want garlic bread with a real kick, here's another way:

Peel a clove of garlic and cut it in half. Brush your bread slices with plain olive oil and toast them under a broiler or on a grill. Rub the toasted bread with the cut garlic and sprinkle lightly with salt. This second method retains the sharp, biting flavor of raw garlic.

GREEN HERB FRITTATA

Like any frittata, this also makes a wonderful picnic dish. It's very good at room temperature, and slices of frittata in a split baguette make a great sandwich.

¾ lb. mixed leafy greens, such as spinach, chard, kale, escarole, etc. (3 cups chopped, packed)
2½ Tbs. fruity green olive oil
2 cloves garlic, chopped
½ tsp. salt, more to taste
1–2 tsp. wine vinegar
10 eggs

fresh-ground pepper to taste
1 cup chopped flat-leaf parsley
3 Tbs. chopped fresh basil or mint, or a combination
⅓ cup fresh-grated Parmesan cheese
1 cup cooked rice

Wash the greens and trim away any tough stems, then chop the leaves coarsely.

Heat 2 tablespoons of olive oil in a large non-stick sauté pan, add the chopped garlic, and stir over medium heat for 2 minutes. Add the chopped greens and a little salt, and sauté, stirring and tossing frequently, until all the greens are wilted and tender, about 5–7 minutes. Sprinkle the greens with a little wine vinegar to bring out their best flavor.

Beat the eggs lightly in a large bowl with ½ teaspoon of salt, some pepper, the chopped herbs, and the Parmesan cheese. Stir in the sautéed greens and the cooked rice.

Heat the remaining ½ tablespoon of olive oil in a 10- or 11-inch non-stick pan. Pour in the frittata mixture, spread it evenly, and lower the heat. Cover the pan and leave the frittata on a very small flame for about 10 minutes before checking it. If the top is still very runny, leave it a few minutes more.

When the top is only slightly runny, put the frittata under a hot broiler for a couple of minutes to finish and brown the top. As soon as the surface is set, remove it from the heat—overcooked eggs get rubbery, so be careful.

Turn the frittata out onto a large plate and cut it in wedges to serve.

Serves 6–8.

BERRY COBBLER

This is a cobbler that I don't mind serving to my kids in any quantity, as it is not inordinately high in fat or in sugar—just enough to be very good. The topping is more like a buttermilk biscuit than a sweet pastry crust. Of course, when you add a scoop of vanilla ice cream, the healthful profile deteriorates, but does it ever taste great!

filling:
½–¾ cup sugar
1 Tbs. cornstarch
½ cup water
2 Tbs. lemon juice
4 cups fresh blackberries, or other
    prepared fruit

topping:
1 cup flour
2 Tbs. sugar
½ tsp. baking soda
1 tsp. baking powder
½ tsp. salt
2–3 Tbs. butter
½ cup buttermilk

Preheat the oven to 400°.

In a fairly large, non-reactive pot, combine ½ cup of sugar, the cornstarch, water, and lemon juice. Stir to dissolve the cornstarch, then add the fruit. Bring this mixture to a boil over medium heat, then simmer for a minute, stirring gently. Taste it, and add a bit more sugar if needed. Pour the berry mixture into a 1½-quart casserole or 8-inch square glass baking dish.

Combine the dry ingredients for the topping in a bowl. Melt the butter and whisk it into the buttermilk, then stir the liquid into the dry mixture, just until it is all combined. The dough will be sticky.

Drop the dough by spoonfuls onto the hot fruit. Bake the cobbler for 20–25 minutes, until the biscuit crust is golden. Serve it hot or warm, with vanilla ice cream.

Serves 6–8.

Note: If you are not using berries, the amount of sugar and lemon juice can vary with the type of fruit used—peaches or nectarines, for example, are much less acidic than berries and will need more lemon. Taste and correct as needed.

Little Dinner Parties

for Spring
and Summer

A RELAXED SUMMER DINNER PARTY

Garlic Crostini with Tapenade

Cold Melon Soup with Mint Cream

*Risotto
with Zucchini Flowers*

*fresh blackberries in
Crème Anglaise*

This is a beautiful, easy dinner based on the foods that
are available only in summertime. To make life comfortable on a
hot day, everything except the risotto is prepared ahead,
and there's not much work to it at all.

The pungent, salty taste of the Tapenade, wonderful
with an apéritif, is the perfect foil for cool, sweet melon soup. Then
a delicate and creamy risotto with flecks of green and gold flowers.
If it's very hot, you could drink white wine throughout—or switch to
a light red. Afterwards, ripe blackberries, one of the great tastes of
summer—although any ripe summer berries would be fine.

Best eaten in a garden, with a slight sunburn on your shoulders . . .

GARLIC CROSTINI

1 or more baguettes, thinly sliced
garlic cloves

olive oil
salt

Slice as much bread as you want, and toast the slices in a medium oven or under a broiler until they are golden on both sides. Rub the toasts very lightly on one side with a cut clove of garlic, then brush with olive oil. Sprinkle the toasts with salt if you like.

Another way to make Garlic Crostini, which I like a lot, is to drop 5–6 cloves of garlic, peeled and slightly bruised, into a cup of green olive oil and let it steep for a few hours. Then discard the garlic cloves and use the oil to brush the hot toasts, omitting the raw garlic rub. This method gives a more subtle garlic flavor.

TAPENADE

½ lb. Kalamata olives (about 1½
   cups)
2 medium cloves garlic
½ cup chopped walnuts
1 tsp. chopped fresh rosemary leaves
½ tsp. chopped fresh thyme leaves

1 Tbs. capers
1 tsp. orange zest
2 Tbs. lemon juice
black pepper to taste
2–4 Tbs. olive oil

Slice the olives off of their pits, and combine them in a food processor with the garlic, walnuts, rosemary, thyme, capers, orange zest, and lemon juice. Process for a few seconds, then again, until you have a chunky paste. Add pepper to taste and trickle in the olive oil as you process again. Add only as much oil as you need to get the consistency you like. The Tapenade should be thick but not stiff.

Serve the Tapenade with crostini—little toasts of French or Italian bread.

Makes about 1¼ cups.

COLD MELON SOUP
WITH MINT CREAM

This is a wonderful soup for a summer dinner party, refreshing, cool, and successful with many varieties of melon. However, don't attempt it if the melon is not absolutely ripe and sweet. The flavor of the melon is the essence of this.

Everybody has a way of choosing a really ripe melon. I believe in sniffing—a ripe melon will be sweetly fragrant. It should also give a little when gently pressed at the stem end.

3 cups water
1 cup sugar
1 large, perfectly ripe melon
    (approx. 6 lbs.)—honeydew,
    Persian, or other juicy, sweet-
    fleshed variety

2 cups good dry white wine
juice of 2 large lemons, strained
3–4 Tbs. finely chopped fresh mint
1 cup heavy cream
additional 1–2 Tbs. sugar if desired

Put the water and sugar in a saucepan and bring it to a simmer, washing down any crystals from the sides of the pan with a brush. When the sugar is completely dissolved, continue simmering the syrup for 3–4 minutes, then allow it to cool completely.

Slice the melon, seed it, and scoop out all the soft, ripe flesh. Purée it in a blender. You should have about 5 cups of melon purée.

Stir the white wine into the melon purée, then start adding the sugar syrup gradually, by ½ cupfuls at first, then even less. Stir and taste each time. You may use 1½ cups of the syrup, or a bit more. When the sweet taste becomes pronounced, add 2 tablespoons of the strained lemon juice. Taste again. Now add a little lemon juice or a little sugar syrup, to achieve just the right tart-sweet balance, without overwhelming the melon flavor.

Remember—every melon is different, every lemon is different, every wine is different. That's why taste buds were invented.

Chill the soup thoroughly; you may want to put it in the freezer for the last 30 minutes before you serve it.

To make the mint cream, add the finely chopped fresh mint to the cream, along with a little sugar if you like, and beat the cream until it barely begins to thicken.

Serve the soup cold, in chilled bowls, with a spoonful of the soft mint cream in the center of each one.

Serves 8.

RISOTTO WITH ZUCCHINI FLOWERS

Why is this so good? I don't know, but it's so much better with the flowers than it would be with just zucchini.

2 Tbs. butter
1½ Tbs. olive oil
½ cup finely chopped shallots
½ cup chopped sweet yellow onion
2 cups chopped zucchini flowers
1 cup chopped baby zucchini
salt to taste
5–6 cups vegetable broth

2 cups Arborio rice
⅓ cup Marsala
¾ cup white wine
1–2 tsp. finely chopped fresh basil
3–4 Tbs. grated Parmesan cheese
pepper to taste
additional Parmesan cheese for the table

Heat the butter and olive oil in a large sauté pan and stir the shallots and onions in it until they are soft. Add the chopped zucchini flowers and baby zucchini. Salt lightly and stir often over medium heat until the vegetables begin to color. Meanwhile, heat the broth in a separate pot and keep it hot on a low flame.

Add the rice to the vegetables and stir constantly for 3–4 minutes, then add the Marsala. As soon as it is absorbed, add the white wine, and when that is almost absorbed, begin adding broth. Add about a cup of broth at a time, and lower the flame so that the liquid is just simmering. Stir occasionally. As soon as the broth is nearly absorbed, add another cupful, stir again, and so on.

After about 20 minutes, have a taste. The rice texture you want is a grain that is creamy on the outside but still quite firm to the tooth inside. Not crunchy, not mushy. The rice should achieve this texture in about 25 minutes of simmering, give or take a bit. Add a final ½ cup or so of broth, stir in the chopped basil and a little cheese, and correct the seasoning with a touch of salt or pepper if needed. Then serve at once, passing more Parmesan cheese.

Serves 6–8.

CRÈME ANGLAISE

(Custard Sauce)

2 cups milk, or part milk, part
   cream
4–5 egg yolks

6 Tbs. sugar
pinch of salt
½ tsp. vanilla extract

Scald the milk and keep it hot. Beat the egg yolks with the sugar and salt until they are pale and thick. Still beating with a whisk, pour the hot milk into the egg yolks in a thin, slow stream.

Return the mixture to very low heat. Use a double boiler or a very heavy-bottomed saucepan on a tiny flame. Stir until the mixture thickens enough to coat a spoon. Add the vanilla and strain. Cover.

Serve warm or cool with fruits and puddings.

Makes about 2½ cups.

A SLIGHTLY MIDDLE EASTERN PILAF DINNER

*Minted Tomato Salad
with Feta Cheese*

Baba Ghanouj

toasted pita triangles

*Wheat and Lentil Pilaf
with Shiitake Mushrooms*

Roasted Potatoes and Fennel

*Yogurt Cheese with Honey
and Fresh Figs*

The pilaf in this dinner is not a Greek or Turkish recipe—it's just something I made up and liked. The various elements of this meal and the way they come together have a Middle Eastern feeling for me.

Tomatoes and mint, while not as familiar as tomatoes and basil, are a wonderful summertime combination. This salad combines ripe tomatoes with both those herbs and feta cheese. It pairs up well with the subtle, smoky flavor of charred eggplant in Baba Ghanouj, served with toasted pita triangles.

The pilaf is not a heavy dish, but it's very satisfying, with the earthy tastes of lentils and mushrooms. With it, a simple dish of roasted vegetables, delicately scented with sweet fennel.

For dessert, Yogurt Cheese with Honey and Fresh Figs, a seductive combination of tastes and textures which requires almost no effort. It does take a little advance planning, though, to drain the yogurt. If you haven't done that, you could substitute mascarpone or crème fraîche.

MINTED TOMATO SALAD
WITH FETA CHEESE

Of course you know that this should be made with ripe, red summer tomatoes, still warm from the vine.

4 cups ripe tomatoes, cut in chunks (about 2½ lbs.)	2 Tbs. chopped fresh basil
1 Tbs. + 1 tsp. olive oil	½ tsp. salt
1 Tbs. balsamic vinegar	4 oz. feta cheese
2 cloves garlic, minced	½ medium red onion
3–4 Tbs. chopped fresh mint	slices of crusty French bread

Wash and trim the tomatoes and cut them in generous chunks—about ½- to 1-inch. Combine them in a bowl with 1 tablespoon of olive oil, the vinegar, minced garlic, 2 tablespoons of chopped mint, and the chopped basil. Sprinkle on a little salt—but not too much, as the feta is likely to be salty.

Mound the tomatoes in the center of a deep platter. Rinse the feta cheese if it's very salty, then break it into rough chunks and arrange them around the tomatoes. Slice the red onion very thinly and scatter the slices over the cheese.

Drizzle the remaining olive oil on the cheese and sprinkle on the rest of the chopped mint. Spoon the salad, with its juices, over slices of crusty French bread.

Serves 6–8 as a first course, or 10–15 as part of a buffet.

BABA GHANOUJ

This is a less rich but exquisitely tasty version of the traditional dish. Be sure you select firm young eggplants. Eggplants that have become overly mature get a bitter taste.

3 lbs. firm young eggplants (about 3
    medium eggplants)
2 medium yellow onions
½ head garlic
1 Tbs. olive oil

½ tsp. salt, more to taste
1½ Tbs. tahine (sesame paste)
3 Tbs. fresh-squeezed lemon juice
pinch of cayenne

optional garnish: lots of fresh cilantro leaves
                additional olive oil if desired

Prick the eggplants here and there with a fork, put them on a big baking sheet and roast them in a 400° oven until they are charred and collapsed—at least an hour. Allow them to cool, then split them lengthwise with a sharp knife and scoop out the flesh, first pulling out and discarding any pockets of dark seeds.

While the eggplants are roasting, chop the onions and peel and mince the garlic. Heat the olive oil in a non-stick pan and cook the onion and garlic in it with ½ teaspoon of salt, stirring often, until they are a deep golden brown—probably at least 45 minutes. The flavor of the dish depends much on this slow caramelizing of the onion and garlic.

Stir the cooked onion and garlic into the eggplant, along with the tahine, lemon juice, and cayenne. Now either chop everything finely until it has the texture you like, or process it a few seconds in a food processor for a smoother finish.

Let it rest 1–2 hours (refrigerate if longer), then taste it and correct the salt and lemon juice if needed. Serve the Baba Ghanouj in a shallow bowl surrounded by lots of cilantro leaves, and pass toasted pita triangles to dip into it. If you're not worried about fat content, you can drizzle more olive oil on top, but it certainly isn't necessary.

Serves 6–8 generously, more if part of a buffet.

WHEAT AND LENTIL PILAF
with Shiitake Mushrooms

This is a delicious hot pilaf to serve with roasted vegetables or sautéed greens, or as an accompaniment to all sorts of things. It also makes a very nice salad when cooled and spooned over an interesting mix of fresh greens, such as Chinese greens or a mix of curly endive and watercress. You may want to sprinkle on a touch more vinegar if using it as a salad. And one of my favorite pita bread sandwiches was made with this pilaf, a spoonful of Baba Ghanouj, and a drizzle of yogurt.

Sprouted wheat and sprouted lentils (as well as other legumes) are available in many health food stores, and I'm seeing them in some upscale supermarkets as well. I get mine at my weekly farmers' market. If you can't easily find sprouted wheat and lentils, use the variation on page 75.

3 medium yellow onions (4 cups chopped)
2 Tbs. olive oil
salt
2 cups sprouted wheat berries (½ lb.)
1¼ cups sprouted lentils

1½ cups spring water
½ lb. shiitake mushrooms (or mixed shiitake and champignon)
½ tsp. dark sesame oil
½–1 tsp. soy sauce
1 Tbs. rice vinegar

Chop the onions rather finely. You should have about 4 cups of chopped onion, which seems like a lot but later will turn out to be just enough. Heat 1½ tablespoons of the olive oil in a large non-stick sauté pan and cook the onions slowly in it, with a sprinkle of salt, until they are caramel-colored. This could take up to an hour.

At the same time, steam the sprouted wheat berries for 45 minutes. Add the steamed wheat to the caramelized onions, along with the lentils, 1½ cups water, and ½ teaspoon salt. Cover the pan tightly and simmer for 20 minutes. Uncover, and if there is any remaining water, let it cook away.

Meanwhile, clean the mushrooms, trim away the tough stems, and cut the caps in ¼-inch dice. In another non-stick pan, heat the remaining ½ tablespoon of olive oil with the sesame oil and sauté the mushrooms in it, stirring often, until they lose their water, dry out, and sizzle. Sprinkle on some soy sauce, toss the mushrooms in it, and cook them a couple minutes more.

Remove the mushrooms from the heat, toss them with the rice vinegar, then stir them into the wheat mixture when you remove the lid.

This is ready to serve as soon as all the liquid is absorbed or evaporated.

This makes 4½–5 cups, or 8 generous servings.

Variation: You can make a very good version of this pilaf with ordinary dry wheatberries and lentils by making the following changes.

For the sprouted wheatberries, substitute ¾ cup dry wheatberries.

For the sprouted lentils, substitute ¾ cup dried lentils.

Simmer the wheatberries in about two quarts water, with a pinch of salt, until they are tender; this could take about two hours. Drain the wheatberries, reserving the liquid, and add enough water to the liquid to make 2½ cups.

Follow the recipe above, using the cooked wheatberries in place of the steamed, sprouted wheat, and the 2½ cups liquid in place of the 1½ cups water. When you combine the wheat, lentils, and liquid with the onions, simmer the mixture for 30–35 minutes instead of the 20 minutes called for, or until the lentils are tender.

ROASTED POTATOES
AND FENNEL

4 medium red-skinned potatoes
    (approx. 2½ lbs.)
2 large fennel bulbs, white only
2 large onions
2 large, ripe tomatoes
8–10 small carrots

1 large bell pepper
½ head garlic
⅔ cup any home-made tomato
    sauce
salt and pepper to taste
2–3 Tbs. olive oil

optional: chopped fresh basil

Scrub, clean, and trim all of the vegetables. The potatoes should be cut in approximately 1-inch cubes, the fennel, onions, and tomatoes about the same or slightly larger. Slender carrots can be cut to the size of your little finger, and the bell pepper sliced into strips or cut in squares. Slice the garlic or chop it coarsely.

Mix everything together in a big bowl with the tomato sauce, some salt and pepper, and the olive oil. Add chopped fresh basil if you like.

Spread the vegetables out on two baking sheets and roast them in a 425° oven, checking them every 7–8 minutes. Stir and turn the vegetables when you see brown or charred spots appearing on top. When all the vegetables are tender—probably about an hour—serve at once.

Serves 6–8.

YOGURT CHEESE WITH HONEY AND FRESH FIGS

With sweet, ripe figs, this is a dish from heaven. However, if fresh figs are unavailable, you could try sliced white peaches (slice them at the last moment), or big, juicy berries, both of which also have that voluptuous quality. Perfect ripeness is essential.

1 recipe Yogurt Cheese (recipe
   follows)

½ cup honey, more to taste
16 large ripe figs

optional garnish: mint sprigs

On each of eight medium-sized dessert plates, put a nice big dollop of freshly stirred Yogurt Cheese. Drizzle at least a tablespoon of honey over it, more if you like.

Cut your figs in half with a sharp knife and split them open, keeping the halves connected at the stem if you want to. Put two figs on each plate next to the Yogurt Cheese. Garnish with mint sprigs if desired.

Serves 8.

YOGURT CHEESE

Yogurt Cheese is nothing more complicated than well-drained plain yogurt. It has a creamy, silky texture, and a flavor similar to cream cheese, though slightly more tangy. It can be spread on bagels, used to make fresh herbed cheese, or sweetened with sugar or honey and eaten with fruit for a wonderful dessert.

**2 quarts plain non-fat yogurt, or a
mixture of non-fat and whole-
milk yogurt**

Use plain yogurt that has no starch or gums added to it.

Line a colander with a triple thickness of damp cheesecloth. Put the yogurt into it and stand the colander in a bowl. Cover with plastic wrap and refrigerate for about 18–20 hours. Drain the liquid from the bowl and discard it once or twice in the course of this process.

If you want an even thicker, denser cheese, pick up the 4 corners of the cheese-cloth, twist them together, then put a weight on top of the cheese and let it drain another few hours.

*2 quarts of yogurt will yield about 2½–3 cups of Yogurt Cheese,
depending on how long you drain it.*

SEVEN GREAT
CHILE PEPPERS

*Part of the fun of chiles, besides their addictive flavor and heat, is the
fact that there are so many of them, and the same chile often goes by different
names in different parts of the country. Don't worry. If the worst thing that
happens to you is that you use an Anaheim (not its real name) when you meant
to use a guajillo (who knows?), then life is good. At least you're eating chiles.*

*These are the chiles I use most frequently. They are usually available
where I live, and the dried pods can be ordered by mail. The mail-order places I
suggest for chiles is the Old Southwest Trading Company, P.O. Box 7545,
Albuquerque, N.M., 87194; telephone (505) 836-0168, and Pendery's, 1221
Manufacturing Street, Dallas, Texas; telephone (214) 741-1870.*

Jalapeño—This is the best-known and most commonly used pepper in
Mexican food—used in fresh salsas, sliced over nachos, pickled whole.
It is even made into fancy jellies.

Jalapeños are used in their fresh form. They are small, smooth,
usually dark green, with a cone-like shape, about 2–3 inches long.
They turn bright red when riper. Jalapeños are medium hot and
have a fantastic, distinctive flavor with their heat. They are widely
available.

jalapeño

Ancho, or *Poblano*—When it is fresh and green, this pepper is
called a poblano, and is frequently used to make *chiles rellenos*, or
stuffed chiles. When it is fully ripened and dried, it becomes a dark
reddish-brown, and is called a *chile ancho*, or "wide pepper," because
the flat, dried pods are almost as wide as they are long. The dried
anchos are an important ingredient of *mole poblano*.

Poblanos are about the size of smaller bell peppers, and are very
mild.

poblano

New Mexican, or *New Mexico*, also still called *Anaheim*
—This chile defines New Mexico and is served in almost every restaurant,
hanging in *ristras* from beams of adobes, perfuming the air during the autumn

roasting season. Once called Anaheim, its name was formally changed to New Mexican recently.

New Mexican chiles are 6–7 inches long, dark green, and later ripening to bright red. They are medium hot and are used in both fresh and dried form. The Ortega company has made canned New Mexican chiles widely available.

Anaheim

Pasilla, sometimes also called *Negro*—because of their very dark color. I have only used the dried pods. They have a mild but rich chile flavor.

Pasillas are usually about 5–6 inches long and fairly narrow, with dark brown wrinkled skin.

dried pasilla

Guajillo—Similar in looks to the New Mexican chile, guajillos are a deep reddish-brown when mature and have a smooth texture. They are 6–7 inches long, little more than an inch wide, and medium hot.

If you can't find guajillos, I would suggest substituting New Mexican chiles, but increasing the quantity a bit, as the New Mexicans are milder.

Serrano—This little chile is noticeably hotter than the familiar jalapeño. It is used fresh to make a delicious hot salsa.

dried guajillo

Serranos are only 1–3 inches long and very narrow. They are dark green when young, ripening to red, though some are orange or yellow. They are very hot.

Chipotle—I'm crazy about chipotles. They are smoke-dried jalapeños, hot and tasty, with a seductive combination of jalapeño flavor and deep, intriguing smokiness. The dried pods are nut-brown, wrinkled, and hard. Sizes vary, but most are 2–3 inches long.

Chipotles are available dried, or canned in an *adobo* sauce. I prefer to use the dried pods, and soak them to get the purest flavor.

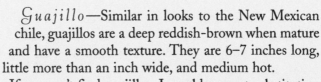

dried chipotle

GUILLERMINA'S CHILE SALSAS

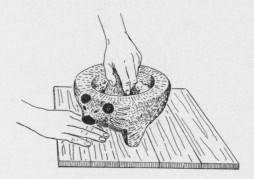

A chile salsa of some kind is the most common condiment in my house. Put a good salsa on your table, freshly made and fragrant in the air around you, and watch your ordinary, everyday food come alive and dance. It really is like turning up the music.

I'm not talking about *moles*, those complex symphonies of flavor involving dozens of ingredients and serious time over a hot stove. I'm talking about the easy salsas that you can throw together at the last minute, the daily salsas, raw or cooked, fiery, brash, dramatic, and refreshing.

One of my favorites is the easiest. Salsa Cruda (see page 240), also sometimes called *pico de gallo*, is just chopped tomatoes, jalapeño chiles, onion, and cilantro, with a little salt. Everything is raw. This is freshness itself, and everyone loves it. Even the kids pile it on their tortilla chips. It is dynamite with guacamole, terrific in burritos or tacos and spooned into hot quesadillas. If you throw it into a hot pan, let it sizzle a moment, then stir in beaten eggs, you have a fast version of Huevos Mexicanos.

The easiest cooked salsas are made by putting dried chiles, onion, garlic, and maybe tomatoes into a pot with a little water and salt, simmering until everything is soft, then spinning it all in a blender for a moment. I sometimes add toasted cumin at the end, or chopped cilantro. This method is almost effortless, and can be adapted to any kind of dried chile pods. A fiery salsa can be made with dried serranos or pequins, a mild one from anchos, and a smoky-hot salsa from chipotles.

I also love salsas made from chiles and fresh tomatillos, scorched on a griddle or grill, and roughly ground up in a mortar. (See Guajillo Chile Salsa, page 31.)

To make a good salsa of this type, there are two pieces of equipment you should have. First, you need a good-sized cast-iron skillet. You could use a heavy stainless steel, Calphalon, or one of the new non-stick finishes, but I recommend the cast-iron pan because after you char the tomatillos you will have to scrub some charcoal off that pan, and cast iron is indestructible.

The other thing you'll want is a *molcajete*, the big, rough stone mortar that can be bought very cheaply in almost any Mexican market. The *molcajete* is a great tool for any kitchen; I use mine almost daily. It's extremely practical for quickly grinding up a spoonful of cumin seed or some other spice, and I like the way it looks on my kitchen counter—it has the traditional little pig's head carved on one side. I'm sure a smart retailer of gourmet cookware will soon have them in a catalogue at ten times the money they cost in the open-air market.

I learned to make these salsas watching my friend Guillermina, who is from Jalisco. One day she threw some green chiles and whole tomatillos into a naked, hot cast-iron pan. For the next ten minutes she'd pass by casually and knock the vegetables around, turning them over as they charred in big blisters and sizzled on the hot iron. The smell of those scorching chiles and tomatillos, rising up through the house, made my tongue drip.

When they were well blackened, she peeled the chiles under running water, pulled out their stems, and tossed them in the *molcajete* with the tomatillos. A few brisk pushes with the stone pestle, and they were salsa. She threw in a big handful of sliced green onions and a bigger one of cilantro, added a dash of salt, gave a few more turns with the stone, and put it on the table. It was sensational. Utterly irresistible. Wow! I thought. That's really cooking. The whole operation had taken less than half an hour.

We dipped our warm tortillas in that salsa and ate it up, and our taste buds danced.

CINCO DE MAYO DINNER

Nopalito Salad
Tamales with Zucchini and Cilantro Filling
Chile Ancho Salsa
Garlic and Cumin Rice
white cheese
Flan with Caramel and Pineapple
(or Strawberry Ice Cream with Triple Sec)
Cafe de Olla

This Mexican meal is authentically delicious and full of surprises, and not very difficult to prepare.

A big Nopalito Salad, served with fresh white cheese and hot tortillas, could be a great lunch by itself. For this menu, serve it in smaller quantities for a starter or alongside the tamales. If you absolutely can't find fresh nopalitos, then substitute lightly steamed tender fresh green beans and increase the lemon juice slightly. It will not be Nopalito Salad, but a very nice salad nevertheless.

The tamales are inspired by some I ate at the Rancho de Chimayo, outside Santa Fe, New Mexico. I more or less reproduced them when I got home. They're savory and piquant, but not spicy, so the most delicate palates can enjoy them. With the tamales I serve a Chile Ancho Salsa that is profound in flavor but likewise not fiery. It is served warm, spooned generously around the tamales. For committed chile-eaters like myself, it is good to offer a really hot sauce as well. Be sure to tell everyone which is which.

After chiles, have a cool and silky flan, presented in a pool of caramel and pineapple sauce. Then serve strong, black Cafe de Olla, fragrant with cinnamon, for a complete experience.

NOPALITO SALAD

If you cannot get nopalitos, a tasty salad can be made with slender green beans steamed until they are just crisp-tender.

3 cups cooked, diced nopalitos
    (for cooking instructions,
    see page 28)
2 medium-sized ripe tomatoes
¾ cup sliced green onions or ½
    sweet yellow onion, finely
    chopped
1–2 Tbs. minced fresh jalapeño
    pepper

¾ cup coarsely chopped fresh
    cilantro leaves
1 cup cooked pinto or black beans
1 Tbs. fresh lemon juice (a few
    drops more if substituting green
    beans for nopalitos)
salt and pepper to taste

garnishes: crumbled fresh white cheese, such as farmer's cheese
            sliced avocados
            fresh chile salsa

The nopalitos, cooked and cooled, can be cut in strips or in ½-inch dice. The tomatoes can be cut in chunks just a little larger than that.

Combine all the ingredients in an ample bowl and toss them together gently but thoroughly; taste and adjust the salt, lemon juice, and jalapeño if needed. The flavor of fresh jalapeños is delicious, but they are hot, so add a little at a time, tasting as you go, until you like the balance.

The salad is best served immediately, but can be kept covered in the refrigerator for 1–2 hours. Spoon the salad onto plates, and garnish each serving with a sprinkling of crumbled fresh farmer's cheese. A mixture of dry farmer's cheese and tangy goat cheese is also wonderful. Fresh avocado slices can be fanned alongside or on top. Then pass the salsa and a basket of fresh hot corn tortillas.

Serves 6.

TAMALES WITH ZUCCHINI AND CILANTRO FILLING

The masa for these tamales is somewhat denser than the one I make for fresh corn tamales. It will hold its texture well with a moist filling and has a nice, savory flavor. It can also be used with any number of other fillings—goat cheese and chipotle sauce, or a *mole*, for instance.

40 large dried corn husks
   (to yield 20)

fresh-ground pepper to taste
⅔ cup chopped fresh cilantro leaves

for the filling:
1 lb. tender young zucchini
1 tsp. salt
1 large yellow onion
4 cloves garlic
8 green onions
1½ Tbs. olive oil
½ cup diced mild green chiles
1 Tbs. lemon juice, more to taste

for the masa:
6 oz. butter, softened (1½ sticks)
3½ cups masa harina
½ tsp. salt
2 tsp. baking powder
½ cup milk
1½ cups vegetable broth, cool or
   lukewarm

To prepare the dried corn husks: Start with at least twice as many dried corn husks as you will need (they usually come in packages of a few dozen). Soak them in hot water for about 30 minutes. When they're soft, rinse them under running water as you separate them, discarding the very small or torn ones. Lay them flat on a plate and keep them covered with a damp tea towel until you need them. The longer torn ones can be torn further, into ½-inch strips, and used for ties.

To prepare the filling: Wash and trim the zucchini and cut it into ¼-inch dice. Toss it with a teaspoon of salt and leave it to drain in a colander for about 30 minutes.

Meanwhile, chop the onion finely, mince the garlic, and trim and thinly slice the green onions. Heat the olive oil in an ample non-stick skillet and sauté all the onions and garlic in it until they begin to color.

When the zucchini have released their water, press them gently in the colander, then add them to the onion mixture. Continue cooking the vegetables, stirring occasionally, until the zucchini are tender and the mixture is quite dry. It is essential to have no excess liquid here.

Stir in the green chiles, lemon juice, some pepper, and the chopped cilantro. Taste, and correct the seasoning if needed.

This makes about 2 cups, or enough filling for at least 20 tamales. Any leftover filling is delicious in omelets, quesadillas, or burritos, or stirred into a vegetable soup.

To prepare the masa: Beat the softened butter in a mixing bowl until it is light and fluffy. Whisk the dry masa harina with the salt and baking powder until well blended. Beat some of the dry mixture into the butter, then the milk, then more of the dry mixture, then some of the broth, and so on until everything is combined.

The prepared masa should have the texture of a tender cookie dough; it should hold its shape well, but not feel dry or crumbly. If it is too dry, add a few more drops of broth, and if too sticky, add a little more masa harina.

This makes enough masa for 18–20 tamales, using slightly less than ¼ cup per tamale.

To assemble the tamales: Lay a prepared corn husk flat on your work surface. Put about ¼ cup of masa in the center of it and spread it slightly. Be sure to leave at least a 1½-inch border on each side and a couple of inches at each end.

Put a rounded tablespoon of filling down the center of the masa, then lift one side of the husk gently over the other until the edges of the masa meet around the filling. Pinch the masa together a little with your fingers, sealing in the filling. Fold the husk lengthwise over the tamale, then fold in the narrow end, then finish rolling up the whole husk, loosely. This makes a tamale that's open on one end. If you have extra-long husks, you can fold the wide end in as well, envelope style, before you finish rolling. Note: forming tamales is tricky the first time, but soon gets much easier, and then becomes a lot of fun.

Tie a thin strip of corn husk around the middle to hold everything together, but not too tightly, as the tamales will expand in cooking. If you have trouble tying strips of corn husk, use plain brown twine, or any other kind of tie that won't react with the food in steaming.

To steam the tamales: Arrange them loosely in a roomy vegetable steamer. If you left the wide end unfolded, be sure to handle them carefully and fit them into the steamer with the open end up. Steam the tamales for 35–45 minutes, then test one. If the masa is cooked through and no longer sticky, they're done. Serve them hot.

Tamales can be prepared a few hours ahead of time and held in the refrigerator, covered, until it's time to steam them—just add a few minutes to the cooking time to take the chill off. They can also be resteamed briefly a day or two later.

This makes 18–20 tamales, enough for 6–8 servings.

CHILE ANCHO SALSA

This is not a spicy salsa, but it is full of deep chile flavor, and can be used in a satisfying quantity.

3 large ancho chile pods
   (about 2 oz.)
1 onion
6 oz. tomatillos
3 cloves garlic

¾ tsp. salt
½ cup cilantro leaves
1 Tbs. cumin seed
water or broth as needed

In a small pot, simmer the ancho pods in just enough water to cover until they are soft and their thin outer skins are curling away. Lift the pods out with a slotted spoon, pull away the skins, pull out the stems and cores, and return the trimmed pods to the water.

Cut the onion into large chunks. Remove the dry husks from the tomatillos and cut them in halves or quarters. Peel the garlic cloves. Add the onion, tomatillos, garlic, salt, and cilantro leaves to the chiles, add a little more water if needed, and simmer everything together for about 15 minutes.

Toast the cumin seeds lightly in a pan, grind them briefly in a mortar, and add them to the vegetables. When all the vegetables are completely soft, purée the salsa in a blender. It should be a coarse purée, thick enough to hold a soft shape in the spoon. This salsa can be thinned with a little water or broth if desired. It keeps well for about a week if tightly covered and refrigerated.

Makes about 3 cups.

GARLIC AND CUMIN RICE

1 medium Spanish onion, finely
   chopped
3 cloves garlic, minced
1 Tbs. olive oil
1 tsp. butter
1 Tbs. whole cumin seed

2 cups long-grain white rice
1 tsp. salt
3 medium red tomatoes, peeled and
   chopped (about 2 cups)
4¼ cups hot water

In a medium-sized non-stick sauté pan, sauté the onions and garlic in the olive oil and butter until the onions are soft and just beginning to color. Meanwhile, toast the cumin seeds in a small pan, over a medium flame, until they release their fragrance. Grind them lightly in a mortar.

Add the rice to the onions and garlic, stir it for 2–3 minutes, then add the cumin, salt, chopped tomatoes, and water. Bring the mixture to a simmer, lower the heat, cover the pan, and leave it to simmer for 20 minutes, longer if you like your rice softer. At the end of the cooking time, turn off the heat and allow to stand, covered, for another 5 minutes, then fluff with a fork before serving.

Makes 6–8 servings.

FLAN WITH CARAMEL AND PINEAPPLE

Flan is ever-present in Mexican and Spanish kitchens, and that's a good thing. A custard with a little caramel sauce, flan is one of the simplest desserts, but when properly made it has a silky texture and purity of flavor that rightly make it a classic. This variation begins with a plain flan, prepared with slightly less sugar than usual, then finishes with a garnish of pineapple in a thin sauce of caramelized sugar and pineapple juice. I love the rich taste of burnt sugar mixed with the slight acidity of the fruit.

1½ cups sugar	½ tsp. vanilla extract
3 cups low-fat or whole milk	1 cup pineapple juice
4 large eggs	1½ cups crushed or chopped canned
pinch of salt	or fresh pineapple

Melt ½ cup of sugar in a heavy-bottomed skillet over a medium flame. When the sugar is entirely melted and a rich golden caramel color, pour the caramel into a 1½-quart baking dish, tilting it around so that the caramel lightly coats both the bottom and the sides.

Scald the milk and remove it from the heat before it boils. Beat the eggs with another ½ cup of sugar, a pinch of salt, and the vanilla until they are smooth, then add the scalded milk in a small stream as you keep beating.

Strain the custard into the prepared baking dish. Place the dish inside a larger baking pan with about an inch of water in it, and bake in a preheated 350° oven for about an hour. If the top seems to be getting too brown, you can cover the flan loosely with a sheet of aluminum foil. It is done when a knife inserted near the center comes out clean.

Remove the baking dish from its water bath and allow the flan to cool, then chill it in the refrigerator.

Meanwhile, melt the final ½ cup of sugar in a medium-sized pan, just as you did at the start. When it is a caramel syrup, remove it from the heat, add about half the pineapple juice, and stand back, as it will boil up and steam dramatically. Let it settle, return it to a low flame, and add the rest of the juice. Stir as it comes to a simmer and the caramel dissolves into the juice. Add the crushed or chopped pineapple and simmer the mixture for 2–3 minutes more, longer if it seems too thin. Then cover it and set aside until you are ready to serve the flan.

To unmold the flan, it helps to dip the bottom of the baking dish into a pan of hot water for a moment. Then run a knife around the edge of the custard to loosen the sides. Invert a large serving platter over the dish and, holding the two securely together, quickly turn them over. The flan will drop onto the serving platter, with a pool of caramel around it.

To serve, spoon the pineapple-caramel sauce around the flan on its platter, to mingle with the pure caramel, or spoon some onto each individual plate next to a slice of flan.

This makes 8 servings.

CAFE DE OLLA

cinnamon sticks
spring water*

coffee beans
piloncillo **(lump cane sugar)**

Cafe de Olla is a strong black coffee made with cinnamon water and sweetened with *pilancillo,* the cone-shaped solid brown cane sugar that is sold in every Mexican market.

Add several sticks of cinnamon to 3 or 4 quarts of water, bring it to a boil, and then leave it to steep for several hours.

Grind your coffee beans and use the cinnamon water to make your coffee in the usual way. For an even stronger cinnamon flavor, add a few broken sticks of cinnamon to the ground beans in the filter.

When the coffee is brewed, add a little *pilancillo* and let it dissolve. This you must do to your own taste. Another way is to serve the cinnamon coffee unsweetened and pass a bowl of *pilancillo,* broken into small pieces, so everyone can sweeten to taste.

*Use tap water only if it is wonderful, otherwise use bottled spring water for this.

PICNIC FOR A SUMMER CONCERT

assorted cured olives

Spinach and Feta Cheese Alligator

White Bean and Tomato Salad

Ratatouille

Panzanella

cheese platter:
Gorgonzola, marinated chèvre,
thin-sliced Parmesan

olive bread, sourdough baguettes, breadsticks

fresh berries, peaches, apricots, and cherries

chocolate-dipped biscotti

coffee

This food is appealing and delicious, and tastes best
at room temperature. And because it's virtually indestructible, it
can easily be transported for a fancy picnic, a tailgate party, or a
dinner in the park before an open-air concert.

This is also a menu that can be easily expanded for a more lavish buffet to serve at home, perhaps to a larger group. You can add some other favorite cold dishes, such as vermicelli with pesto, marinated peppers, a seafood salad, or something from the grill. It's summer food, and goes with everything that's in season.

The Spinach and Feta Cheese Alligator, a big hearty pastry, has a whimsical shape and a savory, chewy filling. Take along a cutting board, and slice the alligator right at the picnic.

A trio of excellent salads go along: White Bean and Tomato Salad, Ratatouille, and Panzanella, a great Tuscan invention made of ripe vegetables and coarse bread. To complete the buffet, serve a little dish of assorted cured olives, a basket of great breads, and a platter of cheeses. I would include one ripe blue-veined cheese, a marinated goat cheese, and one sharp, aged cheese such as Parmesan, aged Jack, or Manchego.

With such good picnic food, you want a good picnic wine— not heavy or serious, but a younger wine with a taste of the fruit. A rosé from Provence, or an Italian white, such as a nice Vernaccia di San Gimignano, would be right. A light red wine would also be fine, especially for an evening picnic in cooler weather.

For dessert, bring along baskets of fresh, ripe summer fruit. You can line a flat wicker tray with vine leaves and fill it with berries, mixing raspberries, blueberries, and small strawberries. Keep boysen- berries and blackberries separate, as they turn to sauce very easily. In another basket, pile up whole apricots, cherries, and peaches.

Serve chocolate-dipped biscotti with the fruit. Fill a thermos with strong, hot coffee, and you will have the perfect ending for a lovely *al fresco* experience, and also be able to stay awake for the concert.

SPINACH AND FETA CHEESE ALLIGATOR

This is similar to Chard and Fennel Pie (page 118). It's a long, narrow pastry in which a filling of greens, potatoes, and herbs is wrapped in a soft bread crust. It's very low in fat and delicious warm or cool, and makes a good buffet or picnic dish when cut in thin slices. I called it an alligator because I made it in the shape of an alligator's head, but you don't have to.

crust:
1½ tsp. dry yeast
1 tsp. sugar
¼ cup warm water
3 cups white flour

1 tsp. salt
1 egg
⅔ cup low-fat milk
1 Tbs. olive oil

filling:
2 Tbs. olive oil
2 cups chopped onion
3 cloves garlic, minced
1 large leek, white and light green only, chopped
¾ cup thinly sliced green onions
1 lb. fresh spinach (2 medium bunches), washed and chopped
2 medium potatoes, peeled and cut in ¼-inch dice

¼ cup chopped fresh dill
1 Tbs. cider vinegar
4 eggs
½ cup low-fat milk
4 oz. feta cheese
3 Tbs. raw rice
¼ cup sliced Kalamata olives
fresh-ground black pepper
salt, if needed

Start the dough first: Dissolve the yeast and sugar in the warm water and leave it a few minutes, until it starts to bubble and foam. Meanwhile, measure 2¾ cups of the flour into a large bowl and stir in the salt. Beat together the egg, milk, and olive oil, stir in the yeast mixture, and then mix the liquid into the flour. Stir it with a big wooden spoon until it forms a dough.

When the stirring gets tough, spread the remaining flour on an ample board and turn the dough out on it. Knead it gently, turning often at first to keep it coated with flour, until it is smooth and becoming elastic. Form the dough into a ball and put it into a lightly oiled bowl. Cover the bowl with a towel and set it aside to rise in a warm place for about an hour, or until doubled.

While it rises, make the filling: Heat the olive oil in a large non-stick skillet and sauté the chopped onions, garlic, and leek in it until the vegetables are soft and beginning to color. Add the green onions, chopped spinach, and potatoes, and toss everything together until the spinach wilts. Cover and keep cooking on low heat for about 10 minutes, or until the potatoes are tender. Uncover, raise the heat, and stir occasionally for a few minutes more, until the excess moisture completely cooks away. Stir in the dill and the cider vinegar, and remove from heat.

Break the eggs into a bowl, reserving 1 yolk to use for a glaze. Beat the eggs with the milk. Crumble the feta cheese.

Transfer the hot vegetable mixture into a cool bowl, and stir in the feta cheese, the raw rice, and the sliced olives. Season with black pepper. Taste, and add salt only if it is needed—the salty cheese and olives may provide enough, so be careful. Finally, stir in the beaten eggs and milk. Let the prepared filling sit for about 15 minutes, to allow the rice and potatoes to soak up some moisture.

Punch down the dough and divide it in half. On a large, floured surface, pat one half of the dough into a rectangle, then gently roll it, turning it over and dusting with more flour to keep it from sticking, until you have an oval about 24 inches long and 8–10 inches across.

Fold the dough in half crosswise and lay it down on an oiled baking sheet. Unfold it, and spoon half the filling down the middle, from the fold line to within an inch of the end.

Beat the reserved egg yolk with a spoonful of water and brush the edges of the dough with it. Fold the other half of the dough over again, laying it evenly on top of the filling and pressing the edges together lightly. Then fold the edges up from underneath, curling the bottom crust over the edge of the top crust, and crimping or pleating it into a pattern. Pierce the dough here and there with a skewer or fork.

If you're feeling especially creative, you can stick on scraps of dough at the appropriate spots for the alligator's eyes. Brush the dough lightly with the egg yolk glaze.

Roll out and fill the second half of the dough, either into an alligator or else just a long, filled loaf. Bake the alligators or loaves at 350° for about 45 minutes. After 25 minutes, reverse their positions in the oven so that they brown evenly. Let them cool slightly before slicing.

Makes 2 alligators, enough to serve 15–20.

WHITE BEAN AND TOMATO SALAD

1 lb. small white beans
pinch of baking soda
½ head garlic, separated into cloves
    and peeled
6–8 sage leaves
3 Tbs. fruity green olive oil
2 tsp. salt
2 large stalks celery
½ medium Maui (sweet) onion
12 Kalamata olives

1 cup sliced or cubed Armenian
    cucumber* (or any cucumber,
    peeled and seeded first)
½ cup coarsely chopped flat-leaf
    parsley
¼ cup coarsely chopped fresh basil
fresh-ground black pepper
3–4 medium-sized vine-ripened
    tomatoes

Soak the beans overnight in plenty of water and a pinch of baking soda. Drain them and put them in a large, heavy-bottomed skillet with enough fresh water to cover them by an inch. Add the peeled garlic cloves, cut in half if they are very large, the sage leaves, and 1 tablespoon of olive oil.

Bring the water to a gentle simmer and regulate the heat to keep it just simmering. After a while, skim some foam off the top. Simmer the beans for 2–3 hours, until they are tender, checking them occasionally to make sure they are still covered with water. Toward the end of the cooking time, gently stir in the salt. Don't overstir the beans or let them boil hard, as you want to maintain their shape.

Allow the beans to cool, then drain off the liquid and either discard it or reserve it for a soup.

Armenian cucumbers are long and thin, with a delicate skin and tiny seeds, so they can be used whole and without peeling. I have seen the same thing sold as European cucumber, and a very similar, if not identical, variety called Japanese cucumber. Any good-tasting cucumber will do, but if it has a tough hide you must peel it.

Trim the celery, halve it lengthwise, and slice it thinly. Coarsely chop half a sweet onion. Slice 12 Kalamata olives off their stones. Cut a thin, Armenian cucumber in half lengthwise and slice thinly enough to fill a cup.

In a large bowl, combine the beans with the celery, onion, olives, cucumber, chopped herbs, 2 tablespoons of olive oil, and fresh-ground black pepper to taste. Mix gently but thoroughly, being careful not to crush the beans.

Just before serving, mound the bean salad in the middle of a platter and surround with freshly cut tomato wedges.

Makes about 8 cups, enough for 12–16 servings.

RATATOUILLE

Ratatouille is the quintessential dish of Provence. It is a dish for late summer, when eggplants and peppers are abundant, and tomatoes at their sweetest. The vegetables are stewed in olive oil, and perfumed with herbs.

I used to make Ratatouille with much more oil, but I like this version better—made with just a little olive oil, and more tomatoes, which provide the liquid for stewing. The result is lighter, with fresh, pure flavors and the concentrated sweetness of the ripe tomatoes.

This recipe yields a big batch, enough for a party, or several meals. I never seem to get tired of Ratatouille, and it's delicious cold, so this big recipe makes sense to me—this way you can stir over the hot stove once and eat at least twice. However, you can also cut the recipe in half.

2 lbs. young, firm eggplants	2 Tbs. olive oil
salt to taste	handful of chopped flat-leaf parsley
2 lbs. zucchini	handful of chopped fresh basil
6 cloves garlic, chopped	1 Tbs. balsamic vinegar
3 large onions, cut in ½-inch pieces	fresh-ground black pepper to taste
1½ lbs. red and green peppers, seeded and cut in ½-inch dice	3 large, red tomatoes, cut in 1-inch pieces
2 cups Summer Tomato Sauce (page 51)	

Peel the eggplants and cut them in ½-inch dice. Toss the cut eggplants with a generous amount of salt and put them in a colander, over a bowl, to drain for at least 45 minutes. Trim the zucchini and cut it into similar-sized pieces. Toss the zucchini with salt and put it in another colander to drain.

While the salted eggplant and squash drain, prepare the other vegetables, as well as the tomato sauce if you don't already have it on hand.

Heat the olive oil in your largest non-stick sauté pan—at least 12 inches. Add the garlic and stir it for 1 minute. Add the chopped onion and a dash of salt and cook over medium heat, stirring frequently, until the onion is soft and just beginning to color.

Briefly rinse the eggplants and zucchini in cold water, and press them gently against their colanders to squeeze out excess moisture. Add the eggplant and zucchini to the onions with a scant teaspoon of salt and sauté, stirring frequently, for 6–7 minutes. Stir in the peppers and the tomato sauce, cover, reduce the flame, and simmer for about 20 minutes.

Uncover the sauté pan. If the Ratatouille looks too much like a soup, simmer it uncovered for a while, stirring often, until it is a thick stew. Add the chopped herbs, a little sprinkle of a good wine vinegar, more salt if needed, and a generous grating of black pepper. Finally, stir in the cut-up tomatoes and simmer for another 2 minutes or so, just to heat them through.

Served cold, this is a great salad. I also like Ratatouille hot over steamed rice, or with pasta. And it's wonderful wrapped in a crepe with a bit of cheese.

Serves 12–15.

PANZANELLA

To make this, you need ripe, juicy tomatoes, and really good bread—a coarse, chewy, country loaf, about a day old.
   Make this salad an hour or two before you're going to eat it.

1 large cucumber	⅓ cup sliced fresh basil leaves
1 green bell pepper	1½ tsp. capers
1 red bell pepper	1 tsp. salt, more to taste
½ small red onion	black pepper to taste
3 large red tomatoes	3 Tbs. fruity green olive oil
1 clove garlic, minced	3 Tbs. balsamic vinegar
¾ cup flat-leaf parsley, loosely packed	½ lb. coarse country bread, a day old

Peel the cucumber, trim off the ends, cut it in half lengthwise, scrape out the seeds, and slice the halves. Trim, core, and quarter the bell peppers, and slice the quarters crosswise very thinly. Slice the red onion lengthwise as thinly as you can.

Rinse the tomatoes and trim out their cores. Cut them into 1-inch pieces, working on a plate so as not to lose a single drop of their juice. This is important to the texture of the salad.

In a large bowl, combine the cucumber, peppers, onion, tomatoes with all their juice, minced garlic, parsley leaves, sliced basil, and capers. Sprinkle on about a teaspoon of salt, grind on some pepper, add the oil and vinegar, and mix everything together gently. It will look rather soupy at this point, and will become more so with the salt and vinegar.

Slice the bread and cut the slices into 1-inch pieces, as you would for a bread pudding or stuffing. You should have about a quart of bread chunks. Add these to the salad, and immediately start lifting and turning the salad ingredients to mix in the bread thoroughly. The bread will start soaking up the dressing and juices at once.

Taste, and correct the seasoning with more salt or pepper if needed. The salad should be moist throughout but not soggy. If it seems too dry, add a drop of oil, vinegar, or fresh tomato pulp. If it seems too wet, add a little more bread. The salad improves with a couple hours of waiting, but by the next day it's too soggy.

Variations: Some nice things to add for a change are very thin slices of fennel bulb, leftover grilled eggplant, cut into pieces, or thinly sliced celery or radishes. Try replacing the capers with a few cured olives, pitted and chopped. Add hearts of romaine, sliced in wide ribbons, or torn radicchio.

Serves 6–8.

MEZZE FOR TEN

Dolmades
(Stuffed Vine Leaves)

Roasted Eggplant Dip

Charred Tomatoes with Garlic and Olives

Hummous

pita bread

Mixed Greek Salad

Yogurt and Potatoes with Mint

figs, apricots, and almonds

Honey Pie

Mezze are the tasty little dishes that start any Middle Eastern meal. They are usually thought of as appetizers, but if you put a few of them together with the right combination of flavors and textures, they become a meal, and, what's more, a meal you will want to linger over, sitting on a shaded terrace and sipping a chilled wine or ice-cold ouzo.

The Roasted Eggplant Dip, Charred Tomatoes with Garlic and Olives, and Hummous are all ideal foods to be scooped up with warm pita bread. You may want one or two other breads with the meal as well—a flatbread, and a big country loaf.

Dolmades—stuffed vine leaves—are also a finger food. The plate is really for the big, colorful salad and the cool yogurt and potato dish. These two go very well side by side: the salad is crunchy and pungent with marinated olives and salty cheese, the yogurt dish slightly creamy and mild.

Most of this food is best at room temperature, and it is served all at once, making it perfect for a long lunch, a late supper, or any other less structured occasion.

Lay a large table: cover it with a bright cloth and arrange all the food in the middle of it, on your most beautiful platters. Add a basket of breads, and a carafe of green olive oil.

Have the ice bucket nearby, with a good white Riesling or Chardonnay, or perhaps a dry rosé from Provence. Ouzo is great, too, although you probably won't want to drink it all evening. I like it frozen, served in very small glasses. It tastes particularly delicious with the stuffed vine leaves, the olives, and the feta cheese. For a refreshing non-alcoholic drink, try iced peppermint tea, sweetened with honey.

You almost have to have figs to end this meal. If fresh figs are not in season, serve dried figs, dried apricots, and almonds, along with a Honey Pie and sweet hot tea or Turkish coffee.

Variations: This menu could be expanded to include grilled fish, chicken, or lamb, or a marinated seafood salad. The number of *mezze* could also be increased for a more elaborate table. Traditional Greek pastries such as *spanakopita* or *tiropita* would be good, as would steamed artichokes with oil and lemon, lentil salad, and tabbouleh.

DOLMADES

(Stuffed Vine Leaves)

½ lb. preserved vine leaves
2 Tbs. + 2 tsp. olive oil
1 medium onion, finely chopped
1 clove garlic, minced
1½ cups long-grain white rice
3–4 Tbs. chopped fresh mint leaves
½ cup chopped fresh dill weed
⅔ cup raisins
⅔ cup pine nuts

3 Tbs. chopped Kalamata olives (or other cured olives)
½ tsp. salt, more to taste
black pepper to taste
6–8 whole cloves garlic
2 cups vegetable broth
1¾ cups water
4–6 Tbs. fresh lemon juice

Remove the vine leaves from the jar carefully, so as not to tear them. Lay them flat in a large bowl and cover them with boiling water. After a minute or two, drain them, then cover them with cold water, let them soak for about 5 minutes, and drain again.

Heat a tablespoon of the olive oil in a non-stick sauté pan and cook the chopped onion and garlic in it for a few minutes, stirring often, until the onion is soft. Put the rice in a bowl, cover it with boiling water, let it soak for 5 minutes, then drain.

In a large mixing bowl, combine the rice, onion and garlic, mint, dill, raisins, pine nuts, olives, ½ teaspoon of salt, and some black pepper. Mix everything together thoroughly.

To wrap the vine leaves, take one at a time and lay it flat on a board, vein side up. Trim off the stem with a sharp knife. Place a heaping tablespoon of the filling almost in the center of the leaf, near the stem end. Fold the bottom of the leaf up over the filling, then fold in the sides, and finish by rolling it up. The leaves should be wrapped neatly, but not very tightly, as the rice will expand when they cook.

When all the filling is used up, line the bottom of a large enameled soup pot or Dutch oven with the remaining leaves. Lay the stuffed vine leaves in the pot, close together and seam side down. Make 2 layers if you need to, fitting the Dolmades together compactly but without crowding. Slice the whole garlic cloves into 2 or 3 pieces each, and tuck them in among the Dolmades.

Pour the vegetable broth and water over the Dolmades, then drizzle the remaining olive oil over them, as well as 2 teaspoons of the lemon juice. Place a flat, heavy plate directly on top of the Dolmades to hold them in place as they cook.

Bring the liquid to a boil, then lower the heat to a simmer, cover the pot tightly, and leave it simmering for about an hour. Almost all the liquid should be absorbed, and the Dolmades plumped up, with the vine leaves stretched tightly around the filling. Allow them to cool, covered, in the pot, then pour the remaining lemon juice over them before serving.

Makes about 50–60 stuffed vine leaves.

ROASTED EGGPLANT DIP

3 medium eggplants (about 3–4 lbs.)	1½ Tbs. butter
salt to taste	½ cup red wine
3 medium yellow onions	pepper to taste
1½ Tbs. olive oil	chopped fresh oregano to taste
	juice of 1 large lemon

Cut the eggplants in half lengthwise, make several incisions in the cut side with a sharp knife, and sprinkle with salt. Lay them cut side down on lightly oiled baking sheets.

Roast the eggplants in a 400° oven for 50–60 minutes, until they are completely soft. Allow them to cool, then scoop out the flesh, scraping out any pockets of dark seeds and discarding them. Chop the pale flesh coarsely.

Chop the onions and cook them slowly in the olive oil and butter until they are caramelized to a deep golden brown. Deglaze the pan with the red wine, let it simmer away, stirring often, and then season to taste with salt, pepper, and a touch of oregano.

Stir the soft brown onions into the chopped eggplant. Taste. Stir in lemon juice, a bit at a time, and keep tasting; correct with a little salt if necessary.

Serve this warm or at room temperature, with lavosh crackers or pita bread.

This makes enough for an ample first course for 6–8 people.

CHARRED TOMATOES WITH GARLIC AND OLIVES

These slow-roasted tomatoes, allowed to char twice, have a terrific intensity of flavor. A bowl of these tomatoes, a bowl of Hummous, and some pita bread make a great appetizer.

4 lbs. ripe red tomatoes	1 tsp. salt
5 cloves garlic	6–8 Kalamata olives
2 Tbs. olive oil	

Put the tomatoes on a baking sheet, and put them directly under a hot broiler. Watch them carefully—as they blister and the skins turn black, turn them over. When the skins are pretty well charred, remove the tomatoes from the oven, peel off the skins (they will almost fall off), and trim out their stem ends.

Cut the tomatoes into rather large pieces and put them back on the baking sheet. Peel the garlic cloves, cut them in half if they're very large, and scatter them among the tomatoes. Drizzle the tomatoes with 1 tablespoon of olive oil, and sprinkle them with salt. Turn the oven down to 400°, and put the tomatoes in the middle. Check them every ½ hour, and as they start to show little charred spots again, stir them up, mixing the blackened spots in.

In about 1½–2 hours, you should have a thickened mass of tomatoes, flecked with dark bits. Remove this from the oven, give it another stir, taste, and add salt only if needed.

Spoon the tomatoes into a shallow serving bowl, smooth the top, and drizzle the remaining tablespoon of olive oil on top. Remove the pits from the olives and chop the olives coarsely. Sprinkle the chopped olives over the tomatoes. Serve with wedges of pita bread.

Makes about 2½ cups.

HUMMOUS

¾ lb. dried garbanzo beans (or
    sprouted garbanzo beans if you
    can get them)
pinch of baking soda
1 tsp. salt, more if needed

reserved liquid from cooking beans
½ cup tahine (sesame seed butter)
6–9 Tbs. fresh lemon juice
4–5 cloves garlic, minced

optional garnish: 1–2 tsp. olive oil

Soak the dried garbanzos overnight in a large bowl of cool water with a pinch of baking soda. Or put the garbanzos in a pot with several quarts of water and a pinch of soda, bring the water to a boil, and let it boil for 5 minutes, then turn off the heat, cover the pot, and let the beans soak for an hour. Drain the soaked beans.

If you are using sprouted garbanzos, you do not need to soak them at all.

Put the beans in a pot with enough lightly salted water to cover the beans by about ½ inch, and boil them gently, covered, until they are very soft. Add water from time to time to keep the beans covered. For Hummous, you want your beans very well cooked, and it may take 2 hours, or even longer. Drain the beans, reserving the cooking water, and allow them to cool a little. After such long cooking, the water will have turned into a thick, almost gelatinous liquid. Set this aside.

Put the garbanzo beans in the container of a food processor with the tahine, about 5 tablespoons of lemon juice, and the minced garlic. Process in pulses of several seconds, scraping down the container with a spatula as needed, until the beans are uniformly ground into a thick paste.

Add as much of the reserved cooking liquid as needed, a little at a time and processing with each addition, until the right texture is achieved. The Hummous should be thick enough to hold a soft shape, but soft enough to scoop up with a piece of pita bread.

Taste, and add more salt and lemon juice as needed. The amount of lemon juice will depend on the acidity of your lemons.

Spoon the Hummous into a shallow bowl, smooth the top, and drizzle very lightly with olive oil if desired. Serve with wedges of pita bread.

Makes about 3 cups.

MIXED GREEK SALAD

1 large cucumber
1 large fennel bulb
1 large red bell pepper
1 large green bell pepper
½ medium red onion
1 cup marinated artichoke hearts,
    well drained
15–20 Kalamata olives
15–20 cured green olives
2 Tbs. fruity green olive oil, more to
    taste

2 Tbs. wine vinegar
handful of dill sprigs
handful of fresh mint leaves
1–2 tsp. chopped fresh oregano
fresh-ground black pepper
12 oz. feta cheese, rinsed and patted
    dry
salt if needed
2 medium tomatoes, cut in thin
    wedges

Peel the cucumber, cut it in half lengthwise, and scrape out the seeds. Slice the cucumber thickly. Trim and quarter the fennel bulb and slice thinly. Trim and core the bell peppers, quarter lengthwise, and slice thickly. Slice the red onion.

Combine the cucumber, fennel, peppers, onion, artichoke hearts, and olives in a large bowl, together with the olive oil and vinegar. Add the dill sprigs and mint leaves—coarsely chopped or left whole, as you prefer—and the chopped oregano. Grind in some black pepper. Break the feta cheese into small chunks and add about ⅔ of it to the bowl. Toss all these things together gently until they are well combined.

Taste, and add some salt only if it is needed; this will depend on the saltiness of your feta cheese. Finally, at the last moment, add the tomato wedges and mix them in.

Pile the salad onto a large platter, and scatter the remaining feta cheese over the top. Garnish the platter with large mint sprigs if you wish.

Even though this salad has no lettuce, and looks as if it would hold up well, it should not be made too far in advance. If you need to work ahead, prepare all the vegetables and herbs, but do not mix them with the wine vinegar or salt until the last moment, as this will cause the cucumbers to weep and the salad will become watery.

Serves 8–10.

YOGURT AND POTATOES WITH MINT

3 lbs. red-skinned potatoes
1 tsp. salt, more to taste
5 green onions, thinly sliced
⅓ cup sliced fresh mint leaves
2 Tbs. olive oil

fresh-ground black pepper
1 quart plain yogurt, whole or
    low-fat
pinch of cayenne

Put the potatoes in a big pot with enough salted water to cover them by a couple of inches. Bring the water to a boil and cook the potatoes until they are completely tender; the time will vary with the size of the potatoes. Drain them and let them cool for about ½ hour, until you can easily handle them.

Peel the skins off the potatoes; they should come off very easily, and don't worry about any little bits that cling. Pick up the still-warm potatoes two at a time, hold them over a large bowl, and crush them with your hands into rough chunks. (Your children will love this part.)

Sprinkle some salt over the potatoes, then add the green onions and mint leaves. Drizzle the olive oil over the potatoes, grind on some black pepper, and mix them up well. Add about half the yogurt and a pinch of cayenne and stir. Now add more yogurt, about ½ cup at a time, until the mixture has the consistency of a thick sauce or pudding. Taste, and correct the seasoning with more salt and pepper if needed.

Serves 8–10.

HONEY PIE

This is something like a cheesecake, though much lighter, and delightfully flavored with honey.

Note: If you don't have Yogurt Cheese on hand, then, several hours before starting, put the yogurt into a colander lined with 3 layers of cheesecloth, and let it drain for 3–4 hours. You should have about 1¼ cups of thickened yogurt.

pastry: 4 oz. butter (1 stick), chilled

1⅓ cups all-purpose flour   1 egg

3 Tbs. sugar   ½ tsp. vanilla

½ tsp. salt

½ tsp. baking powder

filling: ¼ cup honey

4 eggs   ¼ cup sugar

8 oz. cream cheese   ¼ cup flour

1¼ cups Yogurt Cheese, or 2 cups grated zest of 1 orange
    yogurt drained 3–4 hours

To make the pastry: Put the flour, sugar, salt, and baking powder in the container of a food processor and process a few seconds to combine. Cut in the butter and process until the mixture resembles coarse meal. Beat together the egg and the vanilla, and add it to the flour mixture. Process again, just until the dough holds together in one piece.

Lightly butter a 10-inch springform pan. Roll out ⅔ of the pastry to a 10-inch circle. Trim it to the exact size and fit it into the bottom of the cake pan. Roll the remainder of the pastry out into long strips about 1½ inches wide, and form the sides of the crust with them, pressing them together inside the pan, and sealing up the seam between the side and the bottom. Make sure the side of the crust is at least 1½ inches high, of even thickness, and well joined to the bottom part, or your filling could leak when you pour it in. Chill the dough while you prepare the filling.

To make the filling in a food processor: Beat the eggs, then put them in the container of a food processor with the cream cheese, the drained yogurt, honey, and sugar. Process this mixture until it is completely smooth. Add the flour and the grated orange zest and process again, scraping down as necessary, until smooth.

To make the filling by hand: Allow the cream cheese to soften at room temperature, and warm the honey. Beat the eggs. Cream together the cheese, drained yogurt, honey, and sugar until smooth. Beat in the eggs, flour, and orange zest.

Pour the filling into the prepared crust. It should fill this just short of the top. Bake the pie in a preheated 350° oven for 40 minutes, or until a sharp knife inserted near the middle comes out clean.

Place the pan on a rack to cool, and after a few minutes, remove the sides. Allow the pie to cool completely, then chill it.

Serves 10–12.

Fall and Winter

PUMPKIN SOUP
AND CORNBREAD

Wild Rice Salad
with Sesame Oil Dressing

Pumpkin, Potato, and Leek Soup

Honey-Sweetened Buttermilk Cornbread

warm Chunky Applesauce with cream

In the fall and winter we have a lot of soup-based meals.
They're satisfying, nutritious, and unfussy, which counts for a lot
in our house. Soup is a very comforting food in wintertime, and
when a fresh hot bread is added you don't need much more.

A salad with the earthy flavor of wild rice and a hint
of soy sauce in the dressing, complements the rich, golden soup
and slightly sweet cornbread. Chunky Applesauce, served warm, is
like having the best part of an apple pie—personally, I don't miss the
crust. You can add more or less cream, for a richer or lighter dessert.
I make the applesauce in big batches when the apple orchards in our
area are being harvested and apples are at their plentiful best. I put
a large bowlful in the refrigerator and it's gone in a few days.

This is all the kind of family food I like to make in
larger quantities. When the kids bring friends home from school,
or someone drops by, a generous pot of soup on the stove makes
everything easy. And I like to have leftovers. Soup is always
welcome, the rice salad makes a fine lunch, and even the cornbread
is delicious the next morning, sliced and toasted for breakfast.

WILD RICE SALAD

3 cups water
1 tsp. salt
1 cup uncooked wild rice
¾ cup raisins
1 cup dry red wine
2 Tbs. sugar
2–3 small heads radicchio

2 cups shredded arugula
2 cups thinly sliced Belgian endive
5 or 6 fresh basil leaves, cut in thin
 slivers
4 ounces pine nuts
Sesame Oil Dressing to taste
 (recipe follows)

Bring the water to a boil in a medium saucepan, add the salt and the wild rice, lower the heat to a simmer, and cover the saucepan. Simmer the rice, covered, for 45 minutes, then turn off the heat and let it stand for 10 more minutes. Check for texture—the rice should be tender-firm. Drain away any excess water and allow the rice to cool.

Combine the raisins, red wine, and sugar in a small stainless steel or enameled saucepan and simmer for about 10 minutes, then leave to cool gradually. Drain off the excess wine syrup.

Wash the radicchio, reserve 8–10 of the largest nice leaves, and shred the rest. Combine the shredded radicchio with the other greens.

Toast the pine nuts by stirring them in a dry skillet over medium heat for 5–6 minutes, or until they just begin to color and give off a fragrance.

Toss together the cooled rice, the poached raisins, all the greens, and the toasted pine nuts. Shortly before serving, season to taste with Sesame Oil Dressing, then mound the salad in the reserved radicchio leaves to serve.

Serves 8–10.

endive

SESAME OIL DRESSING

3 Tbs. peanut oil
1 Tbs. dark sesame oil
1½ Tbs. balsamic vinegar, or sweet
    rice vinegar

1 tsp. soy sauce
fresh-ground pepper to taste

optional: chopped fresh chives

Combine all the ingredients in a bowl and whisk together briskly, or process in a blender for a few seconds. If using a blender, add the chopped chives after processing, and leave them out if you're not going to use the dressing the same day; they should be added at the last minute.

Makes ⅓ cup dressing.

PUMPKIN, POTATO, AND LEEK SOUP

For this marvelous soup, choose one of the smaller varieties of sweet, dense-textured, and flavorful pumpkins, rather than the big jack-o'-lantern type. Or you could use any of the good winter squashes, such as butternut, Hubbard, Tahitian, etc.

2 lbs. potatoes
2 cups water
1 tsp. salt, more to taste
½ cup fruity white wine
1½ lbs. peeled, cubed pumpkin, or 3
    cups cooked pumpkin purée
3 large leeks, white part only
    (1½ lbs. trimmed weight)

1½ Tbs. butter
2 cups vegetable broth
2 Tbs. lemon juice
2 Tbs. sugar, more or less
white pepper to taste
¼–½ tsp. grated nutmeg
pinch of cinnamon
½ cup cream

garnish: coarsely chopped fresh parsley, cilantro, or chives

Peel and dice the potatoes and put them in a large soup pot with the water, salt, and wine. If you are using fresh, cubed pumpkin, add it now. If you are using purée, wait. Simmer until the vegetables are tender.

Meanwhile, trim, clean, and slice the leeks, and cook them in the butter over a medium flame, stirring often, until they are soft and beginning to color. Add the leeks to the potato mixture, and continue simmering until the vegetables are all very soft—about 45 minutes total cooking time.

Add the vegetable broth, and the pumpkin purée if that's what you're using, and purée the mixture in batches in a blender or food processor until perfectly smooth. Return the purée to the soup pot and season to taste with the lemon juice, sugar, additional salt, and white pepper. How much sugar you need will depend on the variety of pumpkin or squash used—you may need none. When the sweet-sour balance is correct, add a touch of nutmeg and cinnamon, and stir in the cream. Heat thoroughly and serve, sprinkled with some chopped parsley, cilantro, or chives.

Serves 8–10.

HONEY-SWEETENED BUTTERMILK CORNBREAD

1 cup white flour	3 large eggs
1½ cups cornmeal	1⅓ cups buttermilk
½ tsp. baking soda	3 Tbs. honey
1 tsp. baking powder	2 Tbs. melted butter
¾ tsp. salt	

Sift together the flour, cornmeal, soda, baking powder, and salt. Whisk together the eggs, buttermilk, honey, and melted butter. Combine the wet and the dry mixtures, stirring gently just until the lumps are gone.

Pour the batter into a buttered 12-by-15-inch baking dish and bake in a preheated 350° oven for 30–35 minutes, or until a straw inserted in the center of the cornbread comes out clean. Cut into squares and serve hot or warm.

Serves 8.

APPLESAUCE

The most important part is getting good apples. I use a mix of red, yellow, and green apples, whichever flavorful and juicy varieties are in season. I try always to include at least a few of the good baking apples, like golden delicious, which fall apart into a lovely sauce around chunks of the firmer varieties.

I like this applesauce warm, with a bit of cream, for dessert; cold, with a scoop of cottage cheese, for a light lunch.

5 lbs. fresh apples	1 tsp. nutmeg
3 cups spring water	2–4 Tbs. brown sugar
2 tsp. cinnamon	

Wash the apples, quarter them, and core them, but do not peel. Put them in a large non-reactive pot with the spring water and the spices. Bring the water to a boil, then lower the heat and simmer, stirring often with a long-handled wooden spoon, for about 1½ hours, or until the apples have softened to the consistency you like. Sweeten to your taste with a little brown sugar—how much you use will depend on the varieties of apples.

If apple skins don't bother you, you're done. If you want a more refined applesauce, without the skins, take the Applesauce in 2 or 3 batches and push it through an old-fashioned colander or vegetable mill with the big holes. Discard the skins.

This will make about 5 cups of a thick, coarse-textured applesauce with intense flavor.

Chunky Applesauce:

If you want a chunkier applesauce, you cannot press it through a colander to remove the skins. Here is an alternate method that still gets the maximum flavor from the fruit.

Wash, quarter, core, and peel the apples. In a covered saucepan, simmer the peels and cores in the spring water for about 30 minutes, then strain. Discard the peels and cores, and add the peeled apples to the water. Proceed as above in Applesauce recipe and stop when you have achieved the texture you like.

Makes about 5 cups.

Variations: Applesauce can be varied endlessly. Honey can replace the sugar, or sweetener can be omitted entirely. For an even more intense apple flavor, use cider instead of spring water. To give a blander variety of apple some kick, add a tablespoon or two of apple cider vinegar. Another time, try a touch of cloves. For a fancy applesauce, throw a handful of raisins in toward the end of the cooking time.

AUTUMN LUNCH ON THE TERRACE

Salad of Radicchio, Fuji Apples, and Pistachio Nuts

Cavatappi with Potatoes and Herbs

ripe pears, red grapes

Gorgonzola cheese

Biscotti

In our climate, this is a beautiful lunch to have on the terrace on a sunny October weekend. It's just as good for a dinner by the fireplace when evenings start darkening quickly and the air turns cold. The hearty, filling quality of the pasta dish and the flavor of a new crop of apples mixed with the radicchio are just what I want in the fall.

For such a satisfying meal, it doesn't take an enormous effort, and that's the beauty of so many pasta and salad meals. The pasta sauce takes a little time but could be done ahead if you like, the salad is a matter of minutes, and the fruit, cheese, and biscotti can be bought. Because it's uncomplicated, and children will eat most of it (all you can really hope for, in my experience), it's a comfortable family meal as well as a lovely meal to share with company.

SALAD OF RADICCHIO, FUJI APPLES, AND PISTACHIO NUTS

Yes, of course you can use another kind of apple. I'm just crazy about Fujis, with their dense texture and explosive tart-sweet flavor. But any variety that is crisp and has a tart edge will do well, complementing the taste and the color of the radicchio.

1 large head radicchio, or 2 small (1 lb.)
1 large or 2 medium Fuji apples (10–12 oz.)
3 stalks celery
¼ red onion

2–3 Tbs. fruity green olive oil
aged wine vinegar
salt
½ cup lightly toasted shelled pistachio nuts

optional: 1–2 oz. coarsely grated Gruyère or provolone cheese

Wash the radicchio, tear the leaves into bite-sized pieces, and spin it dry in a salad spinner. Quarter, core, and thinly slice the apple. Wash, trim, and thinly slice the celery. Thinly slice the red onion.

Combine the radicchio, apple, celery, onion, and optional cheese in a large salad bowl. Drizzle on a little olive oil and toss. Everything should glisten, but oil should not be dripping off. Sprinkle on a modest amount of vinegar and a little salt and toss again. Taste, and adjust the seasoning if needed.

Mound the salad on plates and sprinkle some pistachio nuts on top of each serving.

Serves 4–6.

radicchio

CAVATAPPI WITH POTATOES AND HERBS

This is comfort food at its greatest, tasty, hearty, and absolutely good for you. Cavatappi are short spiraling tubes, but any of the sturdy, interesting pasta shapes could be used for this—tubetti, rigatoni, etc.

1½ Tbs. olive oil
1 bay leaf
½ tsp. crumbled dried sage leaves
pinch of dried thyme
2 medium carrots, finely chopped
1 thin, inside stalk celery, finely chopped
1 medium onion, peeled and chopped
salt to taste
½ head garlic, peeled and thinly sliced

2–3 medium potatoes (1 lb.), peeled and cut in ½-inch dice
2 cups vegetable broth
⅓ cup chopped flat-leaf parsley
¾ cup dry white wine
5–6 medium tomatoes, peeled and chopped, with their juice (2¼ cups)
fresh-ground black pepper
1 lb. cavatappi, tubetti, or other sturdy pasta
Parmesan or Romano cheese, grated

Heat the olive oil in a large non-stick sauté pan and add the bay leaf, sage, thyme, chopped carrots, chopped celery, chopped onion, and a generous sprinkle of salt. Cook over medium heat, stirring frequently, until the vegetables just begin to color. Add the garlic and stir for another 2 minutes.

Add the diced potatoes, vegetable broth, and parsley to the vegetables in the pan, lower the heat to a simmer, and cook until the potatoes are tender, about 15 minutes.

Add the white wine and the chopped tomatoes, season with additional salt and some fresh-ground black pepper, and continue simmering until the tomatoes are falling apart and the liquid is somewhat reduced.

Meanwhile, bring a very large pot of water to a boil and salt it generously. Cook the pasta in it until it is *al dente*, tender-firm. Drain the pasta and stir it into the potato sauce. Serve at once in warm shallow pasta bowls, and pass the cheese separately.

Serves 6.

A FALL PICNIC
OR A WINTER
SUPPER

Butternut Squash and Pear Soup

Chard and Fennel Pie

Brownies with strawberries and whipped cream

Think about a tailgate party at a football game
or a hike in fall foliage.

Fill your biggest and best thermos with steaming
hot soup. This one is a velvety, sweet-savory concoction perfumed
with cinnamon. The soup makes a wonderful contrast to the
robust Chard and Fennel Pie, redolent of garlic, greens, and salty feta
cheese. It's a sturdy pie, made with bread dough rather than a
crumbly short-crust, so it travels very well, making it ideal for
potlucks or school lunches as well as picnics.

Brownies and juicy strawberries, with some whipped cream
for dipping, are a spectacular finish. Here in California, we have
excellent winter strawberries, and by February the spring berries
arrive in the markets, bright red and enormous. However, any
sweet-tart fruit could take their place—oranges or tangerines,
for example, would be wonderful.

Of course, just because this food can be entirely prepared
ahead of time and packed in a hamper doesn't mean it shouldn't be
eaten at home, by the fireplace. The pie is delicious hot.

BUTTERNUT SQUASH AND PEAR SOUP

I worked out this recipe for my talk about "spa cuisine" at a popular local spa because I wanted to give people something that was very low in fat but tasted luxuriously delicious. The pears add a natural sweetness and silky texture. For a really stripped-down version, you could substitute low-fat milk or yogurt for the half and half.

1 lb. butternut squash* (about 10 oz.
    trimmed and seeded)
1 large yam (about 10 oz.)
2 cups vegetable broth
1½ cups water
1 stick cinnamon
¾ tsp. salt

2 Tbs. butter
2 medium onions, sliced
3 large Anjou or Bartlett pears
⅓ cup dry white wine
¼ cup half and half
white pepper to taste

optional garnish: chopped chives, or sprigs of cilantro

Peel, seed, and dice the squash. Peel and dice the yam. Put them both in a pot with the vegetable broth, water, cinnamon stick, and salt, and simmer until tender, about 40 minutes. Discard the cinnamon stick.

Melt the butter and gently cook the onions in it, stirring occasionally, until it begins to caramelize. Peel, core, and thinly slice the pears, and add them to the onions. Continue cooking for about 5 minutes, stirring often. Add the wine, cover, and simmer for 10 minutes.

Add the pear mixture to the soup and purée everything in a blender in batches. Add the cream and some white pepper, and a bit more salt only if needed. Heat the soup again just to a simmer, but do not boil. Serve plain or garnished with chopped chives or sprigs of cilantro.

Serves 6–8.

If you need to substitute another winter squash for butternut, use acorn or banana squash, but avoid the very sweet ones like Tahitian or Kabocha—the combination of an intensely sweet squash with the pears would upset the balance of flavors.

CHARD AND FENNEL PIE

In our house we call this Victory Pie, because the first time I made it we took it to an exciting election night potluck. It's a big, generous pie, delicious and undoubtedly good for you. And even though it's dark green, for some reason that I can't explain my kids usually eat it.

Note: You will need a 13- or 14-inch round gratin dish to make this pie. If you only have 9- or 10-inch pie dishes, divide both dough and filling in half, and make two pies.

dough:
1½ tsp. dry yeast (½ envelope)
1 tsp. sugar
¼ cup warm water
3 cups white flour

1 tsp. salt
1 egg
⅔ cup low-fat milk
1 Tbs. olive oil

filling:
3 lbs. Swiss chard (about 2 big bunches)
1½ large yellow onions (about 2 cups chopped)
1¼ cups sliced green onions
3 cloves garlic
1 medium fennel bulb
2 Tbs. olive oil
1 Tbs. cider vinegar

2 Tbs. chopped fennel greens
½ cup chopped flat-leaf parsley
pinch of salt
fresh-ground black pepper to taste
4 eggs
½ cup milk
10 oz. feta cheese, crumbled
3 Tbs. uncooked white rice

First make the dough: Dissolve the yeast and sugar in the warm water and leave it a few minutes, until it starts to bubble and foam. Meanwhile, put about 2¾ cups of the flour into a large bowl and stir in the salt. Beat together the egg, milk, and olive oil, stir in the yeast mixture, and then mix the liquid into the flour. Stir it with a big wooden spoon until it forms a dough.

When the stirring gets tough, spread the remaining flour on an ample board and turn the dough out on it. Knead it gently, turning often at first to keep it coated with flour, until it is smooth and becoming elastic. Form the dough into a ball and put it into a lightly oiled bowl. Cover the bowl with a towel and set it aside to rise in a warm, sheltered place for 45 minutes to an hour; it should double in size.

To make the filling: First thoroughly clean the chard, cut off and discard the thick parts of the stems, and chop it coarsely. Peel and chop the onions, and trim and slice the green onions. Mince the garlic cloves, and trim and chop the white part of the fennel bulb.

Heat the olive oil in a large, non-stick sauté pan and cook the onions, green onions, and garlic in it over a medium flame for a few minutes, then add the chopped fennel and keep cooking until the vegetables are soft and beginning to color.

Add the chard by handfuls, tossing it with the hot vegetables to wilt it down, until it's all in the pan. Add the cider vinegar, the fennel greens and parsley, a dash of salt, and some pepper, and keep cooking until the chard is much reduced and all the excess liquid is gone.

Remove the pan from the heat and allow the mixture to cool slightly. Separate one of the eggs, reserving the yolk in a small bowl, then add the other 3 eggs to the remaining white and beat them with the milk. Stir the egg mixture into the cooled vegetables along with the crumbled feta cheese and the uncooked rice. Mix everything together well, taste it, and adjust the salt and pepper if needed.

To assemble and bake: Punch down the risen dough and divide it into two parts, one a bit larger. On a lightly floured board, roll the larger part out into a circle with a diameter 2 inches bigger about than your gratin dish or casserole. Yeast dough is harder to roll out than pastry, because it keeps springing back together. I find it helps to lift it up and stretch it gently over the backs of my hands, just like pizza dough (it's the same thing, really), then lay it down and roll again, adjusting the shape.

Oil a 13- or 14-inch round gratin dish lightly and lay the circle of dough into it, bringing it evenly up the sides and letting the extra inch hang over the edges. Spread the prepared filling inside the dough.

Roll out the smaller piece of dough into a circle just large enough to cover the dish and lay it over the filling. Fold the overhanging edge of bottom crust over the edge of the top crust and pinch them together, making a design if you like.

Beat the reserved egg yolk lightly with a tablespoon of water and brush the glaze over the pie. Poke a few holes in the top crust with a fork and bake the pie at 350° for 45 minutes, or until the crust is golden brown. Cool the pie slightly before cutting it in wedges and serving.

Serves 8–10.

BROWNIES

I have this recipe from my friend and neighbor of many years, Martha Bates Jura, who had it from her mother in Boston. Martha told me that she never could do a thing in the kitchen except this—but she felt this was enough.

4 oz. unsweetened baking chocolate	2 tsp. vanilla
4 oz. butter	1 cup flour
3 eggs	1 cup chopped walnuts
½ tsp. salt	powdered confectioners sugar for
2 cups sugar	dusting

Melt the chocolate and butter together in a heavy-bottomed saucepan. As soon as it is almost all melted, remove it from the heat and allow it to cool slightly.

Beat the eggs with a pinch of salt until they are foamy. Gradually add the sugar and keep beating until the mixture is thick and pale. Beat in the vanilla and the cooled chocolate mixture, then the flour. Stir in the walnuts.

Butter a 13-by-8-inch baking pan, and pour the batter into it, spreading it evenly. Bake at 350° for 25–30 minutes, or until a toothpick inserted in the center comes out nearly clean. The brownies should still be moist and slightly sticky when they come out of the oven; they achieve the right texture as they cool.

Allow the brownies to cool to room temperature, cut into squares, and dust with powdered sugar.

Makes 24 brownies.

A SPAGHETTI
DINNER FOR FALL

White Bean Salad
with Sautéed Radicchio

Spaghetti
with Garlic and Oil

Green Apple Sorbet

The classic pairing of beans and pasta has been perfected
in a hundred variations of *pasta i fagioli*—usually as a soup or a stew.
In this simple meal, the same elements are brought together in
another way. The beans are tossed with sautéed radicchio and a few
other delicious things and served as a substantial antipasto salad.
The pasta that follows is one of the plainest and best—
each strand of spaghetti touched with garlic, oil, and parsley.

To clear the palate after that marvelous dose of
garlic, serve a sorbet made from a new crop of tart green apples.

If you want to dress this dinner up for company,
expand the antipasto by adding another little salad of chopped
tomatoes and basil and perhaps a Simple Focaccia or one of
the other focaccias. Then, with the sorbet, serve some
thin butter cookies or biscotti.

WHITE BEAN SALAD
with Sautéed Radicchio

The flavors of cannellini and radicchio make a very satisfying combination. In this salad, the radicchio is quickly sautéed first, then combined with the beans, and some raw ingredients for a contrast in texture. It's an excellent antipasto salad, or a light main course when served on a bed of greens with some good bread on the side. Also sensational on bruschetta.

3 cups cooked cannellini (or Great Northern white beans)
1 small head radicchio (6 oz.)
2 Tbs. olive oil
1 large clove garlic, minced
dash of salt
4 Tbs. aged red wine vinegar

½ cup chopped celery
¼ medium red onion, sliced very thin
¼ cup slivered cured black olives
½ cup coarsely chopped flat-leaf parsley
fresh-ground black pepper

If using canned beans, drain them and rinse them well, and be very careful when mixing because they tend to be mushy. Beans you have cooked yourself need only be well drained.

Wash the radicchio, cut it in half, then slice into ¼-inch ribbons. Heat a tablespoon of olive oil in a non-stick skillet and throw in half the minced garlic. Stir for a minute, then add the shredded radicchio and a dash of salt. Toss the radicchio in the oil and garlic, over a high flame, for 4 minutes. Remove from the heat and sprinkle on a tablespoon of the wine vinegar. Toss again, then leave to cool slightly.

In a large, shallow bowl, combine the beans with the radicchio, celery, red onion, olives, parsley, and the remaining minced garlic. Drizzle on the rest of the olive oil and vinegar, grind on some fresh black pepper, and mix together gently but thoroughly. The salad improves if left to marinate for an hour or two. Serve cool or at room temperature.

Serves 6 as an appetizer, or 4 as a light main course.

SPAGHETTI WITH GARLIC AND OIL

This is one of those amazingly simple dishes that Italians do so well. Just a few assertive flavors—nothing shy about it, and nothing extra to confuse the issue. Of course, with this kind of food, the all-important rule of good cooking cannot be overstated: use good ingredients! The garlic must be fresh, the parsley must be Italian flat-leaf parsley, the olive oil must be virgin and fruity, full of real olive flavor. And don't even think about using pre-grated, packaged Parmesan cheese or you could get your culinary license revoked.

1 lb. spaghetti
9–10 cloves garlic
3–4 Tbs. fruity green olive oil
salt to taste
¼ tsp. red pepper flakes

¾ cup coarsely chopped flat-leaf
   parsley
lots of fresh-grated Parmesan
   cheese

Put the spaghetti into a big pot of boiling salted water to cook until it is just *al dente*.

While it is cooking, peel and chop the garlic. Heat about 2½ tablespoons of the olive oil in a very large non-stick pan and cook the garlic in it over a low flame, stirring constantly, just until it begins to turn golden. Don't let it brown. Add a dash of salt if you like. Remove the pan from the heat, sprinkle in the red pepper flakes, add the chopped parsley, and set aside.

When the spaghetti is just tender-firm, drain it and add it to the garlic and oil mixture in the pan. Return the pan to a medium flame while you toss the spaghetti with the oil, garlic, pepper flakes, and parsley until everything is well mixed.

Serve immediately on warm plates, and spoon some grated Parmesan cheese over each serving.

This should serve 6, but 4 of us have been known to eat up the whole thing. It's that kind of dish.

GREEN APPLE SORBET

1¼ lbs. crisp green apples (about
    5 cups sliced)
2½ Tbs. fresh lemon juice

1¼ cups water
1¼ cups sugar
dash of cinnamon

Wash the apples well, quarter and core them, then slice the quarters thinly crosswise. Toss the apple slices in a bowl with the lemon juice, until all are evenly coated. Cover the bowl tightly with a lid or with plastic wrap and freeze the apple slices for several hours, or overnight.

Combine the water and sugar in a saucepan and stir gently over medium heat until all the sugar is dissolved. Bring the syrup to a boil and let it boil for a few minutes. Transfer the syrup to a bowl and let it cool completely.

Put the frozen apple slices and cooled syrup into the food processor and purée as smoothly as possible. This purée will always have a little texture from the flecks of green apple peel. Add a little dash of cinnamon—not too much—and give it another spin. Put the purée into an ice cream maker and freeze according to manufacturer's instructions.

This makes about a quart, or 8 servings.

TAMALE PIE

tossed salad
with avocado and cilantro

Tamale Pie

sliced fruit platter

Hot Chipotle Salsa

Cafe de Olla Sorbet

In neighborhoods where good, real tamales are plentiful,
the idea of Tamale Pie is sometimes greeted with laughter,
but never mind—it's a delicious casserole, and has its own place
in the culinary scheme of things.

The basis of my pie is a comforting vegetable stew;
familiar winter vegetables are simmered in a Chile Ancho Salsa
that delivers pure, deep chile flavor yet is mild enough for anyone
(you can spike it with a hotter chile if you want to). Cooked in a big
casserole or gratin dish, the vegetable stew is covered with a rich, thick
crust that gives the dish its name. A masa for tamales
is softened and lightened to a delicate texture with beaten egg
whites. When it is served hot from the oven, bubbling underneath and
crisp on top, with a really hot salsa and a cool fruit salad,
it's hard to beat this for a supper dish.

A tossed salad of your favorite greens, with some avocado
and cilantro, can be served at the same time as the Tamale Pie,
or separately as a first course.

For dessert, you will certainly want something cool and refreshing.
I suggest a sorbet of *cafe de olla*, a perfectly light froth of iced coffee
that happily combines the traditional Mexican flavors of *canela, piloncillo*, and *cafe negro*—cinnamon, brown cane sugar, and strong black
coffee. If you want something rich, serve it garnished with mounds
of whipped cream, and even chocolate curls if you like.

TAMALE PIE

In the Southwest during the mid-sixties, tamale pie was a dish much present in certain magazine recipe sections, and at potluck functions. I think it was one of those inventions intended to make a convenience food out of a traditional, labor-intensive dish. A friend of mine recalls with nostalgia the awful tamale pie of her Arizona childhood—a leaden casserole made mainly from canned foods.

But the idea of a deep-dish pot pie, full of fresh vegetables in a chile-laced broth, with a thick top crust made from masa lightened by beaten egg whites, is very appealing to me, so here's my version of the tamale pie.

for the vegetable stew:
3 medium carrots
1 lb. new white-skinned potatoes
1 medium onion
2 leeks
2 cups vegetable broth
2 cups water
½ tsp. salt

1¾ lbs. Tahitian squash* skinned
1 small bunch green onions
¼ lb. tomatillos
2 cups Chile Ancho Salsa (page 86)
4–5 medium zucchini (¾ lb.)
½ cup cilantro leaves

optional: hot chile salsa to taste, such as Hot Chipotle Salsa, or any kind you like

for the crust:
3 cups fresh corn kernels
1¾ cups milk
2 cups + 2 Tbs. dry masa harina
2½ tsp. baking powder

1¼ tsp. salt
1 cup + 2 Tbs. butter, softened
7 egg whites
6 oz. cheddar cheese

Scrape the carrots and cut them in thick slices. Wash and trim the potatoes and cut them in quarters, or into 1-inch pieces. Cut the onion in 1-inch pieces. Trim and thoroughly wash the leeks, cut them in half lengthwise, and slice them thickly. Combine these vegetables in a large sauté pan with the broth, water, and salt, and simmer for about 15 minutes.

Peel the Tahitian squash and cut it in 1-inch cubes. Trim the green onions and cut them in 1-inch lengths. Peel the dry husks off the tomatillos and cut them in quarters. Add these vegetables to the pan, along with the Chile Ancho Salsa, and simmer, uncovered, for at least another ½ hour, or until all the vegetables

If Tahitian squash is unavailable, use Kabocha, buttercup, one of the Hubbards, or acorn squash. In general, look for the sweetest, most flavorful squash you can find.

are completely tender and the liquid is reduced by about half. You should have a stew, not a soup.

Trim and cut the zucchini in thick slices. Add it to the stew and simmer 5 minutes, then stir in the cilantro leaves. Taste and correct the seasoning if necessary. For a spicier dish, you can add some hot salsa at this point, tasting until you achieve the heat you like. Ladle the stew into a large gratin dish, or into two 8-by-11-inch glass baking dishes.

To prepare the masa: Simmer the corn in the milk for about 6 minutes, or until it's quite soft. Sometimes at this point I reserve a few spoonfuls of the corn kernels, and then stir them into the finished masa for more texture. Purée the mixture in a blender.

Sift together 2 cups of the dry masa, baking powder, and salt. In a large bowl, whip the softened butter with an electric mixer until it is fluffy. Alternately add spoonfuls of the corn purée and the dry mixture, beating each time, until everything is well combined. The masa should be light, fluffy, just firm enough to hold a soft shape. If it seems too dry, beat in a little more milk. If it seems too wet, add a touch more dry masa harina. Fold in the whole corn kernels if you have reserved them.

Beat the egg whites until they are stiff. Stir a third of the beaten whites into the masa to lighten it, then gently fold in the remainder.

Coarsely grate the cheddar cheese and toss it in a bowl with 2 tablespoons of masa harina. Sprinkle the cheese over the vegetables in the gratin dish, then spoon the prepared masa over it evenly.

Bake the pie in a 375° oven for about 40 minutes. The crust should be a bit puffed up and golden brown, and the juices of the vegetable stew bubbling.

Serve at once, with the hot salsa of your choice, and a fruit salad.

Serves 8–10.

Variations: This is a basic pot pie, and many things could be used for the filling. Black Bean Chili would be good, or leftover chili combined with roasted or stewed vegetables. This recipe is based mainly on root vegetables, making it a good winter dish, but other combinations of vegetables could be used in other seasons. Add kidney beans or black beans to the stew, or green chiles to the crust; use crumbled white ranchero cheese instead of cheddar, etc., etc. . . .

HOT CHIPOTLE SALSA

This is a concentrated and intense version of chipotle flavor: a tiny bit will leave a nice, hot afterglow in your mouth. Use it to spike a dish that needs some excitement, to turn up the volume on a milder salsa, or as a dip for tortilla chips.

6 oz. tomatillos (6–8)	5 cloves garlic, peeled
1½ oz. dried chipotle chiles (about 12 chiles, depending on size)	1½ tsp. salt
	4 tsp. cumin seeds
1 large onion, thickly sliced	½ cup chopped cilantro leaves

Peel the dry outer husks from the tomatillos, wash them, and put them on a hot iron pan or a grill. Move them around and turn them frequently as they blister, allowing them to char in big black spots all over, about 10–15 minutes. Then drop them into a bowl of cold water, and take off the charred bits of skin wherever it wants to come off easily. Don't worry about the skin that still clings.

At the same time, put the dried chipotles, onion, garlic, and salt in a nonreactive pot with just enough water to cover. Bring the water to a boil, then simmer for about 15 minutes. Turn off the heat and let the chiles soak for about another 30 minutes, or until they are soft and plumped.

Remove the stems from the chiles, tear the pods open under running water, and discard the seeds.

Combine the tomatillos, chiles, onions, and garlic in the container of a blender, together with as much of the liquid as is needed to purée everything into a thick sauce.

Toast the cumin seeds in a small pan, stirring constantly over medium heat for a minute or two, until the seeds release their fragrance. Grind them roughly in a mortar and add them to the sauce in the blender, processing again briefly.

Add the chopped cilantro leaves, process only if you want the leaves minced into the sauce, and taste. Add salt if needed.

This makes about 3 cups of salsa. It can be kept in the refrigerator, tightly covered, for about a week.

CAFE DE OLLA
SORBET

Mexican *cafe de olla,* a sweet, strong coffee brewed with cinnamon and brown cane sugar, is usually something we enjoy in cooler weather. Traditionally, it's not brewed during heat waves, and yet it's just the flavor I want after a chile-laced Mexican lunch or dinner, so here's the frozen dessert version.

2½ cups spring water
6-in. stick cinnamon, broken up
4 oz. *piloncillo* (solid brown cane
   sugar)

½ cup granulated sugar
about 1½ cups double-strength
   coffee

garnishes: whipped cream
          additional cinnamon sticks

Combine the water and broken-up cinnamon sticks in an enameled or stainless steel pot, bring to a boil, then turn off the heat, add the *piloncillo,* and leave it to steep for at least an hour, longer if possible. Add the granulated sugar to the cinnamon water and bring it slowly to a simmer again, stirring occasionally until all the sugar is completely dissolved. Let the syrup boil gently for 5 minutes, then remove it from the heat.

Meanwhile, brew some double-strength coffee, using excellent beans; you want this to be flavorful, not bitter or acidic. As soon as the coffee is ready, pour it into a measuring cup. Add a cup of the coffee to the cinnamon syrup, stir it, and taste it. Add a little more coffee, a spoonful at a time, until the sweetness of the cinnamon syrup is balanced with the coffee flavor to your taste.

Allow the liquid to cool, then chill it in the refrigerator. Freeze it in an ice cream freezer, according to the manufacturer's instructions. Let it harden in your freezer, packed into a container and tightly covered, for a couple of hours before serving. Serve it in chilled, stemmed glasses, garnished with whipped cream and a cinnamon stick.

This makes about a quart of sorbet.

A WINTER PILAF
DINNER

*Bulgur Pilaf
with Fennel, Raisins, and Pine Nuts*

Oven-Roasted Tahitian Squash

*Red Cabbage
Stewed with Apples and Wine*

steamed fresh lima beans

ripe pears and blue cheese

This meal is built upon an earthy, satisfying pilaf of quick-cooking bulgur. Around it are arranged several vegetables, each with a distinct flavor and character. The bright-red cabbage is tart and fruity; the golden Tahitian squash is effortless to prepare and tastes rich, dense, and sweet; steamed green lima beans are a simple finishing touch. It's a comforting dinner for a fall or winter night. Easy to serve, it all looks nice together, arranged on your biggest dinner plates.

A more elaborate meal can be made of this by adding a nice soup and a superb winter dessert, such as crème caramel or pumpkin cheesecake.

Substitutions: If you can't find Tahitian squash, Kabocha squash could be used, or even acorn or butternut, though these last two might need a drizzle of lemon juice and honey to bring out the flavor. Fresh green limas are ideal, but if they're not available to you, try substituting lightly steamed green beans or sliced Chinese broccoli. The important thing is to keep the flavor and texture simple.

BULGUR PILAF

with Fennel, Raisins, and Pine Nuts

2 medium yellow onions (2 cups
   chopped)
2 small fennel bulbs (1½ cups
   chopped)
2–3 cloves garlic, minced
2 Tbs. olive oil

salt and pepper to taste
2 cups bulgur
4 cups hot vegetable broth
½ cup golden raisins
½ cup pine nuts

optional: 2 Tbs. chopped fresh parsley, or
        2 Tbs. chopped fresh fennel greens

Peel and chop the onions. Trim the fennel bulbs, wash them carefully, and cut them into ½-inch dice. Sauté the onions, fennel, and minced garlic in the olive oil, stirring often, until the vegetables take on a nice golden-brown color. Add some salt and pepper—more or less, depending on the saltiness of the broth you will use.

Add the dry bulgur and stir it in the hot pan with the vegetables for a few minutes. Then add the hot vegetable broth and the raisins.

Pour the whole mixture into a large casserole or gratin dish, cover tightly, and bake it in a 350° oven for 40 minutes.

Meanwhile, toast the pine nuts: Heat them in a small pan, stirring constantly, until they begin to brown. Do not turn away to answer the phone! This only takes a few moments, and they'll burn in an instant if you take your eyes off them. When they are toast-colored and give off a divine fragrance, just set them aside in a bowl.

After 40 minutes, when the pilaf is ready, remove the cover from the pilaf and check to make sure all the liquid has been absorbed. If not, leave it in the oven for a few more minutes. Then fluff the pilaf with a fork and stir in the toasted pine nuts. Sprinkle with the chopped fresh herbs if you like and serve hot.

Serves 10–12.

OVEN-ROASTED TAHITIAN SQUASH

The main job is done at the market. Get the right squash and you don't have to do much more. Tahitian squashes are the great big long ones that curve around into a fishhook shape and have a bulge at the end. They have fairly smooth, light-yellow skin, and range in size from 15 to 50 pounds.

An uncut squash will keep in a cool, dry place for months. Once it is cut, cover the cut end with plastic wrap and refrigerate.

Approximately 5 lbs. Tahitian squash (preferably the neck)	2–3 tsp. olive oil salt to taste

Slice inch-thick rounds evenly from the long neck of a Tahitian squash—this part has no seeds, so you'll have perfect, bright-orange discs. Brush each round lightly on both sides with olive oil. Arrange them on a baking sheet and sprinkle them sparingly with salt.

Roast the squash at 375° for about an hour, turning the slices over halfway through. If you want the tops browned and crusty, put them under the broiler for a few moments at the end, just until they start to color.

Serve hot with pilaf, with rice, or with a mixed vegetable platter and polenta.

Serves 10–12.

RED CABBAGE STEWED WITH APPLES AND WINE

1 medium head red cabbage (about 2 lbs.)	salt and pepper to taste
1 large yellow onion	2 tart green apples, peeled, cored, and grated
2 stalks celery	3 Tbs. chopped flat-leaf parsley
1½ Tbs. olive oil	1¼ cups dry red wine
2–3 cloves garlic, minced	1½ Tbs. red wine vinegar, or 3 Tbs. balsamic vinegar
1 small bay leaf	
¼ tsp. dried thyme	2–3 tsp. brown sugar

Wash the cabbage, cut it into large sections, trim away the core, and shred it either by hand or in a food processor with a slicing disk. Blanch the cabbage in boiling, salted water for 2 minutes, drain it, and set it aside.

Peel and chop the onion. Trim the celery, de-rib it, and dice it finely. Sauté the onion and celery in the olive oil, along with the garlic, until all the vegetables have softened. Add the bay leaf, thyme, and salt and pepper to taste, and continue cooking over medium heat until the onion begins to color.

Stir in the blanched cabbage, grated apple, parsley, and wine. Cover the pan and simmer the mixture over low heat for about 20 minutes. Remove the lid, stir in the wine vinegar and sugar, correct the salt and pepper if needed, and continue cooking, stirring occasionally, for about 30 minutes. The liquid will reduce to a light glaze.

Serves 10–12.

BUCKWHEAT CREPES WITH ONIONS AND APPLES

Wild Mushroom and Charred Tomato Soup

*Buckwheat Crepes
with Onions, Apples, and Cheese*

Cranberry-Jalapeño Sauce

Watercress and Curly Endive Salad

Pear Sorbet and chocolate cookies

or fresh fruit and biscotti

This is a delicious dinner to have with company,
or for a special occasion with your family.

Buckwheat crepes are the basis of many meals in
Brittany. There are restaurants that serve only these crepes,
with a great range of savory and sweet fillings.

These buckwheat crepes are especially evocative of
Brittany to me, because they are filled with a mixture of onions
and apples, moistened with Calvados, and enriched with a little
cheese. The apples add a mysterious quality, a light touch that is not
at first identifiable, but alters the whole character of the dish.

A deeply flavored soup of mushrooms and charred tomatoes
begins the meal, preparing the way for the rich-tasting blend of
melted onions and cheese. A spicy cranberry sauce and a peppery
green salad provide the right contrast with the hot crepes.

Pear Sorbet with chocolate cookies is a dessert of true
elegance, and light enough to be welcome after any meal. If you
have an ice cream freezer, take the time to make this sorbet.
It's very easy, and the result is ambrosial.

WILD MUSHROOM AND CHARRED TOMATO SOUP

2 oz. dried porcini
1 Tbs. + 1 tsp. olive oil
2 Tbs. butter
3 large onions (1½ lbs.), quartered
    and sliced
4 cloves garlic, chopped
1 bay leaf
salt and pepper to taste

½ tsp. dried whole thyme, or 1–2
    tsp. fresh
3 lbs. ripe tomatoes
4 oz. fresh shiitake, or other wild
    mushrooms
1 cup dry red wine
3 cups vegetable broth
½ cup cream

Cover the dried porcini with boiling water and set them aside to soak for at least 30 minutes or longer, until soft.

Heat half the olive oil and half the butter in a large non-stick sauté pan, and add the sliced onions, ¾ of the garlic, the bay leaf, some salt, and the thyme. Regulate the heat and cook slowly, stirring occasionally, until the onions are golden brown—as long as an hour if needed.

Meanwhile, scald and peel the tomatoes, cut them in halves or quarters, and mix them in a large bowl with the remaining olive oil, a sprinkle of salt, and the remaining chopped garlic. Spread them on a baking sheet with edges, and roast in a very hot oven (425–450°), turning once or twice, until charred spots are appearing around their edges.

Check the tomatoes every 10 minutes or so, and then more frequently when they begin to color—remember, you want them subtly charred, not burnt. When they're ready, allow them to cool a little on the pan, then scrape them into a blender and process for a few seconds only; they should be roughly chopped.

When the porcini feel soft and flexible, drain them, reserving the liquid. Rinse them very carefully to get rid of all the sand, and chop any large pieces. Strain the liquid through a paper filter, adding water if needed to make 3 cups. Wash the shiitakes, cut off the stems, and slice them.

Melt the remaining tablespoon of butter in a non-stick pan and sauté all the mushrooms in it until the shiitakes begin to color. Deglaze the pan with the wine, then combine the mushrooms and wine with the caramelized onions in a soup pot.

Add the soaking liquid from the porcini, the vegetable broth, and the tomatoes, and simmer everything together for about 10 minutes to marry the flavors. Taste, and correct the seasoning with salt or pepper if desired. Stir in the cream.

Makes 8–10 servings.

BUCKWHEAT CREPES WITH
ONIONS, APPLES,
AND CHEESE

18–20 Buckwheat Crepes (recipe
   follows)
6 lbs. yellow onions
2 Tbs. olive oil
2 Tbs. butter
1 tsp. salt, more to taste

black pepper
about 4 tart green apples (1½ lbs.,
   pippins or Granny Smiths)
3 Tbs. Calvados
8 oz. grated sharp cheddar cheese

Prepare the Buckwheat Crepes and set aside.

Peel the onions, cut them in half lengthwise, and then slice them thickly. Heat a tablespoon of olive oil and a tablespoon of butter in each of two large non-stick pans, and divide the onions between them. Sprinkle about ½ teaspoon of salt over each batch and cook the onions on medium heat, stirring occasionally, until they are golden brown. This will take about 45 minutes. Add black pepper to taste.

Meanwhile, peel the apples, cut into wedges, and slice the wedges crosswise. When the onions are lightly browned and much reduced in volume, consolidate them into one pan. Add the Calvados to the onions and stir quickly to deglaze the pan. Add the sliced apples, and a touch more salt if needed. Continue cooking, stirring often, until the liquid is entirely gone, the onions are a deep caramel color, and the apples are tender.

Spoon 2–3 rounded tablespoons of the onion mixture across the center of a crepe, then sprinkle about ½ ounce of grated cheese over it. Roll the crepe loosely over the filling and place it seam side down on a buttered baking sheet. Continue filling and rolling crepes until all the onions and cheese are used up. You should have at least 16–18 filled crepes. Reserve any leftover crepes for another use.

Cover the crepes loosely with a piece of aluminum foil, and bake them in a 350° oven for 10–15 minutes, or until they are hot through and the cheese is completely melted. If you have filled the crepes earlier and kept them in the refrigerator for a while, adjust the oven time upward by at least 5 minutes.

Serve the crepes at once, with a green salad or a tart relish.

Serves 8.

BUCKWHEAT CREPES

These buckwheat crepes have a distinctive, nutty flavor, as well as a tenderness that makes them delightful to eat but a bit tricky to handle. If you let them brown before trying to flip them, and work gently when filling them, you'll be fine.

Note: This batter needs to rest at least 2 hours before you make the crepes, so make it in the morning, or the night before—it only takes a few minutes.

1⅓ cups low-fat milk	2 Tbs. vegetable oil, more for the pan
2 eggs	2 Tbs. sugar (slightly more for
2 egg whites	dessert crepes)
½ cup beer	½ tsp. salt
1⅓ cups water	2 cups buckwheat flour

Combine the milk, eggs, egg whites, beer, water, and oil in a blender and process for a few seconds. Add the sugar, salt, and buckwheat flour, and process again until smooth, working in two batches if you need to. Stop and scrape down the sides, and process again.

Put the batter in a bowl, cover it, and refrigerate at least 2 hours, or as long as overnight. Stir the batter up and check its consistency. It should be like heavy cream; you can thin it with a spoonful or two of water if you need to.

To cook the crepes, heat a 9-inch non-stick skillet (a well-seasoned crepe pan can also be used if you have practice). Brush the pan with oil or rub it with a paper towel dipped in oil. Ladle a slight ¼ cup of batter into the hot pan and immediately tilt the pan around to spread the batter evenly over the bottom. Cook the crepe on a medium flame for about 45 seconds, or until the edges are just beginning to brown. Loosen the edges gently with a thin spatula or a butter knife, then turn the crepe over and cook on the other side for 20–30 seconds.

If a crepe sticks, oil the pan a bit more next time, and let the crepe cook slightly longer before turning. You may have a torn crepe or two before your pan temperature and timing are worked out, as these are rather fragile—you'll just have to eat those as you work.

Stack the crepes on a plate as they are finished, and keep them covered with a slightly damp kitchen towel.

Makes about 24 crepes.

Variation: For sweeter crepes, increase the sugar to 2 or 3 tablespoons. These are perfect for dessert, filled with jam or fruit compote.

CRANBERRY-JALAPEÑO SAUCE

12 oz. fresh or frozen cranberries
1 orange
2 Tbs. tequila

½ cup sugar
1 medium jalapeño pepper

Rinse the berries and discard any that are brown and soft. Finely grate the zest only of the orange peel, then cut the orange in half and squeeze out the juice. Add enough water to the orange juice to make one cup of liquid.

Combine the berries, grated orange peel, juice and water, tequila, and sugar in a large non-reactive pot, and bring it to a slow boil, stirring occasionally as the sugar dissolves. Trim the jalapeño, discard the seeds, and chop it finely.

When the berries begin to pop, add the chopped jalapeño and boil everything together for about 5 more minutes, stirring with a long wooden spoon. If the sauce seems too thick, add a little more water.

Remove the sauce from the heat and allow it to cool, stirring now and again to prevent a skin from forming. Spoon it into a pretty dish, and chill if you like.

This delicious, slightly spicy sauce is perfect alongside tamales, with cheese-stuffed crepes, or any similarly rich-flavored dish, or even with your Thanksgiving turkey.

Makes about 2 cups.

WATERCRESS AND CURLY ENDIVE SALAD

This is another of those excellent salads that can be served with wine. The peppery tastes of good watercress and radishes provide bite without acid, and contrast with the sweetness of fennel and raisins. Only a few drops of a fruity vinegar are used, letting the olive oil and walnuts dominate.

Make this salad only when you can get really fresh, dark-green watercress. Watercress is great when just picked, but loses its flavor and character after a few days in the refrigerator.

2 bunches fresh watercress
1–2 heads young curly endive
small handful of fresh basil leaves
small handful of fresh cilantro
1 fennel bulb
5–6 red radishes

½ cup raisins
fruity green olive oil, to taste
2–3 tsp. raspberry vinegar
salt
black pepper
½ cup chopped walnuts

Wash the watercress well to remove any mud, and break off and discard heavy stems. Wash the curly endive and tear it into bite-sized pieces. Spin the greens in a salad spinner to remove excess water. You should have about 10–12 cups of torn greens, loosely packed.

Cut the larger basil leaves in wide strips and leave smaller ones whole. Snip the cilantro leaves off their stems. Clean and trim the fennel bulb, quarter it lengthwise, and cut it in paper-thin slices. Trim and thinly slice the radishes.

Toss together the greens, herbs, fennel, radishes, and raisins. Drizzle on a very small amount of fruity green olive oil and the raspberry vinegar, then add a dash of salt and pepper and toss again until the leaves are all lightly touched with dressing. I use only a couple tablespoons of oil for this salad, as the walnuts add richness.

Sprinkle the chopped walnuts over the salad in the serving bowl, or over each serving.

Serves 8 as a side salad, or small dinner salad.

PEAR SORBET

2½ cups water
1¾ cups sugar
several strips lemon peel
2½ lbs. pears (5–6 medium), ripe
    and juicy but not mushy

3–4 Tbs. fresh lemon juice
3 Tbs. pear brandy

Make a simple sugar syrup by heating the water gently with the sugar, stirring with a wooden spoon, until all the sugar dissolves. Add the lemon peel and simmer the syrup for about 5 minutes.

Peel, core, and slice the pears, removing any blemished areas, and add them immediately to the sugar syrup. Poach them in the syrup, keeping it at a gentle simmer, until they are just tender. Remove the pears and set them aside. Discard the lemon peel.

Measure out 3 cups of the syrup, combine it with the pear slices and 3 tablespoons of lemon juice, and purée in a blender in batches until perfectly smooth.

Taste the purée, and add a little more lemon juice if it seems too sweet. The exact amount of lemon juice will depend on the sweetness of the pears. Stir in the pear brandy.

Chill the mixture first, then freeze according to manufacturer's instructions in an ice cream freezer.

For a divine treat, serve the sorbet with Chocolate-Dipped Biscotti (page 421).

Makes a little more than a quart of sorbet.

AFTER THE HOLIDAYS

A Big Tossed Salad

Winter Vegetable Stew

Simple Couscous

Cranberry Chutney or cranberry sauce

ripe pears

After the holidays, we all want to retreat a little
from food. We probably ate a little more, and a little fancier, than
we normally do. We celebrated! It was fun, but we're carrying the
memory of it on our hips. A certain sluggishness creeps over us.
We feel the need to lighten the load.

It's time for simple food, with true and satisfying flavors
but no heaviness on the palate or elsewhere.

Here it is, both raw and cooked: a bright-flavored tossed salad,
followed by a delicious vegetable stew served with plain couscous and
a dab of cranberry sauce, and then fresh, ripe fruit for dessert.

The salad is big, full of crunchy things, contrasting sweet fennel, hot
radishes, dark greens, and herbs. It can be adapted to what is available
in the green market and needs only a touch of the lightest dressing.

Winter Vegetable Stew is just a great combination of
vegetables simmered together in a reduction of clear broth and white
wine; a little vinegar, honey, and soy sauce are added at the last moment
to form a savory glaze. This stew could be served with almost any rice
or grain, and I chose the easiest one I know—plain couscous, which
I love not only for its ease. Cranberry sauce or chutney is the little
condiment that spikes this combination. If you're tired of
cranberries, almost any tart little relish will do.

A perfectly ripe pear for dessert finishes a meal that is in
every way just what the moment requires.

A BIG TOSSED SALAD

This is not a salad for which a precise formula can be given. The idea is to have a balance of dark and light greens, some pungent and some sweet, with a few very crunchy things for contrast, and perhaps a little taste of fruit as an extra flourish. All the ingredients listed are suggestions.

This salad is made from the good things that are available in colder weather, when tomatoes and basil and sweet peppers are still far away. It has clear, strong flavors and doesn't need much dressing.

greens:
radicchio
curly endive
watercress

arugula
oak leaf or red salad bowl lettuce
small spinach leaves

herbs:
Italian flat-leaf parsley

cilantro
chives

crunchy vegetables:
celery
fennel
radishes

kohlrabi or rutabaga
red onion

garnishes: toasted walnuts, almonds, or pistachios; raisins or dried cranberries

dressing: olive oil and wine vinegar, or Ginger-Sesame Dressing (page 401)

The basic proportions I use are: for every 3 cups or so of mixed, torn greens, add about 1 cup of the more solid ingredients—thinly sliced vegetables, toasted nuts, etc. This ratio gives nice body and texture to the salad.

Select your greens, mixing peppery ones with sweet ones. Wash and trim them as needed, tear into bite-sized pieces, and spin them dry in a salad spinner. Clean the herbs the same way, and add them to the greens—I add a big handful of herbs for a medium-sized bowl of salad, but follow your own taste in this.

Clean and trim the celery, fennel, radishes, kohlrabi, or whatever you like from the crunchy category, cutting it into very thin slices. If you are adding onion, taste it to see how sharp it is, and add it sparingly.

Add the raisins or dried cranberries, and toss everything in a large salad bowl. Dress the salad lightly with your best oil and vinegar, or a touch of Ginger-Sesame Dressing, and toss again. Scatter some toasted nuts on top and serve.

WINTER VEGETABLE STEW

1 medium to large Kabocha squash*
   (3–3½ lbs.)
2 large onions
2 fennel bulbs
2½ Tbs. olive oil
salt and pepper to taste
2 medium russet potatoes
2 cups light vegetable or chicken
   broth
1 cup white wine

2 cloves garlic, finely chopped
1 lb. mushrooms, preferably wild,
   thickly sliced
¼ tsp. cayenne
3 medium tomatoes, peeled and cut
   in chunks
1 bunch kale
3 Tbs. cider vinegar
1–2 Tbs. honey
1 tsp. soy sauce

Cut the squash in half, scrape out all the seeds, and, using your biggest, sharpest knife, cut it into inch-thick slices. Pointing your knife always away from you, cut away the thick green peel, and cut the orange flesh into 1-by-2-inch chunks.

Peel the onions and cut them into thin wedges. Wash and trim the fennel, halve the bulbs lengthwise, and cut them in thick slices.

Heat 1½ tablespoons of olive oil in a large non-stick sauté pan and add the squash, onions, fennel, about ½ teaspoon of salt, and black pepper to taste. Cook the vegetables over medium heat, stirring and turning them often, until the onions and fennel are limp and all the vegetables are beginning to color in spots—about 20 minutes.

Meanwhile, peel and cut the potatoes into 1-inch chunks. Put them in a small pot with the broth and white wine, bring the liquid to an easy boil, and cook them for about 10 minutes.

In another non-stick pan, heat ½ tablespoon of olive oil, add 1 chopped garlic clove, and stir it in the hot oil for a minute. Add the sliced mushrooms, a dash of salt, and the cayenne pepper, and sauté the mushrooms, stirring often, until they release their juice, it cooks away, and the mushrooms are beginning to brown.

Add the mushrooms, the tomatoes, and the potatoes in their broth to the squash mixture. Lower the heat, cover tightly, and let the stew simmer for about 30 minutes. The vegetables should be tender, and the potatoes and squash will fall apart around the edges just enough to thicken the juices slightly. If the mixture seems dry, add a drop of water or white wine.

*If Kabocha squash is unavailable, use buttercup, Hubbard, or acorn squash. In general, look for the most flavorful, dense, and sweetest squash you can find.

Wash the kale thoroughly, slice it off its stems, and cut the leaves into big pieces. Heat the remaining olive oil in the same pan you used for the mushrooms, and stir the rest of the garlic in it for a minute. Add the kale and toss it with the garlic and oil and a little salt just until it wilts, then stir it into the stew.

Add the cider vinegar, honey, and soy sauce to the stew and turn up the flame. Stir everything together for a few minutes as the juices cook down a little and form a glaze. Taste, correct the seasoning with more salt or pepper if needed, and serve on big, deep plates, with couscous or any rice pilaf.

Serves 6–8.

SIMPLE COUSCOUS

3½ cups liquid: a light vegetable broth, or a combination of broth and water

½ tsp. salt, if needed
1 Tbs. butter
2 cups couscous

optional garnish: chopped fresh parsley or cilantro

Bring the liquid to a boil in a medium-sized pot. You can use a delicate vegetable broth, or a combination of half water and half broth. Do not use a broth that is too salty or strongly flavored. Add the salt, if needed, and the butter.

Reduce the heat to a simmer, stir in the couscous, cover the pot tightly, and leave it on the lowest possible heat for 3 minutes. Then turn off the heat and leave the pot covered for another 5 minutes. Uncover and fluff the couscous with a fork before serving.

Serves 8–10.

CRANBERRY CHUTNEY

12 oz. cranberries
¾ cup brown sugar
⅓ cup raisins
½ cup chopped dried pears
1 large, crisp apple, peeled, cored,
    and chopped
¾ cup chopped onion
⅓ cup cider vinegar

2 Tbs. finely chopped fresh ginger
    root
grated zest of 1 lemon
pinch of salt
1½ cups water, more if needed
1½ tsp. whole mustard seed
1–2 small, hot red chiles, dried or
    fresh

Rinse the berries and pick them over, discarding any that are soft and brown. In a large, non-reactive pot, combine the berries with all but the last two ingredients, and bring everything to a slow boil, stirring to dissolve the sugar.

Toast the mustard seeds in a small pan, shaking them over medium heat until they begin to pop and jump. Toast the chiles in a very hot pan or directly over a flame until they blister and turn black in spots, then mince them. Stir the mustard seed and minced chile into the cranberry mixture.

Lower the heat and simmer the chutney for about an hour, stirring occasionally, adding a little more water if the chutney becomes too thick and threatens to scorch.

The chutney can be kept refrigerated and covered for several weeks, or put into canning jars and processed in a hot-water bath for longer storage. Flavor improves after a day or two.

This makes about 4 cups.

ABOUT ROASTING VEGETABLES

My favorite way to cook vegetables at the moment is to roast them. I love grilling things, but this is much easier, and you don't have to have charcoal and get soot all over yourself. Nothing touches water, so nothing can get soggy or lose taste. I get very satisfying results using very little fat; flavors are subtly enriched as juices caramelize, and edges crisp up.

Almost any vegetable that has a solid, as opposed to leafy, texture can be successfully roasted. Of course, everyone's been roasting potatoes forever, but roasted green beans have become a staple in my house now, and have you ever tasted roasted asparagus? Or a pasta sauce made from slowly oven-roasted tomatoes? Or a combination of roasted onions, peppers, squashes, and eggplant? It's like a ratatouille done entirely in the oven, with just a little oil and a great depth to the flavor. Wonderful.

I like to find sympathetic combinations of vegetables, depending on what's in season, roast them all together, and serve them alongside a ladleful of polenta with a dab of tomato sauce or a few slivers of cheese. If the vegetables include some softer, juicier ones, I like to toss them with great big noodles like rigatoni. The denser vegetables, roasted to an almost crispy finish, make a great finger food with drinks. And most any combination can make the taco of your life, wrapped up in a warm corn tortilla with a spoonful of beans and some salsa.

Preparation time is minimal, and you only have to stir the vegetables once or twice while they're in the oven, so life can go on. The whole house smells great, and when you take them out of the oven and serve them, there's so much reward for so little effort.

What's more, they're good cold the next day. Of course, I love them in salad— I toss them with some crisp greens, a splash of oil and vinegar, some chopped herbs, maybe some big gratings of Parmesan or slices of fresh mozzarella, and there's lunch.

The three dinner menus that follow are good examples of different approaches to roasted vegetables. In the first, a combination of vegetables are cut up, mixed up, and all roasted together. The second concentrates on a couple of assertive flavors. The third, Polenta and Roasted Vegetables, presents a whole array of vegetables, roasted simply but separately, for a rustic feast.

Roasted vegetables also turn up in many other menus. See Thanksgiving for Everyone, or Tomato Risotto for the Family.

A RUSTIC AUTUMN DINNER

Fresh Herb Salad

Roasted Autumn Vegetables

Brown and Wild Rice Pilaf

Plum and Walnut Galette

This is a nice menu for the turning of the season, when you want to taste the winter squashes that are turning up in the markets, and to have a glass of red wine. Yet it takes advantage of the late-summer produce that is still abundant in September and October.

A salad that tap-dances with flavors starts the meal. It's full of fresh herbs tossed with tender lettuces, bitter greens, hot radishes—and a touch of honey in the dressing.

After that, one of the simplest and nicest ways to enjoy the time of the harvest—a great platter of assorted vegetables, roasted in the oven until they develop a sweet intensity of flavor, and served with a Brown and Wild Rice Pilaf.

In keeping with the rustic, straightforward style of this dinner, the Plum and Walnut Galette is a generous, juicy tart, casually shaped but bursting with the flavor of autumn plums.

This is not a fussy meal, and can be adapted infinitely as autumn deepens into winter. Almost all the winter vegetables are very suitable for roasting, and the plums in the galette can be replaced with apples or pears later in the season.

FRESH HERB SALAD

This salad has exciting flavors. Handfuls of herbs are mixed with lettuces, green onions, and radishes, and a touch of fruit for contrasting sweetness.

8 cups mixed mild-flavored lettuces

1 bunch dark-green watercress or arugula

½ cup fresh mint leaves, loosely packed

½ cup fresh cilantro leaves, loosely packed

½ cup flat-leaf parsley leaves, loosely packed

½ cup fresh basil leaves, loosely packed

4–5 green onions, sliced paper thin

6 red radishes, thinly sliced

1 large, juicy apple

½ cup raisins

2½ Tbs. fruity green olive oil, or walnut oil

2 Tbs. balsamic vinegar, or sherry vinegar

2 Tbs. honey

2 tsp. Dijon mustard

salt and fresh-ground pepper to taste

Rinse all the greens, tear them into bite-sized pieces if needed, and spin in a salad spinner or blot with towels. Combine the greens, herbs, onions, and radishes in a large salad bowl.

Cut the apple into wedges, core it, and slice the wedges thinly crosswise. If the raisins are very dry, plump them briefly in hot water, then drain. Add the sliced apples and the raisins to the greens. Whisk together the oil, vinegar, honey, and mustard. Pour the dressing over the salad and toss it gently until every leaf glistens. Sprinkle on a little salt and grind on some pepper, toss again, and serve.

Serves 8.

basil

ROASTED AUTUMN VEGETABLES

If Kabocha squash is not available, use any of the other dense, dark-yellow or orange squashes, such as buttercup, acorn, Hubbard, or a Sweet Mama pumpkin.

2 large eggplants (2 lbs.)
salt as needed
1 medium Kabocha squash
   (2–3 lbs. weighed whole)
2 large yellow onions (1 lb.)
3–4 medium bell peppers, red,
   green, or yellow (1½ lbs.)
1½ lbs. small potatoes, preferably
   Yukon Gold or red-skinned
   (about 15–20 new potatoes)

8–10 whole cloves garlic
3 Tbs. fruity green olive oil
2–3 Tbs. fresh rosemary leaves,
   coarsely chopped
1 tsp. dried crushed whole oregano
   leaves
fresh-ground pepper to taste

The whole idea here is to scrub and trim the vegetables and cut them in fairly large pieces of a more or less uniform size so that they will roast evenly.

Trim the eggplants, quarter them lengthwise, then slice about ½ inch thick. Toss the pieces in a bowl with a couple teaspoons of salt and transfer to a colander to drain while you prepare the remaining vegetables.

Cut the Kabocha squash in half, scoop out and discard the seeds, and cut each half into 1-inch wedges. Trim off the skin with a very sharp knife, leaving only the firm, dark-yellow flesh, and cut it in 1-inch squares.

Peel the onions, halve them lengthwise, then cut each half into 6 or 8 chunks. Trim the bell peppers and cut them in pieces about 1 inch square.

Scrub the potatoes, trim away any rough spots, and cut them in ¾-inch dice. Peel the garlic cloves.

Put all the vegetables except the eggplant into your largest bowl, add the olive oil, rosemary, oregano, 1½ teaspoons of salt, and as much fresh pepper as you think you might like. Mix everything together thoroughly. All the vegetables should be lightly coated with oil and herbs. Now rinse and drain the eggplant pieces, and mix them into the other vegetables.

Spread the vegetables out on 2 medium-sized baking sheets, and roast them in a 400° oven for about 1½ hours. After the first 30 minutes, turn them with a spatula, stir them around a bit, and reverse their positions in the oven so the one that was underneath can have a turn on top. Move them around again after 30 minutes, and after that check them every 15 minutes.

They're done when the biggest chunk of squash is tender, when golden brown patches appear here and there, when the peppers look soft and the potatoes have crisp edges—when they just look *done*.

Serves 8–10 generously.

Variation: Substitute 7–8 medium zucchini or crookneck squashes for the eggplant.

BROWN AND WILD RICE PILAF

The chewy texture and sweet, almost nutty flavor of this pilaf make it a very satisfying dish. It is an ideal companion to autumn or winter vegetables, either roasted or stewed.

1½ Tbs. olive oil	1¼ cups long-grain brown rice
1 onion, finely chopped	3 cups vegetable broth
pinch of salt	2¼ cups water
1 cup wild rice	

Warm the olive oil in a medium-sized sauté pan and cook the onion in it with a pinch of salt, stirring often, until the onion is soft and translucent. Add the wild and the brown rice and stir them with the onions for a couple of minutes, then add the broth and water.

Bring the liquid to a simmer, lower the heat, and cover the pan tightly. Leave the rice to simmer for 55 minutes, then turn off the heat and let it stand, without lifting the lid, for another 5 minutes. Fluff the rice up with a fork before serving.

Serves 8.

Leftovers: I made such a tasty little frittata once with some of this leftover pilaf that I thought I'd include the recipe here.

RICE PILAF FRITTATA

1½ Tbs. olive oil
1½ cups chopped white of leek
salt and pepper to taste
2 cups Brown and Wild Rice Pilaf

8 eggs
½ cup fresh-grated Parmesan
cheese

Heat the olive oil in a medium-sized non-stick pan and cook the leeks in it, with a dash of salt and pepper, until they are beginning to color. Add the rice pilaf and stir it over a medium flame until it is thoroughly heated.

Meanwhile, beat the eggs with salt to taste and the Parmesan cheese. Add the hot rice and leek mixture, and immediately stir everything together well.

Wipe the pan clean or start fresh with another one, lightly brushed with olive oil, and pour the egg and rice mixture into it. Turn the heat down low, and cover the pan. Check the frittata after about 10 minutes. If the eggs on top are no longer runny, loosen the frittata gently with a spatula, then invert it onto a plate or lid and slide it back into the pan to brown for a moment on the other side. Serve the frittata warm, cut into wedges.

Serves 6.

PLUM AND WALNUT GALETTE

This is a flat, open-faced tart. It is shaped casually, with the pastry edge pulled over the filling around the sides in loose pleats or folds, leaving the fruit in the center exposed. Under the juicy plums, a layer of sweetened ground nuts and flour absorbs the excess moisture, and adds a nice flavor.

for the pastry:
1⅔ cups all-purpose flour
1½ tsp. sugar
¾ tsp. salt

10 Tbs. unsalted butter (1¼ sticks),
cold
4–5 Tbs. ice water

for the filling:
2½ lbs. sweet plums (12–15 large
plums, 5 cups sliced)
½ cup toasted walnuts

3 Tbs. all-purpose flour
¾ cup sugar

optional: ⅓ cup plum or raspberry preserves, strained

To make the pastry, put the flour, sugar, and salt into the container of a food processor, and add the cold butter, cut into bits. Process very briefly, until the mixture resembles coarse meal. Sprinkle in the ice water, running the processor, just until the pastry starts to hold together—only a few seconds.

Remove the pastry from the processor, form it into a ball, then roll it out on a floured board to a circle or oval about 16 to 18 inches across. Drape the pastry over the rolling pin and transfer it to a large baking sheet. Cover the pastry with a towel or with plastic wrap and chill it for at least 30 minutes.

Slice the plums off their pits into ½-inch wedges. Preheat the oven to 400°. Put the toasted walnuts, 3 tablespoons of flour, and ¼ cup of sugar into the food processor and process into a fine meal.*

Remove the pastry from the refrigerator and spread the walnut mixture evenly over it, leaving a 2-inch border all around. Arrange the plums over the walnut mixture, and sprinkle them evenly with all but 1 teaspoon of the remaining ½ cup of sugar.

If the pastry is still stiff, wait a few minutes for it to reach room temperature and become pliable, in order to avoid cracking. Then fold the 2-inch border of the pastry up over the filling, gathering it into loose folds. The fruit in the center of the pie remains uncovered. Sprinkle the last teaspoon of sugar over the pastry border.

Bake the galette in the bottom half of the hot oven for about an hour. I cover it loosely with foil for the first 30 minutes to keep the crust from browning too much, but that's a matter of taste.

When it is done, remove it from the oven and, while it is still hot, brush the strained preserves over the exposed fruit to make a beautiful, shiny finish (not essential but very pretty). Allow the tart to cool somewhat, then loosen it from the baking sheet with a spatula or knife and slide it onto a cooling rack.

Serve at room temperature from a large, flat platter or board, cut into wedges.

Serves 8–10.

---

*To toast walnuts: Spread the nuts evenly on a baking sheet and toast them in a 250° oven for about 25 minutes, then allow them to cool.

GREEN TOMATOES
AND COUSCOUS

Black Bean Soup

*Roasted Yams
with Green Tomatoes*

Cranberry Couscous

Cinnamon Custard Ice Cream

Yams and cranberries are wonderfully evocative of autumn for us, and this is an unusual but very straightforward way to enjoy them. Because the cranberries are dried, you can use them in any season. However, you must have fresh green tomatoes, which pair up with roasted yams like Fred Astaire and Ginger Rogers.

Savory Black Bean Soup begins the meal, garnished with a hot and smoky sauce made from chipotle chiles. The ice cream that finishes it is a simple custard infused with a subtle touch of cinnamon, and frozen.

This meal can be served with no last-minute fuss. The soup can be prepared ahead, and the ice cream must be. Once the vegetables are cut up, it only takes putting them in the oven 1½ hours before dinner, and turning them over a couple of times. Even the couscous could be partly prepped ahead of time, and in any case, it only takes a few minutes.

BLACK BEAN SOUP

1 lb. black beans
pinch of baking soda
2 large onions
6 cloves garlic
2 bay leaves
6–8 branches cilantro
2 tsp. salt, more to taste
1 Tbs. olive oil
1 Tbs. butter

6 medium carrots, sliced
(2 cups sliced)
3 stalks celery, sliced (1 cup sliced)
2 Tbs. cumin seeds
white pepper to taste
2 tsp. paprika
pinch of cayenne
1 Tbs. cider vinegar

garnishes: fresh limes
cilantro sprigs
Simple Chipotle Sauce (page 247)

Soak the beans overnight in about 3 quarts of water with a pinch of baking soda. In the morning, drain the beans and rinse them, then put them in a large soup pot with enough fresh water to cover them by at least 2 inches. Add ½ an onion, 3 peeled cloves garlic, 2 bay leaves, and a few branches of cilantro. Simmer the beans very gently, keeping them well covered with water, until they are tender, probably about 2 hours. Remove and discard the onion, garlic, bay leaves, and cilantro. Add 2 teaspoons of salt.

Meanwhile, chop the remaining 1½ onions and finely chop the remaining garlic. Heat the oil and butter together in a large non-stick pan and sauté the chopped onion, sliced carrots, sliced celery, and chopped garlic in it, stirring often, until the vegetables are tender and beginning to brown. Add the vegetables to the cooked beans, deglazing the pan with some of the bean liquid.

Toast the cumin seeds lightly in a skillet, then grind them in a mortar and add them to the soup with the remaining ingredients. Simmer everything together for about another ½ hour. Taste and correct the seasoning with a bit more salt, pepper, or cayenne, as needed. Purée the soup in batches in a blender and return to the pot.

Serve the soup hot, passing lime wedges, fresh cilantro sprigs, and Simple Chipotle Sauce as garnishes.

Serves 8–10 generously.

ROASTED YAMS WITH GREEN TOMATOES

The essential thing in this dish is the balance between the dense, sweet yams and the tart, juicy green tomatoes. You could get away with using all green tomatoes if you can't find decent red ones in the fall or winter, and of course the amount of olive oil is very discretionary.

3–4 large yams (2 lbs.)
7–8 medium green tomatoes (2 lbs.)
3 medium red tomatoes
3 medium red onions

6 large cloves garlic
1–2 Tbs. olive oil
salt and pepper to taste

Peel the yams and cut them in ½- or 1-inch dice. Trim the tomatoes and cut them in large chunks. Peel the onions and cut them in 1-inch chunks. Peel the garlic and, if the cloves are very large, cut them in half lengthwise.

Combine all the vegetables in a large bowl, drizzle on the olive oil, add some salt and pepper, and mix well. Spread the vegetables out on two baking sheets, preferably non-stick.

Roast the vegetables at 375° for about 1½ hours, moving them around and turning them twice during the cooking time. They should be very tender, and browning here and there.

Serve with couscous, or with a rice pilaf.

Serves 6–8.

CRANBERRY COUSCOUS

1 large onion
2 tsp. olive oil
2 tsp. butter
salt as needed

3¾ cups vegetable broth
½ cup dried cranberries
2 cups couscous

Peel the onion, cut it lengthwise into 8 wedges, then slice the wedges very thinly crosswise. Heat the olive oil and butter in a large non-stick sauté pan and sauté the onion, with a little salt, until it is lightly browned.

Add the vegetable broth and the dried cranberries and bring the broth to a boil. Lower the heat to a mere simmer, add the couscous, cover the pan, and leave it to simmer for 5 minutes. Remove from the heat and leave covered for another 2–3 minutes, then fluff up the couscous with a fork and serve.

Serves 8–10.

CINNAMON CUSTARD ICE CREAM

2 cups milk
2 cups heavy cream
¾ cup sugar

2 large sticks cinnamon
4 egg yolks, beaten

In a medium-sized, heavy-bottomed saucepan, combine the milk, cream, sugar, and cinnamon sticks. Heat the mixture until it simmers, stirring to dissolve the sugar. Remove from the heat and leave to steep, covered, for 2–3 hours. You can leave the cinnamon to soak in the cream mixture even longer if you want a more defined cinnamon flavor.

Heat the liquid again to just below a simmer. Stir a ladle of the hot liquid into the egg yolks, then whisk the yolks into the cream mixture. Continue stirring over very low heat, never allowing the mixture to boil, until the custard thickens, about 8–10 minutes.

Pour the custard into another container and allow it to cool, then chill it. Remove the cinnamon sticks, strain the custard if needed, and freeze it in an ice cream freezer according to manufacturer's instructions.

This makes slightly more than a quart of ice cream.

POLENTA AND ROASTED VEGETABLES

polenta, plain or grilled

Roasted Whole Garlic

Roasted Radicchio and Endive

Roasted Carrots

Roasted Green Beans with Garlic

Roasted Fennel and Red Onions

Sautéed Winter Greens

Roasted Winter Squash and Apples

fresh fruit plate

biscotti

Here is polenta as an anchor for ten wonderful tastes—
nine vegetables and a little surprise fruit. Polenta served with an
assortment of roasted vegetables is a popular meal for good reason.

The right selection of contrasting vegetables, each roasted to its peak
texture and flavor, is the crowning glory of vegetable roasting. It is
spectacular to look at and spectacular to eat, yet it is simplicity itself.

The entire technique of roasting consists of putting something
in the oven at the correct temperature, leaving it there the right
amount of time, and letting nature take its course.

With this meal, the trick is to divide the vegetables into categories
based on cooking time. Carrots and winter squash go into the oven
first. Then the garlic, the fennel, and the red onions. A little later, you
add the green beans and the apple slices. You finish with the radicchio
and endive, which, being lettuces, wilt quickly at 400°.

Meanwhile, you have stirred the polenta and sautéed the
greens on top of the stove.

Roasting times always vary a little, depending on the size of
things and how well calibrated the oven is, but this kind of food is
very forgiving. If you need to take something out and put it aside
while other things finish roasting, it's no big deal.

You can serve all these vegetables on huge platters,
put an earthenware pot full of polenta on the table, and let all
your guests serve themselves.

The combination of vegetables I propose here can be changed,
reduced, or expanded. I would always want to include garlic and
sautéed greens, and at least one root vegetable or squash, but after
that just be guided by your taste and what's available.

Other good things that could be part of this plate are:

new potatoes	green onions
green or red peppers	turnip wedges
tomato halves	Napa cabbage
sweet potato slices	leeks
zucchini or crookneck squash	mushrooms

ROASTED WHOLE GARLIC

8–10 heads garlic　　　　　　　　　　　**salt to taste**
2 Tbs. olive oil, approx.

There are two ideas about roasting garlic: one is to separate the cloves, and the other to leave the head whole. To roast whole head garlic, first slice off about ½ inch from the sprouting end with a very sharp knife. This will help you to separate the cloves later, when the garlic is soft.

If you're keeping up with kitchen fashion, you can put the trimmed garlic heads into clay garlic roasters, or into the larger onion roaster, or you can arrange them snugly in any casserole or baking dish that is the right size for them. Drizzle a few drops of olive oil over the cut top of each head, and sprinkle them lightly with salt. Put 2 or 3 tablespoons of water in the bottom of the dish.

This is the important part: cover the dish tightly, or the garlic will dry out and become hard. Ideally, the dish should be sealed up. The best method is to use a casserole with a close-fitting cover, or to cover a dish with aluminum foil first and then fit a lid over that to hold it down.

Roast the garlic at 400° for 45 minutes to 1 hour. You should be able to squeeze the soft garlic easily out of a clove.

Serve one head of garlic per person, with plenty of good country bread to spread it on, and be ready for the fact that everyone in the area of about a city block around your house will know what you're having for dinner.

Serves 8–10.

ROASTED RADICCHIO
AND ENDIVE

These two vegetables can easily be roasted together, because they have a similar density.

2 large heads radicchio or 4 small ones 4 Belgian endives	2 Tbs. olive oil salt to taste

Peel away any badly bruised or torn outer leaves, and wash the vegetables. Cut the radicchio into quarters, or, if the heads are very small, into halves. Cut each endive in half lengthwise.

Arrange the radicchio and endive on a baking sheet, cut side up. Brush the olive oil evenly over all the cut parts. Sprinkle them with salt.

Roast the radicchio and endive in a 400° oven for about 15 minutes, or until they feel soft and the tops are beginning to color. They can be finished under a hot broiler for a few moments if you like them a little more charred.

Serves 8.

ROASTED CARROTS

2 lbs. carrots 1½ Tbs. olive oil salt to taste	4–5 Tbs. vegetable broth, more if needed 1 Tbs. fresh lemon juice

Scrape and trim the carrots. If you have thin or very small carrots, you can roast them whole. Otherwise, you will need to cut them into carrot sticks no more than ½ inch thick at their thickest point.

Put the carrots in a bowl and drizzle the olive oil over them. Toss them around until the oil is evenly distributed over all the carrots. Spread them on a shallow baking pan and sprinkle them lightly with salt. Mix together the vegetable broth and lemon juice and sprinkle it over the carrots.

Roast the carrots in a 400° oven for 45 minutes to 1 hour, turning them and moving them around every 20 minutes or so. After a while, the vegetable broth will cook away, and the carrots will begin to color. If they are turning too dark before they are tender, you can add a tiny bit more broth, but you certainly don't want any left by the time they are done.

Serves 8–10

Roasted Green Beans with Garlic (page 220) Roasted Fennel and Red Onions (page 385)

SAUTÉED WINTER GREENS

You can cook a wide variety of winter greens this way. I've done Swiss chard, ruby chard, kale, rapini, Napa cabbage, and, of course, spinach. Cooking times will vary with the density of the greens.

about 2 lbs. greens	**salt to taste**
2 Tbs. fruity green olive oil	**dash of vinegar or lemon juice**
2–3 cloves garlic, peeled and chopped	**black pepper to taste**

Wash the greens thoroughly. Discard any leaves that are yellowed or wilted. Trim off heavy stems, particularly with kale or chard. If your greens are large, cut them into smaller pieces.

Heat the olive oil in your largest non-stick sauté pan and add the chopped garlic. Stir the garlic around in the hot oil for 1 minute, then add as much of the prepared greens as the pan will hold and start turning them gently as they wilt. Continue adding greens and turning them over until you've added them all. Two pounds looks like a lot to start with, but it's amazing how it shrinks.

Salt the greens lightly and keep cooking until there is no excess liquid in the pan. By this time, most greens are completely cooked. With something a little sturdier, like kale, you might have to add a few drops of water and keep cooking for a few minutes more.

Just before serving, toss the greens with a little dash of vinegar, or some lemon juice if you prefer, and grind on a little pepper.

Serves 8–10.

ROASTED WINTER SQUASH AND APPLES

Use Kabocha, delicata, buttercup, blue Hubbard, Tahitian, or ask your green grocer about the best variety of squash available in your area. Use firm, tart apples.

2 lbs. winter squash (about 4 cups cubed)	2 tsp. lemon juice
	1½ Tbs. olive oil
2 lbs. apples	½ tsp. salt

Peel and seed your squash and cut it in large cubes or in slices, whatever works for you. Cut the apples in quarters, and core them, then toss them with the lemon juice.

Put the squash pieces in a big bowl, drizzle them with the olive oil, sprinkle on a little salt, and turn them over and over with your hands until all are lightly and evenly coated with oil.

Combine the squash with the apples and spread them on a baking sheet. Roast them at 400° for about an hour, turning and moving them every 20 minutes or so.

Serves 8–10.

ABOUT WILD MUSHROOMS

A mycologist once said that the world is divided into two types of people—mycophiles and mycophobes. As nations and cultures, we seem to be either fanatics for wild fungus, or else have a dread of it, and there's not much middle ground.

I'm definitely with the mycophiles, by heritage and by personal inclination. I just love wild mushrooms of all sorts, love to find them, love to eat them, and love to cook with them.

I remember on a visit to Poland going mushroom hunting in the cool, deep forest with my relatives. That was when my husband became enamored of wild mushrooms; he later studied them diligently so that he could hunt on his own at home.

I should say here that I do not encourage anyone to find and eat mushrooms on casual information. Do not experiment. There are poisonous mushrooms, and a few of them can kill you, or make you so sick you wish they had. But if you have studied mushrooms or are with someone who has, and you know how to make a positive identification, then collecting mushrooms in the damp and quiet wilderness can be a rewarding experience.

In Poland, as in much of Europe, the forests and meadows are well known to the local inhabitants, and traffic in the woods can be heavy on an autumn morning. The dedicated foragers are there at dawn, baskets on their arms, eyes cast down and scanning. They are there in the cold mist or drizzle, as well as on a bright morning. The first ones in the forest find the prizes. Those who follow in the warmth of the day have to search hard and walk farther to fill their baskets. These are the woods where mushrooms have been harvested for generations, or centuries.

But I have seen a virgin forest. We were in Utah, on our way to a summer workshop in a beautiful, sparsely populated region known for its spectacular mountain landscapes but not for its cuisine. As we were driving into the mountains, my husband suddenly hit the brakes and pulled off the road, his eyes fixed on the forest floor that sloped away from us. "Mushrooms! I see some, right there!"

We got out and tramped into the trees, to a nice, rich stand of what appeared to be boletus, and quite large ones. He was already cutting and gathering when he looked up and exclaimed again. We moved a little farther into the woods, barely away from the road, and stared in speechless wonder. Neither of us had ever seen a forest floor so carpeted with big, glorious, perfectly undisturbed mushrooms. There were thousands. They spread in every direction, as far as we could see.

We rushed back to the car and dumped books and papers out of carry-alls so we could fill them up with fungus. We must have gathered forty or fifty pounds in half an hour, stunned with the knowledge that no one had ever gathered mushrooms there before us. We were in a land of mycophobes.

Later, during the workshop, we went about our business with writers and filmmakers, secretly on fire with the knowledge that in our cabin there were sacks of mushrooms waiting to be made into soup, or pickled the way I had seen my Polish aunt pickle hers. And a funny thing happened. We walked into another cabin for a meeting, and there, on the kitchen counters, all over the tables, on every available surface, mushrooms were laid out on paper towels to dry. The scripts and notebooks were on the floor. It turned out that this filmmaker was Czech.

It was a rare experience, not to be repeated, and probably now there are chic restaurants in that region with chefs who send foragers into the woods. It is becoming easier to buy fresh wild mushrooms in this country than it was even a decade ago. They turn up in gourmet stores, in farmers' markets, and even in supermarkets. Americans are becoming more open to the idea of a delicious little fungus on their dinner plates.

Oyster mushrooms and shiitake mushrooms are cultivated now, so we cannot really call them wild, but they are very tasty indeed, and their ready availability in many markets shows a great improvement over the days when champignons, the little white buttons, were the only thing you could find.

shiitake

I get cultivated Portobello mushrooms at my local farmers' market; they resemble very large field mushrooms. Sometimes I also see chanterelles there, which grow locally in foggy areas near the sea. I've ordered fresh morels from a restaurant supplier in Santa Barbara. If you want something that the good restaurants are getting and don't know where to find it, just ask them who _their_ supplier is. Most of the time they'll be happy to tell you, and many wholesalers are perfectly willing to deal with a home chef—though you might have to drive to the warehouse at odd hours of the morning.

Still the most difficult to get in this country, at least in my area, are _Boletus edulus,_ the greatest of the edible fungi—with the possible exception of truffles. _Boletus_ are called cèpes in France, and porcini—

morel

little pigs—in Italy. Their Italian nickname is becoming more and more frequently used here, and it may one day sound as American as pizza. Better that than what my father called them in Poland: *prawdjiwki*. It means "the real ones," in an affectionate form.

They are the real ones to me, and though they may be expensive and hard to find, it is worth searching them out. Fortunately, dried porcini are more easily available, and while they may seem very costly, their flavor is so intense that even an ounce can add a depth and woodsy perfume to a dish of other fungi.

cèpe

The simplest way to cook most fresh mushrooms is this: Clean them well, and use minimal water if they aren't especially muddy or sandy. If you need to use water, do, but pat them dry on towels. Slice them. Sauté a little garlic into some olive oil or butter, or a combination of the two, and then add the mushrooms. Sauté them until they release their juice and it cooks away. When they are tender, salt and pepper them to your taste and eat them.

This method can be elaborated with the addition of a little chopped parsley, or a dash of wine. Some people like to add a bit of cream at the end. Fresh mushrooms, quickly sautéed in this manner, are great with eggs for breakfast, with a piece of toast or a roll any time, with rice or pasta for dinner. But there are many wonderful ways to cook mushrooms, and I mean to try them all before I die.

The following four dinners are little celebrations of the great culinary gift of fungus. The ragout and the risotto are classic, incomparably good ways to feast on mushrooms in lavish amounts. Wild Mushroom Cobbler is an easy casserole, and in the fourth menu, buckwheat crepes are wrapped around a filling of mushrooms and potatoes.

So, when you have gathered mushrooms, whether you foraged in the woods or at the market, then gather a few fellow mycophiles, open a wonderful bottle of Burgundy, and enjoy a treat that is all the more delightful because it is rare.

Note: For other mushroom dishes, see the Oyster Mushroom Chowder, the Roulade of Fresh Morels, and my own favorite, pure essence of mushrooms, the Wild Mushroom Soup.

A WILD MUSHROOM
DINNER

Gingered Squash and Apple Soup

Ragout of Wild Mushrooms

Rice Pilaf

Cranberry Sauce

Basque Cake

This dinner is elegant in its simplicity. Great seasonal ingredients are cooked and presented in an uncomplicated and satisfying way. The ragout calls for a great bottle of Burgundy, making this a meal for a special occasion. We had a Grands Échézeaux once, and it was memorable. The delicate, buttery pastry at the end also adds a celebratory touch. On the other hand, any time you come into a windfall of fresh wild mushrooms, this can be a wonderful family dinner.

The Gingered Squash and Apple Soup is a golden purée with a lovely flavor kick from fresh ginger and cilantro. It offers a nice introduction to the Ragout of Wild Mushrooms, with its deep woodsy flavors, fully developed by a combination of sautéing and then simmering in red wine. Served with it, a very plain Rice Pilaf and a bright little relish—Cranberry Sauce spiked with orange and cinnamon.

The Basque Cake is nothing more than a sweet short-crust pastry filled with vanilla crème patissière and dusted with powdered sugar. It follows the style of the rest of this meal: no frills, just pure, voluptuous flavor and texture.

Except for the Rice Pilaf, everything in this menu can be made in advance. The soup, ragout, and Cranberry Sauce can be made the day before, and in a pinch so could the cake, though the cake is better made the same day.

GINGERED SQUASH AND APPLE SOUP

You can use almost any of the dark-yellow or orange winter squashes for this, but I like Tahitian for its marvelous flavor. Kabocha, buttercup, acorn, or banana squash—any of them will do, though you may find yourself needing more seasoning with some than others.

2½ lbs. Tahitian squash (unpeeled weight), or other sweet winter squash
2½ Tbs. butter
2 medium red onions, coarsely chopped
1 lb. sweet apples, peeled, cored, and sliced

salt to taste
4½ cups vegetable broth
¾ cup dry white wine
1½ Tbs. minced fresh ginger
2 Tbs. chopped fresh cilantro
pepper to taste

garnish: additional cilantro leaves

Cut the squash in half, or in thick slices, and place cut side down on a lightly oiled baking sheet. Roast in the oven at 375° for 50–60 minutes, or until soft. Cover with foil during roasting if the squash is cut in slices. Let it cool until you can handle it, then scoop out the soft flesh, discarding any seeds, and measure out 3 cups.

In a very large non-stick sauté pan, melt the butter and cook the onions in it over medium heat, stirring often, until they are very soft. Add the apple slices and a little salt, and keep cooking for 15 minutes more, stirring frequently.

Add the cooked squash, vegetable broth, wine, ginger, and chopped cilantro, and simmer for another 15 minutes. Everything should be very soft.

Purée the soup in the blender in batches until perfectly smooth, then add salt and pepper to taste. Serve hot, sprinkled with cilantro leaves.

Of course, a splash of cream could be added for a richer soup, or a spoonful of crème fraîche (page 324) plopped in the center of each bowl, but the pure flavors of the vegetables and fruit are so lively and concentrated in this purée that I prefer it this way.

Serves 6–8.

RAGOUT OF WILD MUSHROOMS

The success of this dish will depend mainly on the flavor and quality of the mushrooms used. It pays to go out of your way to find good wild mushrooms, or the more interesting cultivated varieties, and a combination is more satisfying than all of a kind. You can use porcini, morels, field mushrooms, oyster mushrooms, shiitakes, or other varieties if you live in a good area for mushrooms. Add champignons, the ubiquitous white buttons, if you need to, but try not to use more than half champignons in your mix, as they have the blandest flavor.

1¾ lbs. fresh wild mushrooms, or a combination of wild and cultivated
1 large yellow onion
1 large red onion
1 Tbs. olive oil
2 Tbs. + 1 tsp. butter
3 cloves garlic, chopped
salt and pepper to taste

1 cup dry red wine
1 bay leaf
½ tsp. thyme leaves
2 stalks celery, sliced thinly
pinch of cayenne
1 Tbs. flour
2 cups heated vegetable broth
3 Tbs. chopped flat-leaf parsley

Clean the mushrooms thoroughly, trim off tough or woody stems, and slice the mushrooms or cut them in generous pieces.

Cut the onions in very thin wedges or wide slices. Heat 1 teaspoon of olive oil and 2 teaspoons of butter in a non-stick sauté pan and sauté the onions in it, stirring often, until they begin to soften. Add the chopped garlic and some salt and pepper and continue cooking until the onions and garlic begin to brown. Add half the red wine, the bay leaf and thyme, and the sliced celery. Turn down the heat and simmer gently until the wine cooks away.

Meanwhile, in another non-stick pan, heat 2 teaspoons of olive oil with 2 teaspoons of butter. Sauté the mushrooms in it with a sprinkle of salt and a pinch of cayenne until their excess liquid cooks away and they begin to color. Add the remaining wine, lower the heat, and allow the wine to simmer down. Add the onions to the mushrooms.

Add 1 tablespoon of butter to the pan in which you've sautéed the onions and let it melt. Stir in a tablespoon of flour and keep stirring over medium heat for a few minutes as it turns golden. Whisk in the hot broth and continue whisking as it thickens. Add this sauce to the mushrooms and onions, along with the parsley.

Simmer everything together very gently for about 10 more minutes. Serve with steamed rice or Rice Pilaf.

Serves 6.

Variation: If you can't find any fresh wild mushrooms at all, you could use 1½ pounds of fresh cultivated mushrooms, and about 2 ounces of dried porcini. Cover the porcini with hot water and let them soak until they are soft and pliable, at least ½ hour, then drain, reserving the water. Clean the mushrooms well and slice them. Proceed as above, combining the soaked porcini with the sliced fresh mushrooms. Filter the soaking liquid and add it to the broth.

RICE PILAF

½ cup green onions, thinly sliced
1 Tbs. butter
1½ cups long-grain white rice

3½ cups vegetable broth, heated
salt to taste

optional: chopped flat-leaf parsley, basil, or tarragon
fresh-grated Parmesan cheese

In a medium sauté pan or skillet, sauté the sliced green onions in the butter until they are soft. Add the rice and stir it into the onions and butter for a minute or two. Add the heated broth, and a little salt only if needed.

Cover the pan, lower the heat, and simmer very gently for 25 minutes. Turn off the heat and leave the rice covered for another 5 minutes. Uncover, fluff with a fork, and serve, with or without the optional garnishes.

Serves 6.

CRANBERRY SAUCE

12 oz. fresh cranberries
1 large orange
¾ cup sugar

1 tsp. cinnamon
dash of cloves

Wash the cranberries and discard any that are soft or spoiled.

Finely grate the zest of the orange. Cut away and discard all the white pith, and cut the orange into a few pieces. Put the orange pieces and the grated zest into the container of a blender with enough water to make one cup, and process until the orange is roughly chopped.

Combine the liquid in a heavy-bottomed saucepan with the sugar, cinnamon, and cloves, and bring to a boil, stirring to dissolve the sugar. Add the cranberries, return to a boil, and stir over medium heat for 8–10 minutes. Use a long-handled wooden spoon—this stuff can really spit.

When most of the cranberries have popped and the liquid is somewhat thickened, the sauce is done. Pour it into a serving dish and allow it to cool, then chill.

Serves 6–8 as a garnish.

BASQUE CAKE

This is a lovely cake, made from a delicate, cookie-like pastry filled with crème patissière.

for the crème patissière:
3 large egg yolks
½ cup sugar
⅓ cup flour
pinch of salt

2 cups milk
2 Tbs. cream
1 tsp. pure vanilla extract

for the pastry:
2 cups + 2 Tbs. white flour
½ cup sugar
pinch of salt
1 tsp. baking powder
5 oz. cold butter (10 Tbs.)

grated zest of 1 orange
grated zest of ½ lemon
1 egg
2 Tbs. melted butter
confectioners sugar

Make the crème patissière first, so that it has time to cool completely. Beat the egg yolks with the sugar until they are pale and creamy. Beat in the flour and salt.

Combine the milk, cream, and vanilla in a heavy-bottomed saucepan and heat to a simmer. Beating constantly with a whisk, gradually add the hot milk to the egg yolk mixture. When all the milk has been whisked in, return the mixture to the saucepan and whisk over a medium flame as it returns to a simmer. Continue whisking steadily as the sauce thickens to the consistency of a soft pudding. This will take about 5 minutes.

Transfer the crème patissière to a bowl and allow it to cool completely, giving it a stir with the whisk every now and then to keep the top from drying out.

The pastry can be made in moments with a food processor. Put 2 cups of flour, the sugar, salt, and baking powder into the container of a food processor fitted with the steel blade. Add the cold butter, cut in 6 or 7 pieces, and the grated orange and lemon zest. Process until the mixture resembles coarse cornmeal. Add the egg and process again until a dough forms and begins to hold together.

To make the pastry by hand, sift together 2 cups of flour with the sugar, salt, and baking powder. Add the cold butter, cut in small pieces, and the zest, and cut in the butter with 2 knives or with a pastry cutter until the mixture resembles coarse cornmeal. Lightly beat the egg, add it to the flour mixture, and stir it in with a fork until a dough forms and begins to hold together. Work the dough lightly with your hands for a few moments, just until it can be formed into a ball.

Cover the pastry dough and chill it for about 20 minutes. Divide the dough into 2 equal parts. Roll out the first half of the dough between 2 sheets of wax paper into a circle 12 inches in diameter. Put the rolled pastry away to chill again, still covered with wax paper. Roll the second piece out the same way into a circle about 11 inches in diameter, and allow it to chill again.

Butter a 10-inch springform pan. Gently peel away the wax paper from the larger circle of pastry and fit it into the cake pan, forming an inch-high edge all around. Brush the bottom of the pastry with the melted butter, and dust it lightly with the 2 tablespoons of flour. Fill the pastry with the crème patissière.

Remove the wax paper from the smaller circle of pastry and lay it over the filling. Press the edges of pastry together carefully to seal them, and form a smooth, even rim around the perimeter of the cake. This pastry is very tender, and easy to mold with your fingers.

Bake the cake at 300° for about 45–50 minutes. It should be a light golden brown, and tremble only slightly when moved.

Allow the cake to cool on a rack in its pan for about 10 minutes, then remove the outside of the pan and let the cake finish cooling to room temperature. Dust the top of the cake with sieved confectioners sugar.

Makes one 10-inch cake, 10–12 servings.

WILD MUSHROOM
RISOTTO DINNER

Toasts with Grilled Chèvre

Roasted Beet, Asparagus, and Garlic Salad

Wild Mushroom Risotto

Apple Crisp

Here's a terrific dinner that can be served to company or to family. It can be simplified if need be, or can be as elegant as you want.

It is a good winter dinner, and one of the best things about it is how beautifully it goes with your best red wines. "Buy on bread and sell on cheese" is the wine merchant's motto, and you know why when you bite into creamy, warm goat cheese on a slice of baguette, then sip your wine.

Wild mushrooms are also known for their affinity to red wines. Burgundies and generous Italian Chiantis are our favorites with this risotto.

The salad of roasted beets and asparagus can be served as a course of its own, between the chèvre and the risotto, if you've got someone willing to stand at the stove and stir risotto. If that risotto-stirrer is you, then sip wine and nibble cheese toasts while you stir, and just serve the salad on a smaller plate alongside the bowls of risotto.

Dessert is a refreshing, old-fashioned Apple Crisp.

For a simpler meal, eliminate the Toasts with Grilled Chèvre, and replace the Apple Crisp with a good store-bought ice cream or sorbet.

TOASTS WITH
GRILLED CHÈVRE

This is a very tasty little nibble before dinner, and just the idea of layering butter and cheese this way adds a quality of thrilling recklessness to any event.

1 baguette
butter to taste

8–10 oz. fresh white chèvre
(goat cheese)

Cut the baguette into 18–20 slices, and spread them thinly with softened butter. Arrange the buttered slices on a cookie sheet and toast them in a hot oven (400°) until they are crisp and evenly golden on top, about 7 or 8 minutes.

Allow the toasts to cool slightly, then spread them thickly with a semi-soft fresh goat cheese, using about 2 tablespoons per slice. Put the cheese toasts under a preheated broiler for a few minutes, until the cheese is soft and hot through, about 3 or 4 minutes. Watch them carefully to be sure they don't burn, and serve at once when they are done.

Serves 6–8.

ROASTED BEET, ASPARAGUS,
AND GARLIC SALAD

This is a beautiful salad—rich golds and reds with bright green, all arranged together at the last minute. The flavor is superb as the sweetness of the garlic-infused beets plays against the freshness of asparagus, all of it lightly marinated.

1 lb. red beets (small if possible)
1 lb. golden beets
1 head garlic
1 lb. slender green asparagus
¼ cup + 1 Tbs. olive oil

salt to taste
2 Tbs. balsamic vinegar
¼ cup fresh orange juice
1 Tbs. minced onion
pepper to taste

Trim the beets, leaving an inch of stems, and scrub them well. Break the garlic up into individual cloves, but don't peel them. Put the red beets in one glass baking dish and the golden beets in another, and scatter the garlic cloves evenly between them. Add about ½ cup of water to each dish, cover them tightly with lids or with foil, and cook them in a 400° oven for about 1 hour, until perfectly tender. The time will vary a bit depending on the size of the beets.

Meanwhile, wash the asparagus stalks and trim off any tough ends. Drizzle them with a tablespoon of olive oil, roll them around on a baking sheet until they are evenly coated, spread them out, and sprinkle them with salt. Set aside until the beets are cooked.

When the beets are tender, allow them to cool slightly so you can handle them, then peel and cut them into wedges or slices, keeping them separate.

At the same time, raise the oven temperature to 450° and roast the prepared asparagus stalks for 15–20 minutes, depending on their thickness, until tender but not browned.

Squeeze about 10 cloves of the soft, cooked garlic into a bowl and mash it well with a fork. Add the remaining ¼ cup of olive oil, the balsamic vinegar, orange juice, minced onion, salt, and pepper, and whisk together thoroughly.

In separate bowls, add 2 tablespoons of the dressing each to the red beets, golden beets, and asparagus. Toss gently to coat, and leave the vegetables to marinate for a few hours.

Just before serving, arrange the beets and asparagus on individual plates in attractive random patterns of these spectacular colors. Don't toss them together, or the red beets will stain everything! Serve this salad at room temperature.

Serves 6–8.

WILD MUSHROOM RISOTTO

A delicious risotto can be made with almost any variety of the commonly available edible wild mushrooms, but the ones with the most intense, woodsy flavors are my favorites. I like porcini the best, and if I can get fresh ones I'm thrilled. Because they are not often available where I live, I usually combine a pound of other fresh mushrooms with a small amount of dried porcini to intensify the flavor of the dish, which works very well.

1½ lbs. fresh wild mushrooms
(porcini, morels, shiitake,
Portobello, or other flavorful
varieties), or
1 lb. fresh wild mushrooms
and 1½ oz. dried porcini
(*Boletus edulus*)
6–7 cups vegetable or chicken broth
2 Tbs. olive oil
1 tsp. butter

1 clove garlic, minced
dash of salt
1 medium yellow onion, chopped
1½ cups Arborio rice
⅓ cup Marsala
⅔ cup dry white wine
⅔ cup grated Parmesan cheese,
more for the table
½ cup chopped flat-leaf parsley

Prepare the mushrooms: Clean them carefully under running water to get rid of all the grit, and trim them as needed. Cut them into thin strips or small chunks, depending on the size and variety. If you are using dried porcini, soak them in enough boiling water to cover for about ½ hour, or until they are pliable, then rinse them carefully under running water. Chop them coarsely, and strain the soaking water through a coffee filter. Add the strained water to the broth and set aside.

Heat 1 tablespoon of olive oil and the butter in a non-stick pan, and stir the garlic in it for a minute. Add the prepared fresh mushrooms and a dash of salt, and sauté them, stirring frequently, until they release their moisture. Add the soaked and chopped porcini and keep stirring over medium heat until all the mushrooms are tender and coloring around the edges.

Heat the remaining tablespoon of oil in a large non-stick sauté pan and stir the chopped onion in it over medium heat until it is soft and barely golden. At the same time, heat the broth to a simmer, cover it, and keep it warm.

Add the rice to the sautéed onion and stir together for a few moments. Add the Marsala and keep stirring as it cooks away—this will take a few seconds. Add the white wine, and when it has cooked away, stir in the sautéed mushrooms and about a cup of the hot broth. Adjust the flame so that the broth simmers gently with the rice, and stir it slowly with a wooden spoon.

When the broth has almost all been absorbed, add another cup or so, and continue in the same manner, stirring as often as possible, until most of the broth is used and the rice is *al dente*—tender but firm. It will take about 20 or 25 minutes.

When the rice has reached the right texture, stir in a last ½ cup of broth, ⅔ cup of Parmesan cheese, and the chopped parsley. Serve the risotto at once, in shallow bowls, and pass additional Parmesan cheese at the table.

Serves 6–8.

APPLE CRISP

filling:
3½ lbs. crisp, juicy apples
2 Tbs. fresh lemon juice
½ cup sugar

1 tsp. cinnamon
2 Tbs. all-purpose flour

topping:
½ cup coarsely chopped walnuts
½ cup all-purpose flour
¾ cup dark-brown sugar
½ tsp. cinnamon

3 Tbs. cold butter
1 cup rolled oats
1 egg white

Quarter the apples, peel and core them, and slice them crosswise. Toss the apple slices with the lemon juice, sugar, cinnamon, and flour. Spread the prepared apple mixture evenly in a large, shallow gratin dish.

Spread the chopped walnuts on a cookie sheet and toast them in a 250° oven for about 25 minutes, then remove them and set them aside.

For the topping, combine the flour, brown sugar, and cinnamon in a food processor and process briefly. Add the cold butter, cut in pieces, and process again until the mixture has an evenly grainy texture, with no large chunks of butter. Add the rolled oats and process for a few seconds only. Add the egg white, and process for a few seconds again, until the mixture starts to form clumps.

Using your hands, sprinkle the topping evenly over the apples, breaking apart the largest clumps if necessary. Bake the crisp in a 375° oven for about 35 minutes. The apples should be simmering and the topping crisp and brown.

Allow the crisp to cool slightly, then sprinkle the toasted walnuts over the top and serve. This is best served warm, with a little scoop of vanilla ice cream.

Serves 8.

WILD MUSHROOM COBBLER DINNER

Revised Caesar Salad

Wild Mushroom Cobbler

Cranberry-Jalapeño Sauce

Pumpkin Flan

Deep-dish pot pies are among the homey, familiar foods
that children and adults alike adore, especially when the days close in
with darkness, damp, and chill. I was fooling around with the
idea of a hearty pot pie for supper and started with an assortment of
flavorful mushrooms and lots of onions. Then, because I wanted
to keep it simple and not too heavy, I made a buttermilk biscuit
topping. My children took one look and said, "That's not a pie,
Mom. It's a cobbler." And so it is.

A big plate of cobbler with a spoonful of cranberry sauce is
the center of this meal. A crunchy green salad completes it. While
you can serve any tossed salad you like, I decided on an old
favorite, the Caesar, slightly revised to eliminate the raw egg
and reduce the amount of olive oil a bit.

In keeping with the mood, dessert is a creamy, lovely
Pumpkin Flan—everything a flan should be yet reminiscent of
pumpkin pie. This is a perfect "nursery sweet" but completely elegant
as well. It's even more beautiful than a classic flan when unmolded
onto a platter in its glaze of liquid caramel.

REVISED CAESAR SALAD

The original Caesar salad is an abiding favorite, having survived time, changing fashion, numerous weird and perverse variations, and the certain knowledge that too much oil just isn't good for us. It's a delicious salad, and that's a fact.

But nothing's sacred, that's another fact, so here's a delicious variation. It calls for a lighter hand with the olive oil, and replaces the nearly raw egg with a spoonful of mayonnaise. These are minor changes—the essential flavors of olive oil, lemon juice, Worcestershire, and Parmesan cheese remain clear and true, and the crunchy, home-made garlic croutons are there. It's just a little less of a production to make and a little easier on your health, so now, if you like, *you can have it every day!*

2 cloves garlic
5 Tbs. fruity green olive oil
12–16 slices from a sourdough
    baguette
salt to taste
3–4 heads romaine lettuce, hearts
    only (about 12 cups torn leaves)

3 Tbs. fresh-squeezed lemon juice
1 Tbs. Worcestershire sauce
1–2 Tbs. reduced-fat mayonnaise
⅓–½ cup fresh-grated Parmesan
    cheese
fresh-ground black pepper

Crush the garlic cloves a little with a stone or the flat of a big knife, then peel and chop them coarsely. Combine the garlic in a dish with 2 tablespoons of olive oil and let steep for about 15 minutes.

Cut 12–16 thick slices from a sourdough baguette. You can also use ordinary French bread, but I prefer sourdough. Using a pastry brush, very lightly brush a little garlic oil on both sides of each slice, then sprinkle with salt. Cut the slices into thirds or quarters, spread them on a cookie sheet, and toast them in a 400° oven for 15–20 minutes, or until they are crisp and golden brown around the edges.

Wash the lettuce, set aside the large, dark-green outer leaves for another use, and tear up the crisp, lighter-green inner leaves until you have about 12 moderately packed cups. Spin them dry in a salad spinner and put in a big, wide salad bowl.

In the container of a blender, combine the remaining 3 tablespoons of olive oil, the lemon juice, Worcestershire sauce, a pinch of salt, and 1–2 tablespoons of mayonnaise, depending on how "creamy" you like your dressing. For more assertive garlic taste, add a bit of the chopped garlic you used for the crouton oil. Give this all a brief spin, drizzle it over the lettuce, and toss. Add the grated Parmesan cheese and a few turns of the pepper mill, and toss again. Scatter the croutons over the top, or toss them in with the lettuce, and serve.

Serves 6–8.

WILD MUSHROOM
COBBLER

filling:
2 lbs. red Spanish onions
2½ Tbs. olive oil
2½ Tbs. butter
salt to taste
1 oz. dried porcini
½ lb. fresh porcini or Portobello
    mushrooms
½ lb. fresh oyster mushrooms

2 cloves garlic, chopped
pinch of dried thyme
pinch of cayenne
fresh-ground black pepper to taste
½ cup dry red wine
1½ Tbs. flour
1½ cups low-fat milk, heated

topping:
2 cups all-purpose flour
1 tsp. baking soda
2 tsp. baking powder
1 tsp. salt

4 Tbs. chilled butter
½ cup fresh-grated Parmesan
    cheese
1⅓ cups buttermilk

Prepare the filling: Peel, quarter, and slice the red onions. In a large non-stick skillet, heat a tablespoon of olive oil and a tablespoon of butter, add the onions and a good sprinkle of salt, and cook over low heat, stirring often, for about an hour. The onions will gradually soften and eventually caramelize to a golden-brown color and incredible sweetness.

Pour boiling water to cover over the dried porcini and leave them to soak for at least 30 minutes. Clean, trim, and slice the fresh mushrooms. When the dried porcini are soft, rinse them carefully and chop them finely. Strain the soaking water through a coffee filter and reserve it.

In another large non-stick skillet, heat 1½ tablespoons of olive oil and ½ tablespoon butter. Add the chopped garlic to it and stir for 1 minute, then add the sliced fresh mushrooms and a little salt. Sauté the mushrooms, stirring often, until they start to release their liquid. Add the chopped porcini, a pinch of thyme, a pinch of cayenne, and fresh-ground black pepper to taste, and keep cooking over medium heat until the excess liquid has cooked away, and the mushrooms are sizzling and beginning to color.

Add the red wine, stirring as it cooks away, then add the soaking liquid from the dried mushrooms. Combine the mushrooms with the caramelized onions and simmer them all together for a few minutes.

In a small, heavy-bottomed saucepan, melt the remaining tablespoon of butter and stir in 1½ tablespoons flour. Stir the roux over medium heat for 3 or 4 minutes, until it is golden. Add the heated milk, whisking steadily. Keep stirring with a whisk for several minutes, as the sauce thickens. Stir the white sauce into the onions and mushrooms. Taste, and correct the seasoning with more salt or pepper as needed.

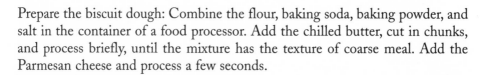

Pour the mushroom mixture into a lightly buttered medium-sized gratin dish, spreading it evenly.

girolle

Prepare the biscuit dough: Combine the flour, baking soda, baking powder, and salt in the container of a food processor. Add the chilled butter, cut in chunks, and process briefly, until the mixture has the texture of coarse meal. Add the Parmesan cheese and process a few seconds.

Transfer the mixture to a bowl and stir in the buttermilk, just until a dough forms. It will be thick and sticky; don't overmix it.

Spoon the biscuit dough onto the mushrooms, distributing it more or less evenly over the top. Bake the cobbler in a preheated 400° oven for about 25 minutes. The biscuit topping should be lightly golden brown.

cèpe

Serve hot, with a green salad, with cranberry sauce or a chutney, or with your favorite relish.

Serves 8.

Cranberry-Jalapeño Sauce (page 138)

PUMPKIN FLAN

This excellent dessert combines some of the best qualities of those two universal favorites, pumpkin pie and flan. It makes a nice change from classic flan, and the flavor of the pumpkin is beautiful with the caramel sauce.

1¾ cups sugar	1¾ cups puréed pumpkin
1¼ cups whole milk	2 tsp. ground cinnamon
1¼ cups evaporated milk	1 tsp. ground ginger
5 large eggs	¼ tsp. allspice
¼ tsp. salt	

Select a 2-quart baking dish, perhaps a soufflé dish or a casserole. Heat the dish in a 400° oven as you melt 1 cup of the sugar in a heavy-bottomed skillet over a medium flame. When the sugar is entirely melted and a rich golden caramel color, put on your thickest pot-holder gloves, take out the heated baking dish, pour the caramel into it, then immediately tilt the dish around so that the caramel coats both the bottom and the sides. Set the prepared dish aside.

Scald all the milk, stopping short of boiling. In a mixing bowl, beat the eggs with the remaining sugar until they are smooth and getting thick. Add the salt, the pumpkin, and the spices, and beat again. Pour the scalded milk through a strainer and add it to the pumpkin mixture, still beating.

Pour the pumpkin mixture into the prepared baking dish, and place that dish in a larger baking pan which has at least an inch of water in it. Put the flan carefully into the oven, lower the heat to 350°, and bake the flan for an hour, or slightly longer. The flan should be golden brown on top, it should tremble only slightly when shaken, and a thin knife inserted in the center should come out clean.

Set the flan on a rack and allow it to cool to room temperature, then cover it tightly and chill it in the refrigerator. To unmold the flan, first loosen the sides by slipping a very thin, sharp knife around the edges. When the flan moves freely in its dish, invert a large serving plate over the baking dish and, holding the 2 securely together, quickly turn them over. The flan will drop out onto the serving platter, and the gleaming brown caramel sauce will pour out around it— a thing of beauty. Cut it into thick wedges to serve, and spoon a little of the sauce over each wedge.

Serves 8.

BUCKWHEAT CREPES WITH WILD MUSHROOMS

Tomatillo and Squash Soup

*Buckwheat Crepes
with Potato and Mushroom Filling*

small green salad

Winter Fruit Compote

Gingerbread Biscotti

I don't think I ever had such an instant hit with a new recipe as I did with this tomatillo-based soup. Everyone who ate it at my dinner party immediately asked for the recipe, and then they all went home and actually *made* it. By week's end, there wasn't a Kabocha squash to be found in our small-town markets.

Buckwheat crepes filled with a hearty mixture of mushrooms, onions, and potatoes are a quintessential winter dish—substantial food, yet not overwhelmingly rich. The distinct flavor and texture of buckwheat is a pleasure. With the wild mushrooms and the little bit of cheese, this is a dish that calls out for a wonderful big red wine. Plates can be garnished with a small side salad, but avoid sharp, piquant dressings, as they fight with the wine.

If you are preparing this meal for company, it is nice to know that most of it can be prepared well ahead of time. The soup, crepes, and compote can all be made the day before with no loss of quality at all. You should, however, rewarm both the crepes and filling before rolling the crepes, and that part should be done just before dinner.

TOMATILLO AND SQUASH SOUP

about 12 medium tomatillos
  (1½ lbs.)
3–4 medium tomatoes, ripe red
  (1 lb.)
10–12 cloves garlic, unpeeled
salt to taste
4 cups peeled and diced Kabocha
  squash* (approx. 2 lbs.
  untrimmed)

4 cups vegetable broth
2 cups water, more if needed
1 Tbs. olive oil
2 large yellow onions, quartered and
  sliced
1 small bunch cilantro, de-stemmed
  and coarsely chopped
2 dried red serrano or other hot
  chiles

Remove and discard the husks from the tomatillos, wash them, and cut in half. Trim the tomatoes and quarter them. Arrange the tomatillos, tomatoes, and all but one clove of the unpeeled garlic on a cookie sheet. Sprinkle lightly with salt and roast in a 450° oven for 35–45 minutes, until the vegetables are soft and beginning to char in spots. Remove and let them cool for a few minutes.

While the vegetables are roasting, combine the diced Kabocha squash, the vegetable broth, and 2 cups of water in an ample soup pot and simmer, covered, for at least 45 minutes, or until the squash is very tender.

At the same time, heat the olive oil in a large non-stick pan and add the onions and the remaining clove of garlic, peeled and minced, and a dash of salt. Cook over medium heat, stirring often, until the onions are caramelized to a dark golden brown.

When the roasted vegetables are ready and cool enough to handle, scrape the red tomatoes off their skins with a spoon. Squeeze the soft garlic out of the cloves and discard the husks. Combine the red tomato pulp, the tomatillos, and the soft garlic in a blender or food processor with a little water, and purée them.

Add the purée to the broth and squash, along with the caramelized onions and the chopped cilantro. If the broth has been greatly reduced during cooking, add back some water.

Toast the dried red chiles in a hot pan or over a flame until they blister or show black spots. Chop them, removing some of the seeds for a milder flavor, and stir them into the soup. Simmer everything together for 5–10 minutes. Serve hot, with warm corn tortillas or any good bread.

Serves 8–10.

If Kabocha squash is unavailable, look for buttercup, Hubbard, or Delicata. In a pinch, you could use an acorn squash.

BUCKWHEAT CREPES
WITH POTATO
AND MUSHROOM FILLING

12–14 large buckwheat crepes
  (page 137)

filling:
1 lb. Portobello or shiitake
  mushrooms
1 Tbs. + 1 tsp. olive oil
1 Tbs. butter
2 cloves garlic, minced
salt to taste

3 large yellow onions, chopped
2 large russet potatoes
½ cup dry white wine
coarsely chopped flat-leaf parsley
fresh-ground black pepper
4 oz. grated Swiss or Fontina cheese

Clean the mushrooms and cut them in ½-inch dice. Heat a tablespoon of olive oil and a teaspoon of butter in a large non-stick skillet and stir the minced garlic in it for a minute. Add the mushrooms and a little salt, and sauté for 10–12 minutes, until they are tender and starting to sizzle.

In another skillet, cook the chopped onions in the remaining olive oil and butter, with a dash of salt, until they are soft and turning golden.

Peel the potatoes and cut them in ½-inch dice. Combine them in a saucepan with the white wine and enough water just barely to cover them, as well as ½ teaspoon of salt. Bring the water to a boil, lower the heat to a simmer, cover the pan tightly, and cook for 10–15 minutes, until the potatoes are just tender. Remove the lid and continue cooking gently, stirring once or twice, until the liquid is reduced and thickened to a sauce. Stir in the sautéed onions and mushrooms, as well as chopped parsley and fresh-ground black pepper to taste.

Allow the potato-mushroom mixture to cool slightly, then fill the crepes. Spoon 2–3 rounded tablespoons of filling across the center of each crepe, then sprinkle a little grated cheese over the filling before rolling or folding the crepe loosely over it. You should have about a dozen filled crepes.

Cover the crepes loosely with aluminum foil and bake in a 350° oven for 10–15 minutes, or until they are hot through and the cheese is completely melted.

Serves 6.

WINTER FRUIT COMPOTE

½ lb. dried nectarines or peaches
   (or a combination)
¼ lb. dried plums
½ lb. dried figs
2½ cups spring water

2 cups dry red wine
peel of 1 lemon
3-inch stick cinnamon
⅓ cup sugar
1 tsp. Pernod

garnish: ice cream

Cut the nectarines or peaches and the plums into wide strips. Leave the figs whole. Combine the fruit in a medium-sized non-reactive pot with the water and the wine. Remember—when cooking with wine, the rule is, if you don't want to drink it, don't cook with it. You don't have to use a rare or expensive wine, but it must be good; its flavor will tell.

Cut the lemon peel off in wide strips, and with a thin, sharp knife slice away the thick white pith and discard. Add the peel to the fruit, along with the cinnamon stick, sugar, and Pernod. Bring everything to a boil, lower the heat, and gently simmer for about 30 minutes. Add a bit more water if needed to keep everything just covered.

The fruit should be soft, but not falling apart. The liquid will have the consistency of a thin syrup, not too sweet and just slightly spicy from the cinnamon and lemon peel. The peel can be left in the syrup while the compote is refrigerated, but should be removed before serving.

Serve warm or cool, in wide, shallow bowls, with a scoop of ice cream added at the last moment. Cinnamon or anise ice cream would be great; so would a good, plain vanilla.

Serves 8–10.

Gingerbread Biscotti (page 420)

Little
Dinner
Parties

for Fall
and Winter

A SIMPLE AUTUMN
DINNER PARTY

Simple Focaccia

cured olives, fennel wedges, celery, radishes

goat cheese

Lima Bean Soup with Herbed Croutons

Torta di Polenta with Three Cheeses

Roasted Tomato Sauce

Parfaits of Fruit and Mascarpone

This straightforward meal consists of a few easy foods that I really like. It's a warming, relaxing meal, good for appetites sharpened by chill air, and a very nice menu for a good bottle of red wine.

A focaccia hot from the oven turns a platter of raw vegetables and some cheese into a great first course. An old-fashioned bowl of steaming lima bean soup with croutons is a universal favorite, and the baked polenta is richly flavored with cheese, then accented with the smoky taste of roasted tomatoes. The flavors are big and hearty, and familiar. A touch of elegance is added by the pretty dessert of sweet, ripe fruit, discreetly layered with mascarpone.

A practical note: Nothing is complicated to serve, and almost all the work can be done in advance, so you can enjoy the meal in the easygoing atmosphere it creates. The polenta just needs to be put in the oven at the right time. The parfaits should be assembled not long before you serve them, but the fruit and the mascarpone can be prepared ahead. Only the vegetables should be cut up at the last minute—
fennel wedges really need to be fresh—but that's a snap.

SIMPLE FOCACCIA

A fresh, warm focaccia is a wonderful addition to almost any meal, and it's not much more trouble to make than stirring up a batch of cornbread. You need to start about 2½ hours before you want to eat, but there's only about 20 minutes of actual work involved.

It's a great thing to serve with an apéritif wine and some olives or chopped tomatoes if you have a gang of people hanging around in the kitchen while you finish cooking dinner. This is a very basic recipe, which can be varied endlessly with herbs and flavorings. Remember, don't make more than you need, because it's only good when it's fresh—but people love it, so you'll need more than you think.

¼ oz. (1 envelope) dry yeast
1¼ cups warm water
pinch of sugar
1 tsp. salt

3 Tbs. olive oil
3–3½ cups flour—white, whole
     wheat, or a combination
coarse sea salt to taste

In a large mixing bowl, dissolve the yeast in the warm water with the sugar, and leave it for about 15 minutes, until it starts to foam. Add the salt and half the olive oil, then start stirring in the flour, a scoop at a time.

When the dough is too stiff to stir with a spoon, turn it out on a well-floured board, sprinkle more flour on top of it, and begin kneading. Knead it gently, working in as much more of the flour as you must to keep it from sticking. When the dough is smooth and elastic, form it into a ball and put it in an oiled bowl, turning it once to coat it. Cover the bowl with a tea towel or with plastic wrap, and leave the dough in a warm place to rise for about 45 minutes, or until almost double in size.

Punch the dough down, lift it out of the bowl onto an oiled baking sheet, and pat or roll it out into a large, thick oval, about 12 × 16 inches. Cover it with a tea towel and leave it to rise again for at least 30 minutes, or until almost doubled.

Brush the focaccia delicately with the remaining olive oil, and sprinkle it with some coarse sea salt. If you like, you can cut shallow diagonal slashes in the top with a sharp knife, in a crisscross pattern. Or dimple the top of the focaccia with your fingertips, but don't be too aggressive—you don't want to punch it down again.

Bake the focaccia in a preheated 450° oven for 20–30 minutes, or until it is golden on top and sounds hollow when the bottom crust is tapped. Cut it in squares and serve it hot or warm.

This makes 1 loaf, and the recipe may be doubled.

LIMA BEAN SOUP

1 lb. dried baby lima beans
pinch of baking soda
1 head garlic
1 large red onion
1 tsp. salt
2–3 sprigs rosemary

1 bay leaf
2 Tbs. green olive oil
3 cups vegetable broth (or chicken
    broth)
fresh-ground black pepper to taste

garnishes: Herbed Croutons (recipe follows)
            grated Parmesan cheese

Soak the beans overnight in plenty of water with a pinch of baking soda in it. Drain and rinse the beans.

Peel the garlic, and peel and coarsely chop the red onion. In a large, heavy-bottomed soup pot, combine the lima beans, 2 quarts water, the salt, rosemary, garlic, onion, bay leaf, and a tablespoon of olive oil. Bring the water to a boil, reduce the heat, and simmer gently for about 2 hours, until the beans are very soft and much of the water is absorbed.

Remove the bay leaf and the stems from the rosemary, then purée the soup in batches in a blender until it is creamy. Add the vegetable broth and heat to simmering, then taste and correct the seasoning with additional salt and some pepper if needed.

Serve hot, drizzled with the remaining olive oil and garnished with Herbed Croutons and Parmesan cheese.

Serves 8.

HERBED CROUTONS

This is one of the best things to do with leftover bread, but you have to get around to it before the bread becomes completely dry. The type of bread is not too important, as long as it's a type you like, and the herbs can be varied.

5 cups bread cubes (white,
sourdough, whole wheat, or
rye, or a mix; fresh or a few days
old, but not dry)
2 Tbs. olive oil

1 tsp. fresh rosemary leaves,
chopped
1 tsp. fresh thyme leaves
1 tsp. minced garlic (optional)
salt and pepper

Cut your bread into cubes of the size you like.

Heat the olive oil, herbs, and garlic in a large, non-stick sauté pan for a minute, then add the bread cubes and immediately start tossing them in the oil until all of them are as evenly coated with oil and herbs as possible; this will never be perfect, but don't worry.

Spread the croutons on a cookie sheet, sprinkle them liberally with salt and, if you like, pepper, and bake them in the oven at 325° for 20–30 minutes, or as long as it takes to make them crispy and golden brown. You might want to move and turn them once during the baking time.

Allow the croutons to cool and use them as you like, in salads and soups.

TORTA DI POLENTA
with Three Cheeses

Polenta can be made plain or fancy. In this version, simple polenta is mixed with a number of savory ingredients, molded into a nice round shape, then baked in the oven and served with a sauce. It's extremely tasty, and does not suffer at all from being prepared hours ahead of time, so is an ideal party dish.

1 large clove garlic, minced
½ cup chopped white of leek
½ cup chopped red onion
2 Tbs. olive oil
4 cups light vegetable broth
1 tsp. butter
1 cup yellow cornmeal (page 230)

1½ oz. fresh white goat cheese
1 oz. smoked Gouda cheese cut in
¼-inch dice
1 oz. Parmesan cheese, grated
salt, if needed

Sauté the garlic, leek, and onion in the olive oil, in a non-stick pan, until they are golden. Heat the broth with the butter, whisk in the cornmeal, and simmer it, stirring constantly with a wooden spoon, for about 10–15 minutes, or until it is thick.

Remove the polenta from the heat and stir in the cooked onions and the goat cheese, then the diced Gouda cheese and the grated Parmesan. Taste, and add salt only if needed. Pour the hot polenta into a buttered deep-dish pie pan or round casserole, and smooth the top. Cover and chill for 45 minutes or longer.

Slide a butter knife around the edges of the polenta to loosen it, then invert it onto a buttered baking sheet. Bake the torta at 400° for 12–15 minutes. It should be hot through and just barely crisping on the outside.

Cut the torta into wedges and serve with Roasted Tomato Sauce.

Serves 6–8.

ROASTED TOMATO SAUCE

For years I thought the simple tomato sauce I made in a skillet, sautéing garlic and tomatoes in a bit of olive oil, was as easy as it could get, but this may be even easier. It takes time in the oven, but hardly any work. More important, roasting tomatoes concentrates their flavor to a dark, rich essence that is a mystical experience for tomato addicts.

4 lbs. very red summer tomatoes
   (12–16 medium tomatoes)
1 lb. sweet onions
5 large cloves garlic

2 Tbs. fruity green olive oil
1 tsp. salt, more to taste
3 Tbs. coarsely chopped fresh basil

Peel the tomatoes in the usual way: Cut a cross in the bottom of each one with a sharp knife and put them into boiling water for 1 minute. Remove them from the hot water directly into cold water, then slip off their skins and trim them over a bowl, catching all the juice.

Cut the tomatoes into large chunks or wedges. Peel and chop the onions. Peel and slice the garlic cloves.

Toss together all the ingredients, including the juice of the tomatoes, and spread it all evenly over a large baking sheet with edges.

Put the tomatoes in a 375° oven and roast them for about 2–2½ hours, stirring once after the first hour, then every 30 minutes or so. Most of the liquid will cook away, and the tomatoes will melt into a soft, thick, slightly caramelized marmalade. It's wonderful.

Serve this on pasta, with rice, on pizza, with polenta, in soups, in a quesadilla, in an omelet—alongside anything that goes well with tomatoes.

Makes 2–2½ cups.

PARFAITS OF FRUIT AND MASCARPONE

I'm suggesting pears and berries for this dessert, but you could use many combinations of soft, ripe fruits. Sliced strawberries, kiwis, seedless grapes, pitted cherries, and cut-up peaches or apricots are all good ideas. You need about 6–7 cups of fruit in all.

4 ripe pears
juice and grated zest of 1 large
    lemon
2 cups raspberries
2 cups blackberries

3–4 Tbs. sugar
1 cup mascarpone
¾ cup cream
¾ cup powdered sugar

garnish: sweet cocoa

Peel and core the pears and cut them into pieces. Sprinkle them with the juice of 1 lemon and toss. Add the berries and the sugar; a drop of cognac or some sympathetically flavored liqueur could be added as well—entirely optional. Mix gently and leave for about 20 minutes.

Stir the mascarpone slowly with a whisk to soften it. Add the cream, powdered sugar, and grated lemon zest. Continue whisking gently only until the mixture is smooth and holds soft shapes. Do not beat this with any vigor, as it can become stiff quickly.

Select 6–8 large goblets or parfait glasses. Put a rounded teaspoon of the mascarpone in the bottom of each glass, then spoon in the macerated fruit. Top with a rounded tablespoon of mascarpone. Dust the top with some sweet cocoa.

Mascarpone is heavenly, but a little goes a long way. Think of it as a garnish to the fruit compote, which is the body of this dessert.

Serves 6–8.

A MOROCCAN
COUSCOUS DINNER

A Relish Plate

Yogurt-Cucumber Dip

pita bread

Roasted Kabocha Squash and Green Tomatoes

Couscous with Moroccan Spices

*Chilled Orange Slices
in Grand Marnier and Cognac*

You will be surprised at how little effort it takes to prepare
this interesting dinner. It looks like a dinner party, but can just as
well be a comfortable family meal.

Each dish is quite simple. A relish plate that includes
mint sprigs and green onions is the traditional start of many Middle
Eastern meals. You could include other fresh herbs, such as basil, and
add multi-colored peppers or other vegetables to make it more elaborate. A fresh Yogurt-Cucumber Dip, flavored with more mint, and
warmed pita bread are served at the same time.

The roasted vegetables and couscous are an easy and plain dish,
until they are enlightened by a sauce of gently fried spices in a
reduction of broth. Then they take on a subtly exotic quality.

Orange slices chilled in a light, sweet syrup are the most
refreshing dessert I know, and pure pleasure after anything rich or
spicy. And because this meal, while delivering both rich and spicy
flavors, is in fact not at all a heavy meal, you might even be tempted
to add vanilla ice cream to those orange slices.

A RELISH PLATE

This can be simple or elaborate, as you wish. For me, the important thing is that there be some balance between the biting, peppery tastes and the cool, cleansing ones. Choose vegetables that are beautiful, fresh, and unblemished, and vary quantities according to the taste of your family or friends.

peppery tastes:
radishes

green onions
pickled peppers

cool tastes:
cucumbers
cherry tomatoes

jicama
sugar peas (eat the whole pod)

somewhere in between:
red or green bell peppers

fennel wedges
mint sprigs

Wash and trim all the vegetables and cut them in spears, wedges, or strips, as desired. Arrange them to look pretty on a big platter, and try to do it as close as possible to the time you will serve it, so the vegetables do not lose their freshness. You can certainly prepare the plate an hour or two ahead of time, but if you do, sprinkle the vegetables with water, cover tightly with plastic wrap, and refrigerate until it's time to serve.

YOGURT-
CUCUMBER DIP

3 cups plain yogurt, or 1 cup yogurt
   + 1 cup Yogurt Cheese
   (page 77)
1½ cups peeled, seeded, and
   chopped cucumbers

½ tsp. salt, more if needed
1 Tbs. chopped fresh dill
1 Tbs. chopped fresh mint

Line a colander with 3 layers of cheesecloth and spoon the yogurt into it. Leave it to drain for several hours so that it is reduced in volume by at least a third. Discard the liquid that drains away. Or, for a quick way to get the same result, combine equal parts of plain yogurt and Yogurt Cheese.

Toss the chopped cucumbers in a bowl with the salt, then leave them in a colander to drain for at least 30 minutes. Rinse them quickly and squeeze out excess moisture.

Combine the drained yogurt, cucumbers, and chopped herbs, mix well, and taste. Add a touch of salt if you feel it is needed. Chill the mixture and stir it up again before serving. Serve with pita bread, cut into wedges and lightly toasted.

Makes about 3 cups.

ROASTED KABOCHA SQUASH AND GREEN TOMATOES

The tart green tomatoes, picked in November here in California, are the perfect foil for sweet Kabocha squash. If you can't find Kabocha, try Tahitian, buttercup, Delicata, or acorn squash if you get good ones in your area. I don't recommend butternut or banana squash for this; you need a sweet and flavorful squash. If you can't get one of these, try another great recipe, Roasted Yams with Green Tomatoes, which is similar to this—and yams are easy to find.

1 medium Kabocha squash (about 3
   lbs., approx. 5 cups cubed)
2 lbs. green tomatoes
1½ lbs. red onions

1¼ lbs. small red-skinned potatoes
6–8 cloves garlic
2 Tbs. olive oil
1–1½ tsp. salt

Peel the squash, seed it, and cut it in ¾-inch cubes. The best method I've found to do this is to cut the squash in half with your biggest, sharpest knife, and scoop out the seeds. Then lay the halves cut side down and slice them in wide strips. Lay the strips on their sides and cut off the thick, hard rind in pieces, then cube the orange flesh. This method allows you to keep the cutting edge of your knife always safely aimed down toward the board, very important when applying pressure to a tough hide.

Cut the green tomatoes in 1-inch chunks. Peel the red onions and cut them in thin wedges. Scrub the potatoes and cut them in pieces no larger than the squash pieces. Peel the garlic cloves and slice the larger ones in half lengthwise.

Toss all the vegetables together with the olive oil and salt until they are evenly coated, spread them on two baking sheets, and roast them at 400° for about 1¼–1½ hours. Stir and turn the vegetables a couple times in the course of the cooking time. They should be perfectly tender, with crisped, browned edges here and there.

Serve the vegetables with Couscous with Moroccan Spices.

Kabocha

Serves 8–10.

COUSCOUS WITH
MOROCCAN SPICES

for the sauce:
1 Tbs. olive oil
½ large onion, chopped (1 cup)
6 cloves garlic, finely chopped
1 tsp. cumin seeds, lightly toasted
    and ground
1 tsp. ground turmeric
½ tsp. cinnamon
½ tsp. ground coriander

¼ tsp. cayenne or red pepper flakes
½ tsp. sweet paprika
2 cups light vegetable broth
3 small red tomatoes, peeled and
    puréed
⅓ cup dried currants
1–2 Tbs. fresh lime or lemon juice

for the couscous:
2 cups vegetable broth
1½ cups water

1 Tbs. butter
½ tsp. salt
2 cups couscous

Heat the olive oil in a non-stick pan and cook the chopped onion and garlic in it until the onion is soft and translucent. Stir in the ground, toasted cumin, turmeric, cinnamon, coriander, cayenne, and paprika. Continue stirring over medium heat for 2–3 minutes, then add the vegetable broth, tomato purée, and currants. Simmer the sauce for 10 minutes.

Remove the sauce from the heat and stir in fresh-squeezed lemon or lime juice to your taste. If you are not planning to use the sauce immediately and want to reheat it before serving, wait to add the citrus juice at the last minute.

To cook the couscous, heat the broth, water, butter, and salt together in a medium skillet until the liquid boils. Reduce to a simmer, add the couscous, cover the skillet tightly, and leave it on lowest heat for 5 minutes. Then remove the pan from the heat and leave it covered for another couple minutes before fluffing the couscous with a fork.

Serve the couscous with roasted vegetables and pass the spicy sauce separately to spoon over it.

Serves 8–10.

CHILLED ORANGE SLICES IN GRAND MARNIER AND COGNAC

This is a very refreshing dessert, perfect after rich or spicy food. It happens to be a non-fat dessert, but that could be solved by adding a scoop of vanilla ice cream.

peel of 1 large orange, julienne cut	8 medium navel oranges
2 cups sugar	2 Tbs. Grand Marnier
2½ cups water	2 Tbs. cognac

Prepare the peel first. Choose a large, firm orange with thick skin and cut away wide strips of the peel, 2–3 inches long. Using a very thin, sharp knife, slice away every bit of the white pith, until you have only the pure orange zest. Cut this lengthwise into matchsticks, discarding the trimmings.

In a medium-sized saucepan, dissolve 2 cups of sugar in 2 cups of water. Add the julienne-cut orange peel and bring the liquid to a boil. Adjust the flame and keep the syrup at a gentle boil for 10–15 minutes.

Meanwhile, peel all the oranges, cutting away all the white pith and outer membrane with a very sharp knife. Cut them crosswise into thick slices, about ⅓ inch, and arrange them in close-fitting layers in a glass dish.

With a slotted spoon or a fork, lift out the strips of orange peel, allowing the syrup to drip off them back into the pan, and lay them out on a sheet of wax paper. Cover them with another sheet, and set them aside. Add the Grand Marnier and the cognac to the syrup in the saucepan, as well as the additional ½ cup of water.

Pour the syrup over the orange slices in the dish; there should be just enough to cover them. If not, try using a dish in which they fit more compactly, or thin the syrup with a tiny bit more water. Cover the dish tightly with plastic wrap and chill the orange slices for several hours or overnight.

Serve the oranges in individual shallow glass bowls, with a little of the syrup poured over several slices, and garnish each serving with a few strips of the candied peel.

Serves 8–10.

STUFFED CORN CREPES IN MOLE

Salad of Curly Endive, Avocado,
Grapefruit, and Fennel

Corn Crepes with Goat Cheese Stuffing
in Mole Poblano

Baked Pears in Caramel Syrup

Once, in Santa Fe, where there is so much good food that it
makes me dizzy to think about it, I had an amazing stuffed poblano
pepper. It was filled with goat cheese, which in turn was studded with
a phantasmagoria of spicy, sweet, and tart flavors. I adapted the idea
of that cheese filling for these corn crepes.

The *mole* sauce is a Mexican classic, combining chiles,
hot and sweet spices, savory onions and garlic, and the richness of
nuts and chocolate, in an exotic and sensational amalgam. Making
mole is easier today than it was in the sixteenth century, when the

nuns in Pueblo ground their spices and pounded almonds by hand in great stone mortars, following formulas that were closely guarded secrets. Where once religious dedication was required, now you just need a food processor, and making *mole* is fun.

What's more, when your family and friends say, "Wow, what's in this sauce?" you can answer, "Chocolate and Chiles."

Because the *mole* and crepes do take some time, the other elements of the menu have been kept very simple. Start with a tossed salad, combining curly endive with avocado, grapefruit, and fennel. Finish with a delicately spiced fruit dessert: pears, baked in a light syrup infused with ginger and cinnamon. But don't hesitate to serve fresh fruit if you'd like to; a perfectly ripe pear, served whole with a little paring knife, is both an elegant and a delicious ending to a meal. Sliced mangoes and papayas, or any sweet melon, would also be an excellent choice.

Leftover **mole:** When you make *mole,* and go to the trouble of assembling all those ingredients, you may as well make a lot. Fortunately it keeps terrifically well. Refrigerated, tightly covered, it will keep for at least 2 weeks. Frozen in a good container, it will keep for several months. And what a useful sauce it is. Spoon it on tacos, stir it into soups and beans, spread it on quesadillas, and serve it with scrambled eggs. In Mexico, it is most frequently used as a basis for a turkey or chicken stew—large pieces of fowl are simmered in *mole* and then served with rice. And finally, it's a nice thing for dipping into with a tortilla chip.

SALAD OF CURLY ENDIVE, AVOCADO, GRAPEFRUIT, AND FENNEL

8 cups torn curly endive (1 large head or 2 small)
2 fennel bulbs (1½ cups sliced)
4 green onions, thinly sliced
½ cup cilantro leaves

1 large avocado
1½–2 Tbs. lemon juice
3 Tbs. fruity green olive oil
salt and pepper to taste
2 large pink or red grapefruits

Wash the curly endive well, tear it into bite-sized pieces, and spin it in a salad spinner or use kitchen towels to remove excess moisture. Wash and trim the fennel bulbs, cut them in half lengthwise, and slice very thinly. In a large salad bowl, toss together the endive, fennel, green onions, and cilantro leaves.

Halve and peel the avocado, slice it, put the slices in a glass dish or bowl, and immediately pour the lemon juice over them. Drizzle the olive oil over the salad greens, add the avocado and lemon juice and a little salt and pepper, and toss the salad very gently with your hands until everything is well combined and lightly coated with dressing.

With a very sharp knife, slice the peel off the grapefruits, cutting away all the white pith, and then pull them apart into sections, peeling away the membranes. Scatter the grapefruit sections over the salad and serve.

Serves 8.

fennel

CORN CREPES WITH GOAT CHEESE STUFFING IN MOLE POBLANO

½ recipe Mole Poblano (recipe
 follows)

for the corn crepes:
3 large eggs
1½ cups milk
¾ cup water
½ tsp. salt

1 cup flour
½ cup masa harina (corn flour)
3 Tbs. melted butter + more for
 the pan

for the stuffing:
1 lb. fresh white goat cheese
3 eggs
1⅔ cups fresh corn kernels
1⅔ cups diced cooked nopalitos*
½ cup golden raisins

½ cup lightly toasted pine nuts
2–3 Tbs. diced green chiles (canned
 Ortega chiles are OK)
salt if needed
melted butter

garnishes: sour cream
            cilantro sprigs

Prepare the Mole Poblano.

To make the crepes: Beat the eggs, milk, water, and salt together, then beat in the white flour, the masa harina, and the melted butter. Or combine all the ingredients in a blender and blend until perfectly smooth, stopping to scrape down the sides as needed. Let the batter rest for at least an hour.

Heat a crepe pan and brush it with butter, then pour in just enough batter to cover the bottom of the pan by quickly tilting it around—a scant ¼ cup. Cook for a minute or two on medium heat, until the crepe is golden brown on the bottom, then gently peel it up and flip it over. Cook the other side until golden and spotted with brown, usually less than a minute. Continue this way until all the batter is used.

Stack the crepes and keep them covered with a slightly damp kitchen towel as you work. The crepes can be made several hours or a day ahead and kept in the

If nopalitos can't be found, use diced small zucchini, lightly sautéed in a little butter and a drop of lemon juice.

refrigerator, tightly covered with plastic wrap. If you refrigerate crepes, allow them to return to room temperature before filling or rolling them. If handling crepes that are still cold, heat a non-stick pan and place each crepe in it for a few seconds to warm it up before filling it; this softens the crepe and keeps it from cracking.

Makes about 18–20 crepes.

To make the filling: Soften the goat cheese with a fork. Lightly beat the eggs and stir them thoroughly into the cheese.

Scald the corn kernels for about a minute, then drain them completely.

Stir together the cheese mixture, the corn kernels, and all the remaining ingredients except the melted butter. Taste, and add salt only if it is really needed.

To assemble and serve the crepes: Lightly butter a large baking sheet. Take one pliable crepe at a time and mound 2 rounded tablespoons of filling down the center of it, leaving plenty of room all around. Roll the crepe over the filling, folding in the sides envelope style as you finish rolling it up. Fill and fold all the crepes this way. Arrange the crepes, seam side down, close together on the prepared baking sheet. Brush their tops lightly with softened or melted butter. Bake the crepes for about 25 minutes at 350°—they will be slightly puffed and golden brown.

Meanwhile, heat the *mole* to a simmer. Spoon about ½ cup of *mole* onto each plate, place one or two of the hot stuffed crepes on top of the *mole,* and garnish with a little dollop of sour cream and a few cilantro sprigs. Serve at once.

*Serves 8–10 as a main course, 18–20 as a little
dish in a series of courses.*

MOLE POBLANO

Mole is to Mexican cuisine what pesto is to Italian—any sauce in which a number of different ingredients are ground or pounded together into a paste. However, the rich, dark *mole* from Pueblo, in which chiles and chocolate combine with a great many other ingredients, is probably the most famous. This recipe is very faithful to the classic version, the main exception being that I eliminate the lard. In my view it's an improvement, as this is already a very rich sauce.

3 oz. dried ancho chiles
3 oz. dried pasilla chiles
2 oz. dried mulato chiles
3–4 cups water
2 cups peeled tomatoes, in their
   juice
2 large onions, peeled and quartered
4 cloves garlic, peeled
1 tsp. salt, more to taste
1½ tsp. coriander seeds
1½ tsp. anise seeds

4 Tbs. sesame seeds, lightly toasted
1 cup blanched almonds
½ cup pine nuts
½ cup raisins
½ tsp. ground cloves
1½ tsp. ground cinnamon
2 cups vegetable broth, more if
   needed
1 cup white grape juice or apple
   juice
1½ oz. unsweetened chocolate

optional: dash of red wine

Remove the stems and seeds from the chiles, wash them, and put them in a non-reactive saucepan with the water, tomatoes, onions, garlic, and salt. Bring the liquid to a boil, then lower the heat and simmer gently for about 30 minutes. Add a little more water if needed to keep all the chiles covered. When the vegetables are soft, purée everything in batches in a blender, and return it to the sauté pan.

Grind the coriander and anise seeds in a stone mortar. Put the sesame seeds, almonds, and pine nuts in a food processor with the steel blade and process until the nuts are ground. Add the ground coriander and anise, the raisins, cloves, and cinnamon, and process again until a thick and sticky paste is formed. Scrape the paste out with a spatula and stir it into the chile purée.

Add the vegetable broth and the fruit juice to the chile sauce and stir as you bring it back to a simmer. Add the chocolate, broken up into pieces. Keep simmering and stirring as the chocolate melts. The *mole* should have the consistency of thick cream. If it seems too thick, you can add a little more broth.

Once when I was making this *mole*, at the very end I added a dash of the Châteauneuf-du-Pape that we planned to serve with it. It was wonderful. So, though it's not traditional and certainly not required, know that you can add a bit of wine to finish it off.

This makes about 2½ quarts of mole.

BAKED PEARS IN
CARAMEL SYRUP

6–8 medium-sized ripe pears	ground ginger
3 Tbs. fresh lemon juice	1 cup sugar
ground cinnamon	

optional garnish: vanilla ice cream, or mascarpone

Cut the pears in half, scoop out their cores, and peel them. Combine the pear halves in a bowl with the lemon juice, moving them around gently until they are coated. Be careful not to bruise the pears.

Choose a baking dish just large enough to hold all the pears in one layer and arrange them cut side down, close together. Drizzle the pears with the lemon juice remaining in the bowl, then sprinkle them with a light dusting of cinnamon and a tiny pinch of ginger.

In a medium-sized, heavy-bottomed saucepan, heat the sugar over medium heat until it melts and begins to turn golden brown. Stir it gently as it completely liquefies, then pour it evenly over all the pear halves. It will bubble and spit a little as it comes in contact with the liquid in the baking dish.

Bake the pears in a 375° oven for 30 minutes, or until the pears are completely tender. A sharp, thin knife inserted near the center of a pear should slide through effortlessly.

The pears will be dotted with brown on top, and the fruit juices will have combined with the caramelized sugar to make an exquisite pool of glistening brown syrup around them.

Baste the pears with a little of this syrup just before serving. Serve them hot or warm, with some syrup spooned around them, and garnish them with a little scoop of vanilla ice cream or a spoonful of mascarpone if you like.

Serves 6–8.

AN INDIAN DINNER

Stewed Garbanzo Beans and Potatoes
in Indian Spices

Fragrant Rice Pilaf
with Currants and Almonds

Yogurt with Cucumber, Mint, Raisins, and Nuts

Green Chile and Mint Chutney

Major Grey's chutney

Naan
or any other Indian bread

fresh sliced fruit with Cardamom Ice Cream

Although it looks very exotic and complex, this is really a pretty
straightforward meal. It is built around a vegetable stew and a rice
dish, with an assortment of condiments and side dishes.

A nice, lightly spiced dish of stewed garbanzo beans
and potatoes is the centerpiece. It has a long list of ingredients, but
most of them are spices which combine to produce a flavor that
has a little kick to it but isn't too hot. The stew is served with a rice
pilaf of great delicacy, perfumed with coriander and cinnamon,
and studded with sweet currants and toasted almonds.

For a little drama and contrast, we add a cool, cool yogurt dish,
a hot, *hot* fresh chutney, and a sweet-sour chutney—my old favorite,
Major Grey's, straight off the shelf of your grocery store.

A bread completes the array of savory foods, which are all
served at once and eaten together on one big plate. The perfect
beverage with this is an ice-cold lager. I've also served an
iced tea blended with berry juice and fresh lemon juice, and a
peppermint tea with honey would be fine as well.

Besides being a delicious meal, this makes a very enjoyable
afternoon of cooking, filling the house with gently exotic fragrances
I'd like to bottle and keep.

On the other hand, if you want to enjoy this meal at a busier
time, preparation can be streamlined: Pita breads, available in markets
almost everywhere, are delicious, and close enough to Naan,
especially when brushed with a little butter, wrapped in foil, and
heated in the oven. Whole wheat tortillas, commonly available
in the Southwest, also can be used; they're almost identical to
chapatis, and only need to be heated on a griddle. And the Cardamom
Ice Cream is a treat, but a good commercial pistachio ice
cream would also be an excellent dessert for this meal.

STEWED GARBANZO BEANS AND POTATOES IN INDIAN SPICES

1 lb. dried garbanzo beans
pinch of baking soda
1½ tsp. salt, more to taste
3 large yellow onions (1½ lbs.)
8–10 cloves garlic
2 Tbs. peanut oil, or vegetable oil
½ Tbs. butter
3–4 large russet potatoes (2 lbs.)
2 Tbs. whole cumin seeds
2 tsp. ground coriander
¼ tsp. cayenne pepper

2 tsp. turmeric
2 tsp. whole mustard seeds
2 small, hot green chiles, trimmed
   and finely chopped
1-inch piece of fresh ginger root,
   peeled and chopped (about
   2 Tbs.)
2 lbs. fresh red tomatoes
¾ cup chopped fresh cilantro leaves
3–4 Tbs. fresh lemon juice
1 Tbs. Major Grey's chutney

Soak the dried garbanzo beans overnight in cold water with a little baking soda before cooking, or just cook them for a longer time, whichever is more convenient for you.

In either case, simmer them in a large pot with enough water to cover them by at least an inch; if you have hard water, add a pinch of baking soda to the water. When the garbanzos are starting to be tender, add about a teaspoon of salt to the water. The cooking time will vary with the age of the beans—it might take an hour or two, or maybe even longer. They're ready when they're tender.

Peel the onions, halve them lengthwise, and cut them in thick slices. Peel and coarsely chop the garlic. Heat the peanut oil and butter in a large, non-stick sauté pan and sauté the onion in it, stirring frequently, until it begins to color. Add the chopped garlic and a dash of salt and keep stirring over medium heat until both onions and garlic are golden brown.

Meanwhile, peel the potatoes and cut them in 1-inch chunks. Toast the cumin seeds lightly in a little pan, stirring and watching until they release their fragrance, then grind them briefly in a stone mortar or a spice grinder.

When the onions and garlic are ready, add the cumin, coriander, cayenne, turmeric, and mustard seeds. Stir over medium heat for about 3 minutes. Add the potatoes, the cooked garbanzo beans, and enough of the cooking liquid from the garbanzos just barely to cover everything in the pan. Bring the liquid to a simmer.

Add ½ teaspoon of salt, the chopped hot green chiles, and the chopped ginger, stir everything, cover the pan, and leave it to simmer for about 15 minutes.

Scald and peel the tomatoes, trim out their cores, and cut them into wedges or big chunks.

Uncover the pan, add the tomatoes, cilantro leaves, fresh lemon juice, and chutney. Simmer the mixture, uncovered, for about another 10–15 minutes. The broth will be thickened, and all the vegetables will be tender, yet still maintaining their separate identities. Taste, and correct the seasoning with a bit more salt or lemon juice if needed.

Serve the stew hot, with a rice pilaf, a chutney or two, and a cool yogurt dish.

Serves 8–10.

FRAGRANT RICE PILAF WITH CURRANTS AND ALMONDS

1 small onion
1 clove garlic
1-inch piece of fresh ginger root
1 Tbs. sesame oil
1 tsp. butter
2 cups long-grain rice
2-inch stick cinnamon, broken in
   little pieces

1 tsp. ground coriander
4¼ cups hot water
1 tsp. salt
½ cup currants
½ cup almonds
2–3 Tbs. sesame seeds

Peel the onion, halve it lengthwise, and cut it in thin slices. Peel and chop the garlic and the ginger root. Heat the sesame oil and the butter in a medium-sized sauté pan and sauté the onion, garlic, and ginger in it, stirring almost constantly, until the onion begins to turn golden brown in spots.

Add the rice, cinnamon stick, and coriander, and continue stirring over heat for a couple of minutes. Stir in the hot water, salt, and currants, cover, lower the heat, and leave the rice to simmer very gently for 25 minutes. Turn off the heat and leave the pan covered for another 5 minutes, then uncover and fluff up the rice with a fork.

While the rice is cooking, spread the almonds on a cookie sheet and toast them in a 350° oven for about 15 minutes; they should be releasing a delightful fragrance and have a very light golden-brown color when broken. Let them cool, then chop them coarsely. Toast the sesame seeds for a few minutes in a little pan on the stove top, stirring them vigilantly, just until they start to turn golden.

To serve, pile the rice pilaf onto a big, beautiful platter, then sprinkle the chopped almonds and the sesame seeds all over it. For a party, garnish the plate with lacy cilantro sprigs or edible flowers.

Serves 8–10.

YOGURT WITH CUCUMBER, MINT, RAISINS, AND NUTS

This is a *raita*, one of the many variations on yogurt that are always present in an Indian meal. It's a lovely side dish to spicy or hot food—soothing, refreshing, and a little bit surprising.

1 quart plain low-fat yogurt	1 large cucumber
¾ cup raisins	¼ cup chopped fresh mint leaves
⅓ cup walnut pieces	plenty of fresh-ground black pepper

Drain the yogurt in a colander, lined with 3 layers of cheesecloth, for about an hour. It will lose about a cup of liquid and gain a nice, thick texture.

Put the raisins in a small pot with enough water to cover them, bring the water to a boil, then turn off the heat and let the raisins soak for an hour.

Toast the walnut pieces in a 350° oven for 10–15 minutes, just until they release their fragrance. Take them out and allow them to cool, then chop them a little if the pieces are very large.

Peel the cucumber, trim off the ends, quarter it lengthwise, and slice out the seeds. Cut into pea-sized bits.

Drain the soaked raisins, pressing them gently in a strainer to squeeze out excess water. Combine the yogurt in a bowl with the chopped mint leaves, raisins, walnuts, cucumber, and a generous amount of fresh-ground black pepper. Stir and taste. Add more black pepper if you like. Some people would add salt to this—you can try it if you want to, but I prefer it without.

This makes about a quart of cooling yogurt raita, *enough for 8–10 servings.*

GREEN CHILE AND MINT CHUTNEY

This is so refreshing and exciting in your mouth that it's well worth the short time it takes to make. The green chiles give it heat, but when fresh cilantro and fresh mint join forces, it's terrific.

6 fresh hot green chiles, such as serranos (about 2 oz.)
1 large clove garlic
1 cup chopped fresh cilantro leaves, packed
⅓ cup chopped fresh mint leaves, packed
⅔ cup chopped green onions
¾ tsp. salt
1 Tbs. whole mustard seeds
3 Tbs. fresh lemon juice

Char the chiles and the unpeeled garlic clove on a hot iron skillet or grill for about 10 minutes, turning them often, until their skins are blackened almost all over. Drop them into a bowl of cool water, then peel both chiles and garlic. Trim the stems off the chiles, and take out their seeds.

In the container of a food processor, combine the chiles, garlic, cilantro, mint, green onions, and salt. Process briefly a few times, scraping down the sides of the container in between.

Heat the mustard seeds in a skillet until they jump and crackle, then remove them to a stone mortar and grind them roughly. Add the mustard to the chiles and herbs, along with the fresh lemon juice, and process again, scraping down as needed, until you have a thick, coarse-textured sauce. Taste, and add a pinch of salt or a drop of lemon juice as needed.

Serve this as a relish with Indian or Middle Eastern foods, or spread it on warm pita toasts for a sensational little appetizer.

Makes about ¾ cup.

NAAN

This is an Indian flatbread, but unlike most flatbreads it is slightly leavened with baking powder. The result is a somewhat thicker, moister bread than a chapati or tortilla. It resembles pita bread, but the yogurt that is used to moisten the dough gives it a wonderfully tangy flavor. Naan are great eaten hot from the oven, but can also be made ahead of time and reheated in foil packets just before serving.

4 cups all-purpose flour, slightly
    more as needed
1 tsp. baking powder

1 tsp. salt
2 cups plain low-fat yogurt

optional: melted butter

Sift together the flour, baking powder, and salt. Stir in the yogurt until the dough is too stiff for a spoon, then knead it in the bowl until it holds together well. Turn it out on a floured board and continue kneading for about 5 minutes, until the dough feels smooth and elastic.

Form the dough into a ball and put it in an oiled bowl, covered with a damp kitchen towel, to rest for an hour or longer.

Take the dough out and cut it into 10 equal pieces. Form each piece into a ball, and press the balls flat into round discs.

Heat a large frying pan or griddle, either seasoned cast iron or a good non-stick finish. Heat your oven to about 500° with the broiler on.

Take 1 piece of dough at a time, and roll it out on a floured board until it is about 8–10 inches across and less than ¼ inch thick. Lay it on the hot griddle and cook it over a medium flame for 4–5 minutes. It will puff up in places, or all over, and there will be some blackish-brown spots on the bottom. Slide a spatula under the naan and transfer it into the oven, directly onto the rack, for a minute or two, just until it finishes puffing up into a balloon and begins to color lightly on top.

Remove the naan from the oven and brush it lightly with melted butter if you like.

Continue this way with all the dough, stacking the breads into a napkin-lined basket. Serve the breads hot, fresh from the oven, or let them cool and wrap them up. To reheat, wrap them in aluminum foil, in packets of 4 or 5 breads, and put them in a 400° oven for 10–15 minutes.

Makes 10 flatbreads, approximately 10 inches across.

CARDAMOM ICE CREAM

A sweet cream, delicately flavored with cinnamon and fragrant cardamom seeds, is cooked with a bit of rice, puréed to a silky texture, and frozen. The result is an ice cream that evokes both the rice pudding of childhood and an aromatic sweet from somewhere faraway and exotic.

3-inch stick cinnamon	1½ cups heavy cream
2–3 cups spring water	¾ cup sugar
1½ tsp. cardamom seeds	¼ cup white rice
2½ cups milk	

First make some cinnamon water by boiling the cinnamon stick with 2 or 3 cups of water for a few minutes, then leaving it to steep for at least an hour. (You only need ¾ cup of cinnamon water for this recipe, but it's a nice thing to have around for making tea or coffee. I sometimes throw a few pieces of cinnamon into a tea kettle so I can have cinnamon water on hand whenever I want it.)

Crush the cardamom seeds in a mortar or grind them in a small spice grinder. In a medium-sized saucepan, combine ¼ cup of cinnamon water, the crushed cardamom seeds, the milk, cream, sugar, and rice. Bring the mixture gently to a simmer, stirring to dissolve the sugar completely. Lower the heat to the smallest possible flame, cover the saucepan, and let the mixture barely simmer for 40 minutes. You can lift the lid occasionally to give it a stir.

Allow the mixture to cool, then purée it in a blender, processing as long as necessary to get a truly smooth texture. It may take a couple of minutes.

Chill the mixture in the refrigerator, then freeze it in an ice cream freezer according to manufacturer's instructions.

Makes approximately a quart of ice cream.

AN INFORMAL
WINTER BUFFET

Baked Rigatoni with Grilled Vegetables

Tuscan White Beans with Chard

Tri-Color Salad

Roasted Green Beans with Garlic

assorted breads

Dessert Table

Cranberry Tart

Chocolate Spongecake with Raspberry Coulis

Chocolate Caramel Nut Tart

strawberries with whipped cream

Apple Crisp

coffee, tea

Twenty or thirty people were going to drop by for dinner after a book-signing party for my freind David Debin. I didn't know how many would turn up, and I was going to be at the bookstore beforehand, drinking champagne with everybody else, so I needed a plan that was festive but loose, with great "do-ahead" factors.

I made several big gratins of Baked Rigatoni with Grilled Vegetables—a hearty, beautiful, and warming dish that could be prepared earlier, put in the oven when we all arrived home, baked while we had a glass of wine, and served bubbling hot half an hour later.

With the gratins I served three salads: some fresh arugula and radicchio for bite, and two bean salads that taste best at room temperature: Tuscan White Beans with Chard, and Roasted Green Beans with Garlic. I added a selection of breads and an extravagant dessert table which included a huge platter of fresh strawberries along with two beautiful tarts, one cake, and a crisp.

The atmosphere was celebratory but relaxed. There was nothing to do at the last minute except pour oil and vinegar on the greens and take the whipped cream out of the refrigerator. And the next day, we had some great leftovers.

Quantities: Expecting about thirty guests, I prepared three gratins, a double recipe of the white beans, and a triple recipe of the green beans. I refilled the Tri-Color Salad as needed, filling the bowl first with prepared greens, then adding oil and vinegar. This is preferred to having a huge quantity ready and dressed all at once, as it may become limp. I made one of each dessert.

If you are preparing this menu for eight or ten guests, make just one of each recipe and select two or three of the desserts—unless you want lots of leftovers in that department.

BAKED RIGATONI WITH GRILLED VEGETABLES

2 large, firm eggplants (2 lbs.)
2 large bell peppers
olive oil for grilling
2 large red onions
2–3 cloves garlic
2 Tbs. olive oil
4 cups peeled, coarsely chopped
    tomatoes

3 Tbs. chopped fresh basil
3 Tbs. chopped flat-leaf parsley
1–2 tsp. chopped fresh oregano
salt and pepper to taste
½ cup dry red wine
1 lb. rigatoni
½ lb. grated mozzarella cheese

Slice the eggplants lengthwise, ½ inch thick. Salt the slices lightly on both sides and leave them to drain for at least 30 minutes. Pat them dry. Cut the peppers in quarters lengthwise and remove the seeds and stems. Brush the vegetables with a small amount of olive oil.

Grill the eggplant over charcoal until it is tender. Grill the peppers, skin side down, until they are charred and blistered. Put the peppers in a paper bag for a few minutes to sweat, then slip off their skins. Cut the vegetables in wide strips and set aside.

Peel, halve, and slice the onions. Peel and chop the garlic. Sauté the onions and garlic in 2 Tbs. olive oil until they begin to color. Add 3 cups of the chopped tomatoes, the chopped herbs, some salt and pepper, and the wine. Simmer the sauce until it has a nice, semi-thick consistency—about 30 minutes.

Cook the rigatoni in a large pot of boiling salted water until it is just barely *al dente*. Drain the pasta and mix it gently but thoroughly with the tomato sauce and the grilled vegetables. Spoon the mixture evenly into a large oiled gratin dish. Scatter the remaining chopped tomatoes over the top, and then the grated mozzarella.

Bake the gratin at 350° for 30–40 minutes, until it is very hot through and beginning to turn color on top. You can put it under the broiler for about a minute at the end if you like the cheese to bubble and brown more. Serve at once, with a good Italian red wine.

Serves 8–10.

TUSCAN WHITE BEANS
WITH CHARD

This is a variation of the slow-cooked Tuscan White Beans with Garlic and Sage that I frequently prepare for an antipasto or a buffet. The beans make a great marriage with chard.

1 lb. small white beans
pinch of baking soda
handful of fresh sage leaves, or 2
   Tbs. dried whole-leaf sage
1 head garlic, separated into cloves
   and peeled

3–4 Tbs. fruity green olive oil
salt
1 lb. fresh green Swiss chard
fresh-ground pepper
juice of 1 or 2 lemons
additional green olive oil for garnish

Soak the beans in cool water for a few hours, or overnight. A pinch of baking soda can be added if you have hard water. Drain the beans and put them in a large, shallow skillet with enough fresh water to cover them by at least 1 inch. Add the sage leaves, the garlic cloves, and about half the olive oil. Bring the water to a boil, then lower the heat and simmer the beans gently until they are tender—this may take anywhere from an hour to all afternoon.

Do not stir the beans more than 2 or 3 times, and then very gently with a wooden spoon. Add water if needed to keep the beans covered at all times. When the beans are beginning to feel tender, add about 2 teaspoons of salt.

Meanwhile, clean the chard, slice away the stems, and cut the firm green leaves into strips about 1 inch wide.

Add the prepared chard to the beans when the beans are just becoming soft, and continue simmering until the beans are done. Stir in the other half of the olive oil and additional salt if it's needed, and grind in some black pepper.

Allow the vegetables to cool slightly, then squeeze in some lemon juice, taste, and add more in discreet amounts until you have the balance you like. Chard comes alive with a touch of acid.

Serve the beans and chard at room temperature in a wide, deep platter, drizzled with a bit more green olive oil.

Serves 10–15.

TRI-COLOR SALAD

This is the simplest of dinner salads, just greens with oil and vinegar, only in this case the "greens" are also red and white. The flavors are great together, and this can be used as a basis for many more elaborate salads.

1 medium bunch arugula
1 medium head radicchio
2–3 heads Belgian endive
2–3 Tbs. fruity green olive oil

balsamic vinegar, or any good wine
    vinegar
salt and pepper to taste

Wash all the greens. Trim the arugula, discarding the thicker stems. Tear the arugula and radicchio into bite-sized pieces. Slice the endive crosswise, discarding any tough inner core. Spin the greens in a salad spinner to get rid of any excess water, and toss them together in a large bowl.

Drizzle on the olive oil and toss the greens again until every leaf glistens. Sprinkle on a few drops of vinegar, and a little salt and pepper, and toss again before serving.

Serves 8–10.

ROASTED GREEN BEANS
WITH GARLIC

If you've never had green beans done this way in the oven, you will be amazed at the flavor it develops. Use only thin, tender *haricots verts* or another stringless variety. Avoid larger, mature beans, as they will be tough.

3 lbs. tender young green beans
1 head garlic

2 Tbs. fruity olive oil
¾ tsp. salt, more to taste

Wash and trim the green beans. Separate and peel the cloves of garlic. Combine the beans, garlic cloves, olive oil, and salt in a large bowl, and mix until all the beans are lightly coated with oil.

Spread the beans and garlic on two large baking sheets and roast them in a 400° oven for about 35–45 minutes. Roasting time will vary with the size of the beans. They are done when they have a somewhat blistered look and are beginning to brown in spots. Try one—if you like it, it's done.

Pile the roasted beans on a platter and serve them hot or at room temperature, as a finger food or on a plate with other foods.

Serves 8–10.

CRANBERRY TART

for the pastry:
1 cup + 2 Tbs. flour
1 stick (4 oz.) cold butter, cut in
    pieces

pinch of salt
2 Tbs. ice water

for the filling:
about 7 cups firm fresh cranberries
¾ cup sugar
zest of 1 large orange, finely grated

dash of cinnamon
⅛ tsp. salt

for the topping:
1 cup flour
1½ cups sugar

1¼ sticks (5 oz.) cold butter, cut in
    pieces

To make the pastry: Combine the flour, cold butter pieces, and salt in the container of a food processor fitted with a steel blade, and process until the mixture resembles coarse meal. Sprinkle the ice water over it and process for a few more seconds, until it starts to hold together. Form the dough into a ball, flatten it somewhat, wrap it in plastic or wax paper, and refrigerate for 30 minutes.

On a large, floured board, roll out the chilled dough into a circle about 12 inches across. It should be less than ¼ inch thick. Lay it carefully into a 10-inch tart pan with a removable bottom. Fit the pastry gently against the fluted sides of the pan and fold in the excess, reinforcing the edge of the shell and leaving it slightly higher than the rim of the pan. Cover the pastry shell and chill again for about 1 hour.

Line the pastry with foil, covering the edges, and fill it with dry beans or rice. Bake it in a 425° oven for 25 minutes. Remove the beans and foil and prick the bottom and sides of the pastry with a fork. Put it back in the oven and bake for another 5–7 minutes, or until it is golden brown.

To make the filling: Wash the cranberries and pick them over carefully, discarding any soft ones. Drain them well, then toss the berries in a bowl with the sugar, orange zest, cinnamon, and salt.

To make the topping: Put the flour and sugar into the food processor fitted with a steel blade, along with the butter, and process until it starts to clump together in walnut-sized bits.

To assemble: Pile the cranberries into the pre-baked pastry crust, mounding them up somewhat in the center. Using your hands, gently press together bits of the topping and then drop them over the berries, covering them pretty evenly. Some of the topping will stay in small clumps, some will fall apart.

Bake the tart at 375° for about 40–45 minutes, or until the topping is golden and the filling bubbles up around the edges. Cool the tart on a rack, and serve at room temperature.

Serves 10–12.

CHOCOLATE SPONGECAKE

This is a virtually fat-free cake, based on egg whites and cocoa. It tastes very chocolatey and stays moist—I love it. I serve it with a fresh berry sauce and whipped cream on the side. Those who want a rich dessert can have one, and those who don't still eat like kings.

2 Tbs. minced dried apricots
¼ cup raisins, chopped
2 Tbs. cognac
2 Tbs. water
½ tsp. almond extract
1 cup white flour
⅔ cup Dutch process cocoa
2 tsp. espresso powder
1 tsp. baking powder

1 tsp. baking soda
½ tsp. cinnamon
pinch of cream of tartar
1 cup plain non-fat yogurt
1⅓ cups packed light-brown sugar
6 large egg whites, at room temperature
confectioners sugar

garnishes: Raspberry Coulis (page 329)
whipped cream

Prepare a 9-inch springform cake pan: oil or butter it lightly and dust it with flour. Preheat the oven to 350°.

Combine the minced dried apricots, chopped raisins, cognac, water, and almond extract in a small skillet and warm over low heat until the liquid begins to steam. Stir it a bit and leave the fruits to macerate while you prepare the batter.

Sift together the dry ingredients, except the brown sugar. In an ample mixing bowl, beat together the yogurt and brown sugar until smooth. In another bowl, whisk or beat the egg whites until they hold firm, glossy peaks.

Stir the macerated fruits and their liquid into the yogurt-sugar mixture. Then stir in the dry ingredients. You will have a stiff batter. Mix in about a third of the egg whites very thoroughly to loosen it, then fold in the remaining whites.

Pile the batter carefully into the prepared pan and bake at 350° for about 35 minutes. Test by inserting a toothpick or a very thin knife near the center; the cake is done when the toothpick comes out clean.

Cool the cake in its pan for about 10–15 minutes, then carefully remove it and cool it completely on a rack. Dust it with confectioners sugar and serve with a fresh berry coulis and with whipped cream on the side.

Serves 8–10.

CHOCOLATE CARAMEL NUT TART

pastry:
1⅓ cups all-purpose flour
2½ Tbs. sugar
½ tsp. salt

4 oz. (1 stick) cold unsalted butter
1 large egg
1 tsp. vanilla

filling:
1 cup whole almonds
1 cup whole hazelnuts
7 oz. best quality bittersweet
    chocolate
¾ cup sweetened condensed milk

½ tsp. pure vanilla extract
½ cup sugar
⅔ cup cream (half and half could be
    used)

Make the pastry first. Combine the flour, sugar, and salt in the container of a food processor. Add the cold butter, cut in pieces, and process until the mixture has the texture of coarse meal. Beat the egg lightly with the vanilla, add it to the flour mixture, and process until the pastry starts to hold together and form a ball.

On a lightly floured board, roll the pastry into a circle about 14 inches across. Lay it into a 12-inch false-bottom tart pan, and fold the excess in to shape a thick fluted edge. Chill the pastry for at least an hour, or overnight.

Prick the chilled pastry here and there with a fork, and then line it with aluminum foil and fill with dry beans or rice. Bake the pastry in a preheated 400° oven for 15 minutes. Remove the dry beans and the foil and bake another 20 minutes. The pastry should be lightly golden. If it is browning too quickly, cover it very loosely with the foil. When it is ready, allow it to cool, then carefully remove it from the pan onto a serving platter.

Meanwhile, spread the almonds and hazelnuts on a cookie sheet and toast them in a 300° oven for about 20 minutes. Allow them to cool until you can handle them, then rub the hazelnuts between your hands to remove as much skin as possible.

Combine the chocolate, cut up in pieces, with the condensed milk and vanilla in a heavy-bottomed saucepan. Heat gently, stirring often, until the chocolate is completely melted and the mixture forms a thick, glossy fudge. Allow the fudge to cool slightly, until it just begins to thicken, then pour it into the prepared tart shell and spread it evenly over the bottom.

To make the caramel sauce, heat the sugar over a medium flame in a heavy-bottomed, enameled saucepan until it begins to melt. Stir it with a fork as it melts completely and just begins to caramelize. Heat the cream to a simmer. Remove the caramelizing sugar from the heat and very carefully stir in the heated cream. It will boil up dramatically, and the caramelized sugar will harden at first, but never fear, it will dissolve back into the cream. Whisk the sugar and cream together over low heat until they form a smooth sauce.

Put the toasted nuts in a bowl, pour the caramel sauce over them, and stir together. Allow this mixture to cool slightly, stirring it up now and then. As the sauce cools it will thicken. After 5–10 minutes, when the caramel forms an even, shiny coat on all the nuts, but before it hardens, spread the nuts over the chocolate layer in the tart shell. Allow the tart to cool to room temperature; if the weather is hot, you can chill it briefly. To serve, cut the tart in thin slices with a very sharp knife.

Serves 10–12.

Apple Crisp (page 176)

Soup Suppers, Pasta Dinners,

and

Other Easy Family Meals

FAMILY DINNER
FROM TUSCANY

Tuscan Salad

*Simple Polenta with goat cheese
and Chunky Tomato Sauce*

seasonal fresh fruit

I could eat this meal at least once a week, and there are times when I do. My children have always loved polenta, the simpler the better, so it's a mainstay in our house. It's one of those easy foods that needs no planning, and it can be combined with any leftover pasta sauce. This version is drizzled with green olive oil, scattered with chunks of feta or fresh white goat cheese, and served with a ladleful of Chunky Tomato Sauce. In the winter I use tomatoes from my garden that I had put up in jars when they were plentiful.

The salad is one of the best—just fresh arugula bathed in the same green olive oil, with big shavings of Parmesan cheese and a spoonful of those good Tuscan White Beans on top. Of course my kids won't eat arugula yet—it's too peppery for them—so sometimes I make two salads, one with sweet butter lettuce or romaine for them and one with arugula for the grown-ups. I suppose the day will come when they'll start eating arugula—and next they'll be drinking our Chianti.

For dessert, we have what we usually have, the best fresh fruit of the season. All in all, if you have a pot of those Tuscan beans on hand, this meal can be prepared in not much more than 30 minutes. If you add a focaccia or other special bread, a bottle of wine, and some biscotti with the fruit, it could be a great casual company meal.

TUSCAN SALAD

This is the salad we always have when we've had Tuscan White Beans with Garlic and Sage the day before.

2–3 bunches fresh arugula (about 2
    quarts when torn)
4–5 Tbs. fruity green olive oil
salt

fresh-ground black pepper
1½–2 cups Tuscan White Beans
    (page 333)
2–3 oz. Parmesan cheese

optional: 1–2 Tbs. balsamic vinegar

Wash the arugula, spin it dry in a salad spinner, trim off the tough stems, and tear it into manageable pieces. Toss it in a bowl with just enough fruity green olive oil to make the leaves glisten. Then add a dash of balsamic vinegar if you like, and a little salt and pepper, and toss again.

Divide the salad between 6 plates and ladle about ⅓ cup of the Tuscan White Beans over each one. Then grate some Parmesan cheese on the coarse side of the grater, making nice big shavings, and scatter them over the salads.

Serves 6–8.

SIMPLE POLENTA

I use a coarse-ground polenta, which I buy in a local Italian deli or in a health food store. It needs longer cooking than the fine grind, but I prefer the texture. I've also had excellent results with cornmeal from the supermarket.

The simplest polenta can be made with water and salt, or a broth can be used for the liquid. Some people like to use a home-made chicken broth. I use a light vegetable broth, and I've been known to use a vegetable broth powder that I keep in the freezer for those times when you just need it. The thing to remember is not to use any broth with a very assertive flavor, as it could take over the delicate taste of the polenta.

8 cups water or vegetable broth
2 cups coarse-ground yellow cornmeal (polenta)

salt to taste
butter or olive oil
½ cup grated Parmesan cheese

garnishes: 6–8 oz. goat cheese, broken into pieces
          Chunky Tomato Sauce (recipe follows)

In a deep saucepan, combine the cold water or broth with the polenta and additional salt if needed. Use about 2 teaspoons of salt if you are using water, otherwise adjust to the saltiness of the broth. You can use slightly less liquid if you want a very firm polenta, which will set up nicely in a pan and can later be sliced and grilled.

Whisk the polenta into the liquid to break up any lumps. Gradually bring the liquid to a boil, stirring often with a long-handled wooden spoon, then lower the heat to a simmer. Continue stirring the polenta over low heat for about 40 minutes, a bit less if you are using the fine-ground cornmeal. Constant stirring is best, but frequent stirring will do if reality so dictates. The polenta will thicken quickly, and has a tendency to splatter, which is why I recommend a deep pot and long-handled spoon.

Before serving, stir in about a tablespoon of butter and about ½ cup of grated Parmesan cheese. Ladle the steaming polenta into shallow bowls, and serve at once, with additional Parmesan cheese, or with a few chunks of goat cheese and a tomato sauce.

Serves 6–8.

Variations: A superb way to enjoy polenta, if you are ever lucky enough to get your hands on a fresh truffle or two, is this—put a rounded tablespoon of mascarpone in the plate, ladle a serving of polenta over it, then scatter shavings of fresh truffle over the polenta. Polenta also goes beautifully with sautéed porcini, or any other mushroom (see also pages 38 and 191).

CHUNKY TOMATO SAUCE

This type of sauce takes only about 15 minutes to make and has a wonderfully fresh, bright flavor.

3 lbs. ripe red tomatoes	salt to taste
2–3 cloves garlic	chopped fresh basil
1 large sweet onion	chopped flat-leaf parsley
2 Tbs. green olive oil	pepper to taste

optional: splash of balsamic vinegar

Plunge the tomatoes into boiling water for no more than a minute, then into a bowl of cold water. Remove their skins, trim them, and cut them into wedges or large chunks, saving all the juice.

Finely chop the garlic and coarsely chop the yellow onion. Heat the olive oil in a large skillet and sauté the garlic and onion in it over high heat, adding a little salt and stirring often, until the onions begin to color.

Add the tomatoes and all their juice to the skillet, and as much chopped basil and parsley as you like. Salt and pepper to taste and stir frequently, still over high heat, until most of the juices have evaporated. If the tomatoes seem to need a little bite, add just a little balsamic vinegar—some tomatoes have less acid than others.

Makes 2½–3 cups.

SOUP AND POPOVERS

tossed green salad

Broccoli Soup

Cheese Popovers

Apple Pudding

Soup is often the basis of a family supper, especially in
the cold and rainy months, when nothing can warm and sustain
the way a steaming bowl of soup can.

In this easy supper, a Broccoli Soup thickened with
potatoes and touched with mustard is paired with Cheese Popovers,
hot out of the oven. The combination makes a nourishing and
delicious meal, with the additional advantage that children are
always enchanted with popovers and the interesting caverns they
find when they tear them open.

A simple green salad before and a juicy Apple Pudding
to finish complete the menu. If you can't find the time to make a
pudding, a bowl of home-made Chunky Applesauce with a little
cream poured over it will do very well.

BROCCOLI SOUP

1¾ lbs. broccoli
3 onions (1½ lbs.)
salt to taste
1 Tbs. olive oil
2½ Tbs. butter
2 russet potatoes (approx. 1 lb.)
1 stalk celery

3 cups water
4 cups vegetable broth
juice of ½ lemon
1½ Tbs. flour
2 cups hot milk
2 Tbs. Dijon mustard
generous pinch of cayenne

optional garnish: sour cream

Trim the broccoli, peel the stems and chop them coarsely, and break the heads into small florets. You should have about 6 cups of broccoli pieces.

Coarsely chop the onions and sauté them with a sprinkle of salt, in a large non-stick sauté pan, in the olive oil and 1 tablespoon of butter, until they are just becoming golden.

Peel and dice the potatoes and chop the celery, and combine them in a soup pot with the water and vegetable broth, and about ½ teaspoon of salt if needed. Bring to a boil, lower the heat, and simmer for 10 minutes. Add the broccoli pieces and the sautéed onions and simmer another 8–10 minutes, until everything is tender. If you like, you can reserve a cup or two of the broccoli florets to steam separately and use as a garnish, or to stir into the soup at the end for greater texture.

When the vegetables are tender, stir in the lemon juice, and then purée the soup in batches in a blender. Don't overprocess: the texture should remain somewhat rough.

Melt the remaining 1½ tablespoons of butter in a heavy-bottomed skillet and stir in the flour. Cook this roux for a few minutes, stirring, until it has a pale-gold color. Whisk in the hot milk, bring the mixture to a boil, then reduce the heat and simmer, stirring or whisking, until it thickens. Whisk in the mustard and the cayenne, and mix the white sauce into the soup.

Bring the soup back to a simmer, taste, and correct the seasoning with more salt, mustard, or cayenne if needed. If you have reserved some steamed broccoli florets, you can stir them in now, or put a few on top of each serving as a garnish.

Serves 10–12.

CHEESE POPOVERS

5 eggs
1⅔ cups milk
1⅔ cups flour
2 Tbs. butter, melted, more
    for muffin cups

½ tsp. salt
⅛ tsp. cayenne
3 Tbs. grated Parmesan cheese
3 oz. grated cheddar or Gruyère
    cheese

Preheat the oven to 400°.

Beat the eggs with the milk, then beat in the flour, melted butter, salt, cayenne, and grated Parmesan cheese. The mixture should be completely smooth. You can also do all this in a few seconds in a blender.

Brush 12–15 non-stick muffin cups lightly with butter. Distribute the grated cheddar or Gruyère cheese among the prepared muffin cups, then pour the popover batter over the cheese, filling each cup about ⅔.

Put the popovers in the oven, immediately reduce the temperature to 375°, and bake the popovers for about 50 minutes. They will balloon up over the rims of the muffin cups, and should be a deep golden brown.

Popovers are best when served hot out of the oven. Just ease them out of the muffin cups. However, if you need to hold them for a little while, loosen them gently, tilt them sideways in their cups to allow some air flow, and cut a small slit in each one with a sharp knife so that steam can escape. Let them cool this way for 10–15 minutes, then serve within the next hour.

Makes 12–15 popovers.

APPLE PUDDING

10–12 medium apples (4 lbs.; Rome, golden delicious, or other pulpy applesauce apples)
2½ cups water*
¾ cup sugar
2 tsp. cinnamon
dash of nutmeg
1½ quarts cubed French bread, cut in ½-inch cubes (½ lb.)

6 Tbs. melted butter
½ cup raisins
4 eggs
2 cups milk
½ tsp. vanilla
⅔ cup chopped walnuts
2 Tbs. brown sugar

garnish: 1–2 cups softly beaten heavy cream

Peel and core the apples, quarter them, and cut the quarters crosswise in thick slices. Combine the prepared apples in a large, non-reactive pot with the water, sugar, cinnamon, and nutmeg. Bring the water to a boil, then lower the heat to medium and let the apples simmer, stirring often, until they are perfectly soft and most of the liquid has cooked away. This may take 30–45 minutes, and some of the apple slices will fall apart into a sauce.

Put the bread cubes in a large mixing bowl. Drizzle the melted butter over the bread and immediately toss the cubes, distributing the butter as evenly as possible. Spread the buttered bread cubes on a baking sheet and toast them in a 400° oven for about 10 minutes, or until they are golden brown.

Return the toasted bread to the big mixing bowl, and stir in the cooked apples and the raisins.

Beat together the eggs, milk, and vanilla, and mix this custard into the apples and bread. Let the pudding mixture stand for a few minutes as the bread absorbs liquid, then give it another stir and spoon it into a large buttered gratin dish. Sprinkle the chopped walnuts and brown sugar over the top.

Bake the pudding at 350° for 40 minutes. Serve it warm, with slightly beaten heavy cream on the side.

Serves 10–15.

---

*Use bottled spring water if your tap water is less than ideal.

TACOS FOR DINNER

Corn and Squash Soup

Black Bean Tacos
with
Salsa Cruda

sliced mangoes, papayas, and pineapple

Living in California, which historically is part of Mexico,
we eat a lot of tacos—and that's a good thing. The corn tortilla is
the principal bread of Mexico, and the taco is like a sandwich:
whatever you want to make it.

In this version, tacos are made with black beans, white cheese,
and a raw salsa, providing what is probably a complete balanced meal
that you can hold in your hand. But the real beauty of it is the
balance of flavors, the sweet corn and savory beans, and the hot
chiles jumping around in your mouth.

The golden soup has a gorgeous flavor and delicacy, but
you must have genuinely fresh corn and one of the good squashes to
do it. Fortunately, Tahitian, Kabocha, blue Hubbard, and other
flavorful varieties like them are becoming more commonly available.

The combination of this soup and the tacos is so good, and when
I wrote down this menu and looked at it, I realized an interesting
thing. Without thinking about it, I had concocted a meal almost
entirely of pre-Columbian ingredients. Corn, squash, black beans,
chiles, tomatoes, and the tropical fruits are all New World foods.

CORN AND SQUASH SOUP

This is a delicious autumn soup, and virtually fat-free. You must use a very good squash and fresh, sweet corn for this, for those are the ingredients that most define the flavor. If you can't get Tahitian squash, try Kabocha, buttercup, or Hubbard. You will not get the same results with butternut or banana squash.

4–5 branches young kale
1 large potato, cut in ½-inch dice
3–4 cups cubed Tahitian squash
1 cup fresh tomatoes, peeled and
    coarsely chopped
¾ cup chopped green onions
1 tsp. salt, more to taste
1½ large onions
1 Tbs. olive oil

1 medium green bell pepper
1 medium red bell pepper
4 large ears sweet corn
3 cups vegetable broth
1½ Tbs. cumin seeds, lightly toasted
    and ground
½ cup coarsely chopped fresh
    cilantro

garnishes: fresh lime or lemon wedges
            chile salsa or chile flakes to taste

Trim the stems from the kale, cut the leaves in half lengthwise, then thickly slice them. Combine the kale, potato, squash, tomatoes, and green onions in a large pot and add enough water to cover and a teaspoon of salt. Simmer these vegetables until the potatoes and squash are tender, about 20 minutes.

Meanwhile, chop the onions and begin sautéing them in the olive oil in a medium non-stick pan. Trim the peppers, cut them in ½-inch dice, and add them to the onions. Sauté the vegetables, stirring often, until the onions begin to brown. At the same time, slice the kernels off the corn—you should have about 4 cups.

When the potatoes are tender, add the sautéed vegetables and the corn kernels to the soup, along with the vegetable broth. Continue simmering for about 10 minutes.

Lightly toast the cumin seeds in a little skillet, then crush them in a mortar and stir them into the soup. Stir in the chopped cilantro leaves. Taste the soup, and correct the seasoning if needed.

Serve the soup with a squeeze of fresh lime or lemon juice, and pass the chile salsa or the chile flakes.

Serves 10.

BLACK BEAN TACOS

Tacos are anything you like folded into a warm corn tortilla. Deep-fried, pre-folded taco shells are an invention of American fast food operations, and until recently they were unheard of in Mexico. The soft taco, on the other hand, is to Mexico as the sandwich is to northern parts—indispensable, and a thing of infinite variety.

 1 recipe Everyday Black Beans
    (recipe follows)
 2 cups crumbled queso ranchero*
 2 cups Salsa Cruda (page 240)

 1 cup chopped fresh cilantro
 2 cups shredded cabbage or lettuce
 18 corn tortillas†

Since tacos should be made the instant before they are eaten, it is best to let folks make their own. Simmer the beans in an open skillet until they are thick enough to spoon into a tortilla. Then line up the beans, cheese, salsa, cilantro, and shredded cabbage or lettuce on the table.

Last, heat the corn tortillas. Put them on a very hot griddle or in a couple of large non-stick pans, doing as many at a time as you can fit. Heat them for about a minute on one side, then about ½ minute on the other. They should be hot, pliable, and releasing a toasty corn fragrance—don't let them get crisp or browned.

As the tortillas are ready, put them immediately into a basket lined and covered with a folded kitchen towel to keep them warm for the few moments between stove top and table. Alternately, wrap a bundle of warm tortillas tightly in foil and keep them warm in a low oven.

To assemble the tacos: spoon about 2 heaping tablespoons of black beans into a warm tortilla, sprinkle on some cheese, add salsa to taste, garnish with chopped cilantro and shredded cabbage or lettuce, fold the tortilla over everything, and eat. Yes, it's a finger food, and might be a touch messy, so be ready to lick your fingers.

Allowing 2–3 tacos per person, this will serve 6–8.

Queso ranchero is a firm, somewhat salty white cheese that crumbles easily. It's extremely common in Mexico and various parts of the Southwest. If it isn't available to you, substitute a mild feta cheese, or a combination of feta and farmer's cheese.
†*If you want to make your own fresh tortillas, see page 34.*

EVERYDAY BLACK
BEANS

This is a very easy recipe that's become a staple in my kitchen because it's so accommodating. The beans are savory but not spicy. They make a perfect taco when spooned into a warm corn tortilla with a little cheese and salsa. They taste great with rice. I love them cold or lukewarm on salads. Puréed with a little broth, they instantly become a delicious soup.

1 lb. dried black beans
pinch of baking soda
3 large yellow onions
6–8 cloves garlic
½ bunch cilantro
salt

1½ Tbs. olive oil
1 large green bell pepper, cored and
    chopped
2 Tbs. cumin seeds
1 Tbs. sweet paprika

Soak the beans overnight in plenty of water with a pinch of baking soda in it. In the morning, drain them, rinse them, and put them in a pot with enough water to cover them by 2 inches, 1 peeled onion, 2 or 3 peeled garlic cloves, and a small handful of cilantro. Simmer the beans gently until they are tender, an hour or two, or however long it takes—beans vary tremendously in cooking time, depending on age. Add a little water if needed to keep them covered, and stir in about a teaspoon of salt toward the end of the cooking time. Remove and discard the onion, garlic cloves, and cilantro.

Chop the remaining onions and garlic, and sauté them in the olive oil in a large non-stick pan until they are limp. Add the chopped bell pepper and continue cooking, stirring often, until all the vegetables are beginning to color.

Meanwhile, lightly toast the cumin in a small pan, then quickly crush it in a mortar. Chop about 2 tablespoons of cilantro leaves. Add the cumin and paprika to the vegetables, then stir in the beans with their remaining liquid, the chopped cilantro, and a little more salt to your taste. Simmer the beans with the vegetables and spices until the liquid has thickened a bit and you like the consistency.

Makes about 5½ cups, or 6–8 servings.

SALSA CRUDA

This is also called *pico de gallo,* or *salsa fresca.* It is the staple item of the south-western table, the garnish that accompanies almost anything. A simple combination of freshly chopped tomatoes, onions, chiles, and cilantro, it depends on the excellence and freshness of its few ingredients.

6–8 medium-sized vine-ripe
    tomatoes (2 lbs.)
½ medium yellow onion (sweet
    varieties are best)

2–3 fresh jalapeño chiles
½ cup chopped cilantro
salt to taste

optional: 1–2 tsp. lemon juice
        cumin seeds, toasted and crushed

Cut the tomatoes into small dice, using a sharp, serrated knife. Don't use the food processor for this, as it will turn the tomatoes into soup. If the tomatoes are very, very juicy, you could drain them a few minutes in a colander.

Finely chop the onion. Cut the jalapeños in half lengthwise, remove the ribs and seeds, and chop them finely. Remove the cilantro leaves from their stems and chop them roughly.

Toss all these things in a bowl, add salt to your taste, and lemon if you like. Sometimes I add a little toasted, crushed cumin, and sometimes not, depending on my mood and the time.

Makes about 4 cups, which is less than you think.

jalapeño

STEWED WHITE BEANS WITH BABY POTATOES

tossed green salad

White Beans with Baby Potatoes and Herbs

Parmesan and Rosemary Focaccia

fruit sorbets

Dinner in a bowl is not only an attractive idea during our busier times, sometimes it's a downright necessity. But plain food can be wonderful—sometimes more delicious and satisfying than any elaborate meal. This bowlful of beans with potatoes and tomatoes, all swimming in a savory broth, fills that bill for me.

It's an easy thing to make, although the beans take their unhurried hours of simmering. If you can't be around the house, that part could be done in a crockpot, following manufacturer's instructions.

Also in keeping with the down-home style, this is a generous recipe—you'll have more than you need for one dinner, but with a dish like this, you want leftovers. Combine some with pasta for an instant *pasta i fagioli*.

I paired these beans and potatoes with a focaccia, one of the easiest yeast breads and the perfect flavor to accompany cannellini, but any good chewy, crusty bread is fine. Your favorite green salad can be added as starter.

For dessert, refreshing fruit sorbets are perfect. This kind of comforting peasant food is filling, and a heavy dessert could be too much. An old-fashioned baked apple would be just as nice, or a bowl of fresh seasonal fruit with some walnuts and a wedge of cheese.

WHITE BEANS WITH BABY POTATOES AND HERBS

1 lb. dried white cannellini (or
    Great Northern white beans)
pinch of baking soda
½ head garlic, parted into cloves
    and peeled
1 tsp. crumbled dried sage
3 Tbs. olive oil
salt to taste
2 lbs. very small red-skinned
    potatoes
6 cloves garlic, minced

½ cup chopped flat-leaf parsley
2 tsp. chopped fresh rosemary leaves
1 bay leaf
pinch of oregano
¼ tsp. crushed red pepper
2 lbs. ripe tomatoes, peeled and cut
    in chunks
1 cup water
1 cup vegetable broth
pepper to taste

optional garnish: grated Parmesan cheese

Wash the beans and put them in a large, shallow saucepan with water to cover and a pinch of baking soda. Bring the water to a boil, let it boil for 5 minutes, then remove the beans from the heat and let them soak for an hour. Drain and rinse the beans and return them to the saucepan with water to cover by 2 inches. Add ½ head of peeled garlic cloves, a teaspoon of crumbled sage leaves, and about a tablespoon of olive oil.

Simmer the beans gently until they are tender, anywhere from 1 to 3 hours. Add more water as needed to keep the beans covered, and toward the end of the cooking time add about ½ teaspoon of salt, or more to taste.

Put the baby potatoes in a pot of cold, salted water, bring it to a boil, and cook them until they are just tender, 10–15 minutes, depending on their size.

Meanwhile, heat the remaining 2 tablespoons of olive oil in a large non-stick sauté pan, and stir the minced garlic in it for a minute or two over medium heat. Add the parsley, rosemary, bay leaf, oregano, and crushed red pepper. Continue stirring for 3 or 4 minutes, then add the tomatoes, water, and vegetable broth. Add some salt and pepper to taste and simmer the mixture for 10 minutes.

Add the cooked beans with their remaining broth and the cooked potatoes to the herb mixture. Let everything heat through together, then spoon it into generous bowls, pouring a little of the herb-scented broth over each serving.

Pass grated Parmesan cheese to sprinkle on top, and have big hunks of chewy country bread with this for a perfect supper.

Serves 8–10.

PARMESAN AND ROSEMARY FOCACCIA

Parmesan cheese marries well with many herbs. It's good with basil in pesto, delicious with parsley in spaghetti *aglio e olio,* and here it sings with rosemary in a fragrant bread. Start this bread about 3 hours before dinner and serve it warm—it will vanish.

¼ oz. (1 envelope) dry yeast
1¼ cups warm water
½ tsp. sugar or honey
1 tsp. salt
2 Tbs. fruity green olive oil
1½ Tbs. chopped fresh rosemary
  leaves

3½ cups unbleached white flour,
  approx.
1 cup fresh-grated Parmesan cheese
½ tsp. coarse salt

In a large mixing bowl, dissolve the yeast in the warm water with the sugar or honey. When it starts to foam, stir in the salt, 1 tablespoon of the olive oil, the chopped rosemary, as much of the flour as it takes to make a thick batter, and half the Parmesan cheese.

Continue adding flour and stirring until the dough is too stiff for a spoon, then turn it out on a floured board. Knead it gently, sprinkling it liberally with more flour to keep it from sticking, until it is smooth and elastic, about 10 minutes.

Form the dough into a ball, and put it in a large, oiled bowl, turning it to coat it with oil. Cover the bowl with a tea towel and leave the dough to rise in a warm place for about an hour, or until more or less doubled in size.

Punch the dough down, lift it out of the bowl, and lay it onto an oiled baking sheet. Pat it out into a large oval of uniform thickness, about 16 × 12 inches. Cover it loosely with a tea towel again and leave it to rise for about 30 minutes, until almost doubled.

Brush the focaccia very gently with the remaining olive oil, and sprinkle it with the remaining Parmesan cheese and the coarse salt. If you like, you can cut a few diagonal slashes in it with a sharp knife, or dimple it here and there with your fingers. Bake it in a preheated 400° oven about 35 minutes, or until it is golden brown on top and sounds hollow when the bottom crust is tapped. Let it cool on a rack for just a few minutes, then cut it in squares and serve.

Serves 6–8.

A CASSEROLE SUPPER

Rice and Corn Salad

Hubbard Squash Flan

Simple Chipotle Sauce

warm tortillas or sourdough bread

fresh fruit in season

A salad and a casserole are a good, homely combination
that has been done a thousand times, and this is yet another.

In this case, the salad is rice and corn, crunchy and a little
bit spicy. The casserole is Hubbard Squash Flan, a generous, savory
pudding of sweet winter squash, semolina, and eggs, punctuated
with flecks of blue cheese and walnuts. A sauce made of my favorite
chiles, the smoky chipotle, is served on the side. In the tradition
of casseroles, this is make-ahead food, but there is no
compromise of flavor.

The same Hubbard Squash Flan could also be served with a very
simple green salad, and the chipotle sauce could be replaced by any
salsa or relish you like—try cranberry sauce, or piccalilli.

RICE AND CORN SALAD

This is a refreshing salad of bright colors and flavors—citrus, cumin, and cilantro with the sweetness of corn. It's good as a tostada topping, in tacos, with black beans, and just fine on its own.

2 Tbs. olive oil
¾ lb. zucchini (3 medium), cut in ½-inch dice
salt to taste
juice of 2 large lemons
4 medium ears fresh sweet corn (2 cups kernels)
1 Tbs. cumin seeds
4 cups cooked long-grain white rice
¾ cup coarsely chopped cilantro leaves
1 large sweet red pepper, trimmed and cut in ¼-inch dice
½ cup diced roasted Anaheim chiles (Ortega chiles are OK)
½ cup thinly sliced green onions

Heat a tablespoon of the olive oil in a non-stick pan. Add the zucchini, lightly salted, and sauté it over very high heat, tossing and stirring constantly, until it is flecked with brown spots—about 7–8 minutes. Remove it from the heat, sprinkle about 2 tablespoons of the lemon juice over it, and toss again.

Plunge the shucked corn into boiling salted water for 5 minutes, then remove it and let it cool slightly before slicing the kernels off with a sharp knife. Measure out 2 cups.

Heat the cumin seeds in a little skillet, stirring constantly, until they release a toasty aroma, then crush them in a mortar.

In a large bowl, combine the zucchini, corn, cumin seeds, rice, cilantro, diced red pepper, diced chiles, and green onions. Toss everything together with the remaining olive oil, and as much more lemon juice and salt as you like. Let the salad chill in the refrigerator, in a covered bowl, for about an hour.

Serves 6–8.

HUBBARD SQUASH FLAN

There are so many kinds of squash available now that it can get confusing. On the other hand, there's a lot of good eating to be had. I made this flan with blue Hubbard squash, which looks like something from the moon, but the sweet, bright-golden flesh is delicious.

If blue Hubbard is not around in your neighborhood, look for Tahitian squash, Kabocha, buttercup, or any of the very sweet and flavorful winter varieties.

2½ cups thick purée of cooked squash	2 Tbs. molasses
1 tsp. salt	½ tsp. nutmeg
2½ cups milk	½ tsp. cinnamon
⅓ cup semolina	1 medium onion
⅓ cup cornmeal	½ tsp. ground ginger
1 Tbs. + 2 tsp. butter	¼ cup small walnut pieces
5 eggs, beaten	1½ oz. Roquefort cheese, crumbled

To cook any winter squash into a purée, seed and peel it and cut the flesh into pieces. Simmer the squash in a heavy-bottomed pot with about 1 inch of water and a little salt, tightly covered, until it is falling apart. Lift the lid and give it a stir now and then, adding a little water if necessary. When the squash is completely tender, remove the lid, raise the heat, and stir constantly as you cook away all the excess moisture. Then mash the pulp with a potato masher or purée it in a food processor. The finished purée should have the consistency of a thick applesauce. Another method is to roast squash in the oven (see page 384).

Heat the milk in a medium-sized saucepan and whisk in the semolina, cornmeal, and 2 teaspoons of butter. Continue stirring with a whisk or a wooden spoon until the mixture thickens, then remove it from the heat, let it cool for about 5 minutes, and whisk in the beaten eggs a little at a time.

Stir in the squash purée, the molasses, ½ teaspoon of salt, nutmeg, and cinnamon. Whisk all this together or process it in a blender for a few seconds—the mixture should be silky smooth, with no lumps. Taste, and add more salt if needed.

Peel and quarter the onion and slice it rather thickly. Sauté the onion in a tablespoon of butter with the ginger and a dash of salt until it begins to color. Lower the heat and keep cooking the onion until it is an even caramel color.

Stir the walnut pieces and the crumbled cheese gently into the squash mixture; the cheese should not get too mushy and blend into the custard, but rather should stay in distinct lumps. Pour the mixture into a large, shallow, buttered baking dish, and scatter the sautéed onions over the top. Put the flan into a pre-heated 400° oven; after 10 minutes, lower the heat to 350° and bake for 40–45 minutes more.

Serve the flan hot or warm, with some Simple Chipotle Sauce on the side.

Serves 6–8.

SIMPLE CHIPOTLE SAUCE

Chipotle chiles have become quite fashionable now, and it's high time. These searingly hot and smoky nuggets, in reality nothing more mysterious than smoked jalapeños, have been a favorite of mine for years. I buy them in their simple, dried form at the big *mercado* in East L.A., pounds at a time, and keep a huge jar of them on my kitchen counter. More commonly available are chipotle chiles in cans, pickled in *adobo* sauce, but that is not the pure chipotle. Seek out a market that carries Mexican products and get the dried ones for the true effect.

This sauce is so fast, easy, and good that it is a staple in my kitchen. It keeps for about a week refrigerated.

3–4 dried chipotle chiles	½ tsp. salt
2 medium tomatoes, peeled	⅓ cup cilantro leaves, coarsely
½ large sweet onion	chopped
4 cloves garlic	1 Tbs. cumin seeds

In a small non-reactive skillet, pour enough hot water over the chipotle chiles to cover them and let them soften for a few minutes. Take them out, pull out their stems and remove the main cluster of seeds, and return them to the skillet.

Cut the peeled tomatoes in wedges, and the onion into large chunks. Peel the garlic. Add the tomatoes, garlic, salt, and cilantro leaves to the chiles. Add a little more water if needed, just barely to cover the vegetables, and simmer it all for about 30 minutes.

Toast the cumin seeds lightly in a small pan, then grind them in a mortar and add them to the chile mixture. When everything is soft, purée the mixture in a blender. Taste, add a bit of salt if needed, and you're done. Serve the sauce warm or cold, with quesadillas, with soup, with beans, with any kind of taco or enchilada, as a dip for tortilla chips, or with your morning eggs for a real wake-up call.

This makes 1–1½ cups of sauce.

A SALAD AND CHOWDER DINNER

*Salad of Bitter Greens
with Gorgonzola Cheese and Walnuts*

Oyster Mushroom Chowder

Fast Buttermilk Yeast Rolls

Apple and Pear Crumble

The salad is substantial, interesting, and on the fancy side.
With a garnish of spiced figs, it could qualify for what used to be
called a "company meal." The rest of the food is very straightforward
and homey, though—you could substitute a salad of whatever you
have on hand and eat this dinner any night of the week, with the
children, at the kitchen table. On the other hand, share it with
friends and they'll appreciate you.

After the pungent, complex flavors of the salad, the
Oyster Mushroom Chowder makes a pleasing change, with delicate
tastes and a rich texture. The Fast Buttermilk Yeast Rolls use a
speeded-up version of yeast dough, simple to make but allowing you
to enjoy that fresh-baked quality that you can't get any other way.
Serve them with both the salad and the chowder. Finish with Apple
and Pear Crumble, a seasonal favorite.

Both the chowder and the crumble can be prepared
ahead of time, if need be, but don't put the crumble in the oven
until shortly before dinner, so that you can enjoy it hot.

SALAD OF BITTER GREENS

with Gorgonzola Cheese and Walnuts

12 oz. arugula (2 large bunches)
1 medium head radicchio (about
    ¼ lb.)
½ head curly endive (about ¼ lb.)
12 large fresh basil leaves
¼ red onion, cut in slivers

6 oz. Gorgonzola cheese
¾ cup walnut pieces, lightly toasted
2 Tbs. fruity green olive oil
1 Tbs. walnut oil
sprinkle of balsamic vinegar
salt and pepper to taste

garnish: 16 Figs Marinated in Spiced Wine (recipe follows)

Wash and trim all the salad greens, spin them dry in a salad spinner, and tear them into manageable pieces. Combine the greens in a large bowl with the slivered red onion.

Break the cheese into pea-sized nuggets and scatter it over the greens. If the walnut pieces are very large, chop them just a little, then add them to the salad. Drizzle on the olive oil and walnut oil, and toss everything together gently. Add a few drops of balsamic vinegar and some salt and fresh-ground black pepper, and toss again.

Divide the salad among 8 large salad plates and garnish each plate with 2 of the marinated figs.

Serves 8.

FIGS MARINATED IN
SPICED WINE

1 lb. dried figs (preferably not the
    ones on a string)
2½–3 cups dry red wine
¼ cup balsamic vinegar

½ cup sugar
1 stick cinnamon
6–7 whole cloves

Pierce the figs in several places with the tip of a sharp, narrow knife or with the tines of a fork.

Combine the wine, vinegar, sugar, and spices in an enameled saucepan and heat, stirring, until the sugar is completely dissolved. Add the figs and simmer gently for about 30 minutes. Remove from the heat and allow the figs to steep in the wine for several hours at room temperature, or overnight in the refrigerator. The figs can be kept for several days, in their marinade, refrigerated in a covered container. Or they can be drained and used at once.

Makes about a pint of spiced figs.

OYSTER MUSHROOM CHOWDER

2 large yellow onions
1 Tbs. olive oil
1 Tbs. butter
salt to taste
1 lb. well-cleaned fresh oyster mushrooms
¾ cup dry white wine
1¾ lbs. russet potatoes (3 medium)
3 cups water
1 cup chopped leeks, white part only
1 stalk celery, trimmed and chopped

1 bay leaf
½ tsp. dried thyme leaves
2 cups vegetable broth
2 Tbs. Marsala
½ cup finely diced sweet red pepper
pinch of cayenne
pinch of fresh-ground black pepper
2 cups milk (low-fat if desired)
¼ cup heavy cream
chopped cilantro

Peel the onions, cut them in half lengthwise, and slice them in very thin wedges. In a large non-stick sauté pan, cook the onions slowly in the oil and butter and a little salt until they begin to color.

Add the sliced oyster mushrooms and keep cooking on medium-low heat, stirring often, until the mushrooms are turning golden brown. This may take about ½ hour. Add half the white wine and continue stirring as it cooks away. When the mushrooms are dry and crackling in the pan and turning an even deeper brown, add the remainder of the wine, and let it cook away again. This long, slow cooking of the onions and mushrooms develops a flavor that is worth waiting for.

Meanwhile, peel the potatoes, quarter them lengthwise, and slice them thinly. Put them in a pot with 3 cups of cold water, ½ teaspoon of salt, the chopped leeks, chopped celery, bay leaf, and thyme. Bring the water to a boil, then lower the heat and let it simmer for about 20 minutes. The potatoes should be very soft.

Add the potato mixture to the mushrooms, along with the vegetable broth, Marsala, diced red pepper, cayenne pepper, and black pepper. Simmer everything together for about another 10 minutes, then stir in the milk and cream, and about a tablespoon of chopped cilantro. Correct the seasoning with salt and more pepper if needed.

Serve the chowder hot, with additional chopped cilantro to sprinkle on top.

Serves 6–8.

FAST BUTTERMILK YEAST ROLLS

Yeast-leavened bread has a quality of its own that cannot be duplicated with any amount of soda or baking powder, but it usually takes hours to make. These rolls are a hybrid: a combination of leavenings is used, as well as a greater amount of yeast and higher temperatures, to speed the process. The result is a delightful, soft dinner roll, with the inimitable character of a yeast roll but in about a third of the time.

1¼ cups buttermilk	1 Tbs. sugar
¼ cup water	1 tsp. salt
1 Tbs. butter	½ tsp. baking soda
3 cups all-purpose flour	½ cup rolled oats
½ oz. dry yeast (2 envelopes)	

Heat the buttermilk, water, and butter together, stirring over a low flame just until the butter begins to melt. Remove from heat and pour the liquid into another container. Stir as the butter finishes melting. The liquid should feel hot to the touch, but not scalding.

Sift together 2½ cups of flour with the yeast, sugar, salt, and baking soda. Stir in the oats. Mix the warm liquid into the dry mixture, and stir until a sticky dough forms.

Sprinkle the remaining flour on a board and turn the dough out on it, coating the dough with the flour. Knead it gently for about 5 minutes, working in more flour as you go. The dough should remain fairly soft, but become much smoother and more elastic.

Form the dough into a rope about 20 inches long, then cut it into 12 equal pieces. Shape each piece into a ball, pulling the sides down and pinching together the bottom.

Arrange the balls on a buttered baking sheet, seam side down, and cover them with a tea towel. Or put the balls of dough close together in a buttered 10-inch cake pan; they will grow together as they rise, forming a "loaf" of rolls that will easily pull apart. Either way, leave the rolls to rise in a warm, sheltered place for about an hour.

Bake the rolls in a preheated 350° oven for 20–22 minutes, or until they are lightly browned and sound hollow when the bottom is tapped.

Cool the rolls on a rack for a few minutes before serving.

Makes a dozen rolls.

APPLE AND PEAR CRUMBLE

Here's a simple, homely dessert to make when fall fruits are plentiful and freshly picked. This should be eaten warm, so prepare it ahead if you need to, but put it in the oven about an hour before you want to serve it. For a divine experience, have a scoop of vanilla ice cream alongside.

filling:
4–5 medium apples, mixed sweet
   and tart (2 lbs.)
4–5 medium pears (2 lbs.)
3 Tbs. lemon juice

½ cup sugar
½ cup raisins
dash of nutmeg
dash of cinnamon

crumble:
⅔ cup white flour
¾ cup brown sugar
pinch of salt
1 tsp. cinnamon
¼ tsp. nutmeg

5 Tbs. butter
2 Tbs. ice water
1 cup rolled oats, or slightly more to
   taste

Peel and core the apples and pears, quarter them, and slice them crosswise about ¼ inch thick. Toss them in a bowl with the lemon juice, sugar, raisins, and just a whiff of nutmeg and cinnamon.

Combine the flour, sugar, salt, and spices in the container of a food processor fitted with the steel blade. Process for a few seconds. Then cut the butter into chunks, add it to the dry mixture, and process again until the mixture resembles coarse cornmeal. There should be no large bits of butter left.

Sprinkle in the ice water and process again, about 5 or 6 seconds, until the crumble mixture is holding together and forming little clumps. Add the rolled oats and pulse for a few seconds only, just enough to mix everything together but not so much that you grind up the oats. If the mixture seems too sticky, add a bit more oats.

If you are not using a food processor, mix together all the dry ingredients thoroughly, then rub softened butter in with your fingers until the mixture feels like very coarse cornmeal. Sprinkle the ice water over it and toss together with forks until it is all well combined and starting to clump together.

Spread the apples evenly in a large glass or ceramic gratin dish—I use a 13-inch round, or a 9-by-14-inch oval—and scatter the topping evenly over them, leaving some of it in larger chunks and letting some crumble finely.

Bake the crumble at 375° for about 40–45 minutes, or until the top is crisp and brown and the juice of the apples is bubbling up around the edges. Serve it hot or warm, with vanilla ice cream, with crème fraîche (page 324), with whipped cream, or all by itself.

Serves 8–10.

Variation: I have also made this with summer fruits. I used a combination of peaches, nectarines, apricots, and plums—a total of 4 pounds. The result was slightly more tart and much juicier, but a great success. If you want to thicken the juices a little, dissolve 2 teaspoons of cornstarch in the lemon juice before stirring it into the fruit.

FIVE EASY PASTA DINNERS

A Bowl of Noodles

Pasta with Cream Cheese and Pistachio Nuts

Penne with Oyster Mushrooms and Chinese Broccoli

Greek Pasta Casserole

Rigatoni with Garlic, Olives, and Raw Tomatoes

There is nothing like a good plate of pasta. First of all, I just love it. Furthermore, everyone else loves it, too. Of all the foods I know, pasta is the one most likely to be met with universal enthusiasm at any given moment. It presents itself in infinite variety, and on top of all that, it's healthy.

That would be reason enough to have pasta every day, but it also is *fast and easy*. It's the most satisfying hot meal to prepare when you have little time to think about it and less to do it, but want real food.

So here, as a friend to the working mother, the impromptu host, or anyone who needs a friend, are five pasta dinners. Each is a little different, each answers a particular need. With perhaps one exception, each could stand alone as a meal; a loaf of bread and something good to drink, and you're in business. A fresh green salad could be added to the plan, and would be nice, but is not required. A plate of fresh fruit, whatever is in season, makes an ideal ending, as does a scoop of sorbet and a cookie from the cookie jar.

In other parts of this book you'll find more pasta dishes that should also be in everyone's repertoire—pasta with simple tomato sauce, with garlic and oil, with fresh herbs, with goat cheese and chard. They are all suggested in specific menu combinations, but any of them can also be treated in exactly the same way as the recipes given here.

A BOWL OF NOODLES

We've all had times when we've walked into the kitchen at dinnertime, tired and distracted, and just grabbed whatever was at hand and thrown it together in some fashion to make a meal. Sometimes it works. This time it came together into a brothy bowl of noodles with lightly cooked, fragrant, fresh-tasting vegetables, just hitting the spot. I wrote it down at once, and have enjoyed it many times since.

Only the simplest of salads is needed, because there are so many vegetables in the bowl.

5 cloves garlic, chopped
1 bunch green onions, sliced
1½ Tbs. olive oil
1 lb. fresh mushrooms, sliced
   (shiitake, oyster, or whatever you
   have)
splash of white wine
1 lb. fresh spinach leaves, whole or
   sliced

6 cups light vegetable broth
   (chicken broth would be OK)
salt and pepper to taste
1 lb. fettucine or linguine
1½ lbs. tomatoes, peeled and
   chopped

garnishes: grated Parmesan cheese
            red pepper flakes

Put a pot of water on to boil for the pasta.

In a large non-stick sauté pan, toss the garlic and green onions in the heated olive oil for a couple of minutes. Add the sliced mushrooms and sauté everything together, stirring often, until the onions and mushrooms begin to color and everything smells great.

Pour in a little white wine, then add the spinach leaves, the broth, and salt and pepper to taste. Bring it to a boil, lower the heat, and let the soup simmer for a few minutes.

Meanwhile, cook the fettucine or linguine in plenty of boiling, salted water until it is *al dente,* then drain.

About 2 minutes before serving, add the chopped tomatoes to the broth. Taste, and correct the seasoning with more salt or pepper if needed.

Using generous soup bowls, put a serving of cooked pasta into each bowl, then ladle a cup or so of broth and vegetables over it. Serve at once, passing Parmesan cheese and red pepper flakes at the table.

Serves 6–8.

PASTA WITH CREAM CHEESE AND PISTACHIO NUTS

I made this in a few minutes for my children when they didn't want to eat the "grown-up" pasta I was preparing. But the grown-ups had no qualms about eating this right along with theirs. It was a forbidden pleasure, with all that cream cheese! It's delicious, and very pretty too, with the light-green pistachios against the white sauce.

I would serve a plate of crudités while the pasta is cooking, the kind that children will eat—carrot sticks, cucumber spears, celery, and sugar snap peas. Some children love cherry tomatoes, and mine will eat lightly steamed broccoli on occasion.

1 lb. rigatoni (or the pasta of your choice)
2½ Tbs. butter
6 oz. cream cheese

1¼ cups milk
½ cup shelled, roasted pistachio nuts

Put the pasta on to cook in a big pot of boiling salted water.

Melt the butter in a large sauté pan, and add the cream cheese, broken into chunks. Stir it over medium heat with a wooden spoon as it softens. Add the milk and keep stirring, and in a little while you'll have a smooth, creamy sauce.

When the pasta is *al dente,* drain it and add it to the cream cheese sauce. Stir until all the pasta is coated with sauce, then serve on warmed plates. Sprinkle each serving with some pistachio nuts. Now, wasn't that easy?

Serves 6–8.

PENNE WITH OYSTER MUSHROOMS AND CHINESE BROCCOLI

I started buying Chinese broccoli at the farmers' market, and for a while I practically abandoned the ordinary heads of broccoli I used to get. I love the flavor of this, and I like using the stems, the leaves, and the little flower buds for a real variety of texture. Oyster mushrooms are cultivated, and are pretty widely available now—I see them frequently at my local supermarket.

These ingredients combine well and add a whisper of Asian influence to what is essentially an Italian dish. We drink Chianti with it and this seems to work just fine. A salad of mild-flavored lettuces would go well this, and fresh sweet oranges for dessert.

¾ lb. fresh oyster mushrooms	1 tsp. rice vinegar
1 medium yellow onion	about 1 tsp. soy sauce
2 cloves garlic	1 lb. penne noodles
2–3 Tbs. olive oil	2–3 fresh red tomatoes
salt and pepper to taste	¾ cup pine nuts, lightly toasted
2 medium bunches Chinese broccoli (approx. 1¼ lbs.)	fresh-grated Parmesan cheese as needed

Clean the mushrooms gently but thoroughly, and cut them in wide strips. Chop the onion and garlic.

Heat half the olive oil in an ample non-stick pan and sauté the onions and garlic in it for a few minutes. Add the oyster mushrooms and continue cooking over high heat, stirring occasionally, until the mushrooms release their water, it cooks away, and they begin to color. Lower the heat to medium, add salt and pepper to taste, and stir more frequently until both mushrooms and onions are flecked with golden-brown spots. This may take up to 30 minutes, depending on your flame. Remove the mushrooms from the heat.

Meanwhile, wash the broccoli, trim off the tough ends, and peel the thick bottoms of the stalks as you would asparagus. Slice the stalks diagonally about ½ inch thick and put them aside. Cut off the florets and cut the largest leaves and thin stems into big pieces.

Heat the remaining olive oil in another non-stick pan or wok, and stir-fry the broccoli stems in it for a few minutes. Add the leaves and flowers and continue stirring over high heat until the leaves are wilted and the stems are beginning to color. Sprinkle on the rice vinegar and soy sauce and toss together for a moment. Remove from heat.

Cook the penne noodles in several quarts of boiling salted water until they are just *al dente*. While the pasta is cooking, cut the tomatoes in ½-inch cubes. A couple of minutes before the pasta is ready (you're tasting it, right?), toss the mushrooms over high heat again for a moment, then add the cut-up tomatoes and stir just until the tomatoes are heated through. Add the broccoli to the mushrooms.

When the pasta is *al dente,* drain it and add it immediately to the vegetables. Toss everything together in the hot pan and serve at once on warm plates, passing toasted pine nuts and Parmesan cheese to scatter over each serving.

Serves 6.

GREEK PASTA CASSEROLE

This is a big, oven-baked dish that takes a little more preparation than some other pastas, but the great thing is that it can all be done completely ahead of time, and just put in the oven about 40 minutes before you serve it. This makes it a great party dish, and it's much easier to put together than lasagne. Have fresh baguettes or a big Greek loaf with sesame seeds, some red wine, and, for dessert, ripe melons cut into wedges.

This recipe can, of course, be cut in half.

1 large eggplant (at least 1 lb.)	⅔ cup dry red wine
2 large green or red bell peppers	1 Tbs. chopped fresh Greek
3 lbs. ripe red tomatoes	oregano or 1 tsp. dried (more to
2 large yellow onions	taste)
2 large cloves garlic	2 lbs. shell pasta
3 Tbs. fruity green olive oil	⅔ cup sliced Kalamata olives
1 cup sun-dried tomatoes, halved	¾ lb. Bulgarian feta, coarsely
or sliced	crumbled*
salt and pepper	

I use fresh Bulgarian feta cheese, which I prefer to the Greek; the one I get seems a little creamier and less aggressively salty. Ask at your favorite deli which feta is the mildest. If you are buying packaged feta at the supermarket, try the French one. Strictly speaking, it is not really feta, as it is made with sheep's milk rather than goat's milk, but it's very good.

Trim the eggplant and slice it ⅓ inch thick, crosswise. Salt the slices lightly on both sides and leave them in a non-reactive tray to drain for about 30 minutes. Rinse the eggplant quickly and blot it dry on paper towels, pressing gently. Cut the eggplant slices into cubes.

Trim and seed the bell peppers, cut them to a similar size, and set aside.

While the eggplant is draining, scald the ripe tomatoes, slip off their skins, and cut them into medium-sized wedges. Coarsely chop the onions and finely chop the garlic. Sauté the onions and garlic in 2 tablespoons of the olive oil over a high flame, stirring often, until they begin to color. Add both the ripe and dried tomatoes, and a little salt and pepper, and simmer for a few minutes. Add the wine and about a tablespoon of chopped fresh oregano, and simmer about 5–6 more minutes, until the liquid is slightly reduced.

Heat the remaining tablespoon of olive oil in a heavy-bottomed, non-stick pan and sauté the eggplant and peppers with a sprinkle of salt and pepper, until the vegetables are tender and the eggplant is beginning to color.

Cook the pasta in vigorously boiling salted water just until it is *al dente,* then drain.

In your largest bowl, combine the cooked pasta, the tomato sauce, the sautéed eggplant and peppers, the sliced olives, and half the feta cheese. Using big wooden spoons or your hands, mix everything together well.

Spoon the mixture into two large, oiled gratin dishes, or one enormous one. Scatter the remaining feta cheese over the top. At this point, you can cover the dishes tightly and refrigerate them for a day with no harm done.

Cover the dishes with foil, and bake at 350° for about 20 minutes if the mixture is still warm, or about 35–40 minutes if it has been refrigerated. Remove the foil for the last 5 minutes, and raise the heat to brown the cheese slightly.

Serve hot, with a green salad, a wonderful bread, and a full-bodied red wine.

Serves 16.

RIGATONI WITH GARLIC, OLIVES, AND RAW TOMATOES

This is a summer dish; everything in the sauce is barely cooked or not cooked at all. Pungent, salty olives, garlic, hot peppers, and the freshness of herbs combine with juicy raw tomatoes. Salad is almost redundant. I'd like a chewy, dense country bread and some creamy goat cheese with this, and then lots of peaches, apricots, and cherries.

1 lb. rigatoni	½ tsp. red pepper flakes, more to
3 Tbs. olive oil	taste
5 cloves garlic, chopped	2 lbs. ripe tomatoes, peeled and cut
½ cup sliced Kalamata olives	in ½-inch dice
⅓ cup coarsely chopped fresh basil	salt to taste
⅔ cup coarsely chopped flat-leaf	coarse-grated Parmesan cheese
parsley	fresh-ground black pepper

Cook the rigatoni in a large pot of boiling salted water until it is *al dente*.

While the pasta is cooking, heat 2 tablespoons of olive oil in a large non-stick sauté pan. Sauté the chopped garlic in it for just a minute or two—you want to take the raw edge away, but don't let it brown. Add the sliced olives, chopped herbs, and red pepper flakes to the garlic and remove the pan from the heat.

Just before draining the pasta, add the diced tomatoes to the pan and toss them with the other ingredients over high heat for about a minute, just to warm them and start releasing their juices. Add a sprinkle of salt if the olives are not too salty.

Drain the pasta, add it to the tomato mixture in the pan with the remaining tablespoon of olive oil, and fold everything together thoroughly. Serve at once on warmed plates, and pass a generous bowl of coarse-grated Parmesan cheese and a pepper grinder.

Serves 6.

DINNER IN A BOWL

Sometimes basic is best, and that's what the following four menus are. Each one is a hearty, nourishing bowl of soup, paired with the right bread. A dessert can be added to fancy up a meal like this, but a piece of good, ripe fruit and a sliver of cheese are always welcome.

These are the easiest meals in winter, and satisfy in many ways, even before you eat them. Cook a big soup on a dark, cold day and comforting aromas fill each part of the house. The heart of the home is beating, and everyone is reassured. If you bake bread or muffins—even the easiest popovers—this effect is multiplied.

And there is no more restorative food when you sit down to eat on a raw and blustery day than that steaming bowl of home-made soup and the fragrant loaf, warm from the oven. It replenishes the body and cheers the spirit. Add a glass of wine and the cares of the day melt. By the time you're having the pear and the cheese, all's well.

So it is not surprising that we sit down to a big bowl of soup often on a winter day, as do so many other families I know. Here is a series of family meals based on that welcoming bowl.

All the soups here are of a type—the rib-sticking, appetite-quenching main course soup, full of vegetables and full of taste. The breads are all quick breads—only one is yeast-leavened and even that is a batter bread. For those times when it's just about getting dinner on the table before you drop dead, these menus can be really stripped down: a good country bread from a bakery to replace home-baked bread, fresh fruit for dessert, a glass of wine, and you're fine.

FOUR EASY SOUP DINNERS

Guillermina's Lentil Soup

Jalapeño and Cheese Cornbread
or
pumpernickel bread
and a slice of smoked cheese

Greens and Garlic Soup

Toasted Polenta Slices
or
sourdough bread and hummous

Leek and Potato Soup

Irish Soda Bread
and cheddar cheese
or
olive bread and fresh goat cheese

Sweet Potato and Corn Soup

Tomato and Onion Batter Bread
or
baguettes with any pesto or tapenade

GUILLERMINA'S LENTIL SOUP

As Laurie Colwin once pointed out, lentils never let you down. They're good plain or complicated, marrying easily with almost anything. This big, nourishing lentil and vegetable soup has been the *soupe du jour* in my house on many blustery days. I first watched my friend and fellow cook Guillermina make it. She never measured anything, never even thought about it. One day I asked her to tell me the recipe so I could write it down.

"Do you put chard in? Or spinach?"

"Yes."

"Which one?"

"Which one do you have?"

"How about potatoes?"

"OK."

"But how many?"

"How many do you want?"

"Do you use green onions or yellow onions?"

"Which ones do you like?"

"Just make the soup, and I'll watch."

1 lb. lentils	1 large bell pepper
2 tsp. salt, more to taste	3–4 leeks, white only (about 3 cups
3 medium carrots	chopped)
2 stalks celery	2 Tbs. olive oil
½ bunch cilantro	4 cloves garlic, minced
6 green onions	2 Tbs. cumin seeds
8–10 chard leaves, chopped (or 2	fresh-ground black pepper to taste
cups chopped spinach)	pinch of cayenne
2 medium potatoes (about 1¼ lbs.)	juice of 1 lemon
2–3 ripe tomatoes	

Boil the lentils in about 3½ quarts water, with a teaspoon of salt, for about 30 minutes.

Meanwhile: peel and slice the carrots; trim and slice the celery; wash the cilantro well and remove the leaves, discarding the stems; trim and slice the green onions; wash the chard leaves, remove the tough part of the stems, and coarsely chop the leaves; scrub the potatoes and cut in ¾-inch dice; peel and coarsely chop the tomatoes; trim and seed the bell pepper and coarsely dice it; clean and chop the leeks.

Heat the olive oil in a medium-sized skillet and sauté the leeks, green onions, and garlic in it, stirring often, until softened and beginning to color. Add the chard and cook a few minutes more. Then add the sautéed mixture, as well as all the other vegetables and another teaspoon of salt, to the lentils. Continue simmering the soup for another 30 minutes.

Toast the cumin seeds in a small skillet, stirring constantly, until they release their fragrance. Grind them in a mortar and add them to the soup, along with fresh-ground black pepper to taste, a good pinch of cayenne, and the juice of a lemon.

Simmer the soup a few minutes more, or until all the vegetables are tender. Taste and correct the seasoning if needed.

This is a big soup—it will yield 12–15 servings, but you'll want to have that much, because people will have seconds, and you'll want it around the next day, and you'll be putting it in thermoses for kids' lunches. . . .

JALAPEÑO AND CHEESE CORNBREAD

Cornmeal and flour, jalapeño peppers, cheddar cheese, onions, fresh corn, milk and eggs—this bread is the entire food pyramid in one dish. When you mix it up and bake it, it comes out crunchy, chewy, a little bit spicy, and a little bit sweet—in short, just a great cornbread. The jalapeños, searingly hot when raw, lose a lot of their fire when baked in a batter, so don't be afraid to use them.

1⅓ cups white flour	2 cups fresh or frozen corn kernels
2½ cups yellow cornmeal	3 Tbs. butter
2 tsp. salt	3 eggs
5 tsp. baking powder	4 fresh jalapeño peppers
2 Tbs. sugar	½ cup chopped onion
2 cups low-fat milk	4 oz. coarsely grated cheddar cheese

Sift together into a mixing bowl the flour, cornmeal, salt, baking powder, and sugar.

Heat together the milk, corn kernels, and butter, until the butter melts. Scoop out some of the corn kernels and set them aside, then process the mixture briefly in a blender, just enough to chop up the corn roughly. Add back the whole corn kernels.

Beat the eggs in a bowl, and beat in the warm milk and corn mixture. Stir the liquid into the dry ingredients. Seed and chop the jalapeños, and stir them into the batter, along with the chopped onions and grated cheese.

Spoon the mixture evenly into a large (9-by-13-inch) buttered baking dish. Bake at 425° for about 35 minutes, or until the bread is puffed up, the top is golden brown, and a thin knife inserted near the middle comes out clean. Serve hot or warm, cut in squares.

Serves 8–10.

GREENS AND GARLIC SOUP

This soup packs a punch. It starts with a whole head of garlic and moves on to stronger flavors from there, making the kind of robust, assertive bowlful you want on a cold winter day. With a good bread and maybe some Hummous, it's a meal.

I've made it with a combination of Napa cabbage, chard, and spinach, and another time with a mix of chard and kale. For best results, use 2–3 kinds of greens, mixing stronger flavors with milder ones.

1 head garlic, separated into cloves, peeled and chopped
1 onion, chopped
2 Tbs. fruity green olive oil
1 bunch (12 oz.) *each* young kale and chard, or 1½ lbs. mixed other leafy greens, such as escarole, spinach, rapini, Napa cabbage, etc.

1½ lbs. russet potatoes, peeled and diced
2 cups water
salt and pepper to taste
8 cups vegetable broth (or low-salt chicken broth)
¾ cup white wine
3 Tbs. rice vinegar

garnishes: additional olive oil
hot red chile pepper flakes
6 oz. feta cheese, crumbled

Sauté the garlic and onion in the olive oil in a large non-stick pan, until they begin to color. Wash the greens, trim away any tough stems and ribs, and shred the leaves with a sharp knife. If you're using one of the sturdier greens, such as kale or escarole, add it to the pan when the garlic starts to turn golden, and sauté them together for a few minutes, stirring often.

Meanwhile, combine the diced potatoes, water, salt and pepper to taste, and vegetable broth in a soup pot and bring to a boil. When the potatoes are tender, add the garlic and onion mixture, all the shredded greens, the white wine, and the rice vinegar. Simmer everything together for about 30 minutes, then taste and correct the seasoning if needed.

Put on the table a carafe of good green olive oil, some dried red chile flakes, and a bowl of crumbled feta cheese, then serve steaming bowls of soup. The best way is with a little of everything: a tiny drizzle of the oil, a sprinkle of chile, and a spoonful of crumbled feta in the middle.

Serves 10.

TOASTED POLENTA SLICES

This is essentially a dish made from leftover polenta. Cold polenta is cut into slices and used instead of bread for making Parmesan cheese toasts. Any kind of polenta can be used, as long as it's thick enough to cool to a solid consistency. If you're starting from scratch, prepare the polenta earlier in the day so that it has time to become firm.

leftover polenta, chilled in a loaf pan, or 1 recipe Simple Polenta (page 230), made with 2¼ cups dry polenta

olive oil
Parmesan cheese

Make the polenta as always, using the slightly larger quantity of dry polenta to make it thicker. When it's ready, pour it into glass loaf pans and allow it to cool completely, then chill it in the refrigerator.

When the polenta is completely firm, turn it out of the pans and cut it into ¾-inch slices, as you would a loaf of bread. Cut the slices in half or into triangles if they are very large.

Lay the slices on lightly oiled cookie sheets, and brush them with a very small amount of olive oil. Sprinkle them with a little Parmesan cheese.

Bake the polenta on the lower rack of a 375° oven for 3–5 minutes, until they are hot through, then put them under the broiler for a moment, watching them carefully, until lightly browned on top.

Serve hot, with a soup or stew, or alongside grilled vegetables.

Serves 8–10, if using a whole recipe of polenta.

Variation: Brush the polenta slices with olive oil in which you have crushed some garlic, lightly salt them, and omit the cheese. For spicy flavor, sprinkle on some hot red pepper flakes.

LEEK AND POTATO SOUP

This is genuine comfort food—one of the simplest and best soups, in any of its variations. The recipe given here has a large yield and can be cut in half, but for me it's a big-pot kind of soup, the kind I like to have around for a couple of days because no one gets tired of it.

5 cups sliced leeks, white and light green only (1½ lbs. trimmed weight)	1 tsp. salt
	4 cups vegetable broth
	2–3 Tbs. chopped fresh dill
1½ Tbs. butter	2–3 Tbs. chopped fresh parsley
4 lbs. russet potatoes	juice of ½ lemon
4 cups water	fresh-ground black pepper

optional: milk or cream to taste

Thoroughly wash the leeks, quarter them lengthwise, and slice them thinly. Melt the butter in a large non-stick skillet and cook the leeks in it over medium heat, stirring often, until they are limp and just hinting at the idea of coloring.

Meanwhile, peel the potatoes and cut them in ½-inch dice. Combine them in a saucepan with the 4 cups of water and the salt, adding a little more water only if needed to cover them. Bring the water to a boil, lower the heat, and simmer the potatoes until they are completely tender.

For a more intense potato flavor, cook the peels in a separate pot, in just enough water to cover. When the potatoes are tender, strain the water off the peels and add it to the soup.

Add the cooked leeks to the potatoes, along with the vegetable broth, chopped herbs, lemon juice, and pepper. Cook everything together for about 10 more minutes, then taste and correct the seasoning with more salt or pepper if desired.

If you like a chunky soup, it's ready. If you want it less chunky, use a potato masher. If you want it smooth, purée it in the blender in batches, but be sure to blend very briefly, as potatoes suffer from overprocessing. For a creamier soup, stir in a little milk or cream now.

Makes about 3½ quarts, or about 12 servings.

IRISH SODA BREAD

I've revised this recipe a little over the years. This version has a little butter, some rolled oats, and raisins.

1¾ cups buttermilk	1¼ tsp. salt
1 egg	1½ cups white flour
2 Tbs. melted butter	1½ cups whole wheat flour
1 tsp. baking soda	1 cup rolled oats
3 tsp. baking powder	½ cup raisins

Beat together the buttermilk, the egg, and the melted butter.

Sift together the baking soda, baking powder, salt, white flour, and whole wheat flour. Stir in the rolled oats and the raisins, and then the buttermilk mixture.

Turn the dough out on a well-floured board and knead it gently, dusting with a bit more flour to keep it from sticking, just until it all holds together. Divide the dough into 2 parts and form each part into a smooth ball.

Place the loaves on a buttered baking sheet, press down slightly, and cut a shallow cross in the top of each one.

Bake the loaves for 35–40 minutes at 375°. Allow the loaves to cool slightly on a rack before cutting them, if you can stand to wait. They will smell so delicious that you may have to cut right into them, but they will tear a little until they've had time to cool off.

Makes 2 medium loaves.

SWEET POTATO AND CORN SOUP

1 large yellow onion, chopped
1½ Tbs. butter
salt to taste
2 lbs. sweet potatoes
2 cups water
4 cups vegetable broth
3 cups yellow or white sweet corn kernels

1 medium red bell pepper, finely diced
1 small fresh jalapeño pepper, finely chopped
1 cup milk
juice of ½ lemon
pinch of cayenne
2–3 Tbs. cream

garnish: chopped cilantro leaves

Cook the onion slowly in the butter, with a little salt, stirring often, until it is golden brown. At the same time, peel and dice the sweet potatoes, combine them in a pot with the water and the vegetable broth, and simmer until the potatoes are tender, about 20–30 minutes. Add the caramelized onions to the soup, deglaze the onion pan with a little of the broth, and add it back, then purée this mixture in batches in a blender.

Return the purée to the pot and add the corn kernels, diced red bell pepper, chopped jalapeño, and milk. Simmer until the peppers and corn are tender. Stir in the lemon juice and cayenne, taste, and correct the seasoning if needed. Finish the soup with a little cream.

Serve hot, garnished with coarsely chopped cilantro leaves.

Serves 8.

TOMATO AND ONION BATTER BREAD

¼ cup chopped sun-dried tomatoes
1 cup hot water
2 large onions
3½ Tbs. olive oil, more for the pans
2 tsp. salt
1½ lbs. fresh red tomatoes, scalded
    and peeled

1 cup whole wheat flour
4 cups all-purpose flour, approx.
2 envelopes dry yeast
2 Tbs. sugar

Put the sun-dried tomatoes in a bowl with a cup of hot water and leave them to soak for at least ½ hour.

Peel the onions, quarter them lengthwise, and slice them. Heat 1½ tablespoons of olive oil in a non-stick pan and add the onions and a teaspoon of salt. Cook the onions in the oil over medium heat, stirring very often, until they are golden brown all over, then set them aside until needed.

Cut the fresh tomatoes into chunks, working over a bowl so as not to lose their juice. Simmer them in their own juice for 5–10 minutes, just until they are tender and their juice is slightly thickened. You should have 2 cups of chunky sauce. Combine the cooked fresh tomatoes, the soaked sun-dried tomatoes with their water, 2 tablespoons of olive oil, and a teaspoon of salt in a bowl and allow the mixture to cool slightly.

In the bowl of a food processor, fitted with the short plastic blade, combine the whole wheat flour and 1½ cups of the white flour with the yeast and sugar, and spin briefly to blend. Add the tomatoes and liquid, and process for several seconds at a time, scraping the sides down with a spatula in between, until you have a soft batter. Start adding the remaining flour, a little at a time, and process briefly after each addition. Continue adding flour only until the batter is thick and elastic but not yet stiff. Add the cooked onions and process for a few seconds only.

To prepare the batter by hand, combine the whole wheat flour and 1½ cups of the white flour with the yeast and sugar in a large mixing bowl and stir with a whisk to blend. Add the tomatoes and liquid and beat vigorously with a wooden spoon for several minutes. Add as much of the remaining flour as is needed, a little at a time, beating it in thoroughly each time, until the batter is thick and elastic. You should use almost all the 5 cups of flour. Add the cooked onions and stir them into the batter.

Generously oil two deep-dish pie pans, or one large oblong baking dish, about 9 by 12 inches. Using a large spoon or spatula, scoop the batter out into the prepared pans. It should be thick enough to hold a shape, but softer and stickier than a dough that you would knead. Spread the batter evenly in the pans, and push it into the corners. The surface will remain rough, which is fine.

Cover the pans with plastic wrap and leave the loaves to rise for about 45 minutes. The batter will nearly double in size.

Bake the bread in a preheated 375° oven for 35–40 minutes, or until it is lightly browned on top and the bottom sounds hollow when tapped. A thin knife inserted near the middle should come out dry.

Let the bread cool on a rack for a little while, then cut it into wedges or squares to serve.

Makes 2 normal loaves, or 1 very large loaf.

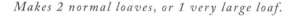

WHAT DO CHILDREN EAT?

How do children actually stay alive and keep growing, since they refuse to eat almost everything? This is the question I keep asking myself, and every other mother I know asks the same.

You may think that, because I write about food, my children come docilely to the table and eat everything that is put in front of them. Not so. My children, like yours, turn up their noses at almost everything I cook. Then, just when I've given up in despair, and cooked one thing for them and something entirely different for the adults, they come and snatch the adult food from our plates.

Why will a child who categorically refuses to touch anything green suddenly eat watercress sandwiches? Or Japanese seaweed? The same kid will painstakingly pick the raisins out of his coffee cake and leave them on the plate. He will demand to have his pasta completely plain, without even butter on it, but pizza can have everything. Probably they are programmed this way just to keep us paying attention.

One thing is clear—kids are so quirky that the marvelous solutions devised by one mother may be perfectly useless to another. Nevertheless, here is what I have observed in eleven years of fascinated observation.

My children will eat many kinds of Mediterranean foods. I think there are two reasons why. First, we live in a Mediterranean sort of climate, so we are surrounded by that kind of produce, that style of cooking. Second, it's just awfully good. They will eat pasta, polenta, and risotto as often as I make them.

They will eat Mexican food erratically. They love tortillas and tamales, but there are times when they will not eat food that has even one atom of chile in it, and other times when they unaccountably lap up hot salsa.

They will always, always eat quesadillas. Quesadillas have saved them from starvation and me from a nervous breakdown many times.

They will eat crepes if the fillings are not too weird. Jam is always all right. Cheese and mushrooms are fine, but nothing green will be accepted inside a crepe; that is considered a betrayal of the whole idea of crepes.

Rice and couscous are almost always accepted. Beans get the nod from one, vehement refusal from the other.

Fruit is either passionately devoured or completely ignored. Sometimes we go through intense fads for yogurt smoothies. Salads will turn to compost before they get a second look. And sometimes my children demand sausages, or hamburgers, or steak!

So what are we to do? My basic approach is to offer them a variety of healthy and tasty things, and then let them do pretty much what they want. (If after three years they have not touched a vegetable, I will go ahead and force them to eat one.) When they ask for sausage, I send them out to a restaurant with their father. Let them eat sausage. Eventually, they will work out for themselves how they want to eat, anyway, just as we all do. And I teach them to cook anything they are interested in learning.

Meanwhile, I let them eat the grain-based diet they seem to prefer. I bake bread when I can. I make a hundred quesadillas and plates of fruit. I give them carrot sticks and smoothies, and make pasta, risotto, and polenta as often as possible.

Here is the "children's menu" of an ideal restaurant, as it would be written by *my* children:

1. Quesadillas and a fruit plate.
2. Spaghetti with a little butter and cheese, or with nothing at all. Steamed broccoli on the side.
3. Baked potatoes with everything on the side—sour cream or cottage cheese, butter, green onions, and so on.
4. Plain polenta, with grated Parmesan on the side. Carrot sticks and snap peas.
5. Tomato and rice soup. Muffins.
6. Pizza.
7. Fruit Smoothie.

Here are four recipes that you can stencil on the refrigerator door for the baby-sitter.

Quesadillas

Take a plain flour tortilla and heat it in an ungreased skillet for a few seconds on each side. Sprinkle about 1 ounce of grated Monterey Jack or cheddar cheese over one half of it, and fold the other half over the cheese. Keep toasting it in the skillet for about a minute, turning once, until both sides are golden and the cheese is melted. Serve at once.

Cheese Toasts

I think in the Midwest the quesadilla might be replaced by one of my childhood favorites (I grew up in Michigan), the toasted cheese sandwich. I used to make them the classic way, buttering the outside of a plain cheese sandwich and grilling it in a pan. Now I pile grated cheese on top of a thick slice of good bread and put it in the toaster oven until the cheese bubbles.

Almost Instant Tomato and Rice Soup

You can start from scratch and make this soup in about ½ hour. Or you can start with a tomato sauce you have made before, and some leftover cooked rice, and be done in a minute.

Combine 2–3 cups of good, home-made tomato sauce (but nothing fancy) with an equal amount of delicate vegetable broth or chicken broth. Add a slightly smaller amount of cooked rice, white or brown. Let everything simmer together for a couple of minutes. Serve with cheese toasts or any kind of bread.

You can add a little milk or cream. This makes a rather thick soup, becoming more porridge-like as the rice expands, and they love it that way.

Fruit Smoothie

Put into a blender 1 banana, a few strawberries, sliced peaches, or other soft fruit, about ½ cup (or a little more) of milk or yogurt, a little honey, and a drop of vanilla. Purée. Add 2 or 3 ice cubes and process until the ice cubes are completely ground up. Pour and serve.

Pizza

This is one for you to make when you're ready for détente. You make it. They eat it. There's peace in the house. It's plain cheese pizza, the abiding favorite of my two sons.

There are great techniques for making pizza. You can put a stone tile in your oven, and slide the pizza onto it with a peel, but not everyone has such things. These instructions are for anyone with an oven and a cookie sheet. They will result in a very good pizza, and your children will adore you for it. It takes a not very demanding hour to do.

for the dough:
½ cup milk
¾ cup hot water
1 Tbs. dry yeast (1 envelope)
1 tsp. sugar
1 tsp. salt

1 Tbs. rye flour
about 3 cups white flour
a little olive oil
a little cornmeal

for the sauce:
1½ lbs. red tomatoes
2 cloves garlic, minced
1 Tbs. olive oil
salt to taste
1 Tbs. chopped fresh basil

¼ tsp. dried oregano
¼ tsp. dried thyme
¼ tsp. dried marjoram
2–3 Tbs. tomato paste, or sun-dried
    tomato paste

optional: dash of balsamic vinegar

garnish: ½ lb. part-skim mozzarella cheese, grated

In a large mixing bowl, combine the milk and the hot water. Add the yeast to this lukewarm liquid, along with the sugar and salt. Wait for a few minutes to see if it begins to froth, then stir in the rye flour and about 2½ cups of the white flour. Stir until a thick dough forms.

Sprinkle the rest of the flour on a board and turn the dough out on it. Knead the dough for about 10 minutes, working in as much more flour as it wants to become smooth and elastic. Form the dough into a ball and put it in a lightly oiled bowl, turning it over once, then cover the bowl with a kitchen towel and leave it in a warm place to rise for about 45–50 minutes.

While the dough rises, prepare the sauce. Scald the tomatoes, peel them and core them, then process them briefly in a blender to make a rough purée. Sauté the garlic in the olive oil for a minute or two, then add the tomatoes, some salt, and the herbs. Stir occasionally over fairly high heat until the tomatoes cook down to a thick, dark red. Stir in the tomato paste, and the vinegar if you want it. Taste, and correct the seasoning. You should have about 1½ cups of sauce.

Lightly oil 2 pizza pans or large cookie sheets, and sprinkle them with cornmeal. Preheat the oven to 550°, and be sure one of the racks is in the lowest position.

Punch down the dough and cut it into 2 equal parts. Form each part into a smooth ball. Take one of the balls and pat it, stretch it, roll it, and otherwise per-suade it to be a circle about 13 inches across. It will want to spring back at first, but it will comply, don't worry. If it's very stubborn, leave it to relax for 5 or 10 minutes. Do the same to the other ball, and lay the finished circles of dough on the prepared baking sheets.

Spread half the sauce over each circle, and then sprinkle on the cheese. Bake at 550°, on the lowest rack, for about 12–14 minutes, or until the crust is lightly browned around the edges and the cheese is bubbling. For an extra-crispy crust, slide the pizza off the baking sheet directly onto the oven rack for the last few minutes of baking.

Slice each pizza into 8 wedges and eat while they are hot.

Serves 4–8, depending on how you feel about pizza.

Salad Lunches, a Brunch, and Tea

A SALAD BOWL LUNCH ON THE PATIO

Salad with Sautéed Mushrooms

*Semolina Focaccia
with Onion and Garlic*

Gorgonzola cheese

Clafouti with Apricots

This is a true salad-eater's lunch—wonderful greens and lots of them. The salad starts with a mix of spinach, arugula, curly endive, watercress, and delicate young lettuces; on top there's a generous scattering of wild mushrooms, seared in hot oil with garlic and ginger. The combination is refreshing, surprising, and delicious.

With a cool main-dish salad, it's nice to serve a focaccia warm from the oven, and a little wedge of Gorgonzola cheese. Add a glass of cold white wine and it's just what you'll want on a hot, sunny day.

Since the meal is light, you can have a dessert with a little more substance. I like the Clafouti with Apricots, but you can make a clafouti with whatever fruit is best at the time.

SALAD WITH SAUTÉED MUSHROOMS

sautéed mushrooms:
1 lb. oyster mushrooms
½ lb. fresh shiitake mushrooms
2 Tbs. olive oil
1 tsp. dark sesame oil

4 cloves garlic, minced
2 Tbs. minced fresh ginger
2–3 Tbs. rice vinegar
2 tsp. soy sauce

salad greens—a total of 12 packed
    cups torn greens, such as:
1 bunch frisée (young curly endive)
1 head baby red romaine
1 head curly leaf or butter lettuce

1 large bunch watercress or arugula
⅓ cup thinly sliced spring onions
1 cup de-stemmed cilantro leaves

dressing:
olive oil
dark sesame oil

wine vinegar
salt and pepper

garnishes: cilantro sprigs
        big gratings of Manchego or Parmesan cheese

Clean and trim all the mushrooms carefully, and cut the large ones into ½-inch strips.

Heat the olive oil and sesame oil in a large non-stick skillet, add the minced garlic and ginger, and stir for a minute or so, until the garlic begins to soften. Add the mushrooms and toss over a medium-high flame until they start to give up their moisture. Continue cooking the mushrooms, stirring frequently, until they are tender and beginning to brown in spots.

Wash, spin, and tear all the greens, and combine them in a large salad bowl. Use any combination of lettuces you like, but remember that you need a balance between sweet, delicately flavored lettuces and peppery greens such as watercress or arugula. The cilantro is essential.

Dress the salad sparingly with olive oil and a trace of dark sesame oil, a little splash of wine vinegar, and some salt and pepper. Toss it until each leaf glistens, taste, and correct the seasoning if needed. Divide the salad greens among 8 plates.

When the mushrooms are starting to color, drizzle on the rice vinegar and soy sauce and toss the mushrooms with the seasonings for a few moments. Divide the warm mushrooms evenly over the 8 salads, garnish with cilantro sprigs, grated cheese, or both, and serve at once.

Serves 4–6 as a light main dish for lunch, or 8 as a first course.

SEMOLINA FOCACCIA

with Onion and Garlic

¼ oz. (1 envelope) yeast
1¼ cups warm water
½ tsp. sugar or honey
3 Tbs. fruity green olive oil
1 large yellow onion, finely chopped

2 cloves garlic, finely chopped
1 tsp. salt
2 cups semolina flour*
1½ cups unbleached white flour,
  approx.

In a large mixing bowl, dissolve the yeast in the warm water with the sugar or honey, and put it aside for a few minutes. Meanwhile, heat 2 tablespoons of the olive oil in a non-stick skillet and cook the chopped onion and garlic in it over a low flame, stirring constantly, just until they soften. Put it aside to cool.

When the yeast begins to foam, stir in the teaspoon of salt, the onions and garlic in their oil, and the semolina, about ½ cup at a time. Keep stirring with a wooden spoon as you add white flour, little by little, until the mixture is too stiff for a spoon.

Turn the dough out onto a floured board and knead it gently, working in as much of the white flour as it wants to absorb, until it feels quite smooth and elastic. Continue sprinkling it with flour as needed to keep it from sticking.

Form the dough into a ball and put it into an oiled bowl, turning to coat it on all sides. Cover it with a tea towel and leave it in a warm place to rise for about 1½ hours, or until the dough has doubled in size.

Punch it down, lift it out of the bowl, and lay it in an oiled jelly roll pan (15½ by 10½ inches). Pat the dough evenly into the pan, out to the edges and corners. Cover it loosely and leave it to rise again, this time about 45 minutes, until almost doubled.

Brush the focaccia with the remaining olive oil, dimple the top with your fingertips if you like, and bake it in a preheated 400° oven for about 35 minutes, or until it is golden brown on top and the bottom crust sounds hollow when tapped. Let it cool for just a few minutes on a rack.

Cut the focaccia in squares and serve it hot or warm.

Focaccia, like cornbread or biscuits, really should be eaten shortly after it is out of the oven. This one, however, makes a delicious toast the next day. Cut it in ½-inch slices and grill or toast in a toaster oven until golden.

Makes 1 large loaf.

*See note on page 50.

CLAFOUTI WITH APRICOTS

A clafouti is a pudding-like dessert, made by pouring a pancake batter over fruit and baking it in a hot oven. It's quick and easy, and best eaten hot or warm, dusted with powdered sugar.

2 lbs. ripe apricots
2 Tbs. butter, melted, more for the
    baking dish
¾ cup + 2 Tbs. sugar
1¼ cups flour
1 tsp. baking powder

pinch of salt
4 eggs
1¾ cups warmed milk
1 tsp. vanilla
grated zest of 1 lemon

garnishes: powdered sugar
            cream

Wash and dry the apricots, then cut them in half and remove their stones. Preheat the oven to 425°. Butter a large, shallow baking dish (I use a 14-inch round gratin), sprinkle it with 2 tablespoons of sugar, and arrange the apricots in one layer, close together, cut side down. Put them in the oven for 10 minutes; they should just begin to release their juice.

Sift together the flour, baking powder, and salt. Beat the eggs with the remaining sugar until fluffy, then beat in the flour mixture, the warmed milk, melted butter, vanilla, and lemon zest to make a smooth batter.

Take the apricots out of the oven and pour the batter over them evenly. Push them down with a spatula if they float up, gently pressing out any trapped air. Put the dish back into the center of the oven and reduce the heat to 400°.

Bake the clafouti for about 35 minutes, but check it after 15. This clafouti has a little baking powder in the batter, so don't be surprised to see it rising in high, billowy shapes. If the edges are browning quickly, lay a sheet of aluminum foil loosely over the top for the remaining time.

The clafouti will sink gradually when you take it out of the oven. Serve it warm, sprinkled generously with sifted powdered sugar. A little cream poured around it on the plate also goes very well.

Serves 8.

SALAD LUNCH FOR A HOT DAY

*Cold Peach and Nectarine Soup
with Honey-Sweetened Yogurt*

Salad with Wheat Pilaf and Red Grapes

Roquefort cheese

French bread or crackers

Coffee Granita

Make this salad the day after you've had pilaf for dinner. With leftovers on hand, this meal is almost effortless. I designed it for a very hot day, when no one wants to cook and no one cares to eat anything hot, but perhaps there's company coming or there's another reason why something nicer than a carton of yogurt is called for. Well, here it is.

Everything can be prepared ahead and, assuming the existence of the leftover pilaf, it takes no heat and very little time. The soup takes 15 minutes to prepare, then goes into the refrigerator. All the elements of the salad can be prepped ahead, to be dressed and assembled at the last moment. The granita is waiting in the freezer.

Now go for a swim, shower and change, spend about five more minutes by your refrigerator, and you're ready to serve a beautiful lunch. Set a table outside, in a shady spot if you have one, and open a bottle of chilled wine. The whole meal is refreshing, and none of it overly filling.

COLD PEACH AND NECTARINE SOUP
with Honey-Sweetened Yogurt

This soup is almost instant. It's whipped together in the blender and chilled, and is divinely refreshing in the dog days of August—or, in our case, September.

3 cups sliced, peeled peaches (about 2 lbs.)
3 cups sliced, peeled nectarines (about 2 lbs.)
3 cups plain low-fat yogurt

¼ cup + 3 Tbs. honey
2 Tbs. fresh lemon juice
2 Tbs. Marsala
½ tsp. cinnamon

optional garnish: mint sprigs

Use fully ripe, juicy peaches and nectarines. Working in batches, purée the fruit in a blender with 2 cups of the yogurt, 3 tablespoons of honey, the lemon juice, Marsala, and cinnamon. Chill the mixture well. (When I'm in a hurry, I put it in the freezer in a stainless steel bowl and give it a stir with a whisk every 15 minutes or so. It will be very cold in about an hour.)

Whisk together the remaining cup of yogurt with the remaining ¼ cup of honey, and chill.

Ladle the soup into shallow bowls and put a spoonful of the honey-sweetened yogurt in the center of each serving. Garnish with mint sprigs if you happen to have some mint around.

Serves 6.

SALAD WITH WHEAT PILAF AND RED GRAPES

This is really a delicious salad, combining the pungency of fresh greens with the rich chewiness of wheat and browned onions, and the sweetness of grapes. It makes a nice first course, and because the pilaf is quite substantial, it can also be the centerpiece of a summer lunch with no change except portion size.

12 cups mixed tender salad greens, torn if large
1 large cucumber (1½ cups sliced)
2 small sweet red peppers (1½ cups sliced)
½ cup sunflower seed sprouts, or any mild-flavored sprouts
½ cup radish sprouts, or ⅓ cup very thinly sliced radishes

3 Tbs. virgin olive oil
1½ Tbs. balsamic vinegar
salt to taste
3 cups Wheat and Lentil Pilaf, cooled (page 74)
⅔ cup toasted almonds, coarsely chopped
3 cups seedless red grapes

The mix of salad greens is important—use tender young lettuces and herbs, and be sure you have a balance of peppery flavors with the delicate, sweet ones. Mesclun, which is a mix of many salad greens, is quite widely available now, but if you don't have it you can start with red and green salad bowl lettuce or tender butter lettuce, add some young curly endive and some arugula or watercress, and a bit of radicchio if you can get it. Wash all the greens, remove heavy stems, if any, and spin the leaves dry in a salad spinner. Tear everything into bite-sized pieces. You should have 3 quarts, loosely packed.

Peel the cucumber, quarter it lengthwise, and slice thinly. Trim the sweet peppers, quarter them lengthwise, and then cut crosswise in matchsticks.

In a large bowl, toss the greens with the cucumber, peppers, sprouts, olive oil, vinegar, and a touch of salt.

Using ample salad plates, divide the various ingredients equally among them: first a mound of greens, and on top of that a large spoonful of pilaf, then a tablespoon or more of chopped almonds scattered over everything. Finally, arrange some red grapes casually around the perimeter of the greens, and serve.

Serves 6 as a light entree, or 8–10 as a first course.

COFFEE GRANITA

4 cups hot espresso, or triple-
    strength drip coffee
½ cup sugar

3 thin strips lemon peel, or orange
    peel
2 Tbs. Triple Sec, or Grand Marnier

optional garnish: whipped cream, or vanilla ice cream

Be sure to use very strong coffee. Stir the sugar and the citrus peel into the coffee. Allow it to cool, then chill it. Stir in the Triple Sec or Grand Marnier.

Put the coffee in a big, shallow bowl, or into old-fashioned ice-cube trays with the dividers removed. Put it in the freezer, and every ½ hour or so take it out and stir it up well with a fork, scraping the ice down from the sides and breaking it up. Do this until the coffee has turned into a mass of coarse ice crystals, something like a rough-textured sorbet.

The granita can be kept in the freezer, tightly covered, for several days.

Serve the granita piled into sorbet goblets, alone or with whipped cream on top. Or place a small scoop of vanilla ice cream in the glass and then spoon the granita around it.

Serves 6–8.

A FRENCH SOUP
AND SALAD LUNCH

Cream of Carrot Soup

*Haricots Verts, Red Potato,
and Cucumber Salad*

Goat Cheese Toasts

Rustic Plum Pie or white peaches

Here's a lunch that takes me straight back to France,
to an ancient stone table under a tree at the edge of the big lawn
behind our little rented house at Beaureport.

Each nearby village had a market day, and so nearly every
day you could drive a few kilometers and find seasonal vegetables,
fresh farmhouse cheeses, beautiful fruits, and flowers for the table. In
the hot Provençal afternoons, we sat at the stone table, eating meals
of easy summer food, drinking ice-cold rosé from Tavel.

The Cream of Carrot Soup is a classic purée. Sprinkle it with
chopped chives or mint from the garden. After the soup, a big plate
of salad that can only be had in summer, when *haricots verts* are plentiful and cucumbers sweet. They're mixed with new red potatoes cut
in big chunks, and everything is scattered with fresh dill.

Along with the salad, serve toasted country bread with hot goat
cheese melting on top of it. Of course, one of the delicious Tavel
rosés, well chilled, would be perfect with this.

For dessert, have either an easy fruit pie or a bowl of
ripe, perfumed white peaches. These peaches have a short season,
and are very delicate, so they don't travel well, but when you find
them at the peak of their ripeness, juicy and fragrant, buy
as many as you can—they'll make your day.

CREAM OF CARROT SOUP

1 cup chopped white of leek
2 large yellow onions, chopped
4 Tbs. butter
2 generous lbs. sweet carrots
3 cups water
3 cups vegetable broth
5 Tbs. uncooked white rice
pinch of sugar

1 tsp. salt
½ tsp. crushed dried thyme
1 small bay leaf
pinch of cayenne
1½ cups milk
⅓ cup cream
dash of nutmeg

garnish: chopped fresh chives

In a large, heavy saucepan, sauté the leeks and onions in the butter, stirring often, until they are golden. Meanwhile, peel and thinly slice the carrots. Add the carrots, water, broth, rice, sugar, salt, herbs, and cayenne to the onion mixture. Cover and simmer for about 40 minutes, or until the carrots and rice are completely mushy soft.

Remove the bay leaf and purée the soup in batches in a blender or food processor until it is velvety smooth. Return the soup to the rinsed saucepan and stir in the milk, cream, and a sprinkle of nutmeg. Heat the soup through, stirring gently, then taste and correct the seasoning with another pinch of salt or nutmeg. Sprinkle each serving with chopped fresh chives.

Serves 8–10 generously. This may be more than you need for one meal, but a soup like this one is a nice thing to have left over for lunch the next day.

HARICOTS VERTS, RED POTATO, AND CUCUMBER SALAD

This salad came into my head at the farmers' market one day as I bought a huge bunch of fresh dill, and then all the things I like best with dill. It's an excellent salad for picnics, and keeps well for a day or two in the refrigerator. But the thin, tender French green beans are important to this—don't try to cheat with any larger, tougher beans.

1½ lbs. small red-skinned potatoes (about the size of walnuts)

1 lb. *haricots verts* (French green beans)

½ lb. small English or Persian cucumbers

½ cup coarsely chopped fresh dill weed

¼ cup finely chopped red onion

2 Tbs. fruity olive oil

2 Tbs. fresh lemon juice

½ tsp. salt

½ tsp. sugar

1 tsp. Dijon mustard

fresh-ground pepper to taste

Scrub the potatoes clean and trim away any rough spots. Cut in half potatoes that are larger in size than a walnut. Salt the potatoes lightly and steam them for about 15 minutes, or until tender. Let them cool.

Wash and trim the *haricots verts* and steam them for 5–7 minutes, or until tender-crisp. Let them cool.

If you have the slender, thin-skinned cucumbers, wash them, trim off the ends, and slice them about ⅛ inch thick. There's no need to peel or seed this variety. If you can only find the larger, thick-skinned cucumbers, you will need a bit more by weight, peel them, halve them lengthwise, and scrape out the seeds before slicing them.

Combine the potatoes, green beans, sliced cucumbers, coarsely chopped dill, and chopped red onion in a large bowl. Whisk together the olive oil, lemon juice, salt, sugar, Dijon mustard, and a dash of pepper. Pour the dressing over the vegetables and toss together gently but thoroughly. Try not to break up the potatoes.

Allow the salad to rest in the refrigerator for an hour or so, then taste, and correct the seasoning with more salt, pepper, or lemon juice if needed.

This serves 6–8 generously, or up to 10 in smaller servings.

GOAT CHEESE TOASTS

16–20 slices from a baguette
butter to taste

8 oz. white goat cheese (Montrachet
type)

Cut the French bread into slices about ½ inch thick, and butter them lightly. Toast the buttered slices under a broiler or in a toaster oven until they are just golden and slightly crisp—do not let them get brown.

Spread a thick slice of the goat cheese evenly over each toast. Arrange the toasts on a baking sheet and bake them in a hot oven for about 2 minutes to soften the cheese, then put them under a broiler until the cheese begins to turn golden brown in spots. Serve at once.

Serves 8.

RUSTIC PLUM PIE

for the pastry:
1⅓ cups flour
1 tsp. salt
1 tsp. sugar

½ cup cold butter (1 stick)
3–4 Tbs. ice water

for the filling:
6 cups sliced plums (about 3½ lbs.)
⅔ cup sugar
3 Tbs. cornstarch

dash of cinnamon
¼ tsp. almond extract
1 egg

Combine the flour, salt, and sugar in the bowl of a food processor, and cut in the cold butter in chunks. Process briefly, until the mixture resembles coarse meal. Process again while trickling in the ice water, just until the pastry pulls together and starts forming a ball. Do not add more water than necessary to reach this stage.

On a lightly floured board, roll the dough out into a circle about 14 inches in diameter. Transfer it to a baking sheet, cover it with plastic wrap, and put it away to chill for an hour or longer.

Wash the plums and slice them off their stones into thin wedges. In a dry bowl, whisk together the sugar and cornstarch until there are no lumps left. Add the prepared plums, the cinnamon, and the almond extract, and mix well. Let the fruit sit for about 20 minutes.

Preheat the oven to 450°. Remove the pastry from the refrigerator and give it a few minutes to soften. It should be cool but pliable, to prevent cracking. Center the pastry over a 10-inch deep-dish pie pan and fit it gently into the curve of the pan, pushing out all air bubbles and letting the excess pastry hang over the sides.

Whisk the egg in a bowl and brush the inside of the pie shell with it. Stir up the plums, then pour them into the prepared pie crust, distributing them evenly. You can make a pattern in the center with plum wedges, or just leave it random.

You should have about a 2-inch border of pastry overhanging the edge of the pan. You can trim it a little to make it more even, or just leave it ragged around the edges as I do. Fold this edge in over the fruit, pleating it loosely as you go round. You will have a rustic-looking pie, something like a deep-dish galette. Only about a 5-inch circle of fruit will show in the middle.

Brush the pastry edge with the remaining egg, and put the pie into the lower half of the oven. Lay a sheet of aluminum foil loosely over the top of it, and bake for 20 minutes. Lower the heat to 375° and bake for another 40 minutes, removing the foil for the last 10 or 15 minutes to brown the crust. The fruit will be bubbling vigorously when you remove the pie.

Let the pie cool on a rack for a while, then serve it while it's still warm if you can. Enjoy it alone or with a scoop of vanilla ice cream. This is a juicy pie, so have a spoon ready as well as a pie server.

Serves 8.

A NOODLE SALAD LUNCH

papaya halves
with fresh lime wedges

Asian Noodle Salad

Lemon Cheesecake Ice Cream
with blueberries

A salad made of nutty-flavored soba noodles, tossed
with a combination of vegetables and mushrooms in a sesame and
ginger dressing, makes the centerpiece of this cold lunch. The
noodle salad is not overly spicy, but flecks of hot red pepper, ginger,
and garlic keep it lively. A Gewürztraminer or a fruity white
Riesling would be just right with this.

The salad is a subtle complex of tastes and textures, so the
other parts of the meal should be kept as simple as possible—
ripe papaya halves with lime wedges for a starter, and one of my
favorites, Lemon Cheesecake Ice Cream, for dessert.

ASIAN NOODLE SALAD

½ lb. *haricots verts* (French green
    beans), or thin asparagus
2 Tbs. peanut oil
salt to taste
6 oz. finger-sized zucchini, or small
    zucchini quartered lengthwise
½ lb. oyster mushrooms
½ large onion
1–2 cloves garlic
1 tsp. dark sesame oil
¼ cup rice wine

1½ cups shredded Napa cabbage
2 Tbs. minced fresh ginger
2–3 Tbs. rice vinegar
soy sauce
1 lb. soba noodles
½ cup thinly sliced green onions
2 small hot red peppers, minced
    (1 Tbs. approx.)
⅔ cup cilantro leaves, coarsely
    chopped

dressing:
1 Tbs. sesame oil, more to taste

2½ Tbs. rice vinegar, more to taste
2 Tbs. soy sauce, more to taste

garnishes: cilantro sprigs
             thin strips of red chile pepper
             sesame seeds

Trim the ends off the *haricots verts;* if using asparagus, trim off the tough parts
of the stalks and cut each stalk in half. Toss the vegetables with a teaspoon of
peanut oil and a little salt, and spread them out on a cookie sheet. Quarter the
zucchini lengthwise, toss it with another teaspoon of the oil and some salt, and
spread on another cookie sheet.

Roast the prepared vegetables in a 400° oven for 15–20 minutes, just until tender and barely beginning to color. Remove and allow to cool.

Meanwhile, cut the oyster mushrooms in ½-inch strips, and thinly slice the
onion and mince the garlic. Heat the remaining peanut oil and a teaspoon of
sesame oil in a non-stick sauté pan, and sauté the mushrooms, onion, and garlic in it until they are lightly browned. Add 2 tablespoons of rice wine to the pan
and continue to stir the vegetables for another minute. Remove the mushroom
mixture from the pan and set it aside.

Add the shredded cabbage to the pan, along with the minced ginger, and sauté
it over medium heat until it is limp and starting to color. Add the remaining rice

wine, the rice vinegar, and a dash of soy sauce, and keep tossing the cabbage over medium heat until the excess liquid is gone.

Cook the noodles in an ample amount of boiling, salted water until they are *al dente*. Drain them, then plunge them into ice water for a moment and drain again.

In a large bowl, combine the drained noodles, the roasted vegetables, the mushroom mixture, cabbage, sliced green onions, minced peppers, and cilantro. Add sesame oil, rice vinegar, and soy sauce to taste and toss gently until everything is lightly coated with the dressing. Serve at room temperature and garnish with cilantro sprigs, strips of chile pepper, and sesame seeds.

Serves 6–8.

LEMON CHEESECAKE
ICE CREAM

Because this is made with more buttermilk than cream, it is not as fatty as conventional ice cream, and it has the delicious, tangy taste of cheesecake. It's sensational with ripe summer blueberries.

¼ cup fresh-squeezed lemon juice	⅓ cup water
grated zest of 2 lemons (yellow only)	½ cup heavy cream
	½ cup milk
¾ cup + 1 Tbs. sugar	1 cup low-fat buttermilk

In a small enameled saucepan, combine the lemon juice, zest, sugar, and water. Heat to a simmer and stir until the sugar is completely dissolved. Cool the syrup, then chill it.

Combine the chilled lemon syrup with the cream, milk, and buttermilk, and freeze according to manufacturer's instructions in an ice cream freezer.

This makes about a quart of ice cream.

A TOSTADA LUNCH

Black Bean Tostadas
with nopalitos, ranchero cheese, radishes
and Guacamole

fruit platter

Strawberry Ice Cream with Triple Sec

A tostada lunch has the casual and relaxed quality of a
picnic, whether it is eaten inside or out. Everyone makes their own
tostadas, the way they like them. Bowls of tasty things are passed
back and forth, you pick up tostadas in your hands to eat them, and
things drip a little so fingers have to be licked.

Savory black beans and crumbly white cheese, on a
crisply toasted corn tortilla, are the foundation. After that, all sorts
of toppings are added. Purists like a dab of salsa, or a few sliced
radishes. Others pile nopalitos on top of guacamole, adding
sliced green onions, dousing it all with salsa, and decorating the top
with cilantro. Having guests assemble their own tostadas is important
not only because it's fun, but because freshness is essential when
combining juicy toppings with crispy tortillas.

These are not so big, so you can
have two or three, made different ways.

With spicy food, I always serve fruit. After Black Bean Tostadas I
like more fruit for dessert, in the form of a terrific home-made
ice cream with strawberries and Triple Sec.

BLACK BEAN TOSTADAS

These are not to be confused with restaurant tostadas—mounds of salad piled inside a deep-fried flour tortilla "bowl." The tostadas I make are much smaller, crisp-toasted corn tortillas spread with delicious things, and they can be picked up and eaten out of hand.

If you don't have nopalitos, don't worry. Make tostadas anyway, substituting some other green vegetable, perhaps sautéed zucchini with a squeeze of lemon.

20–24 corn tortillas	12 oz. ranchero cheese, crumbled
olive oil	1 cup thinly sliced radishes
salt	1 cup thinly sliced green onions
2 lbs. fresh nopalitos (substitute	1 cup chopped cilantro leaves
zucchini if nopalitos unavailable)	Hot Chipotle Salsa (page 128), or
1 recipe Everyday Black Beans	Guajillo Chile Salsa (page 31)
(page 239)	Guacamole (recipe follows)

Everything you need for tostadas can be prepared ahead of time if you like, but it is important to assemble them a second before you eat them.

Lay the corn tortillas out on cookie sheets. Brush them very lightly with olive oil and sprinkle with a little salt. Shortly before you're going to eat, toast the tortillas for a few minutes under a hot broiler. Watch them carefully and remove them as soon as they start to turn golden brown in spots. Pile them in a basket, where they will become very crisp as they cool.

Prepare your nopalitos, if you're lucky enough to have them. Slice off the spines, cut the nopalitos in ¼-inch strips, and mix them up with a little salt. Put them in a big non-stick sauté pan over a high flame and cook them, stirring and turning often, until their excess juices cook away and they begin to color in spots. If you don't have nopalitos, cut up some zucchini, and sauté them lightly in a tiny bit of butter and a little lemon juice.

Have your black beans warm and ready in a bowl. Put everything on the table, and assemble the tostadas like this:

Spread about 2 rounded tablespoons of black beans on a crisp tortilla. Sprinkle crumbled ranchero cheese over the beans. Now add whatever toppings appeal to you, just as you would on a pizza. The combinations are endless, but what always works for me is the basic layer of black beans and ranchero cheese followed by something green or crunchy, and then something spicy. Some of my favorites:

Black beans, ranchero cheese, lots of nopalitos, a little guacamole, a
  dab of chipotle salsa

Black beans, ranchero cheese, thin-sliced radishes

Black beans, ranchero cheese, green onions, radishes, and cilantro

Black beans, guacamole, chipotle salsa, ranchero cheese

*The amounts given here are enough for 6–8 people,
depending on what other food is served.*

GUACAMOLE

Here is the most basic Guacamole, and it should be freshly made. You can elaborate this with the addition of chiles, hot salsas, or tomatoes. I cannot give exact proportions, as the acidity of lemons and the size and ripeness of avocados will vary.

2 large ripe avocados
2–3 Tbs. fresh lemon juice
salt to taste

3–4 Tbs. thinly sliced green onions
chopped cilantro leaves

Cut the avocados in half lengthwise, take out the pits, and scoop the soft flesh out into a bowl. Immediately add some lemon juice and mash the avocado with it. Add salt to taste, some thinly sliced green onions, and as much chopped cilantro as you like. Taste, and add more lemon if needed. Serve the Guacamole as soon as possible, with corn tortillas or chips, and as a topping for tostadas.

Makes about 2 cups.

STRAWBERRY ICE CREAM
WITH TRIPLE SEC

½ cup heavy cream
½ cup milk
1¼ cups sugar
½ tsp. vanilla

1 quart sliced ripe strawberries
2 Tbs. lemon juice
1–2 Tbs. Triple Sec
1 cup buttermilk

Scald the cream and milk with ¾ cup of sugar and the vanilla, stirring until the sugar is completely dissolved. Allow the mixture to cool, then chill it. Crush the strawberries with the remaining ½ cup of sugar, the lemon juice, and Triple Sec. Pulse this mixture in a food processor until it is a rough purée. You want a little texture, but no great big chunks of strawberry. Chill the processed strawberries.

Combine the cream mixture, the strawberries, and the buttermilk, and freeze according to manufacturer's instructions in an ice cream freezer.

This makes about 1½ quarts of intensely flavored ice cream, with a texture somewhere between true ice cream and sorbet.

NOTHING FANCY
BRUNCH

Mimosas

fresh-squeezed orange juice

Ortega Chile Potatoes

Huevos Mexicanos

fresh corn tortillas

Salsa Cruda

Molletes

Teddy's Fruit Salad

Buttermilk Coffee Cake

coffee

I've heard brunch praised as the most interesting
and relaxed of meals, and dismissed as an aberration.
Well, let's lighten up, folks.

What I like about brunch is that anything goes.
Breakfast foods, lunch foods (and, truthfully, some of those might
be dinner foods), fruit juices, wine, coffee—they're all part
of brunch. Of course, that's exactly the spirit of anarchy that drives
some people crazy, but I remember what Duke Ellington said
about serious music versus popular music: "If it sounds good, it *is*
good." The same is true if it tastes good, and I've eaten all these
foods in the middle of a nice Sunday, and it *was* good.

Brunches ultimately fall to the side of either the great,
hearty breakfast, or the big, fancy buffet lunch, and this one is
solidly in the breakfast camp.

There's nothing fancy here, nothing held warm in a
chafing dish, only simple foods prepared just before they're eaten.
If that sounds tricky for a company meal, let me hasten to add that
all the component parts can be prepared well ahead of time, and you
only need a few minutes at the stove before serving.

It starts with the classic brunch drink, a Mimosa. Ice-
cold champagne mixed with fresh-squeezed orange juice is equally
welcome after hiking in the mountains all morning or sleeping till
noon. Next, two great skillet dishes, Ortega Chile Potatoes and
Huevos Mexicanos. The potatoes are savory with onions, mild chiles,
and cheese, and the eggs snappy with serrano or jalapeño chiles.
Both can be served straight from the skillets in which they're made.

To accompany the hearty hot foods serve warm corn tortillas,
your favorite salsa, fresh fruit, a sweet and easy coffee cake, and my
personal favorite, Molletes—crusty rolls toasted and topped with
warm refried beans and melted cheese.

MIMOSAS

This refreshing beverage is the traditional drink of a California brunch. There are only 2 ingredients, so they must both be excellent. You don't need to buy the most expensive vintage champagne, but you should be willing to drink it even without the orange juice (and someone is sure to do just that).

fresh-squeezed orange juice   ice-cold champagne

Strain the orange juice to remove the heavy pulp, chill it thoroughly, and keep it cold without adding ice. Have the champagne completely chilled as well, and keep the bottle in an ice bucket.

Mix the Mimosas a moment before they are to be consumed. Half fill a champagne flute with juice, then fill to the top with champagne.

ORTEGA CHILE POTATOES

This is roadside diner food the way you wish it would taste in the roadside diner. My father-in-law, Rudy, described it to me one day, and I made a panful right away, which the whole family ate for lunch. It's an old-fashioned skillet dish that combines potatoes, Monterey Jack cheese, and Ortega chiles, one of the few foods I buy in a can.

Use the smaller red-skinned potatoes if you can, for their taste and their texture. If they're unavailable, use the white-skinned variety.

3½ lbs. small red-skinned potatoes
2 Tbs. olive oil
2 large onions, chopped
1 clove garlic, finely chopped
salt and pepper to taste
½ cup chopped Ortega chiles, or

fresh green Anaheim chiles roasted, peeled, and chopped, or more to taste
4–5 oz. grated Monterey Jack cheese, to taste

Boil the unpeeled potatoes in salted water until they are just tender—the time will depend on their size. Drain them and allow them to cool. Cut them up in 1-inch chunks.

Heat the olive oil in a large non-stick sauté pan, and sauté the chopped onion in it until it softens. Add the garlic, and stir for a minute. Add the potatoes and some salt and pepper.

Sauté the potatoes with the onions and garlic, stirring and turning gently but often, until they are becoming browned and crisp in spots. Stir in the chopped Ortega chiles and continue turning over medium-high heat for another 2 minutes.

Spread the potato mixture evenly in the pan, sprinkle the grated cheese over the top, cover tightly, and turn off the heat. Wait 2 minutes; the steam will melt the cheese over the potatoes in a delectable way. Then lift the lid and serve.

Serves 8.

HUEVOS MEXICANOS

For a traditional Mexican breakfast, serve these eggs with refried beans, warm corn tortillas, fresh fruit, hot chile salsa, and cafe con leche or hot chocolate.

This recipe gives the amounts for 4 servings. For 8 servings, double the quantities, but do the cooking in 2 pans. It's easier, and the texture of the eggs will be good.

8 eggs	2 jalapeño chiles, trimmed and
salt to taste	finely chopped
black pepper to taste	1 medium onion, chopped
½ cup chopped cilantro leaves	1 cup chopped fresh tomatoes,
1 tsp. olive oil	drained
1 Tbs. butter	

Beat the eggs with salt, pepper, and cilantro. Heat the oil and butter in a non-stick sauté pan, add the jalapeño chiles and chopped onion, and stir and cook for about 5 minutes, just until the onion is translucent and soft.

Add the drained tomatoes, stir them just until they are hot through, then add the eggs. Scramble the eggs over a medium-low flame until the eggs are set, then serve at once with warm corn tortillas.

Serves 4.

Salsa Cruda (page 240)

MOLLETES

These provide a great way for using leftover refried beans the next morning, and they are just delicious.

8 small, crusty French rolls (I like sourdough rolls)
2½ Tbs. butter
2 cups Refried Pinto Beans (page 32)

4 oz. grated cheddar or Monterey Jack cheese

optional: roasted, chopped green chiles, hot or mild

Split the rolls in half lengthwise and butter them lightly. Toast them in a toaster oven or under the broiler just until they start to turn golden.

Spread a generous, heaping tablespoon of warm refried beans on each toasted roll, covering it as completely as you can to prevent the edges from scorching when you toast it again. Sprinkle a little grated cheese over the beans. Put the rolls back in the toaster oven or under the broiler for about 2 minutes, or until the beans are hot through and the cheese is melted and bubbling. Serve at once with hot coffee or chocolate.

These can be made spicy to taste by stirring some chopped green chiles into the refried beans. I prefer them without the chiles, although I am a great fan of chiles in general, but don't be afraid to try.

Serves 8.

TEDDY'S FRUIT SALAD

No one needs a recipe for fruit salad. But just because it perfectly captures the spirit of fruit salad, here is one written by my son Teddy when he was 6 years old, for a little cookbook his school was putting together.

Just as he wrote it:

You need a medium sized bowl. Cut off the green part of at least 10 strawberries and put them in. Cut up some apricots. Any amount. And put them in. Put some mint leaves. One branch. And put some mango in. Cut up some peach. Drop it in. Cut up some honeydew. And drop it in. That's it. The end.

And in fact, if you do just that, you will have an excellent fruit salad.

BUTTERMILK COFFEE CAKE

This easy coffee cake is made with blueberries and walnuts, but I've made the same cake substituting chopped fresh apple and raisins, with excellent results.

1⅔ cups white flour	3 Tbs. melted butter
4 tsp. baking powder	1 tsp. vanilla
pinch of salt	1 cup fresh or frozen blueberries
½ cup sugar	
½ tsp. cinnamon	topping:
½ cup rolled oats	¼ cup rolled oats
¼ cup finely chopped walnuts	3 Tbs. brown sugar
1 large egg	¼ tsp. cinnamon
1 cup buttermilk	1 Tbs. softened butter

Sift together the flour, baking powder, salt, sugar, and ½ teaspoon of cinnamon. Stir in the ½ cup of rolled oats and the chopped walnuts.

In another bowl, beat the egg with the buttermilk, melted butter, and vanilla. Stir the wet mixture into the dry one, just until a batter is formed. If using fresh blueberries, rinse them and pat them dry. Stir the fresh or frozen blueberries gently into the batter.

Spoon the batter into a buttered 8-inch square baking pan. In a small bowl, combine all the topping ingredients and rub them together with your fingers until you have a crumbly mixture. Sprinkle this over the batter in the pan.

Bake the cake at 400° for about 40 minutes, or until a toothpick inserted near the center comes out clean. Allow the cake to cool slightly, then cut it into squares to serve.

Serves 9–12.

THE CALIFORNIA TEA

Tea is not a meal where I live. Tea is something you drink if you don't drink coffee, or else it's an event.

Afternoon tea is an exotic idea here, associated with white gloves, cold weather, and polite conversation, all of which are things we believe in but some of us have never actually encountered.

In California, a pretty tea party can have the irresistible charm of something taking place in a storybook. Reality is left at the door, or at the garden gate, since gardens in bloom are the best venue for this sort of thing.

I once went to a very grand tea which was part of a fund-raising event for the local film society. I knew nearly everyone there, but didn't recognize a soul; the ladies were all in hats! And never have I seen such a stupendous array of lovely foods laid out on doilies.

A tea of that kind is sometimes mistakenly called a high tea here. It sounds right, and many people have had no reason to find out that high tea does not translate to *haute cuisine*. In fact, my British friends have informed me, a real high tea might be something on the order of fried fish and chips with a mug of strong, inky brew, served at a rather early dinner hour and taking its place as the evening meal. The correct name for the white glove and doily event is "afternoon tea," but never mind—we love our tea events, and I think they are gradually evolving into a genre of their own. Maybe we'll call them California tea.

A FANCY TEA

*Watercress Sandwiches on
Oat Bread with Maple Syrup*

*Chopped Egg and Dill Sandwiches
on pumpernickel bread*

Avocado Sandwiches on whole grain bread

*Three-Grain Cranberry Bread
with butter or Pumpkin Butter*

*Buttermilk Scones with
Sweetened Yogurt Cream and strawberries*

Russian Tea Cakes

Darjeeling or Earl Grey tea

dry sherry

This tea party stays pretty close to the traditional style of an
English tea. There are savory sandwiches—watercress, and egg with dill,
and, because this is California, avocado. On the slightly sweet side are
scones with strawberries and something reminiscent of clotted cream, as
well as a very good cranberry bread with all-American Pumpkin Butter.
And for dessert, Russian Tea Cakes, the best cookie ever made.

All this should be served with a fragrant tea, freshly
brewed in an ample teapot, and very, very hot. And, as much as
I love a good cup of tea, I think it's nice to have a little something
more on hand for an occasion like this. For that little something,
I suggest a medium-dry sherry. Finally, since this is a California tea,
a bottle of champagne is never out of place.

AN EASY TEA

For a simpler tea, something small for a couple of friends,
here is a pared-down version.

Watercress Sandwiches
on whole grain bread

Buttermilk Scones
with
Sweetened Yogurt Cream
and strawberries

Russian Tea Cakes

Darjeeling or Earl Grey tea

dry sherry

This is a very nice yet sensible sort of tea that can
be put together with a minimum of effort.

It provides the peppery bite of watercress, the pleasure of
fresh-baked scones (which are a snap to make) with ripe strawberries
and cream, and those sensational cookies, which could be replaced by
something good from the bakery in a pinch. All the elements are
there, in a restrained way that is actually very appealing.

WATERCRESS SANDWICHES

8 slices Oat Bread with Maple
    Syrup (page 308), or any
    good, fine-textured sandwich
    bread

2–3 oz. cream cheese
2 cups watercress sprigs, gently
    packed

Spread each of the freshly cut slices of bread thinly with cream cheese. You can use reduced-fat cream cheese with perfect results; Yogurt Cheese would be fine also, though I wouldn't recommend non-fat Yogurt Cheese, which is a little too tart.

Take ½ cup of clean, dry watercress sprigs, with all the heavy stems removed, and arrange them more or less evenly over a slice of bread. Cover with another slice, so that the watercress is held between cream cheese on both sides. This is a practical necessity as well as a tasty plan, since the sandwich would fall apart without the cementing properties of the cream cheese.

Construct all the sandwiches this way, then trim away the crusts if you must, and cut each of the 4 sandwiches in half diagonally, making 8 triangles. Keep them well covered with plastic wrap until serving time.

Makes 8 small watercress sandwiches.

AVOCADO SANDWICHES

2 ripe medium-sized avocados
1 Tbs. mayonnaise
2 tsp. fresh lemon juice
salt to taste

fresh-ground pepper to taste
finely chopped chives
8 thin slices whole grain bread

Cut the avocados in half lengthwise and take out the pits. Scoop out the soft flesh and immediately add the mayonnaise and lemon juice, and a little salt and pepper. Mash everything together, taste, and add more salt as needed. Stir in some chopped chives.

Spread 4 slices of bread evenly with the avocado mixture, and cover with the other 4 slices. Cut each sandwich in half.

Makes 8 small sandwiches.

OAT BREAD WITH MAPLE SYRUP

My children love this bread, so I make it often. Once a whole loaf disappeared when I left it cooling on a rack in the kitchen. It's a crossover bread—loved by kids and grown-ups alike. A little bit of maple syrup enriches the flavor without making it noticeably sweet.

This is an excellent bread for sandwiches and for toast.

2 cups water
1 cup milk
1½ cups rolled oats
1 package dry yeast
¼ cup pure maple syrup

2 tsp. salt
2 Tbs. butter, melted and cooled
3 cups unbleached white flour
3 cups whole wheat bread flour

Heat the water and milk together until scalding, and pour the liquid over the oats in a large bowl. Leave it to soak for about an hour.

Sprinkle the yeast over the oatmeal, which should be tepid, and stir it in. Then stir in the maple syrup, the salt, the melted butter, and the white flour. You will have a thick batter that can still be stirred with a big wooden spoon. Cover it with a tea towel or with plastic wrap and leave it in a warm place to rise for about an hour.

Stir the batter down and start adding the whole wheat flour, about ½ cup at a time, stirring it in well. When the dough is too stiff for a spoon, turn it out on a well-floured board, sprinkle more flour on top, and begin kneading. Keep adding sprinkles of flour as long as the dough is sticky, but not past that point. Knead it until it is elastic and firm, and responds quickly to your push.

Divide the dough into 2 equal parts and shape them into loaves. Put the loaves into medium-sized, buttered loaf pans or on buttered baking sheets, and cover them loosely with a tea towel. Leave them in a warm place to rise for just under an hour, or until about doubled.

Bake the loaves in a preheated 350° oven for about 45–50 minutes. Check them along the way—if they're getting too dark, lay a piece of aluminum foil over them. They should be golden brown and sound hollow when tapped on the bottom crust.

Remove the loaves from the pans and cool them on racks before slicing.

Makes 2 loaves.

CHOPPED EGG AND DILL SANDWICHES

4 hard-cooked eggs
1 stalk celery, finely chopped
2 Tbs. minced sweet pickles
1½ Tbs. mayonnaise
1–2 tsp. prepared mustard
pinch of cayenne

¼ cup chopped fresh dill
salt to taste
fresh-ground black pepper to taste
8 thin slices pumpernickel bread
radish sprouts, or sunflower sprouts

Peel the eggs and chop them rather finely. Combine them in a bowl with the chopped celery and minced sweet pickles. Mix together the mayonnaise, mustard, cayenne, and dill, and add this to the eggs, mixing everything together thoroughly. Taste, and add salt and pepper as needed until the balance is right for you.

Spread this mixture evenly over 4 of the bread slices, and cover them with the other 4. Cut each of the sandwiches in half, crosswise or diagonally, depending on the shape of the bread.

Lift the top off each sandwich, and place a few radish sprouts so that they peek out over the edge of the bread in a decorative frill, then replace the top neatly.

Makes 8 small sandwiches.

THREE-GRAIN CRANBERRY BREAD

This bread is very easy and fast to make, not too sweet, and for a quick bread it is uncommonly low in fat. The dense, red-speckled slices look festive and taste great alone or with cream cheese.

1 cup white flour
1 cup rye flour
1 tsp. salt
1 tsp. baking soda
1½ tsp. baking powder

1¼ cups rolled oats
1⅓ cups buttermilk
¼ cup dark molasses
1 cup dried cranberries
⅓ cup chopped walnuts

Prepare 2 small loaf pans: butter them, line them with wax paper, and butter the wax paper. Preheat the oven to 350°.

Sift the 2 flours together with the salt, baking soda, and baking powder. Stir in the rolled oats. Mix together the buttermilk and molasses, and stir the wet mixture into the dry one, along with the cranberries and chopped walnuts.

Spoon the batter into the prepared pans, smooth it out, and bake at 350° for about 50 minutes, or until a toothpick inserted in the center of a loaf comes out clean. Allow the loaves to cool in their pans for a few minutes, then remove them to racks and let them cool further before slicing.

Serve with butter or Pumpkin Butter (page 417).

Makes 2 small loaves.

BUTTERMILK SCONES

This recipe calls for walnuts and raisins in a light-textured scone that is just sweet enough. The raisins could be replaced with currants, dried cranberries, dried cherries, or dried blueberries.

2½ cups white flour, approx.	2 Tbs. toasted wheat germ
3 Tbs. sugar	¼ cup finely chopped walnuts
2 tsp. baking powder	½ cup raisins
½ tsp. salt	1 cup buttermilk
2½ Tbs. cold butter	

Combine 2 cups of flour, the sugar, baking powder, and salt in the container of a food processor and add the cold butter, cut into several pieces. Process briefly, until the mixture resembles a coarse meal.

Transfer it to a bowl, and stir in the wheat germ, walnuts, and raisins. Add the buttermilk and stir just until a thick batter forms.

Turn the batter out onto a well-floured board, sprinkle a little more flour on top of it, flour your hands, and gently pull it together into a ball. Keeping it always well dredged in flour, fold the dough a couple of times to smooth it out. I don't even want to call this kneading. The secret to having light-textured scones is simply not to overhandle this moist, sticky dough.

Cut the dough in half, form each part into a ball, then pat each ball into an even circle a little less than 1 inch thick. With a sharp knife, cut each circle into 6 wedges. Lift the wedges with a spatula onto a buttered baking sheet.

Bake the scones in a preheated 425° oven for about 18–20 minutes, or until golden brown on top. Take them out of the oven and immediately transfer them to a rack to cool slightly, then serve. These are best eaten warm.

Makes 12 scones.

SWEETENED YOGURT CREAM

This combination of yogurt and cream is reminiscent of crème fraîche (page 324), and of English clotted cream, but is not quite as heavy as either, making it much more enjoyable to eat.

1 cup low-fat yogurt	½ cup whipping cream
1 cup non-fat yogurt	½ cup powdered sugar

Stir together the 2 yogurts and pour them into a colander lined with 3 or 4 layers of cheesecloth, set over a bowl. Leave it to drain for several hours. You should end up with about 1¼ cups of thickened yogurt, with the texture of sour cream.

Beat the whipping cream in a bowl until it starts to hold a soft shape. Add the powdered sugar and continue beating until the cream just begins to hold a stiff shape. Beat in the drained yogurt.

Serve with any fresh, ripe berries.

Makes about 2 cups.

RUSSIAN TEA CAKES

I have this recipe from my sister, Eve Lowry, but it's one of those fabulous recipes that have been around for a long time and are claimed by many nations. I've seen almost the identical thing called Mexican wedding cookies, and a crescent-shaped version of it called a Turkish something or other.

My sister is a registered dietitian, and spends most of her time developing low-fat food and providing educational tools about healthy diets to doctors and hospitals. I think it's very funny that among her family she is absolutely *famous* for these cookies, and everyone waits for the Christmas box that arrives each year. It proves that there is such a thing as a balanced life.

1 cup sweet butter, softened
½ cup powdered sugar
1½ tsp. vanilla
½ teaspoon almond extract
¼ tsp. salt

¾ cup chopped pecans or walnuts
2¼ cups all-purpose white flour
additional powdered sugar as
    needed

Combine the butter, ½ cup of powdered sugar, vanilla, almond extract, and salt in the container of a food processor, and cream everything until it is light and fluffy. Add the nuts and process in short pulses until the nuts are chopped finely. Add the flour and process in pulses until the dough is just combined.

Turn the dough out onto a large sheet of wax paper. It will be quite soft. Use the paper to shape the dough into a cube, then wrap it and refrigerate for an hour or two, until the dough is firm enough to slice easily into small cubes without losing its shape. You can keep the dough in the refrigerator, well wrapped, for several days. However, when it gets completely chilled, you need to take it out and let it warm up a little before slicing, as it will be brittle.

Preheat the oven to 400°. Using a thin-bladed knife, cut ½-inch slices off the cube, then cut each slice into ½-inch cubes. You can roll the cubes into balls if you want to take the time; we leave them square.

Put the cookies on ungreased cookie sheets, about ½ inch apart, or on parchment-lined sheets. Bake them, one sheet at a time, in the upper part of the oven, for about 10–12 minutes, or until they just barely start turning color.

My sister points out that they should not brown, but they taste better if they develop a slightly golden color on top. They do have a tendency to get dark brown on the bottom while the top still looks raw, so you just have to check every minute or so after the first 10 minutes, until you get the time right for your particular oven.

When done, remove them from the oven and allow them to cool on the cookie sheet for 2 minutes. Then put half a box of powdered sugar into a bowl, add about 20 warm cookies at a time, and toss them around gently until they are well coated with sugar. Spread them out on wax paper to cool, and when they have cooled completely, roll them in powdered sugar one more time.

This makes about 4 dozen cookies.

The Last Word

I must give one last variation on the tea theme. In summer, when tomatoes are dark red and sweet, the tomato sandwich is one of the great treats of life. It makes a superb replacement for the watercress sandwich, which is out of season in that weather.

TOMATO SANDWICHES
FOR A SUMMERTIME TEA

Cut slices from a dense-textured loaf of French bread. Butter the slices thinly and sprinkle them with a little chopped parsley or basil. Cut perfectly ripe tomatoes into thick slices, and use only the big middle slices, which match the size of the bread. Place one fat tomato slice on each piece of buttered and herbed bread, sprinkle on some salt and a few more herbs, and serve.

Celebrations
and
Feasts

A GALA DINNER
FOR LATE SPRING

Garlic Crostini
with
Sun-Dried Tomato Pesto
and Fresh Cheese with Basil Pesto

Cold Plum Soup

Salad of Peppery Greens
with Baked Goat Cheese and Olives

Roulade of Fresh Morels

Pink Grapefruit Sorbet

Cornmeal Griddlecakes
with Sweet Chipotle Sauce,
Nopalitos, Crème fraîche, and Pine Nuts

White Peach Mousse in Chocolate Collars,
with Raspberry Coulis
and Fresh Berries

Toward the end of May, when we can still get nopalitos and morels, and the first summer fruits are appearing, this extravagant meal can be prepared to celebrate a milestone in someone's life— or just to have more fun at a dinner party than you've ever had before.

It's eclectic and interesting, cheerfully crossing cultural lines.

We start in Provence with Garlic Crostini, spread with two pungent versions of pesto. A champagne apéritif on the terrace would be perfect here—even if the terrace is only in your mind. Then skip to Eastern Europe for Cold Plum Soup, served with a delicate white Riesling—a refreshing pause between the garlicky appetizer and the peppery-salty salad that follows.

The first hot course is Roulade of Fresh Morels, a classic dish, subtle and rich with the incomparable taste of morels. That richness is gently erased by a dab of Pink Grapefruit Sorbet, and then the taste buds are really awakened by the sweet and fiery flavors from the Southwest: corn and chiles, with cactus and pine nuts. These chiles are slightly tempered, however, so you can enjoy a big, spicy, flavorful red wine for a great finale.

The dessert is a real concoction. It's the kind of thing that is often left in the "don't try this at home" category, along with the spun sugar swans, but if you're an experienced cook, I say why not? It's absolutely wonderful.

Garlic Crostini (page 67)

SUN-DRIED TOMATO PESTO

3 oz. sun-dried tomatoes (about 1¼
   cups rehydrated)
¼ cup pine nuts
¼ cup walnut pieces
¼ cup fruity green olive oil
½ cup chopped fresh basil

2 Tbs. balsamic vinegar
2 Tbs. reserved water from soaking
   tomatoes, or as needed
¼ cup grated Parmesan cheese
pinch of tarragon
salt and fresh-ground pepper

optional: 1–2 garlic cloves

Put the dried tomatoes in a small pot with enough water to cover them, bring to a boil, reduce the heat, and simmer for a minute, then remove from heat and leave them to soak for about an hour. Drain the tomatoes, reserving the excess water.

If you want the taste of garlic in this pesto, peel a couple of garlic cloves, bruise them slightly, and leave them in the olive oil for about 30 minutes before using it.

Combine all the ingredients in a food processor and process for a few seconds at a time, scraping down the sides in between, until you have a thick, coarse-textured pulp. Taste, correct the seasoning with more salt and pepper if needed, and moisten the mixture with a little of the reserved tomato water if it seems too thick.

Serve at room temperature with Garlic Crostini (page 67), plain crackers, French bread, etc.

This makes about 2 cups of an intensely flavored, dark-red paste.

Variations: This paste also combines well with goat cheese or cream cheese, and when thinned a bit makes a nice sauce for pasta or a good addition to salad dressing.

FRESH CHEESE WITH BASIL PESTO

5–6 oz. fresh white goat cheese
2 oz. cream cheese
4 oz. ricotta, or soft farmer's cheese

¼–½ cup Fresh Basil Pesto (recipe follows)

Allow the goat cheese and cream cheese to soften at room temperature, then combine all the ingredients in a bowl and beat with an electric mixer until smooth, or process briefly in a food processor. Mound the cheese on a serving plate and garnish with basil leaves. Serve cool but not cold, with crackers, crostini, or bread.

Makes about 1½ cups of cheese.

FRESH BASIL PESTO

5 oz. fresh basil leaves (about 2 cups leaves, packed)
½ cup pine nuts
½ cup freshly grated Parmesan cheese

2 cloves garlic
5 Tbs. fruity green olive oil
salt and fresh-ground pepper to taste

If you need to wash the basil leaves, spin them in a salad spinner or dry them in kitchen towels before proceeding. Remove any large or thick stems.

In the container of a food processor or blender, combine the basil leaves, pine nuts, cheese, and garlic, and process until the nuts and garlic are finely chopped. Add the olive oil and process again, scraping down the sides of the container as necessary, until you have a paste of the consistency you like. Add salt and fresh-ground black pepper to your taste.

Makes about 1½ cups.

COLD PLUM SOUP

3 lbs. Santa Rosa plums (or mixed
    red and purple plums)
2 cups water
2 cups dry red table wine
juice and grated zest of 1 large
    lemon

1¼ cups sugar, more if needed
1 3-inch stick cinnamon
1 Tbs. cornstarch
2 Tbs. powdered sugar
1 cup light sour cream

Wash the plums, cut them off their stones, and put them in a large non-reactive pot with the water, wine, lemon juice, lemon zest, sugar, and cinnamon. Bring to a boil, then lower the heat and simmer for 45 minutes.

Strain the cooked soup through a colander, stirring it down with a wooden spoon until the pulp remaining in the colander is mostly skins. Discard the skins, purée the soup in a blender in batches, and return it to the rinsed pot. Taste and correct the seasoning with a bit more sugar or lemon juice if needed. The soup should be both slightly sweet and slightly tart.

Dissolve the cornstarch in ¼ cup of cold water, and stir it into the soup. Bring the soup back to a boil and keep it boiling for 2 minutes, or until it clarifies. Allow it to cool, then chill it thoroughly.

Whisk the powdered sugar into the sour cream, and serve the soup in shallow, chilled bowls with a spoonful of the sour cream in the center of each one.

Serves 8.

SALAD OF PEPPERY GREENS
with Baked Goat Cheese and Olives

Do not scorn warm goat cheese salad simply because it has enjoyed such popularity in recent times. Some things become popular for a good reason. This is marvelous.

2 bunches arugula
1 small head young curly endive
1 small head radicchio
3–4 heads Belgian endive
handful of fresh basil leaves
1 10-oz. log of fresh white goat
    cheese

⅔ cup fruity green olive oil
½ cup fine dry breadcrumbs
½ cup coarse-ground walnuts
3–4 Tbs. balsamic vinegar
salt and pepper
25–30 cured black olives

optional garnish: marinated sun-dried tomatoes

Wash and trim the arugula, curly endive, and radicchio, spin dry in a salad spinner, and tear into manageable pieces. Wash the Belgian endive and slice it crosswise. Cut the basil leaves into slivers.

Cut the log of goat cheese into 8 thick circles of equal size. Pour ⅓ cup of olive oil into a small bowl. In another bowl, combine the breadcrumbs and ground walnuts. Take one goat cheese slice at a time, coat it lightly with the olive oil, then dip it on all sides into the breadcrumb mixture, pressing gently, until the goat cheese is wearing a nice little coat of crumbs and walnuts. Arrange the coated goat cheeses on a stainless steel baking sheet.

About 10 minutes before you are ready to serve the salad, preheat your oven to 400°. Toss the salad greens together in a big bowl with the remaining ⅓ cup of olive oil, some balsamic vinegar, and salt and pepper to taste. Divide the salad among 8 large plates.

Bake the goat cheeses in the preheated oven for 5 minutes, then check them. Their crusts should just be turning golden brown. Leave them for another minute or two if necessary, but watch them carefully, because they can turn dark awfully fast once they warm up.

Remove the goat cheeses from the oven and, working quickly but carefully, pick up one at a time with a spatula and slide it out onto the center of a salad. Remember, they are very soft now. Garnish each salad with a few olives, and marinated sun-dried tomatoes if desired. Serve at once.

Serves 8.

ROULADE OF
FRESH MORELS

Morels are among the most highly prized of the wild mushrooms, and have been an important part of French cuisine since anyone can remember. They are a seasonal delicacy, available in the spring after the rains. Ours come from the damp Northwest—Washington or Oregon—and are well worth the price when they turn up at the farmers' market.

the morel filling:
¾ lb. fresh morels
4 Tbs. butter
½ cup minced onions
2 Tbs. cognac
salt to taste

white pepper to taste
½ tsp. paprika
3 medium-sized tomatoes
¼ cup heavy cream

the roulade base:
1¼ lbs. zucchini
1 tsp. salt, more to taste
½ cup butter
⅓ cup chopped onion
⅔ cup flour

1 cup warm milk
4 eggs, separated
½ cup grated Parmesan cheese
about ½ cup fine, dry breadcrumbs

garnishes: melted butter
   additional grated Parmesan cheese

To make the filling: Clean the morels carefully under running water until you are certain there is no sand trapped in any of them. Trim away any soft or damaged parts and chop them coarsely.

Melt the butter in a large skillet and sauté the minced onion in it for a few minutes, until it just begins to color. Add the chopped morels and cook over medium heat, stirring often, until they release their water and it cooks away. Add the cognac and stir for another minute or so. Then salt and pepper to taste and add the paprika.

Meanwhile, drop the tomatoes into boiling water for about 45 seconds, then remove them and slip off their skins. Purée the tomatoes in a blender and pass the purée through a sieve to eliminate the seeds. You should have about a cup of fresh tomato pulp.

Lower the heat under the morels, pour in the tomato pulp, and simmer the mixture, continuing to stir it often, until it is reduced to a thick consistency, able to hold a soft shape. Stir in the cream, heat through, and set aside.

To make the roulade: Wash and grate the zucchini and toss it with a teaspoon of salt. Leave it in a colander to drain for 20 minutes, then gently squeeze out the excess moisture.

Melt the butter in a medium saucepan and sauté the onions in it until they are just beginning to color. Add the flour and stir constantly over low heat until the flour is golden, about 4–5 minutes. Add the warm milk and stir vigorously until the mixture is smooth and thick.

Remove the saucepan from the heat and let the mixture cool for 5 minutes. Beat in the 4 egg yolks, one at a time. Then stir in the grated, drained zucchini and ½ cup of grated Parmesan cheese.

Beat the 4 egg whites until they hold peaks. Stir half the egg whites into the zucchini mixture, then gently fold in the other half.

Butter a 10-by-14-inch jelly roll pan and sprinkle it with fine, dry breadcrumbs. Be sure every bit of the pan is coated with butter and breadcrumbs or you could have trouble turning out the roulade. Carefully spoon the egg-zucchini-cheese mixture into the prepared pan and spread it gently over the entire surface, taking care not to smear the breadcrumb coating.

Bake in a preheated 375° oven for 15–18 minutes, or until it is puffed and coming away from the sides.

Lift the edges of the roulade gently with a spatula to be sure that it will come up. Then, using pot holders or gloves to protect your hands, stretch a tea towel over the top of the pan, and swiftly turn the pan over onto a flat surface. The roulade should drop right out onto the tea towel.

While it is still warm, spread the roulade with the morel filling, leaving a 1½-inch border on one of the long sides. Starting at the edge with the border, and using the tea towel to help you lift the edge of the roulade evenly, roll it up just like a jelly roll. Using long spatulas, lift the roulade carefully onto a baking sheet, and return it to the oven for about 5 minutes to heat through.

Slice the roulade with a thin, sharp knife and lay 2 slices on each plate, bottom to bottom. Drizzle each serving with melted butter and pass the grated Parmesan separately.

Serves 8 generously, or 10–12 as an appetizer.

PINK GRAPEFRUIT SORBET

1⅓ cups water
1⅓ cups sugar
2½ cups strained fresh pink
grapefruit juice

4–6 Tbs. strained fresh lemon juice
1–2 tsp. grenadine
2 tsp. Pernod

Living in a citrus-growing area, I've found out how much these fruits change once they're off the tree. Use the freshest fruit you can get your hands on. If you're fortunate enough to have a tree or know someone who does, pick the grapefruits when you're ready to squeeze the juice and make the sorbet. You'll have a great treat.

Combine the water and sugar in a small saucepan and bring it to a simmer over a medium flame. Stir until all the sugar is dissolved. Allow the syrup to cool, then chill it for at least an hour.

Squeeze and strain the grapefruit juice and the lemon juice, and chill them in separate containers.

Combine the syrup with the grapefruit juice, 1 teaspoon of grenadine, 4 tablespoons of lemon juice, and the Pernod. Taste. Now add more lemon juice if needed—this will depend on the acidity of all the fruit. Remember, this sorbet should not be too sweet. Add more grenadine if you want it to be pinker.

Chill the mixture for 2 hours, then freeze it in an ice cream maker, according to manufacturer's instructions.

Makes a little more than a quart of sorbet.

CORNMEAL GRIDDLECAKES WITH SWEET CHIPOTLE SAUCE,
Nopalitos, Crème Fraîche, and Pine Nuts

1 lb. fresh nopalitos
⅔ cup pine nuts
16 Cornmeal Griddlecakes (recipe
follows)

3 cups Sweet Chipotle Sauce
(page 326)
2 cups crème fraîche*

garnish: cilantro sprigs

*Crème fraîche, the French version of sour cream, is now available here in many cheese stores and specialty food shops. However, a delicious facsimile can be made by whisking together equal parts of sour cream and sweet heavy cream, and leaving the mixture in a bowl at room temperature, covered with a plate, for several hours or overnight.

Prepare the nopalitos according to directions (page 28) and keep them hot in their water until the last minute.

If nopalitos are impossible to obtain, use red and green bell peppers, or sweet Italian peppers. Cut them in thin strips and sauté briefly in a little olive oil.

Toast the pine nuts by stirring them in a dry skillet over a medium flame for 5–6 minutes, until they begin to turn golden brown and release a toasty fragrance.

If the griddlecakes were prepared earlier, put them under a hot broiler now to reheat. Warm the Sweet Chipotle Sauce until it just simmers. Stir up the crème fraîche to soften it. Drain the nopalitos.

Put 2 hot griddlecakes on each of 8 large plates. Pour a ladleful of warm Sweet Chipotle Sauce alongside the griddlecakes on one side, and spoon some crème fraîche on the other side. Lay about ½ cup of drained nopalito strips over the griddlecakes, and scatter toasted pine nuts over the entire plate. Garnish the plates with big cilantro sprigs and serve at once.

Serves 8.

CORNMEAL GRIDDLECAKES

My favorite way to serve these is with Sweet Chipotle Sauce and crème fraîche (page 324), garnished with nopalitos and pine nuts, as in this menu. But they're also wonderful with sautéed mushrooms and tomato sauce, or topped with a little melted cheese and served alongside oven-roasted vegetables. My boys like them best snatched from the griddle and eaten while running away.

2 large eggs, separated	1 cup yellow cornmeal
¼ cup butter, melted and cooled	4 tsp. double-acting baking powder
1 cup milk	1 tsp. salt
½ cup cream, heavy or light	vegetable oil for frying
1 cup all-purpose white flour	

Combine the egg yolks, melted butter, milk, and cream in a bowl and whisk together lightly. In another bowl, sift together all the dry ingredients. Add the egg yolk mixture to the cornmeal mixture and stir just until the wet and dry ingredients are combined; do not overmix.

Beat the egg whites, which should be at room temperature, until they hold stiff peaks, and then fold them gently into the batter. (Cold egg whites can be warmed quickly by putting them in a bowl, then setting that bowl into a larger bowl of hot water, and whisking the whites for about a minute.)

Heat a griddle or large frying pan until a drop of water sizzles on it, and brush it lightly with oil. Drop the batter onto the griddle by scant ¼ cups, and cook for about 1½ minutes on one side, until the bottom is golden brown, then flip and cook briefly on the other side.

The griddlecakes can be served at once, or they can be cooled on racks, wrapped tightly in plastic, and held for a day or so. To reheat them, lay them out on a cookie sheet and allow them to come to room temperature. Then put them under a hot broiler, about 5–6 inches away, for about 1½ minutes on each side, or until just heated through. Serve at once.

Makes 16 medium-sized griddlecakes, enough for 8 servings in this menu, or 4–6 servings if fewer other dishes are being served.

SWEET CHIPOTLE SAUCE

In this recipe, the smoky spiciness of chipotle chiles is offset by sweet red peppers and a touch of honey.

The sauce keeps well refrigerated. I often double the recipe, and serve it with tortilla chips, on quesadillas, with eggs, with tamales—with most any Mexican food.

2 cloves garlic
1 medium yellow onion
10 medium-sized dried New
    Mexican chile pods
    (about 4 oz. dried)
2 dried chipotle chiles
1 cup water
½ cup white grape juice or apple
    juice

2 cups cooked tomatoes with their
    juice
1 tsp. salt, more to taste
1½ cups roasted and peeled sweet
    red peppers
1 Tbs. lemon juice
1 Tbs. honey

Peel the garlic and peel and quarter the onion. Pull the stems and seeds out of all the chile pods and wash them. Put the garlic, onion, chiles, water, fruit juice, tomatoes, and salt in a large non-reactive pot and simmer gently for at least 30 minutes and up to an hour, until the chiles are pulpy and soft.

Add the roasted and peeled sweet red peppers—you can use the ones sold in jars in Italian groceries, or roast and peel your own.

Purée the mixture in batches in a blender or a food processor until it is perfectly smooth. Stir in the lemon juice and honey, and taste. The sauce should be spicy but not searingly hot, with a slightly sweet taste under the chile flavor.

Makes about 5 cups.

WHITE PEACH MOUSSE IN CHOCOLATE COLLARS
with Raspberry Coulis and Fresh Berries

1 recipe White Peach Mousse
   (recipe follows)
1 recipe Raspberry Coulis
   (page 329)

8 dark chocolate collars or cups

garnishes: fresh raspberries and blackberries
        chocolate curls and mint sprigs

This is one of those fantasy desserts, more likely to be found in a restaurant than at home, but now and again it's fun to do something wild.

I devised it for a fancy dinner I prepared as a fund-raising event for my boys' school. My crew and I slaved over it. We called it the peach mousse from hell, because it was so tricky to get the acid balance right without breaking down the texture of the mousse; because we had to send out for a good candy thermometer, as I hadn't used mine in so long that I couldn't find it; and because our arms were falling off from all the beating of egg whites. Of course, we were making enough for 120 people—it's easier for 8. Anyway, the dessert was such a spectacular success that I pass the recipe along here with warning for the inexperienced.

I had the bittersweet chocolate collars made to order by a wonderful chocolatier who has a small shop near where I live, and who makes everything by hand. You could use pre-formed dark chocolate cups, which are available at some specialty shops, or make your own by learning some of the chocolatier's art. In any case, what you need are thin chocolate containers into which you can mound the peach mousse.

To assemble the dessert: Place the chocolate rings or cups in the centers of 8 large dessert plates. Spoon some chilled Raspberry Coulis around the chocolate, and mound the peach mousse inside it. Scatter a few berries in the coulis, and tuck a mint sprig in each serving of mousse. Serve at once.

Serves 8.

WHITE PEACH MOUSSE

5–6 medium white peaches, to make
    1½ cups peach purée
3–4 tsp. lemon juice
1½ tsp. gelatin
⅔ cup whipping cream
3 egg whites at room temperature

pinch of salt
pinch of cream of tartar
⅔ cup sugar
½ tsp. almond extract
grated zest of 1 orange (about
    1 tsp.)

garnishes: chocolate curls and mint sprigs

Peel and purée the peaches and add just enough lemon juice to bring out their best flavor. Cover and chill.

Sprinkle the gelatin into ¼ cup of water and allow it to soften. Set it aside.

Whip the cream until it thickens so that it forms soft peaks when it falls back into the bowl. Set it aside in the refrigerator. Beat the egg whites with the salt and cream of tartar until they form soft peaks.

In a heavy saucepan, dissolve the sugar over medium heat in ¼ cup of water. Bring the syrup to a boil, swirling the pan a little to wash down any crystals from the sides. Cook it over a medium flame until it reaches the soft ball stage (238°).

Start beating the egg whites again with an electric mixer, on high speed, and pour the hot syrup into the egg whites in a thin, steady stream. As soon as the syrup is incorporated into the egg whites, and while the mixture is still hot, beat in the softened gelatin. Continue to beat at moderate speed until the mixture has cooled to room temperature, about 10–15 minutes.

Stir the almond extract and the orange zest into the peach purée, then pour the purée and the whipped cream over the meringue, and fold everything together gently but thoroughly with a spatula.

Chill the mousse for several hours. It is then ready to spoon into chocolate collars if you're doing the elaborate recipe on page 327, or it can be served in parfait glasses, garnished with chocolate curls and mint leaves.

Serves 8–10.

RASPBERRY COULIS

2 pints fresh or frozen raspberries   ¼–½ cup sugar

Purée the berries and sugar together in a blender or food processor, then strain through a sieve. Taste and adjust the sugar if needed. Chill the coulis, covered, until needed. This can be prepared ahead and stored in the refrigerator for a day or two.

Makes 2½–3 cups.

A SUMMER BUFFET
FOR A CROWD

Roasted Green Bean Salad

Tuscan White Beans
with Garlic and Sage

Olives and Feta Cheese with Oregano

Pasta with Olive Oil
and Fresh Herbs

Fresh-Chopped Tomatoes with Basil

Chard and Parsley Frittata

Marinated Grilled Eggplant

Rosemary Focaccia

Sun-Dried Tomato Pesto

salad of mixed greens

assorted cheeses

summer fruits with
Honey-Sweetened Mascarpone

assorted biscotti

An afternoon or evening party, in a garden, on a terrace, or anywhere, suitable for a crowd, casual or elegant—this is the kind of food everyone I know really likes the best. I cooked this exact menu once for about fifty people, doubling and tripling recipes, and then was able to enjoy the party myself. Everything is largely prepared ahead, and it's all delicious at room temperature, so there is a minimum of bother at serving time. The green beans, pasta, and frittata could be served hot or warm, but won't be harmed at all by cooling down.

This is a party that can be easily expanded or scaled down, depending on the numbers, and on your style. As given here, it will feed fifteen to twenty people. If you're having guests with mixed tastes, you can add a platter of prosciutto and melons, some spit-roasted chickens, or a big seafood salad—any of these would fit in perfectly. If it's a gala occasion, a spectacular cake could be added at the end. If it's a smaller group or a less ambitious time, the ten dishes could simply be pruned to six or seven and the home-made focaccia replaced by breads from a good bakery.

It's also a great menu for leftovers. Don't worry about making too much of anything. I just start recombining things, and eat this way for days. The herbed pasta can be put together with leftover chopped tomatoes and other vegetables for a lovely pasta salad. Or drop it into a broth with the white beans for an easy *pasta i fagioli*. Put slices of frittata into split and toasted focaccia with a dab of tomato pesto for a terrific sandwich. And so on.

ROASTED GREEN
BEAN SALAD

2 lbs. thin, tender green beans (like
    haricots verts)
1 head garlic
3 Tbs. green olive oil

salt and pepper to taste
2 large, ripe red tomatoes
a little balsamic vinegar
2 Tbs. chopped fresh basil leaves

Wash and trim the green beans, and separate and peel the cloves of garlic. Reserve one small clove of garlic and toss the remaining garlic and the beans in a bowl with half the olive oil, salt to taste, and a few grinds of black pepper. Spread them evenly over 2 baking sheets and roast them in a 400° oven for about 40 minutes. Stir and turn the beans at least once in the course of roasting them.

The roasting time will vary with the size of the beans. They are done when they have a somewhat wrinkled and blistered look, with light-brown spots here and there. A marvelous toasty fragrance will alert you.

While the beans are roasting, peel the tomatoes and chop them, keeping all their juice. Mince the reserved clove of garlic. Combine the tomatoes, their juice, the garlic, the remaining olive oil, some balsamic vinegar, a little salt and pepper, and the chopped basil. Crush everything together a bit to blend the flavors.

When the beans are ready, transfer them to a big, shallow bowl and pour the tomato dressing over them. Serve hot, warm, or at room temperature.

*This serves 6–8 as a first course, more in a buffet,
but I always wish I made more.*

Variations: I have also served these roasted beans without the tomato dressing, just tossing them with a little additional oil and a few drops of balsamic vinegar. Sometimes I even omit the vinegar. Then they become a finger food, perfect for snacking in the kitchen with cheese crostini and a glass of wine while I finish cooking dinner. (See Roasted Green Beans with Garlic in the Informal Winter Buffet menu.)

TUSCAN WHITE BEANS
with Garlic and Sage

1 lb. small white beans
handful of fresh sage leaves, or
   2 Tbs. dried whole-leaf sage
1 head garlic, separated and peeled

3–4 Tbs. fruity green olive oil
salt
fresh-ground pepper

Soak the beans in cool water for a few hours, or overnight if you have the time. A pinch of soda can be added to the water if it's hard.

Drain the beans and put them in a large, shallow skillet, with enough fresh water to cover them by an inch. Add the sage leaves, the garlic cloves, and a tablespoon of olive oil. Bring the water to a boil, then lower the heat to a gentle simmer.

Allow the beans to simmer this way until they are tender—this may take an hour, or 2, or 3. As always with dried beans, the cooking time varies quite a bit depending on the freshness of the beans.

Do not stir more than 2 or 3 times, and then gently, with a wooden spoon. If the water evaporates too much, carefully add more, always keeping the beans covered. The trick is just to leave the beans alone on that low flame for the right amount of time, so that they are soft to the bite but firm to the eye—you don't want them to fall apart into a mush.

Shortly before they're done, when they are just beginning to be tender, add about 2 teaspoons of salt. When they are soft, and the cooking water has become a savory, sage-and-garlic-perfumed broth, pour beans and broth into a wide, shallow bowl, drizzle with 2–3 tablespoons of the best green olive oil, grind on some black pepper, and serve.

These are delicious as an antipasto, either warm or at room temperature, and also excellent cold in salads. Spoon them over bruschetta for a typical Tuscan dish, or add them to Pasta with Olive Oil and Fresh Herbs for an instant *pasta i fagioli*. And if you have lots of leftovers, these make a great soup; just purée them in a light broth (chicken broth will do if you don't have vegetable broth) with a bit of leftover rice or on their own. Then add a few slivers of any cooked greens and some croutons—delicious.

Serves 6–8 in a small dinner, more in a buffet.

OLIVES AND FETA CHEESE
WITH OREGANO

1 pint cured olives, various kinds   olive oil
1½ lbs. feta cheese, Bulgarian or   fresh oregano
    Greek

optional garnishes: oregano branches or mint sprigs

Choose 2 or 3 types of cured olives. Kalamata olives are very good and quite easily available, so I use them often. I also like to get big green cured olives that you can find in good Mediterranean delis. Tiny black Niçoise olives are a nice addition, but very salty. About a pint of olives altogether will be enough, unless your friends are all Greek.

I use fresh Bulgarian feta cheese, which I prefer to the Greek; the one I get seems a little creamier and less aggressively salty. Ask at your favorite deli which feta is the mildest. If you are buying packaged feta at the supermarket, try the French one. Strictly speaking, it is not really feta, as it is made with sheep's milk rather than goat's milk, but it's very good.

Slice the feta cheese and then break it into large chunks. Arrange the various olives and the feta pieces on a platter, all mixed up, or any way you like. Drizzle a tiny bit of green olive oil on the feta, and scatter chopped fresh oregano over everything.

You can garnish this platter with oregano branches or mint sprigs.

Serves 15–20 in this menu.

Variation: Another nice presentation is to line the platter with rinsed vine leaves and arrange the olives and cheese on top.

PASTA WITH OLIVE OIL
AND FRESH HERBS

This is a nice, easy pasta for warm weather. You can use a variety of different summer herbs, such as basil, Italian flat-leaf parsley, summer savory, thyme, oregano, as well as chives or rosemary in moderation. Use the more assertive herbs sparingly, and follow your nose. The formula here is a combination that I've used and particularly liked. The fragrance of the fresh herbs and olive oil is delightful, and this dish is good at room temperature as well as hot.

½ cup chopped fresh basil
½ cup chopped flat-leaf Italian
    parsley
1 Tbs. chopped fresh oregano

1 Tbs. chopped fresh thyme
¼ cup fruity green olive oil
salt and pepper to taste
1 lb. spaghetti or linguine

garnishes: Parmesan cheese and toasted pine nuts, or slivers of Kalamata olives

optional: 1 small clove garlic, minced

Combine the chopped fresh herbs in a large ceramic bowl with the olive oil and a little salt and pepper. Add the optional minced garlic to the herbs if you want it. Cook the pasta in boiling salted water until it is *al dente,* then drain and immediately toss with the herbs and oil. Correct the seasoning if you need to, and serve.

This is delicious with some coarse-grated Parmesan cheese and a few toasted pine nuts scattered over it. It's also nice with slivers of cured black olives, or some red pepper flakes.

Serves 6–8, more in a buffet.

FRESH-CHOPPED TOMATOES WITH BASIL

During the late summer days, when I pick a big basket of ripe tomatoes almost every day, my favorite way to start dinner is with a bowl of these tomatoes, cut up just a few minutes before they're served, along with some focaccia, goat cheese, and a glass of wine. Sometimes it turns out to be both the starter and the finisher, as we just have another helping and another glass. . . . Make this only if you have great, vine-ripened tomatoes and fresh herbs.

3 lbs. ripe red tomatoes (about 4
    cups chopped)
2–3 Tbs. chopped fresh basil
2 Tbs. chopped flat-leaf parsley

1 clove garlic, minced
2–3 Tbs. fruity green olive oil
1 Tbs. balsamic vinegar
salt and pepper to taste

Wash and trim the tomatoes and cut them into ½-inch dice. Chop the fresh herbs and mix them into the tomatoes along with the garlic, oil, and vinegar. Taste as you mix in some salt and pepper, as tomatoes can vary and some need less salt than others.

These tomatoes get quite soupy with their own juices, especially if you use a naturally juicy variety such as beefsteak, so serve them in little bowls with a good country bread to soak up the marinade. They're perfect spooned over bruschetta—grilled bread brushed with olive oil. They can be served at once, or kept covered at cool room temperature for 1–2 hours. They will keep longer in the refrigerator, but I really hate to put a great vine-ripened tomato into the refrigerator, and would only do it if I feared fermentation, as tomatoes lose both texture and flavor when refrigerated.

Serves 6–8 as an appetizer.

CHARD AND PARSLEY FRITTATA

All of the dark, leafy greens, such as chard or spinach, go well with eggs. The taste of parsley does wonders for them, too, and so does Parmesan cheese. Be sure you use the flat-leafed Italian parsley, which has a much more pronounced flavor than the curly type.

1 medium onion (about a cup, chopped)	4 Tbs. Parmesan cheese
1 clove garlic	1 cup chopped flat-leaf parsley (packed)
1 large potato	fresh-ground pepper
1½ Tbs. olive oil	2½ cups chopped Swiss chard (packed)
1 tsp. salt	1 tsp. cider vinegar
8–9 eggs	

Chop the onion, mince the garlic, and scrub the potato and cut it in ¼-inch dice. Heat the olive oil in a 12-inch skillet, preferably a good non-stick type. Sauté the onion and garlic for a few minutes, then add the diced potato and about ½ teaspoon of salt, and continue cooking over medium heat, stirring often, for about 10 minutes. The vegetables will be starting to brown.

Meanwhile, beat the eggs with the Parmesan cheese, the parsley, the remaining salt, and some pepper, and set aside. Add the chopped chard to the pan, sprinkle it with the cider vinegar, and toss it with the other vegetables until it is thoroughly wilted.

Pour the egg mixture into the vegetable mixture and give it a quick stir to make sure everything is more or less evenly distributed. Adjust the flame until it is very low, cover the pan, and let the frittata cook slowly for about 10–15 minutes, or until the eggs are completely set.

Loosen the frittata gently with a spatula until it slides freely in the pan, then invert it onto a flat lid or platter and slide it back into the pan to brown on the other side, just for a minute or two. Turn it out onto a platter and serve warm or cool, cut into wedges.

Serves 6–8, more if cut in thin wedges for a large antipasto buffet.

MARINATED GRILLED EGGPLANT

3 large purple eggplants (about
  3½–4½ lbs.)
salt
2 cloves garlic
¼ cup olive oil

¼ cup balsamic vinegar
fresh-ground pepper
½ large red onion, very thinly sliced
3 Tbs. slivered fresh basil

Wash the eggplants and cut them crosswise in ½-inch slices. Salt the slices lightly on both sides and leave them on a glass platter or tray for ½–1 hour to release their excess water. Pat the slices dry between paper towels, squeezing gently.

Mince or press the garlic cloves and stir them into the olive oil. Brush the eggplant slices lightly on both sides with the garlic oil, and grill them over hot coals until they are charred in spots and tender throughout.

In a large glass or ceramic dish, arrange half the eggplant slices close together in one layer. Prick them here and there with a fork, sprinkle them with about half the balsamic vinegar, and salt and pepper them lightly. Scatter half the onion slices and half the slivered basil over them. Repeat with the remaining eggplant and other ingredients.

Cover the dish tightly with plastic wrap and leave the eggplant at room temperature for a couple of hours, or in the refrigerator if longer.

Serve cool or at room temperature as a first course or as part of a buffet. This also makes a great sandwich, with a thick slice of ripe summer tomato and some fresh mozzarella, on a coarse country bread.

Serves 6–8, more if served with many dishes.

ROSEMARY FOCACCIA

1 Tbs. dry yeast (1 envelope)
1 cup warm water
pinch of sugar
2 cups unbleached white flour
¾ cup whole wheat flour
1 tsp. salt

3 Tbs. olive oil
2 Tbs. coarsely chopped fresh
   rosemary, or 1 Tbs. dried
3 Tbs. cornmeal
coarse sea salt

Dissolve the yeast in the warm water and sugar. Put the 2 flours in a mixing bowl and begin stirring in the yeast mixture and salt, a little at a time, until you have a soft batter. Stir in 1 tablespoon of the olive oil and half of the chopped rosemary. Then continue adding flour until the dough is too stiff to stir.

Spread the remaining flour on a board, turn the dough out on it, and knead it gently for just a few minutes, working in only enough of the flour to keep it from sticking.

Form the dough into a ball, put it in an oiled bowl, and turn it once. Then cover the bowl with a towel and leave the dough to rise for 30–40 minutes, or until almost doubled. Meanwhile, oil a baking sheet and dust it with the cornmeal.

Punch down the dough and lay it on the board, then roll it into an oval about ¾ inch thick. Do not work the dough a lot at this point. Transfer the focaccia to the prepared baking sheet, cover it with a towel, and leave it to rise for about 30 minutes.

If you like, you can cut shallow crisscross patterns in the top of the focaccia with a sharp serrated knife and pull it apart a little to show the pattern. Or skip the cutting, and use your fingers to dimple it in a random pattern.

Brush the focaccia with the remaining 2 tablespoons of olive oil, sprinkle it with the remaining rosemary and about ½ teaspoon of coarse salt, and bake it in the middle of the oven at 450° for about 18 minutes. It should be turning golden brown on top. Serve the focaccia hot or warm, cut into squares.

This makes the equivalent of 1 small loaf of bread.
It's easy to double this recipe, and I usually do, as my son Teddy
can eat one of these by himself.

Sun-Dried Tomato Pesto (page 318)

HONEY-SWEETENED MASCARPONE

2 cups mascarpone   **6–8 Tbs. honey**

Allow the mascarpone to come to room temperature, then stir it gently with a whisk until it is softened. Drizzle in the honey, and continue whisking slowly until smooth. Once the honey is incorporated, the mascarpone can be served at once, or cooled again.

Serve the sweetened mascarpone in small portions alongside summer fruits such as berries, sliced peaches, or figs.

Makes about 2½ cups.

A CELEBRATION
DINNER

Bruschetta
with Caramelized Fennel and Onion

Salad of Arugula and Persimmons
with Walnuts and Roquefort Cheese

Eggplant Pancakes
in Sweet Red Pepper Purée

Rosemary Sorbet

Grilled Polenta
with Grilled Fresh Porcini

Warm Chocolate Cakes
with Crème Anglaise and Boysenberry Sauce

Visiting dignitaries? Did someone finally get married?
Publish a great book? Win the Nobel prize? Just get elected
president? Finish a dissertation? Actually, if I can get fresh
porcini, that's reason enough to have a party. I remember traveling
in northern Italy in the autumn, and seeing the big baskets
full of giant fresh porcini proudly displayed in the entrances of
restaurants. No need to look at the menu. We'd select our porcini
and have them simply grilled, with a little garlic and parsley.
Often they were accompanied by some polenta. I have never
found a better way to have porcini.

In this meal, rustic country dishes alternate
with more refined ones, but the flavors are all assertive,
pungent, earthy, and interesting.

First the taste of caramelized fennel with onion—
aromatic and a little mysterious. Then peppery arugula with
one of my favorite fruits, the sweet but crisp Fuyu persimmon,
in my favorite autumn salad. The Eggplant Pancakes have
a smoky delicacy, punctuated by salty feta cheese and Greek olives.
Rosemary Sorbet perfectly cools and cleanses the palate, and
will amaze your guests with its subtle perfume and flavor. And
it leaves you hungry again, ready for the marvelous, woodsy
porcini. The dessert is extravagant, and you must wait a while
for it, as it is baked at the last minute.

This is a great dinner for red wines, from beginning to end.

BRUSCHETTA WITH CARAMELIZED FENNEL AND ONION

4–5 large yellow onions (6 cups
    sliced)
4–5 large, trimmed white fennel
    bulbs (6 cups sliced)
2 Tbs. olive oil
1 Tbs. butter

salt to taste
½ cup slivered Kalamata olives
⅓–½ cup white wine, to taste
fresh-ground black pepper to taste
1 loaf crusty, coarse-textured Italian
    bread

optional garnish: sprigs of watercress

Peel the onions, quarter them lengthwise, and slice them thickly. Trim and clean the fennel bulbs and slice them to a similar size.

In a heavy-bottomed non-stick pan, heat the olive oil and butter. Add the onion and fennel, salt it lightly, and cook over medium heat, stirring often, until the vegetables are a beautiful golden brown. This may take 45 minutes to 1 hour.

Stir in the slivers of Kalamata olives and the white wine. Continue stirring until the wine is completely absorbed. Taste and correct the seasoning with salt or fresh-ground black pepper if needed.

Meanwhile, slice the bread about ½ inch thick. If it's a large loaf, cut the slices down to about 3 by 2 inches. Toast the slices in a 400° oven or on a grill over hot coals until they are crisp and golden brown on both sides. Brush them lightly with olive oil.

Put 2 toasts on each plate and spoon the hot fennel and onion mixture over them. Garnish the plates with sprigs of watercress if desired, and serve at once.

I find the taste of caramelized fennel and onion intoxicating. It can be varied with a shaving of Parmesan cheese, or you can up the ante on the fennel by toasting some fennel seeds, crushing them, and stirring them in. This dish is sensational with a glass of red wine.

Serves 8–10.

SALAD OF ARUGULA
AND PERSIMMONS
with Walnuts and Roquefort Cheese

In California, persimmons are plentiful in the fall and early winter, and recipes for persimmon cookies, persimmon puddings, and persimmon breads abound in our Junior League cookbooks. Until recently, only Hachiya persimmons were commonly found; they're the ones which have to be completely soft and jelly-like before they can be eaten. At the moment when they look ready for the compost—that's when you eat them or bake the cookies.

But now Fuyu persimmons have taken the markets by storm. They are eaten while hard and crisp, like apples. Their sweetness is delightful in a salad next to the peppery snap of arugula and watercress.

If Fuyu persimmons are not available to you, you can use pears that are still just slightly firm, or one of the varieties of crisp Asian pears that are now becoming much more available.

3 good-sized bunches of arugula (about 1½ quarts, torn)
1 small head radicchio
1 small bunch watercress
2 medium Fuyu persimmons
½ cup thinly sliced sweet onion (like Maui or Texas Trophies)

½ medium red bell pepper
1 small sweet yellow pepper
½ lb. Roquefort cheese
½ cup walnut pieces
3–4 Tbs. green olive oil
2–3 Tbs. balsamic vinegar
salt and pepper to taste

optional: ⅓–½ cup raisins

Wash the arugula, radicchio, and watercress, spin them dry in a salad spinner, and tear into manageable pieces. Peel and quarter the persimmons, cut out the cores, and slice them thinly crosswise. Quarter and very thinly slice the onion and the red bell pepper. Cut the yellow pepper into thin rings, trimming out the ribs. Break the Roquefort cheese into little chunks.

Combine all the vegetables, fruits, cheese, and nuts in a large bowl. Drizzle on the olive oil and toss gently until every leaf glistens. Add a splash of balsamic vinegar and a little salt and pepper, toss again, and serve.

Makes 8 generous salads, or 10–12 small ones.

EGGPLANT PANCAKES
in Sweet Red Pepper Purée

about 4 lbs. eggplant (3 large)
2 Tbs. olive oil
salt
1 cup finely chopped onion
3 large cloves garlic, minced
3 large eggs
¼ cup flour
pinch of dried oregano

fresh-ground pepper
additional olive oil for frying
Sweet Red Pepper Purée (recipe
   follows)
16 Kalamata olives, sliced off of
   their pits
½ lb. feta cheese, crumbled

garnish: fresh mint sprigs

Pierce the eggplants in several places with a fork, brush them with a bit of olive oil, and roast them on baking sheets in a 400° oven for about an hour, or until they are completely soft and collapsing. Cut them open, let them cool a bit, then carefully remove and discard any pockets of dark seeds. Scoop out the pale flesh, toss it in a bowl with about a teaspoon of salt, and leave it in a colander to drain for an hour or more. Transfer the eggplant to a board, chop it coarsely, then put it in a large mixing bowl.

In a small, heavy non-stick skillet, sauté the onion and garlic in a tablespoon of olive oil until soft and translucent. Whisk together the eggs and the flour. Add the onion mixture, the egg mixture, and the oregano to the eggplant, and mix thoroughly. Add more salt and some fresh-ground pepper to taste.

Brush a large, heavy-bottomed non-stick skillet with olive oil and heat it over a medium flame. Place heaping tablespoonfuls of the eggplant batter evenly in the skillet, shaping them into 3-inch pancakes. Cook the pancakes until they are lightly colored on both sides, about 7–8 minutes total, and turn them very carefully.

Spoon a little warm Sweet Red Pepper Purée on each plate, and place 2–3 pancakes on top of it. Scatter some sliced olives and crumbled feta over the pancakes, and garnish with mint sprigs.

This serves 8 generously.

SWEET RED PEPPER PURÉE

2 cups chopped sweet onions
1 Tbs. olive oil
salt
2 cups roasted and peeled sweet red
    peppers (page 14)

3 Tbs. cider vinegar, more to taste
3 Tbs. brown sugar, more to taste

In a heavy-bottomed non-stick skillet, cook the onions in the olive oil over low heat until they are a light-golden color. Salt lightly. In a blender or food processor, combine the caramelized onions, the peppers, the vinegar, and the sugar, and process until you have a smooth purée. Add salt to taste, and correct the sweet-sour balance with a little more vinegar or sugar if needed.

Warm the sauce gently before serving.

Makes about 1½ pints of sauce.

ROSEMARY SORBET

rosemary syrup:
1 cup sugar
2½ cups water

⅓ cup chopped fresh rosemary
    leaves

to make the sorbet:
2½ cups rosemary syrup
2 cups good white Riesling

3–4 Tbs. fresh lemon juice, strained

Dissolve the sugar in the water, add the rosemary, and bring to a boil in a stainless steel or enamel pot. Lower the heat and simmer for 5 minutes. Cool and allow to steep for at least several hours, or overnight. Strain the syrup through a very fine sieve.

Combine 2½ cups of cooled rosemary syrup with the wine and taste. Add the lemon juice a bit at a time, stirring and tasting as you go, until there's enough of an acidic little bite to make the mixture interesting. This sorbet is not meant to be overly sweet, and how much lemon juice you use will depend on how sour the lemons are, and how fruity or dry the wine.

Chill the mixture, and then freeze it in an ice cream maker, according to manufacturer's directions.

This should be served in small scoops. Chill the sorbet glasses first.

Makes about a quart of sorbet.

GRILLED POLENTA WITH GRILLED FRESH PORCINI

1 recipe Simple Polenta (page 230)
2–3 lbs. fresh porcini (*Boletus edulus*)
½ cup fruity olive oil

2 cloves garlic, minced
½ cup flat-leaf Italian parsley, finely chopped
salt and pepper to taste

Prepare the polenta according to directions, using 2¼ cups of cornmeal instead of 2, and when it is cooked pour it into 2 shallow ceramic or glass tart dishes, quickly smoothing the top. It should be no more than ¾ inch thick. Allow the polenta to cool until it is completely firm. Then turn it out of its dishes onto a board and cut it into wedges.

Clean the porcini thoroughly, trimming away any soft spots and the hard bottoms of the stems. Separate the stems from the caps, and slice the stems lengthwise once or twice, depending on their thickness.

Whisk together the olive oil, minced garlic, and half of the parsley, and brush this mixture over both sides of the porcini. Salt and pepper them lightly.

Brush the polenta wedges with olive oil and grill them over hot coals until they are golden brown and hot through—about 4–6 minutes on each side.

Grill the porcini over the coals alongside the polenta if they are large. If they are small and you fear that they will drop into the coals, you can use one of the wire-mesh racks that are used to grill flaky fish or small shrimp, or you can put them under a hot broiler. They'll need 3–4 minutes on a side, depending on how thick they are, and should be golden brown on the outside, tender and juicy on the inside.

Serve the polenta wedges and porcini at once, sprinkled with the remaining chopped parsley.

Serves 8.

WARM CHOCOLATE CAKES

with Crème Anglaise and Boysenberry Sauce

This is a lovely dessert for a special occasion. The little cakes are served warm, and the insides remain soft, like puddings, spilling out when the cakes are cut with a fork. Use only the very best chocolate for these.

6 oz. best-quality semi-sweet
    chocolate
6 oz. unsalted butter (12 Tbs.)
5 eggs, at room temperature

½ cup sugar
pinch of salt
6 Tbs. flour

garnishes: powdered sugar
          Boysenberry Sauce (recipe follows)
          fresh berries
          whipped cream or Crème Anglaise

Prepare 8 5-oz. baking dishes; I like to use the ordinary little Pyrex dishes with the slightly rounded bottoms, the kind you can buy in any supermarket, but I've also used small soufflé dishes. Butter the dishes well, then dust them with flour.

In a heavy-bottomed saucepan, melt together the chocolate and the butter over low heat, stirring often, until you have a perfectly smooth sauce. In a mixing bowl, beat the eggs with the sugar and a little pinch of salt for about 6–8 minutes, or until they are thick and creamy. Beat in the flour, a tablespoon at a time, then slowly beat in the melted chocolate and butter.

Pour the batter into the 8 prepared baking dishes. Bake the cakes in a preheated 325° oven for 11–12 minutes. The edges of the cakes will be firm, and the centers will still look soft, and tremble slightly when you tap the edge of the dish.

While the cakes are baking, prepare the plates on which you will serve them, and any garnishes. As soon as the cakes are ready, invert them onto large dessert plates and lift off the baking dishes. Dust the cakes lightly with powdered sugar, and spoon a little Boysenberry Sauce around each one. Garnish with fresh berries if you like.

Serve the cakes as soon as possible after removing them from the oven. Pass whipped cream or Crème Anglaise separately.

Serves 8.

BOYSENBERRY SAUCE

2 pints fresh boysenberries   ½ cup sugar
spring water   lemon juice if needed

Combine the clean boysenberries in a non-reactive saucepan with about ½ cup of spring water and about ½ cup of sugar. Simmer them, stirring, for about 5 minutes. Taste. If they are sour, add a little more sugar. If they are too sweet, add a squirt of lemon juice, then simmer again for a few minutes. If the liquid seems too thick, add a bit more water; it all depends on the juiciness of the berries.

Makes about 4 cups of sauce.

Crème Anglaise (page 70)

A SMALL WINE TASTING

With the White Wines

crostini with *Lima Bean Purée*

olives

Salad of Endive, Fennel, Roquefort, and Celery

Tomato and Onion Focaccia

goat cheese

With the Red Wines

Toasted Walnuts with Rosemary and Sage

Wild Mushroom Pâté with baguettes

Bocconcini di Parma

cheese tray: Blue Castello, Camembert

pastries

fresh fruit

nougats

coffee

A wine tasting can be a very interesting and pleasant way to have a little party. I'm not talking about a professional wine tasting, in which ratings are created which spell success or doom for particular vintages, but rather a tasting for fun-loving oenophiles, in which we learn a little something that we didn't know before, and a good time is had by all. In other words, we drink the wine, we don't spit it out.

This type of wine tasting can take several forms. A vertical tasting is a specific comparison of one wine through several vintages. Or you can compare the same kind of wine from one year but different vineyards.

On the other hand, we once had a tasting to introduce a few eager amateurs to some wines that they normally had little opportunity to taste, from several of the greatest wine regions of the world.

After a couple of fine California Chardonnays to begin with, we went to the serious reds: a Bordeaux, a Burgundy, a California Cabernet Sauvignon, and an Italian wine. These were the wines we drank that evening.

white wines
1990 Stony Hill Napa Valley Chardonnay
1990 Kistler Dutton Ranch Chardonnay (Sonoma Valley)

red wines
1982 Chateau Léoville-Lascases
1988 Chamertin-Clos-de-Béze, Jadot
1986 Dunn Howell Mountain Cabernet Sauvignon
1985 Brunello di Montalcino, Poggio Antico

My mission was to provide some food that would accompany but not overwhelm the wines. Bread and cheese instantly came to mind, but I wanted some variety, and when the tasting was all done I wanted it to add up to a meal.

For the white wines, I arranged a little picnic of my favorite tastes from Italy and Provence—a wine-friendly salad, crostini, a focaccia, and some cheese.

With the red wines, my choices were traditional. Toasted walnuts, wild mushrooms, and soft-ripened cheeses are flavors that will always be embraced by red wine. The bocconcini, crepes rolled around a delicate filling, were the only food served hot.

After the wines, we had a few sweet and refreshing nibbles with coffee, and everyone went to bed happy in the wee hours.

LIMA BEAN PURÉE

This garlicky purée is nice to have on crostini, with a drizzle of green olive oil and a sprinkle of chopped parsley. It's very light, and makes a nice change from the somewhat richer tapenades, pestos, and cheeses that are often served on toast or crackers with an apéritif. A few cured olives alongside are perfect.

1 lb. dry lima beans
pinch of baking soda
salt
¼ cup olive oil
5 cloves garlic, chopped

2 tsp. chopped fresh rosemary leaves
pinch of red pepper flakes
1–2 Tbs. fresh lemon juice
fresh-ground black pepper to taste

garnishes: additional olive oil
chopped flat-leaf parsley

Soak the lima beans overnight in plenty of water with a pinch of baking soda in it. Drain them, rinse them, and put them in a heavy-bottomed pot with water to cover by at least 2 inches. Bring the water to a boil, then lower the heat and simmer the beans for at least an hour, and perhaps longer, until they are perfectly tender.

Add more water, if necessary, to keep the beans just covered. Toward the end of the cooking time, add about a teaspoon of salt, or more to taste.

In a small skillet, combine 1 tablespoon of the olive oil, about a third of the garlic, the chopped rosemary, and the red pepper flakes. Warm the oil and herbs on medium heat, stirring constantly, for about 2 minutes.

Drain the cooked lima beans, reserving the liquid. Combine them in a food processor or blender with ½ cup of their cooking liquid and the warm oil with herbs, and purée. Add the remaining minced garlic, the unheated olive oil, a tablespoon of lemon juice, and salt and pepper to your taste, and process again until everything is thoroughly blended. Taste, and correct the seasoning with a touch more salt or lemon juice if you like. If the purée seems too thick, add a little more of the cooking liquid. It should be light, but hold a shape.

Allow the purée to cool. Spread it in a pretty, shallow bowl, drizzle some fruity olive oil on top, and sprinkle with chopped parsley. Serve the purée with toasted or grilled bread.

Makes about 5 cups.

Leftovers: Once I made this purée to serve among several other dishes, and had a lot of it left over the next day. Having no time to cook dinner, I combined the purée with a few cups of ready vegetable broth and some leftover cooked tomatoes. I put half a pound of radiatori (any chunky pasta would do) in a pot to boil, and when the pasta was barely cooked I added it to the soup. It was a delicious *pasta i fagioli.* With a little cheese on top and a slice of bread, it made a great 10-minute supper.

SALAD OF ENDIVE, FENNEL, ROQUEFORT, AND CELERY

This is the right salad to serve in a meal when you'd like to keep enjoying your wine with every bite. Salads usually fight with the wine, but this one, enriched with a bit of Roquefort cheese and some toasted almonds, and with virtually no acid in the dressing, is very agreeable.

1½ cups thinly sliced fennel bulb
   (2 medium bulbs)
3 cups sliced Belgian endives
1½ cups thinly sliced celery
1 cup shredded radicchio
3 oz. Roquefort cheese

fruity green olive oil
a few drops balsamic vinegar
salt to taste
⅔ cup coarsely chopped toasted
   almonds (with skins)

Combine the fennel, endive, celery, and radicchio in a large bowl. Break the Roquefort cheese into lumps and scatter them over the salad.

Drizzle on a little green olive oil and toss everything together. The vegetables should be barely glistening with oil, not dripping, and the cheese must be dispersed through the salad. Add a few drops of balsamic vinegar, and a dash of salt if you feel it's needed, and toss again.

Scatter the chopped toasted almonds over the salad and serve.

Serves 6–8.

TOMATO AND ONION FOCACCIA

Use a good, home-made tomato sauce for this, cooked down until it's thick. This is delicious with tapenade and a glass of wine.

3 Tbs. fruity green olive oil
2 large yellow onions, coarsely
    chopped
1–1½ tsp. salt
1¼ cups warm water

1 tsp. dry yeast
1 tsp. sugar
4½ cups white flour
½ cup thick, puréed tomato sauce

Heat 2 tablespoons of the olive oil in a non-stick pan and cook the chopped onions in it, with a sprinkle of salt. Stir them often over a medium flame until they are limp and golden. Allow them to cool slightly.

Meanwhile, put the warm water in a large mixing bowl and sprinkle the yeast over it. Stir in the sugar and leave the mixture in a warm place for a few minutes, until it begins to froth and foam. Stir in the salt and about 2½ cups of flour, making a soft sponge. Leave the sponge to rise, covered with a kitchen towel, for about 30 minutes.

Stir down the sponge and add the tomato sauce and the cooked onions. Stir in more flour, until the dough is too stiff to be stirred with a spoon.

Turn the dough out onto a heavily floured board and begin kneading in as much of the remaining flour as is necessary. Knead gently until the dough is smooth and beginning to pull back. It should still be soft.

Form the dough into a ball. Keeping the board well floured and turning the dough once or twice, roll it out to a large oval, about an inch thick. Lightly oil a baking sheet, preferably one with edges, and lay the loaf on it. Poke dimples in the bread with your fingers if you like. Cover the dough and let it rise about 40 minutes, or until it is almost doubled in bulk.

Brush the top of the bread very gently with the remaining olive oil, and bake the focaccia in a preheated 400° oven for about 35 minutes.

Remove it from the pan with the help of a large spatula and transfer it to a wire rack to cool slightly, then cut it in squares to serve.

Makes 1 large loaf.

TOASTED WALNUTS WITH ROSEMARY AND SAGE

1 Tbs. olive oil
1 Tbs. butter
2 Tbs. finely chopped fresh
    rosemary leaves

½ tsp. rubbed sage
1 tsp. sweet paprika
¾ tsp. salt
12 oz. walnut halves, or large pieces

Heat the oil and butter together in a large skillet. Stir in the herbs and salt. Add the walnuts and toss them in the herb mixture until they are evenly coated.

Spread the walnuts out on a baking sheet and toast them in a 300° oven for 20–30 minutes, stirring and turning them once or twice. They should be fragrant and somewhat darker in color, but never blackened.

Allow them to cool to room temperature, then bite into one to make sure they are crisp. If not, they need a few more minutes in the oven.

These are delicious to nibble with an apéritif, or with cheese and a great glass of red wine at the end of a meal.

Makes about 2½ cups.

WILD MUSHROOM PÂTÉ

1 oz. dried porcini (*Boletus edulus*)
1 cup vegetable broth
1 Tbs. olive oil
1½ Tbs. butter
¾ cup chopped shallots
2 large onions, chopped
salt and pepper to taste
1¼ lbs. fresh wild mushrooms—you
    can use oyster mushrooms, field
    mushrooms, or a mix of shiitakes
    and champignons if wild ones
    are scarce

¼ tsp. thyme
pinch of cayenne
½ cup port wine
½ cup dry red wine
2 cups day-old bread, torn into
    small pieces
¼ cup chopped parsley

morel

Pour boiling water over the dried porcini and let them soak for about 30 minutes. Drain them, reserving the water, and wash them well. Strain the water through a paper filter to eliminate all the grit and add it to the vegetable broth. You will have 1½ to 2 cups of broth altogether. Chop the porcini.

Heat the oil and butter in a large non-stick sauté pan, and sauté the shallots and onions in it with a bit of salt until they are golden brown.

Wash and chop all the fresh mushrooms, and add them to the caramelized onions along with the chopped porcini, thyme, cayenne, and a little more salt and some pepper. Continue cooking, stirring occasionally, while the mushrooms release their water and the water cooks away. Stir more frequently as they begin to color.

When the mushrooms are browning and beginning to stick to the pan, pour in the port wine to deglaze it. When that has cooked away, repeat with the dry red wine.

Add the torn bread, the chopped parsley, and about a cup of the vegetable broth. Lower the heat and keep stirring as the bread softens and absorbs the liquid. Add a little more broth if needed. The pâté mixture should be thick but moist.

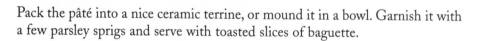

Remove the mixture from the heat and allow it to cool somewhat, then put it all through the medium blade of the food mill. If you want a less chunky texture, you could put some of it through the fine blade.

shiitake

Pack the pâté into a nice ceramic terrine, or mound it in a bowl. Garnish it with a few parsley sprigs and serve with toasted slices of baguette.

Makes about 3 cups.

BOCCONCINI DI PARMA

Traditional bocconcini are made with no onion or parsley, just cheese, eggs, and butter. I like this variation, and another one I made once, in which I added chopped truffles to the cheese mixture instead of onions. All of them are fantastic.

1 recipe of basic crepes (page 21)
2½ lbs. fresh ricotta cheese (about 5 cups)
1½ cups finely chopped onion
7 Tbs. softened butter
4 whole eggs

2 cups grated Parmesan cheese
salt and finely ground black pepper, if needed
3 Tbs. finely chopped flat-leaf parsley

Make the crepes ahead of time and have them ready, at room temperature.

Drain the ricotta cheese for about 30 minutes in a colander lined with a double thickness of cheesecloth. While it's draining, sauté the finely chopped onion in 2 tablespoons of the butter, stirring often, until it is golden. Beat the eggs lightly. Combine in a bowl the drained ricotta, eggs, Parmesan cheese, sautéed onion, and the remaining 5 tablespoons of softened butter. Mix everything together well, then taste and add salt and finely ground black pepper to taste. Stir in the chopped parsley.

Lay one crepe at a time on a board and spread about 3 heaping tablespoons of filling down the middle of it. Roll the crepe up around the filling, making a cylinder. Lay the rolled crepes, seam side down, on a platter, cover with plastic wrap, and chill in the refrigerator for at least 30 minutes.

Butter a large gratin dish, or a 9-by-13-inch baking dish. Take the chilled, rolled crepes and lay them on a board. With a very sharp knife, cut each crepe into 4 even pieces. Arrange the cut crepes in the buttered gratin dish, standing up side-by-side, and close together.

Bake the bocconcini for about 25 minutes at 375°, and serve hot.

Serves 8–10.

A FORMAL DINNER PARTY

for late summer

crostini with
Mushroom Tapenade

Tomato and Provolone Tart

*Cantaloupe and Nectarine Soup
with Raspberry Purée*

*Salad with Wheat Pilaf
and Red Grapes*

*Sweet Corn Soufflé
with Tomato and Garlic Fondue*

Chocolate and Chile Torte

Orange and Mango Sorbet

coffee

This meal captures the voluptuous feeling of summer for me.
It starts with a taste of salty Provençal olives, ripe tomatoes, strong
cheese—and a glass of cold white wine. Already I want to be
outside, in soft evening air.

Combining the formality of a five-course dinner with a
relaxed outdoor setting has been refined to an art in the south of
France, and you can do it too. Set a table somewhere on a balcony
or in a garden, with white linen and your best china. Put wild
flowers in a jug next to crystal glasses. Then let this dinner unfold
in its leisurely pace through the evening and into the summer night.

The appetizers are finger food, and pungent tastes
like tapenade are perfect with a slightly fruity champagne apéritif.
The cooling fruit soup, which is the first sit-down course, is
beautiful as well as delicious: you can paint a picture in each bowl,
placing dots and spirals of raspberry purée on the pale orange
of cantaloupes and nectarines. It's a delightful thing to come from
apéritifs to the table and find these soup-paintings. The
salad that follows, with a chewy, nutty pilaf mounded on
greens, is hearty without being heavy.

The only hot course in this meal is a puffy corn soufflé
with tomato and garlic fondue, the essence of summer garden
flavors. To have the hot soufflé coming out of the oven at exactly
the right moment, put it in just as you're sitting down to eat soup.
You can linger comfortably over two courses that have been
prepared ahead, then serve the soufflé in its perfection.

A grand dessert ends this dinner. Some people accuse
me of being unable to serve a meal without some chile in it
somewhere. This is not true—but I did find a way to bring some
in here, in the Chocolate and Chile Torte. Don't be afraid to try
this. It's no spicier than a good gingerbread, and a scoop of
Orange and Mango Sorbet is heavenly alongside it. End a
summer celebration with little fireworks in your mouth.

MUSHROOM TAPENADE

A variety of mushrooms lends an earthy richness to the familiar pungency of tapenade. Serve this with thin slices of baguette, toasted crisp. It's delicious with a fruity wine or your favorite apéritif.

½ lb. champignon mushrooms
¼ lb. shiitake mushrooms
¼ lb. oyster mushrooms
3 Tbs. olive oil
½ head garlic, peeled and chopped
1 tsp. dried thyme
pinch of dried oregano

pinch of cayenne
¼ tsp. salt
fresh-ground black pepper
⅔ cup dry red wine
½ cup chopped flat-leaf parsley
½ cup sliced Kalamata olives
2 Tbs. fresh lemon juice

optional garnishes: additional olive oil
parsley leaves
additional olives

Clean and chop all the mushrooms. Heat 2 tablespoons of olive oil in a non-stick skillet, add the garlic, and stir it for about a minute. Add the mushrooms, thyme, oregano, cayenne, salt, and pepper, and stir over high heat until the mushrooms release their liquid and it begins to reduce. Add the wine, and continue to stir frequently. Cook the mixture down until it sizzles in the pan and the mushrooms begin to color.

Combine the mushroom mixture in the food processor with the parsley, olives, lemon juice, and the remaining olive oil. Pulse for 1–2 seconds at a time until it is chopped to your taste. I like it to be spreadable, but not mushy.

Serve the tapenade in a shallow bowl, with a basket of crostini—crisply toasted or grilled baguette slices. If you like, you can smooth the top, drizzle on some more green olive oil, and garnish with parsley leaves and whole olives.

Makes about 2 cups.

TOMATO AND PROVOLONE TART

This tart is made with the same kind of cream cheese pastry I've used for years to make pierogi. It's delicious, and a slightly guilty pleasure. The mustard marries the tastes of the tomatoes and the provolone cheese in an unexpected and delightful way. Be sure to get real Italian provolone cheese, as it's quite different from the bland domestic version.

pastry dough:
½ lb. butter
½ lb. cream cheese
¾ tsp. salt
1 tsp. crushed dried thyme or
    rosemary

2 cups white flour, more for rolling
    out
3 Tbs. cold white wine

topping:
1 Tbs. olive oil
3 Tbs. Dijon mustard
4–5 ripe red tomatoes (2 lbs.), thinly
    sliced

salt as needed
4 oz. grated provolone cheese
3 Tbs. thinly sliced fresh basil leaves
fresh-ground pepper

Cut the butter and cream cheese into chunks and combine them in the food processor with the salt, thyme or rosemary, and flour. Blend until the mixture has a dry and crumbly look. Sprinkle in the white wine and blend again until the pastry forms and holds together. Shape the pastry into a thick rectangle, wrap it well, and chill it in the refrigerator for an hour.

On a lightly floured board, roll the pastry out to a 14-by-18-inch rectangle, about ¼ inch thick. Brush the olive oil onto a 12-by-16-inch cookie sheet with edges. Fit the pastry into the pan, folding it up against the sides and trimming away the excess.

Prick the pastry here and there with a fork, then bake it in a 375° oven for 25 minutes, or until light golden brown. Let it cool slightly. Brush the pastry evenly with the mustard. Arrange the tomato slices over the mustard. Sprinkle the tomatoes with a touch of salt and the grated provolone, and finally the sliced basil leaves. Grind on a little black pepper.

Bake the tart, again at 375°, for about 20 minutes, or until the cheese is bubbling. Let the tart cool for a few minutes only, then cut it into 2-inch squares while it is still warm.

Serves 10–12 as a first course, 20 as part of a buffet.

Note: Leftovers are very popular, and especially tasty when popped into the toaster oven for a moment first.

CANTALOUPE
AND NECTARINE SOUP
with Raspberry Purée

4 lbs. cantaloupe (2 medium
   melons, 4 cups cubed flesh)
2 lbs. nectarines (2½ cups sliced)
5–7 Tbs. lemon juice
3–4 Tbs. honey

1½ cups plain yogurt
2 Tbs. chopped fresh mint leaves
1 pint raspberries
2–3 Tbs. sugar

Choose the fruit with great care. Use only sweet, intensely flavorful cantaloupes, and ripe, juicy nectarines. There is nothing here to obscure the flavor of the fruit, only a few tweaks to heighten it.

Peel and seed the cantaloupes and cut the flesh in cubes. You should have about 4 cups. Peel and slice the nectarines. You should have about 2½ cups. Purée all the fruit, with 5 tablespoons of fresh lemon juice, 3 tablespoons of honey, and the yogurt, until it is entirely smooth.

Taste the mixture and stir in a little more lemon juice or a little more honey—or both—until you have just the right sweet-tart balance. You must do this by taste; all fruit varies in sugar content, and lemons vary widely in acidity. When it tastes just fabulous, stir in the chopped mint and refrigerate the soup in a covered container for several hours.

Purée the raspberries and force the purée through a fine sieve to eliminate the seeds. Add a little sugar and stir until it's dissolved. Chill the sweetened purée.

Serve the soup in chilled bowls, and drizzle patterns of raspberry purée in each one.

Serves 8.

Salad with Wheat Pilaf and Red Grapes (page 284)

SWEET CORN SOUFFLÉ

3 Tbs. + 2 tsp. butter
1 large onion, chopped
salt
1 cup milk
2 cups fresh sweet corn kernels
    (5–6 ears)
¼ cup white flour
4 egg yolks

6 egg whites
⅓ cup thinly sliced green onions
4 oz. aged cheddar cheese, cut in
    ¼-inch cubes
pinch of cayenne
black pepper to taste
pinch of cream of tartar

garnish: Tomato and Garlic Fondue (recipe follows)

Melt 2 teaspoons of butter in a small non-stick skillet and sauté the chopped onion in it, with a sprinkle of salt, until it begins to color. Remove the onion and set it aside.

Heat the milk just to scalding point. In a blender, purée half the corn kernels with the hot milk.

Melt 3 tablespoons of butter in a heavy-bottomed saucepan, and stir the flour into it. Keep stirring with a wooden spoon over medium heat until the roux is golden and foaming, about 2–3 minutes. Then whisk in the hot milk and corn purée. Lower the heat and continue stirring with the whisk until the sauce thickens.

Remove the sauce from the heat and whisk in the egg yolks, one at a time. Return the saucepan to a very low flame and keep stirring steadily for about 2 more minutes. The egg whites, meanwhile, should be left in a bowl to warm to room temperature.

Allow the mixture to cool slightly, then stir in half the sautéed onions, the sliced green onions, the cubed cheese, a pinch of cayenne, the remaining corn kernels, and some salt and pepper to taste. (At this point, the soufflé mixture could be covered and held for several hours in the refrigerator. Allow it to return to room temperature before proceeding.)

Prepare an 8-cup soufflé dish by forming a collar out of aluminum foil or heavy brown paper and tying it around the dish with strong twine. The collar should extend about 2 inches above the rim of the soufflé dish. Butter the dish and the inside of the collar. Preheat the oven to 425°.

Beat the egg whites with a pinch of cream of tartar and a little salt until they hold stiff peaks. Stir about a third of the beaten whites into the corn mixture to lighten it, then gently fold in the remainder. Don't overmix.

Pile the soufflé mixture into the prepared dish, and sprinkle the remaining sautéed onions over the top. Bake the soufflé in the center of the oven for 25 minutes. It should be crusty and brown on top, but wiggle slightly when moved. The inside will still be creamy and slightly runny. Serve it at once, and scoop out some of the crusty part and some of the saucy inside for each serving. Garnish each plate with a generous spoonful of Tomato and Garlic Fondue.

Serves 6–8.

TOMATO AND GARLIC FONDUE

This is so basic that you almost can't even call it a sauce. It's the perfect little condiment for a lot of things, redolent of garlic and intense tomato flavor.

4–5 large, very red tomatoes	2 Tbs. fruity green olive oil
6 cloves garlic, peeled and chopped	salt to taste

Scald the tomatoes, peel and core them, and trim them, and cut them in wedges or large chunks.

Sauté the minced garlic in the olive oil until it barely begins to turn color. Add the tomato chunks with all their juice, and a little salt, and cook until the juices are reduced and the tomatoes are saucy rather than soupy. The texture will vary with the variety of tomatoes, but they should melt into a pleasant softness without completely losing their identity.

Makes about 2 cups.

CHOCOLATE AND CHILE TORTE

Mole Poblano, the famous chile and chocolate sauce of Mexico, combines those two essentially American flavors, and numerous other spices, with a strong emphasis on the chile. In this wonderful cake, the ratio is reversed, and Pasilla Chile Paste adds a subtle kick to the rich chocolate flavor. The effect is something like that of a true gingerbread, sweet but genuinely spicy. If you don't tell people what it is, they never guess.

butter and flour for cake pan
1 cup toasted almonds, with skins
⅓ cup brown sugar
2 Tbs. ground cinnamon
¼ tsp. ground cloves
2 tsp. anise seeds, crushed in a
　mortar
½ tsp. salt
9 oz. dark (semi-sweet) chocolate

3 Tbs. thick Pasilla Chile Paste
　(recipe follows)
4 egg yolks
5 egg whites, at room temperature
½ cup granulated white sugar
2 Tbs. unsalted butter
2 Tbs. cream
1 Tbs. light corn syrup

Butter a 9-inch springform cake pan, and line the bottom with a circle of buttered wax paper. Dust the pan with flour, tapping out the excess.

In the container of the food processor, fitted with the steel blade, blend together the almonds, brown sugar, spices, and salt until the texture resembles cornmeal. Add 5 ounces of the chocolate, broken into bits, and blend again until the chocolate is finely ground. Add the chile paste and the 4 egg yolks and pulse briefly, then scrape the mixture out into an ample bowl.

In a separate bowl, beat the egg whites with a pinch of salt until they hold soft peaks. Gradually beat in the granulated sugar and continue beating until the whites hold stiff peaks.

Stir about a third of this meringue thoroughly into the chocolate mixture to lighten it, then carefully fold in the remainder. Keep folding gently just until there are no large streaks of egg white left.

Pour the batter into the prepared pan, smooth the top with a spatula, and bake the torte in the center of a preheated 325° oven for 50–55 minutes, or until it tests done. Let the torte cool a while in the pan, then remove it, invert it onto a wire rack, and let it finish cooling.

In a double boiler or a steel bowl set over a pot of simmering water, melt the remaining 4 ounces of chocolate with the butter, cream, and corn syrup. Stir until completely smooth. Let this glaze cool until it is medium-warm.

Set the torte, on its rack, over a large platter or a sheet of wax paper, and pour the glaze over it. Smooth the glaze with a spatula and let it drizzle down the sides. It thickens as it cools, so you can adjust the look to your liking.

Transfer the torte carefully to a beautiful serving platter, and allow it to stand at cool room temperature for 2–3 hours. The glaze should set and remain glossy.

Serve each slice of torte accompanied by a scoop of Orange and Mango Sorbet, or some other refreshing fruit ice.

This is a moist cake, and keeps well for a couple of days if covered with plastic wrap. You'll enjoy having some leftovers of this.

Serves 16.

PASILLA CHILE PASTE

5–6 dried pasilla chile pods

Rinse the pasilla chile pods, break them open, pull out their stems and seeds, and put them in a small saucepan with water just to cover. Bring the water to a boil, lower the heat to a simmer for a few minutes, then remove from the heat and leave the pods to soak for 30 minutes.

Purée the softened chile pods in a blender or food processor with enough of the remaining water to form a soft but thick paste. Put the purée through a strainer, measure out 3 tablespoons, and reserve the rest for another use, storing it in a tightly covered jar in the refrigerator.

Note: When working with chiles, wear rubber gloves, or wash your hands very thoroughly afterwards. I find that rubbing my hands first with vegetable oil, and then washing them several times with soap and water, is very effective for removing chile oil.

ORANGE AND MANGO SORBET

½ cup sugar
½ cup water
2 large ripe mangoes (2 cups sliced)
1½ cups fresh-squeezed orange
  juice

5 Tbs. fresh-squeezed lemon juice
finely grated zest of 1 large orange

In a small saucepan, dissolve the sugar in the water, bring it to a boil, and let it boil for 5 minutes. Allow the syrup to cool, then chill it.

Peel and slice the mangoes, and purée them with the orange juice, lemon juice, and orange zest. Stir the sugar syrup into the purée, a little at a time, until the sweet-tart balance is right.

Freeze the mixture according to manufacturer's instructions in an ice cream freezer.

Makes about 1½ pints of sorbet.

EASTER
BRUNCH

crostini with
Eggplant and Olive Relish

Spinach, Green Garlic, and Mushroom Pie

painted eggs

Beet Salad in Raspberry Vinaigrette

Onion and Thyme Flan

Roasted Asparagus with
Herb-Roasted Baby Potatoes

Yogurt Cheese with honey

fresh strawberries

hot cross buns

Easter Baba

Gypsy Mazurek

At our house, Easter means brunch on the terrace with
several families, lots of kids, lots of beautiful food laid
out on a buffet, and Easter egg wars.

The centerpiece of this brunch is a hearty spinach
and mushroom pie, a big, wonderful-looking thing with a bread-like
crust, something like an open calzone. Around it, I serve a bounty
of spring vegetables—bright-green asparagus, pink and gold beets
with their leaves, little potatoes, and sweet onions in a flan.

There's flavorful Eggplant and Olive Relish to nibble with a cracker
and a glass of champagne, and there are sweet strawberries and Polish
pastries to linger over into the afternoon with a cup of coffee.

Most important, there are painted eggs. After the traditional
egg hunt, everyone comes to the table and a big basket of painted
hard-cooked eggs is passed around. We all choose our weapons
for the egg war, and challenges are called out. The rules are simple:
pointy end against pointy, blunt against blunt, the challenger usually
does the hitting. The longest surviving egg wins. I don't need to say
that the kids love this little event, and wait for it all year. Once only,
one of my boys made a mistake and painted an egg that was still raw.

After the hilarity, there's a toast, and then food for as
long as anyone likes. Most years we're lucky, the weather is
beautiful, and we sit outside under the trees for hours.

On a practical note: most of the work for this brunch can
be done the day before. The pie should be baked on Easter morning,
but the filling can be done Saturday. The asparagus and potatoes
take about 10 minutes preparation time before they go into the oven,
and even the flan can be made the night before and then
rewarmed slightly before being unmolded onto a platter.

This is also a meal that adapts well to a potluck style.
Almost anything seasonal that someone might bring along
to a brunch will fit right in.

EGGPLANT AND OLIVE RELISH

3 medium eggplants (about
   3–4 lbs.)
3–4 medium tomatoes (1 lb.)
¾ cup coarsely chopped Kalamata
   olives, or a combination of black
   and green cured olives

lemon juice to taste
fresh-ground black pepper
2–3 Tbs. chopped flat-leaf parsley

Prick the eggplants with a fork, put them on a cookie sheet, and roast them in a 400° oven for at least an hour, or until they are soft enough to collapse when pushed. At the same time, quarter the tomatoes, arrange them skin side down on another baking sheet, and roast until they are blackened around the edges and most of the excess juice has cooked away, also about an hour.

When the eggplants have cooled enough so you can handle them, split them open and scoop the flesh out of the skins with a spoon. Scrape away and discard any clusters of very dark seeds. Allow the eggplant to drain in a colander for about ½ hour, then chop it coarsely.

When the tomatoes are ready, use a spoon to remove the tomato pulp gently from the skins. Discard the skins and stir the pulp into the eggplant.

Add the chopped olives to the eggplant and tomatoes. Stir and taste. Add a few drops of lemon juice and some black pepper, and stir in the chopped parsley. You should not need any salt, as the olives will provide enough.

Serve the relish warm or at room temperature, with crostini, plain crackers, or pita bread.

Makes about 2 cups of relish.

SPINACH, GREEN GARLIC, AND MUSHROOM PIE

Somewhere between calzone and quiche, and bigger than either one, is this substantial bread-like pastry filled with ricotta cheese, spinach, plenty of garlic, and sautéed oyster mushrooms. It's tasty when hot, and just as good at room temperature, and, because of its sturdy consistency, travels well to picnics.

Green garlic looks like slightly larger green onions. It's garlic that hasn't bulbed yet, and it has a milder, fresher taste. If you can't find it, use a combination of green onions and bulb garlic.

for the dough:
1 Tbs. dry yeast (1 envelope)
1 tsp. sugar
¾ cup lukewarm water
2¾–3¼ cups all-purpose flour

1 tsp. salt
2 eggs
1½ Tbs. olive oil

for the filling:
¾ lb. fresh spinach
1 cup sliced green garlic, or 1 cup
    sliced green onions and 2 cloves
    garlic, chopped
2 Tbs. olive oil
salt and pepper to taste
1–2 tsp. lemon juice

1 egg
1 lb. ricotta cheese
½ cup grated Parmesan cheese
2 cups thinly sliced white of leek
½ lb. oyster mushrooms
2 Tbs. white vermouth

In a small bowl, dissolve the yeast and the sugar in the lukewarm water and leave it for 10–15 minutes, until it begins to foam. Mix 2¾ cups of flour with the salt in a medium-sized mixing bowl.

Beat one egg lightly into the yeast mixture, and stir in the olive oil. Pour the liquid into the flour and mix with a wooden spoon until a ragged dough forms. Turn the dough out on a board lightly sprinkled with flour and knead it until it is smooth, about 5–6 minutes. If the dough feels very moist and sticks to the board, sprinkle on a little more flour, but don't let the dough get too dry.

Form the dough into a ball and put it into a lightly oiled bowl, turning it over once. Cover the bowl with a towel or with plastic wrap and leave the dough in a warm place to rise for about 45 minutes, or until doubled in volume.

Meanwhile, prepare the filling. Wash the spinach very well, remove tough stems, and chop it coarsely. Clean and slice the green garlic, or slice the green onion and finely chop the garlic.

Heat a tablespoon of olive oil in a large non-stick sauté pan and sauté the green garlic, or green onions and garlic, in it until limp. Add the spinach and some salt and pepper. Continue cooking, stirring often, until the spinach is completely wilted, all the excess water has cooked away, and it begins to sizzle. Remove from the heat, and toss the spinach mixture with 1–2 teaspoons of lemon juice.

Beat the egg into the ricotta cheese and stir in the Parmesan cheese, then the cooked spinach.

In another large non-stick pan, heat the remaining tablespoon of olive oil and sauté the leeks in it until they begin to be spotted with gold. Add the oyster mushrooms and continue sautéing, stirring often, until the mushrooms are also just beginning to color. Add salt and pepper to taste, and the vermouth, and stir as the vermouth cooks away. Remove from heat.

When the dough is fully risen, punch it down and set it aside to rest for a few minutes. Then roll it out gently on a lightly floured board, to an oval about 21 by 15 inches. Very lightly oil a large cookie sheet and sprinkle it with cornmeal. Lift the oval of dough and lay it down evenly on the cookie sheet; the edges of the dough may overhang the cookie sheet, which is fine.

Spread the ricotta cheese and spinach mixture over the dough, leaving a border of about 3 inches all the way around. Spread the cooked oyster mushrooms evenly over the spinach mixture.

Pull the edges of the dough up over the filling, pleating or folding them as you like. Beat the remaining egg with a spoonful of water and brush the dough lightly with it.

Bake at 400° for about 35 minutes. Check after 25 minutes, and if the crust is looking very dark, cover it lightly with a sheet of foil for the remaining time. It should be glossy and golden brown.

Allow the pie to cool slightly in its pan before removing it to a board and slicing it into wedges or squares.

Serves 8–10 as a main course, more as an appetizer.

BEET SALAD IN RASPBERRY VINAIGRETTE

Raspberry vinegar and a little honey give this salad a surprising delicacy. This salad uses both the beets and their greens, so choose young beets that have fresh, crisp greens.

2 bunches young beets (1½ lbs. without tops)
8 whole cloves garlic, unpeeled
3 cups sliced beet greens, packed
1 Tbs. olive oil
2 cloves garlic, minced

2 Tbs. honey
3 Tbs. raspberry vinegar
1 large stalk celery, diced
¼ cup finely chopped red onion
salt and pepper to taste

garnish: ½ cup crumbled Roquefort cheese or feta cheese

Cut the greens off the beets, leaving about ½ inch of stem, reserve the greens, and scrub the beets well. Arrange the damp beets close together on a sheet of heavy-duty aluminum foil and scatter 8 unpeeled garlic cloves over them. Wrap the beets in the foil, folding over and crimping the edges to make a tight seal. Bake the beets in the foil packet in a 400° oven for about 1 hour and 15 minutes.

Meanwhile, wash the beet greens, discard those that are anything less than fresh and lovely, and cut off the stems. Slice the greens in ½-inch strips; you should have at least 3 cups firmly packed.

Heat the olive oil in a non-stick sauté pan, add the minced garlic, stir for ½ minute, then add the sliced beet greens and a sprinkle of salt. Toss over a medium flame until the greens are completely wilted and sizzling in the pan, about 5–6 minutes. Remove the pan from the heat.

In a small bowl, whisk together the honey and the raspberry vinegar. Drizzle 2 tablespoons of this mixture over the beet greens in the warm pan and toss to combine thoroughly.

When the beets are cool enough to handle, slip off their skins and cut them into slices or chunks. Squeeze out the soft garlic, mash it with a fork, and whisk it into the remaining vinegar-honey mixture. Pour this over the beets in a bowl, and add the diced celery, chopped red onion, salt and pepper to taste, and the sautéed greens. Mix everything together well.

Serve the salad warm or at room temperature, alone or on a bed of tender young curly endive. Garnish each serving with a sprinkle of crumbled cheese.

Serves 6.

ONION AND THYME FLAN

This is a marvelous concentration of sweet onions, married with a simple custard of eggs, milk, and cheese. The secret is in starting with good, sweet onions, and cooking them slowly for a long time.

Some of the better-known sweet onions are Vidalia, Texas Sweet, and Maui onions, but these days everyone is claiming to have the sweetest onion in the world.

3½ lbs. sweet onions	2 Tbs. sherry or Marsala
1 tsp. olive oil	5 eggs
1½ Tbs. butter	1½ cups milk (low-fat milk is fine)
1½ tsp. salt	2 oz. Gruyère cheese, grated
1 tsp. dried thyme	2 oz. Parmesan cheese, grated
½ tsp. white pepper	

Peel and chop the onions. In a large non-stick sauté pan, heat the olive oil and butter, then add the onions and most of the salt, and begin stirring over medium heat. After a few minutes, lower the flame, and keep cooking the onions very slowly, stirring often, for about an hour.

It is essential to take your time in this process. The onions must not brown, but rather soften and melt slowly, and finally reduce to about a quarter of their original volume. Allow them to turn a pale shade of gold, then add the thyme and white pepper, and stir a few more minutes. Add the sherry or Marsala, and stir again until the liquid has completely cooked away. Remove the onions from the heat and let them cool slightly.

Whisk together the eggs and milk with a pinch of salt, then stir in the grated cheeses and the cooked onions.

Butter 1 large, straight-sided baking dish, or 10 individual ramekins. If you are using 1 baking dish, such as a medium gratin dish or large soufflé dish, and plan to unmold the flan to serve it, line the bottom of the dish with a buttered piece of wax paper or parchment, cut to fit.

Pour the custard mixture into the prepared dish or ramekins. Place the baking dish or ramekins into a larger baking pan in which there is about an inch of water. Bake in a 350° oven for about 40–45 minutes for 1 large dish, about 25 minutes for individual ramekins. The flan is ready when the top is golden brown, the custard no longer trembles when the pan is jiggled, and a thin knife inserted near the middle comes out clean.

Remove the flan from its water bath, and allow to cool slightly before serving. The flan can be served hot, warm, or at room temperature. The large flan can be served in its baking dish, and spooned out casually, or it can be unmolded, served on a platter and cut into wedges.

To unmold, slide a thin knife blade around the sides to loosen. Give the dish a little shake to check that the flan is moving freely. Place a large plate over the top of the baking dish, hold them together tightly, and flip. The flan will drop out onto the plate. Peel away the wax paper. Now invert a serving platter over the flan and flip it again, revealing its nicely browned top.

Serves 10–12.

ROASTED ASPARAGUS

3 lbs. thin green asparagus	salt to taste
2 Tbs. olive oil	10 cloves garlic, peeled

optional: lemon juice or a fruity vinegar

Wash the asparagus and snap off the tough ends of the stalks. Drizzle the olive oil over the asparagus, sprinkle on some salt, and roll the asparagus around until all of it is evenly, lightly coated with oil. Spread the asparagus out on baking sheets, and tuck peeled garlic cloves in among it, here and there.

Roast at 400° for 20–30 minutes, depending on the thickness of the stalks. Check after 10 or 15 minutes, and when you see them getting a slightly blistered look, move the stalks around and turn them over.

The roasting time will vary. How long you leave the asparagus in the oven depends on how thick the stalks are, and even more on how you like them. Sometimes I like them just tender. Other times I like to let the thin tips get golden brown and crispy. When thin asparagus is roasted to this further stage, it makes an excellent finger food.

Serve the asparagus hot or at room temperature. You can sprinkle it with a few drops of lemon juice or a fruity vinegar if you like. I've used raspberry vinegar this way, and also a grapefruit vinegar once, which was very good.

Serves 10–12.

HERB-ROASTED
BABY POTATOES

Here's one of those easy, practical things that are just delicious. These potatoes are best when they're hot, but also very good at room temperature. They are wonderful with eggs for breakfast, and make a delicious nibble with a glass of wine. I can make a meal of these with a green salad and a little slice of cheese.

3 lbs. baby red-skinned potatoes   salt to taste
   (the size of walnuts)
2 tsp. olive oil
1–2 Tbs. herbes de Provence
   (thyme, rosemary, basil, savory,
   marjoram)

Wash the potatoes thoroughly, scrubbing with a vegetable brush. Trim away any soft or damaged spots, and let the potatoes dry in a colander or on a tea towel. If some of the potatoes are much larger than others, cut them in half.

Put the potatoes in a bowl, drizzle them with the olive oil, and sprinkle on the crushed herbs and as much salt as you'd like, then tumble them around with your hands until all are evenly coated with oil and herbs—2 teaspoons of oil really is enough! If you use more, the potatoes will be heavy, and taste greasy at room temperature.

Spread the prepared potatoes evenly on a non-stick cookie sheet and roast them in the middle of a 400° oven for about 45 minutes to an hour. After the first 30 minutes, move them around and turn them over.

When the potatoes are tender, you can serve them at once or let them cool to room temperature.

Serves 6–8.

Yogurt Cheese (page 77)

EASTER BABA

A sweet, rich yeast bread is an Easter tradition over most of Europe. This one is the Polish baba that I have eaten every Easter since I can remember. My mother made it by hand, slapping the glossy batter against the side of the bowl, and later worrying whether the butter-laden cake would rise properly.

The recipe to which she referred, in an old Polish cookbook with yellowed pages, called for sixty egg yolks and about two pounds of butter. I have made a few modifications, in the amount of egg yolks as well as in some technique, but it is still a very traditional recipe, and the result is a true baba.

I serve it with Easter brunch or breakfast. It makes a fabulous coffee cake any time, and a slice of freshly baked baba with some crème fraîche and berries is a fine dessert.

2 eggs
2 egg yolks
1¼ cups sugar
2 cups warm milk
2 envelopes dry yeast (2 Tbs.)
5–5½ cups white flour
pinch of ground cardamom

1 tsp. pure vanilla extract
½ tsp. salt
4 oz. butter (1 stick), softened
1 cup plump raisins
¾ cup finely chopped blanched
   almonds
confectioners sugar

Start by making a sponge: In a large mixing bowl, beat the eggs, egg yolks, and 2 tablespoons of sugar until creamy and light. Beat in the warm milk, the yeast, and about half the flour. Cover the bowl with a towel or with plastic wrap and leave it in a warm place until the sponge rises to at least double its volume.

Stir down the sponge, and use an electric mixer to beat in the remaining sugar, the cardamom, vanilla, salt, and softened butter. Start beating in more flour, about ½ cup at a time, until the batter becomes too thick to use an electric mixer. Continue adding flour, beating it in now with a wooden spoon, until the batter starts to take on the consistency of a very soft dough. Do not let it get stiff.

Beat this dough vigorously with a wooden spoon, slapping it against the side of the bowl and giving the bowl an occasional turn, until the dough starts to pull away in a shiny, elastic mass. The consistency will be somewhere between a batter and a bread dough. It will fall *slowly* from the wooden spoon when lifted.

Work the raisins and chopped almonds into the dough, and let it rest as you prepare the pan.

Butter a large springform pan, and line the bottom with a round of buttered parchment or wax paper, cut to fit. Spoon the soft dough into the prepared pan, spreading it evenly. It should come no more than halfway up the side of the pan. Cover the pan with a towel or with plastic wrap, and put it away in a warm place to rise.

This rich dough will rise slowly, but after 1½ hours or so, it should reach the top of the pan. Find the warmest, stillest spot in your kitchen to help it along—an oven with a pilot light is great.

When the baba has doubled in size, preheat the oven to 325°, and bake it for about 1 hour and 15 minutes. After the first 20 minutes, lay a sheet of aluminum foil or plain brown paper loosely over the top to keep it from browning too much. It should rise in a beautiful dome shape above the edge of the cake pan. When it is done, it should sound hollow when tapped, and a thin blade inserted near the middle should come out perfectly clean.

Remove the baba from the oven and let it cool slowly on a rack before removing the sides of the pan and lifting it off the bottom. Dust the top with confectioners sugar. Do not slice the baba until it is completely cooled, then cut it in thin wedges to serve.

Serves 12–15.

GYPSY MAZUREK

We had several kinds of mazurek for Easter when I was little, and this was always my favorite. The flat, slightly crumbly pastry holds masses of raisins and almonds, and is cut into bars or squares to serve, making one of the nicest cookies I know.

10 egg yolks	1½ cups plump dark raisins
2 whole eggs	1½ cups golden raisins
2 cups + 2 Tbs. sugar	1 cup currants
pinch of salt	8 oz. blanched almonds, coarsely
½ tsp. nutmeg	chopped
¼ tsp. almond extract	3 Tbs. finely chopped candied
1¾ cups flour	orange peel

In a large mixing bowl, beat the egg yolks and eggs until they are foamy. Gradually add the sugar, and keep beating until the mixture is thick and cream-colored. Add the salt, nutmeg, and almond extract, and then stir in the flour, a little at a time, until you have a smooth batter. Stir in all the dried fruit, the chopped almonds, and the orange peel.

Prepare 2 medium-sized cookie sheets with sides. Butter the sheets, and line them with buttered parchment. Spoon the batter onto the parchment and spread it evenly, about ½ inch thick. If your cookie sheets are large and you don't have enough batter to fill two, simply fill one to the edges, and the other one as far as you can, maintaining an even thickness; the batter will hold its shape.

Bake the pastries at 325° for about 25–30 minutes. When done, the top will be a pale-amber color, and the pastry will sound hollow when tapped. Remove them from the oven carefully. Don't bend the cookie sheets, as the pastry is fragile at this point. If the crusty top cracks a little, don't worry.

Allow the mazurek to cool, then slide it onto a board, trim away any dark or uneven edges, and cut into 1-by-2-inch bars, or into squares. The cookies can be kept for a week in a tightly covered container, with wax paper between the layers. If you want less brittle, chewier cookies, put an apple slice in the container with them, and replace it every couple of days.

Makes about 5 dozen cookies.

THANKSGIVING
FOR EVERYONE

crudité platter: radishes, carrot sticks, celery,
jicama, sliced kohlrabi, cucumber spears,
raw fennel, olives, peppers

Yogurt Cheese with Garlic and Herbs
crackers, sliced baguette

Cheddar Cheese Straws

Polenta Torta with Roasted Squash

Sautéed Spinach and Garlic

Roasted Fennel and Red Onions

Stewed Green Tomatoes with Red Jalapeños

Roasted Pearl Onions and Green Beans

Cranberry, Orange, and Red Wine Sauce

Gratin of Baked Yams with Pineapple

roast turkey

Bread Stuffing with Apples and Walnuts

Mashed Potatoes with Roasted Garlic

Apple Pie

Pumpkin Cheesecake with Caramelized
Walnut and Ginger Sauce
or pumpkin pie with whipped cream

coffee

I don't know about you, but I don't live in an ideal world where everyone behaves the same way or wants the same thing. In my world—in my very own family, in fact—some are vegetarians and some want to eat meat. Some are even harder to define— the sortavegetarians, I call them.

So, when a holiday like Thanksgiving comes around, I like to share a feast that is in the spirit of the celebration; it's a good time for us all to get together and accommodate each other.

With this harvest menu, a true vegetarian can have a memorable meal, yet tradition is satisfied and the turkey-eaters are content. I designed it around a great polenta dish, a torta made with caramelized onions and roasted squash. It's a beautiful golden thing, on a big platter, surrounded by dark-green sautéed spinach. Along with the polenta and spinach, I serve an array of fall vegetables, each one prepared its own way but always staying on the simple side, letting their individual characters and flavors shine.

Roasted Fennel and Red Onions develop a rich, deep flavor, and so do the green beans and pearl onions. The sautéed spinach with a whole lot of garlic just seems essential with the polenta. To counterpoint these flavors, I make an easy little stew of green tomatoes, tart and slightly spicy, and a cranberry sauce with oranges, cinnamon, and red wine.

Every one of these dishes crosses over
beautifully into a turkey dinner, and the bread stuffing
can be baked in casseroles so that everyone may enjoy it.
The savory menu is finished with the two tubers that are
de rigueur: the yams are baked and baked again with pineapple,
and the potatoes mashed with garlic. Everything goes
with everything, and everyone is happy.

This all seems like a lot of food, but that's what harvest festivals
like Thanksgiving are all about. Still, it's nice to be able to
try everything without feeling like a stuffed turkey yourself, so I've
kept most of the dishes high in flavor but quite low in fat.

The appetizers are all "walking around" food, the
kind of thing that can be put out on a sideboard or a
coffee table and nibbled through the course of the afternoon.
They go well with champagne, with football, and with kids
running in and out of a house. The desserts are a very
traditional Apple Pie and Pumpkin Cheesecake
or your favorite pumpkin pie.

Yields in the individual recipes are estimated at
eight to ten servings, but in the context of a meal like this,
with many more than the usual number of dishes, you can
count on feeding at least a dozen comfortably.

YOGURT CHEESE WITH GARLIC AND HERBS

1 cup thick Yogurt Cheese (page 77)
2 Tbs. chopped fresh dill weed
2 Tbs. chopped fresh parsley

1 clove garlic, minced
fresh-ground black pepper to taste
salt to taste

Mix everything together thoroughly and press into a small crock or mound on a plate. Chill for a few hours, allowing the flavors to marry. Serve with crostini, or with any good crackers.

This makes about a cup, and can be kept, tightly covered and refrigerated, for several days.

CHEDDAR CHEESE STRAWS

Long, thin, buttery pastries flavored with lots of cheddar cheese and a little snap of cayenne and mustard, these are a favorite with adults and kids alike. Their flavor can be dressed up with the addition of red pepper flakes, cracked black pepper, or a little Parmesan or blue cheese. But this recipe is the very tasty basic version.

2 cups flour
¾ tsp. salt
½ tsp. cayenne pepper
½ cup butter (1 stick), cut in pieces
¾ lb. grated sharp cheddar cheese
    (about 3½ cups)

4 Tbs. cold water, more if needed
1 tsp. prepared mustard
1 tsp. Worcestershire sauce

In the container of a food processor, combine the flour, salt, cayenne, butter, and grated cheese, and process until the mixture resembles coarse meal.

In a small bowl, whisk together the cold water, mustard, and Worcestershire sauce. Drizzle this over the mixture in the food processor and pulse for a few seconds at a time, until the pastry pulls together into a ball. Add a few drops more cold water if you need to, and do not overprocess.

Take the pastry out, divide it into 2 equal parts, and roll each part out between 2 sheets of wax paper into rectangles about 8 by 16 inches, and about ⅛ inch thick. Put the thin pastry sheets, still covered with wax paper, into the refrigerator to chill for at least an hour.

Peel back the top sheet of paper and slice the pastry sheets crosswise into strips about ⅓ inch wide. Transfer the strips to baking sheets, either buttered or lined with parchment. Bake at 400° for about 10 minutes, or until the straws are golden and beginning to brown at the ends. Let the straws cool on a rack for a few minutes before serving.

This makes about 80–90 thin cheese straws, or enough for 10–15 people, but if children are involved, I suggest a double batch.

A Practical Note: You can make this pastry several days ahead of time and keep it in the refrigerator, well wrapped. Then slice and bake the straws not too long before you want to serve them. To recrisp leftover straws, put them in a hot oven for a minute or two.

POLENTA TORTA WITH ROASTED SQUASH

2 large Spanish onions, chopped
1 Tbs. olive oil, plus more to brush
    on top of torta
1 tsp. butter
salt to taste
pinch of dried thyme
2 Tbs. Marsala
3 cups vegetable broth

3 cups water
1½ cups coarse-ground polenta
2 cups thick purée of roasted
    squash, such as Kabocha, butter-
    cup, Tahitian, or other flavorful
    variety (procedure follows)
2 oz. fresh white goat cheese

garnish: Parmesan cheese

In a large non-stick pan, cook the chopped onions slowly in the olive oil and butter, with a generous sprinkle of salt and a pinch of thyme, until they are very soft and golden brown, about 45 minutes. Stir them from time to time, and when they are caramelized add the Marsala, swirling it around quickly to deglaze the pan.

While the onions are browning, combine the vegetable broth, water, and polenta in a large pot and bring the liquid to a boil, stirring with a whisk. Reduce the heat to a simmer and cook the polenta, stirring frequently, for at least 30 minutes, or until it is very thick. Stir in the caramelized onions, the puréed roasted squash, and the goat cheese.

Keep stirring over low heat until the cheese is melted and everything is well blended. Taste and correct the seasoning with a bit of salt if needed.

Pour the polenta into a big round casserole or shallow bowl and allow it to cool completely and set. You can refrigerate it, tightly covered, for a day or so at this point. Unmold the polenta torta onto a baking sheet, brush it with olive oil, and bake it in a 375° oven for about 45 minutes.

Transfer the polenta to a large serving platter, surround it with sautéed spinach or roasted vegetables, and cut it in wedges to serve. Pass grated Parmesan cheese.

Serves 8–10.

To Roast Winter Squash

Any of the hard winter squashes can be roasted in their skins in a hot oven. If the squash is very large, cut it in half, scrape out the seeds, and place it cut side down in a large baking pan. For Tahitian squash, cut it in 2-inch-thick slices, and cover them with aluminum foil. Very small squashes can be roasted whole— just prick their skins several times with a fork.

Roast squashes at 400° until they are soft enough to collapse easily when pushed with a wooden spoon. The time will vary with the size of the squash, but think in terms of an hour or more.

When the squash is tender, allow it to cool, then scoop out the soft flesh with a spoon. If the squash seems watery, cook it down in a non-stick pan until it has the desired thick texture.

SAUTÉED SPINACH
AND GARLIC

This couldn't be simpler, and couldn't be better. Use good, fresh spinach, and do not be afraid of too much garlic.

4–5 bunches fresh spinach (about 2 lbs.)
2–3 Tbs. fruity green olive oil

½ head garlic, peeled and chopped
salt to taste
dash of rice vinegar or lemon juice

Wash the spinach well in several changes of water, until all the mud and grit are gone. Discard any leaves that are yellowed and trim off the heavier stems. Shake the spinach in a kitchen towel or spin it in a salad spinner.

Cook the spinach down in 2 batches: Heat half the olive oil in a large non-stick sauté pan and add half the chopped garlic. Stir the garlic around in the hot oil for a minute, then add as much spinach as the pan will hold and start turning it gently as it wilts. Continue adding spinach and turning it over until you've used half of it. Salt it to your taste and keep cooking until there is no excess liquid in the pan.

Remove the sautéed spinach into a bowl and repeat the procedure with the remaining olive oil, garlic, and spinach. Eventually, that mountain of spinach will become 2–3 cups. When the second batch has cooked down, add back the first batch and sauté all of it together for a few moments until everything is hot. Just before serving, toss the spinach with a little dash of rice vinegar, or some lemon juice if you prefer.

Serves 8–10.

ROASTED FENNEL AND RED ONIONS

Fennel and onions both develop a deep, sweet flavor when roasted. They are superb with polenta, and in combination with other vegetables.

6 large bulbs fennel
3 large red onions

2 Tbs. olive oil
salt to taste

Slice the stalks off the fennel and peel off the top, thick layer. Wash the fennel well, then quarter it lengthwise and trim out the root end. Cut each quarter into halves or thirds.

Peel the onions and cut them into chunks similar in size to the fennel. Combine the vegetables in a large bowl, drizzle with olive oil, and sprinkle generously with salt. Toss them together until everything is evenly, lightly coated with olive oil.

Spread the vegetables out on a large baking sheet with edges. Roast the fennel and onions in a 375° oven for 45 minutes to 1 hour, turning them over after about 20 minutes, and every 10–15 minutes after that. The vegetables should be soft through and well browned in spots. Serve hot.

Serves 8–10.

STEWED GREEN TOMATOES WITH RED JALAPEÑOS

The beauty of this easy little stew is the way the sour green tomatoes combine with the sweetness of onions and a little kick of heat from red jalapeños. It's not a terribly hot dish, just lively. You can use green jalapeños if you can't find red ones, but the red ones are prettier.

Serve this with polenta or tamales, add it to quesadillas, or use it as a relish with any mild-flavored dish that could use some spicing up.

10–12 green tomatoes (3 lbs.)	1 Tbs. olive oil
3 large yellow onions (4 cups chopped)	2–3 red jalapeño peppers
2 cloves garlic	1 small bunch cilantro
	1 tsp. salt, more to taste

Blanch the tomatoes by dropping them into boiling water one by one for about 45 seconds, then retrieve them and slip off their skins. Trim out their cores and cut them in large chunks. Chop the onions and mince the garlic.

Heat the olive oil in a large non-stick sauté pan and stir the onions and garlic into it. Cook them over medium heat, stirring often, until the onions are limp and translucent. Add the green tomatoes.

Trim the jalapeño peppers and scrape out the seeds if you want a little less heat, then chop them finely. Work carefully (see note on page 365), and wash your hands well afterwards. Remove the cilantro leaves from their stems and discard the stems.

Add the jalapeños, cilantro, and salt to the tomatoes and continue simmering until the tomatoes are soft and any excess liquid has simmered away. If the mixture dries out too quickly, just add a drop of water. Taste and correct the seasoning if needed.

Makes enough for 8–10 servings.

ROASTED PEARL ONIONS AND GREEN BEANS

1½ lbs. pearl onions, either white or yellow, or both
2 Tbs. olive oil
salt to taste
1½ lbs. slender green beans
6 cloves garlic

Drop the onions into boiling water and let them boil for about 2 minutes, then drain them and let them cool. Peel the onions, trimming them at the stem end and slipping off their skins. Drizzle 1 tablespoon of the olive oil over the onions, sprinkle them with salt, and mix until all the onions are lightly coated with oil.

Spread the onions in a shallow baking pan and roast them in a 375° oven for 45 minutes to 1 hour, depending on their size, and moving them around once or twice during that time.

Meanwhile, wash and trim the green beans. Peel the garlic cloves and slice them in half lengthwise if they are large. In a bowl, toss together the green beans, garlic, the remaining olive oil, and some salt.

Spread the green beans and garlic out on a large, shallow baking pan and roast them in the same oven with the onions for 30–45 minutes. Turn them once or twice during the cooking time, and remove them when they are tender and spotted here and there with dark brown.

Roasting the onions and the green beans in two separate pans allows you to remove each one from the oven when it is done, and not overcook one for the sake of the other. When both the onions and the beans are ready, mix them together, add a dash of salt if needed, and pile them on a serving platter.

Serves 8–10.

CRANBERRY, ORANGE, AND RED WINE SAUCE

Lately there has been a fashion for complicated cranberry sauces full of exotic ingredients. This is understandable, because cranberries are delicious, and if you eat them frequently you want a little variety. However, some of these concoctions stray a little too far from the pure taste of the cranberry for me.

This sauce uses oranges, cinnamon, and red wine to complement the flavor of the berries, without overwhelming them. It's a refreshing relish as part of your Thanksgiving feast, but it could also be served as a light dessert with just a touch of sweetened whipped cream.

1½ lbs. fresh cranberries	⅓ cup dry red wine
1 cup orange juice	1¾ cups sugar
½ cup water	½ tsp. cinnamon
grated zest of 1 orange	pinch of cloves

Wash the cranberries and pick them over, throwing away any that are too soft or discolored. Combine all the ingredients in a large non-reactive pot and bring to a boil, stirring with a long-handled wooden spoon. Reduce the heat and simmer for 10 minutes, stirring frequently. The sauce should be thick and glossy.

Allow the sauce to cool, stirring now and then to keep a skin from forming on top, then transfer to a beautiful serving dish.

This makes enough for 8–10 generous servings, or 20 average servings.

GRATIN OF BAKED YAMS WITH PINEAPPLE

Yams and pineapple just go together. It's a natural affinity, I think, like apples and cinnamon, or spinach and cheese. In this dish, the pairing has been stripped down to bare essentials, making a lighter version of a traditional favorite.

3½ lbs. yams (6 medium-sized
   yams)
salt to taste
1½ cups crushed pineapple, with
   juice

3 Tbs. brown sugar
1 Tbs. butter, plus more for the
   gratin dish

Wash the yams, prick them several times with a fork, and arrange them in a roasting pan. Roast them in a 400° oven for at least an hour, maybe a bit more if they are very large. They should be completely soft and release a syrupy juice when pierced with a fork.

Remove the yams from the oven and allow them to cool until you can easily handle them. Then cut them in half and scoop them out of their skins with a spoon, or peel them, whichever is easier for you. Discard the skins, and mash the pulp with the juices in the roasting pan. Salt the yams to your taste.

Stir the crushed pineapple and brown sugar into the yams. Lightly butter a large, shallow gratin dish, and spoon the yam mixture into it. I like to smooth the top and then score it with a large fork into a pretty pattern. Cut a tablespoon of butter into pea-sized pieces and dot the top of the yams.

Bake the yams again in a 350° oven for about 30 minutes, until they are hot through and browning on top.

Serves 8–12.

BREAD STUFFING WITH APPLES AND WALNUTS
(for turkey, or for a casserole)

When my husband roasts a turkey, I usually make this bread stuffing to go with it. It is excellent for stuffing a turkey, but can also be baked separately in a casserole, and thus enjoyed by meat-eaters and vegetarians alike. Greg likes to roast his turkey on a spit, with no stuffing in it, just a handful of herbs and garlic, so that suits him just fine.

    Use whatever bread you like. I like a coarse-textured country-style white bread, but you could use a whole wheat bread, sourdough, or some of this and some of that. The bread can be fresh, stale, or perfectly dry—the only difference will be in the amount of broth you use. Trim off the crusts if they are very crusty, or leave them if you want extra texture—anything goes!

¾ cup butter
2 cups chopped onion
2 cups sliced or chopped celery
1–2 tsp. salt
pepper to taste
3 tsp. dried sage
1 tsp. dried marjoram
3 tsp. poultry seasoning
½ cup chopped fresh parsley

2–3 Tbs. cider vinegar
4 quarts of ½-inch bread cubes
4 cups chopped, peeled green apples
1½ cups raisins
1½ cups lightly toasted walnuts, finely chopped
2 cups vegetable broth, or chicken broth, or both

Melt the butter in a large skillet and sauté the chopped onion and celery in it until they are soft and just starting to color. Add about a teaspoon of salt, pepper to your taste, the herbs, and the cider vinegar. Stir well and remove from the heat.

In a very large mixing bowl, combine the bread cubes, chopped apples, raisins, and chopped walnuts. Add the sautéed vegetables and herbs with all their butter, and toss everything together until it is thoroughly combined.

Drizzle on about half the broth, toss again, and test. You are aiming for a mixture that is soft and moist throughout, but not soggy or soupy. Keep adding broth, a little at a time, mixing everything up well after each addition, until you have the consistency you like. The amount of broth used will vary quite a bit, depending on what kind of bread is used and how dry it is.

If you are roasting a turkey, and plan to bake the stuffing separately but want the flavor of the turkey in it, you could add some drippings in place of part of the broth. In that case, however, cut down a little on the butter. If, on the other hand, you plan to stuff a turkey, leave the stuffing just a little on the dry side.

When the texture feels right, taste and correct the seasoning with more salt or pepper if needed.

Spoon the stuffing into two buttered casseroles, or one very large one, cover well, and bake at 350° for about 45 minutes. Or spoon it into a turkey that has been prepared for roasting.

This makes about 4 quarts of stuffing, enough for a 16–20-lb. turkey, or two medium casseroles. It's more than enough for 10 people, but you'll want to have leftovers. (It's Thanksgiving—you have to have leftovers.)

MASHED POTATOES WITH
ROASTED GARLIC

1 head garlic	1 Tbs. butter
1–2 tsp. olive oil	¾ cup buttermilk
3 lbs. russet potatoes	salt and pepper to taste

Separate the garlic cloves, but do not peel them. Pile them on a piece of aluminum foil, drizzle with olive oil, and fold the foil over them to form a sealed packet. Bake the garlic in a 375° oven for about 45 minutes, or until the cloves are soft.

Peel the potatoes and cut them into 2-inch chunks. If you prefer your mashed potatoes with their skins, just scrub them, trim them, and cut them up. Put the potatoes in a pot with enough well-salted cold water to cover them by ½ inch, bring the water to a slow boil, and cook them until they are completely tender. Drain the potatoes, reserving the cooking water. Return the drained potatoes to the pot.

Squeeze the soft garlic out of the cloves and discard the skins. Press the garlic through a strainer and add the pulp to the potatoes, along with the butter, buttermilk, and salt and pepper to your taste. Mash thoroughly with a potato masher while the potatoes are still steaming hot. Add a little of the cooking water if the potatoes seem too dry. (The rest of the water can be saved and used for making bread if you're so inclined.) Taste, and adjust the seasoning.

Serves 6–8.

APPLE PIE

pastry:
2½ cups flour
½ tsp. salt

5 oz. cold butter (1¼ sticks)
3–4 Tbs. cold water

filling:
2½ lbs. tart green apples
½ cup sugar
1 tsp. cinnamon

pinch of nutmeg
2 Tbs. flour
2 Tbs. lemon juice

crumble topping:
½ cup brown sugar
3 Tbs. softened butter

2 Tbs. flour

To make the pastry, put the flour and salt in the container of a food processor, and add the chilled butter, cut in slices. Process until the mixture resembles coarse meal. Add a little cold water at a time, through the feeder tube, as you process, just until the pastry begins to hold together. Remove the pastry, form it into a ball, wrap it well, and chill it.

Peel the apples, cut them in quarters, trim out the cores, and cut the quarters crosswise into thick slices. Mix together the sugar, cinnamon, nutmeg, and flour. Put the apple slices in a bowl, sprinkle the dry mixture over them, and toss until it is evenly distributed. Add the lemon juice and toss again.

Roll the pastry out into a circle about 14 inches across. Line a large, deep-dish pie pan with the pastry, and trim off the excess, leaving about ½ inch hanging over. Fold the extra ½ inch in and crimp it to make a nice, high edge.

Combine the brown sugar, softened butter, and 2 tablespoons of flour in a small bowl and rub it together with four fingers until it forms a crumbly paste.

Fill the prepared pie shell with the apples, and sprinkle the crumble topping over them. Roll and cut leftover pastry into strips and lay a few of them decoratively over the top of the pie.

Bake the pie in a preheated 350° oven for about 1 hour and 15 minutes. Cover it loosely with a piece of foil for the first 45 minutes to keep it from browning too much.

Allow the pie to cool to lukewarm before serving.

Serves 8–10.

PUMPKIN CHEESECAKE
with Caramelized Walnut and Ginger Sauce

crust:
1½ cups graham cracker crumbs
4 Tbs. butter, melted

filling:
3 8-oz. packages cream cheese
1½ cups sugar
1½ cups cooked pumpkin, canned
   or fresh (cooking instructions
   follow)
1 tsp. allspice

3 Tbs. sugar
1 egg white, lightly beaten

2 tsp. cinnamon
¼ tsp. nutmeg
pinch of cloves
4 eggs
4 Tbs. heavy cream
1 recipe Caramelized Walnut and
   Ginger Sauce (recipe follows)

Prepare the crust by mixing together the graham cracker crumbs, melted butter, and sugar, then stirring in the lightly beaten egg white. Press the crust into the bottom and partly up the sides of a 10-inch springform pan. Flatten it evenly with a potato masher, or with your fingers.

Beat the cream cheese with the sugar until it is somewhat fluffy. Remove about ¾ cup of this mixture and set it aside in the refrigerator in a tightly covered container.

To the remainder of the cream cheese mixture, add the pumpkin and spices and beat thoroughly, then beat in the eggs, one at a time. Pour the filling into the crust and bake in a preheated 350° oven for 1 hour and 15 minutes. The center of the cake will still move slightly when shaken.

Remove the cheesecake from the oven and allow it to cool on a rack for 15 minutes, then run a very thin, sharp knife around the sides to loosen it. Let the cake finish cooling, then cover it tightly and chill it for 6 hours, or overnight.

Remove the reserved cream cheese mixture from the refrigerator and allow it to reach room temperature. Whisk in the 4 tablespoons of cream until smooth.

Remove the sides of the cake pan, and spread the cream cheese smoothly over the top of the cheesecake.

Cut the cheesecake in wedges with a very sharp knife, wiping the knife between slices, and spoon Caramelized Walnut and Ginger Sauce over the top of each serving.

Serves 12.

To Cook Fresh Pumpkin

The easiest way to cook fresh pumpkin is to bake it in a hot oven (375°) until it is soft throughout. If you are baking an entire pumpkin, prick it in a few places with a fork and put it on a baking sheet to catch any juices. If you're baking a wedge or slice of a large pumpkin, scrape out the seeds, then wrap the piece well in aluminum foil and bake until soft. The time will vary with the size of the pumpkin, but count on at least an hour.

When the pumpkin gives easily to slight pressure, it's done. Cut it open, allow it to cool somewhat, then scoop out and discard the seeds. Scrape all the soft flesh off the skin and drain it in a sieve for about 15 minutes, then purée or mash it. You will have a thick pulp which can be used for pies or soups, or for Pumpkin Butter.

CARAMELIZED WALNUT
AND
GINGER SAUCE

⅓ cup sugar
1 cup hot water
1 cup coarsely chopped toasted
   walnuts

¼ cup finely chopped crystallized
   ginger

Heat the sugar in a small, heavy-bottomed pot until it melts and turns light golden brown. Add the hot water carefully; the caramel will "seize up" in contact with the liquid, and there may be some spattering. Lower the heat and simmer the liquid, stirring occasionally, until the caramel completely dissolves into it, making a thin syrup.

Stir the chopped walnuts and ginger into the syrup, remove it from the heat, and allow it to cool somewhat before serving.

Spoon the sauce, in small quantities, over slices of Pumpkin Cheesecake, or over vanilla ice cream.

GREG'S SPIT-ROASTED TURKEY

*(Confessions of a Self-Taught Spit-Roaster —*GREG NAVA*)*

On a holiday like Thanksgiving, we have a lot of people around the house with different eating habits. So Anna cooks a feast of vegetarian dishes, and my job is cooking the turkey. Everyone is happy, and even the vegetarians usually want to try my great spit-roasted turkey.

Spit-roasting a turkey is an adventure. It is exciting and medieval, and can result in the most delicious turkey you've ever eaten. But if you want everything timed and planned down to the minute, then read no further. An open fire, together with the varying size and construction of birds, can result in wildly differing cooking times.

Use a timetable only to give you a general idea of cooking time, but don't try to spit-roast a turkey according to a timetable; it will only result in disaster. You must use a good meat thermometer and, when the temperature is right, believe that the turkey is ready. Your guests may be eating an hour earlier or an hour later than anticipated, and sometimes it takes sangfroid to pull the turkey off the spit when it cooks quickly, but experience has taught me—believe the thermometer.

So why spit-roast, if it's so unpredictable? Mainly because nothing can compare with the flavor an open charcoal fire imparts, especially if you use mesquite. And since the turkey is constantly turning, it is always basting itself, resulting in a moist and succulent roasted turkey. To me, this is the way roasted turkey was meant to taste!

First of all, always use a fresh turkey, with no chemical additives. I can't emphasize this enough. Prepare the turkey as usual for any roasting. Wash it inside and out, and rub the cavity with lemon. Rub the outside of the turkey with a little butter, and salt it.

I think it is better not to stuff the bird. You can bake your stuffing separately in a casserole. It's better for the turkey, and people who don't eat meat can still enjoy the stuffing. I like to go outside and pick handfuls of wild rosemary, and stuff the branches into the cavity, along with several cloves of crushed garlic. I slice more garlic into thin slivers and push it under the skin of the turkey. I sew the cavity closed using string and trussing pins.

Trussing the turkey is extremely important for spit-roasting. The tighter the turkey is held together, the juicier and better the result. I use a free-form approach, tying the legs together first, then looping string around the whole bird and tying it up very tightly.

Putting the turkey on the spit itself is also critical to the success of the whole operation. Spear the turkey so that its weight is balanced as evenly as possible around the spit. Most spit-roasting outfits provide weights to balance the bird. Hand-tighten the forks which hold the turkey on the spit, and then test the turning of the turkey. Adjust the weight until the bird *turns evenly*—or it won't cook evenly. Once the bird is turning evenly, stop and tighten the forks with a pair of pliers so the turkey won't slip.

Now put the charcoal into the rear rack of the spit-roaster. I think that mesquite gives the best flavor, especially when combined with the fresh rosemary. But mesquite constantly pops and shoots out hot embers, so I stand a fireplace screen in front of the barbecue to protect passers-by.

After the first hour of roasting, you will need a pan below the turkey to catch the drippings. You can occasionally baste the bird with these drippings if you want to. In general you will find that there will be far less juice released than with an oven-roasted turkey.

I like to cook up a broth with the giblets and liver to use for the sauce later. Put them in a saucepan along with an onion stuck with a couple of cloves, 1 teaspoon of dried tarragon, 1 clove of garlic, and a sprig of parsley. Cover with water and simmer for a long time. Then skim thoroughly and strain.

Taking the temperature of the turkey is tricky. Plunge the thermometer deep into the turkey without touching the bone. Take the temperature of the white meat at the breast, and the dark meat at the thigh, and do it on both sides of the turkey. No matter how evenly the bird may be turning, parts of it will have been in front of the fire longer than others, and the four temperatures will vary.

White meat is perfectly done between 170° and 175°, dark meat between 180° and 185°. Now comes the judgment call. With four different temperatures, and with dark and white meat needing different temperatures, when do you call it done?

My experience has shown me that dark meat isn't underdone at 175°, but white meat is dry at 185°. I always favor cooking for the white meat, since that's what most people eat first, and the dark meat generally gets reheated. If the white meat is registering 175° in both breasts, I always pull the turkey. If one breast is reading 172° and the other breast is reading 180°, I pull the bird. No matter what, I never let either breast get above 180°. Nothing is worse than dry white meat.

The turkey should rest between 20 and 30 minutes before being carved. While the bird is resting, I deglaze the drippings in the pan with plenty of Madeira. I add the deglazed juices to the strained giblet broth in a saucepan and reduce it to taste, and that's my delicious brown sauce.

Once you get the hang of it, spit-roasting is easy. Most of the time the turkey is just spinning away and needs little attention, so you have more time to have a drink with your friends.

NEW YEAR'S EVE

caviar and toast points

*Watercress and Radicchio Salad
with Ginger-Sesame Dressing*

Timbales of Tahitian Squash and Pears

Rosemary Sorbet

*Wild Mushroom Soup
with Cream Cheese Pierogi*

Pineapple Meringue Torte

Sometimes a moment comes when you want to serve
a meal for gentlemen in tuxedoes and ladies in glittering dresses.
This is the one. Chill the Dom Pérignon, and bring up your great
wines. This meal is sophisticated in a fun way, with exquisite flavors
in unusual combinations, but nothing odd just for the sake of being
odd. And if anyone asks why the soup is the last savory course and
not the first, and why there's a sorbet in the middle instead of for
dessert, just tell them it's because you're a genius.

The Wild Mushroom Soup is actually one of my own absolutely
favorite things to eat. I prepare it every Christmas Eve, and at other
times when I can get my hands on some good porcini. The deep,
woodsy flavor of the mushrooms is complemented by little, meltingly
tender Cream Cheese Pierogi, with traditional Polish fillings.

The soup certainly merits being the centerpiece of a meal for many reasons, but one of them is that it pairs superbly with the finest red wine, so it makes sense to build up to it in a meal, rather than try to follow it with something. With this menu, you can start with champagne, move on to a lovely Riesling with the timbales, then peak with a great, aged red as companion to the Wild Mushroom Soup.

If you like caviar, then by all means start with caviar and toast points with that glass of iced champagne. If not, you'll still get plenty to eat. First there is Watercress and Radicchio Salad. It sets you up for the delicate Timbales of Tahitian Squash and Pears that follow, a dish that is both savory and sweet, and perfect with a fruity wine.

Then there is a little surprise—dainty scoops of Rosemary Sorbet are served to clear the palate before the mushroom soup and the rich pierogi. This is a refreshing thing to do, an idea much used in multi-course meals in France, and if you've never tried a palate-clearing sorbet, do try it and see what fun it is.

Now, although you've had some very interesting tastes, you haven't eaten too much yet, so you can really enjoy the splendid combination of the Wild Mushroom Soup with a great Burgundy. Of course, after all that, an elegant dessert seems in order, but nothing too rich. A tart or pastry would be superfluous after the pierogi, but the Pineapple Meringue Torte fits the bill exactly. It's marvelous looking, tastes sweet and delicious, but is extremely light— and much easier to make than you would think.

I enjoy a meal like this, full of little twists and surprises. It has a genuine celebratory feel and yet does not leave you groaning with a sense of excess afterwards. With a meal like this one, you can see the old year out lavishly, and enjoy the start of the new year the next day.

Leftovers: Don't hesitate to make lots of pierogi. You will enjoy them for several days. And although I think of this as a very grown-up meal, I find that my children actually like a lot of this food, and most of all the pierogi, which they will eat at any time of day and take to school in lunch boxes. Pierogi are best if reheated a bit in the oven, but this is not altogether necessary.

WATERCRESS AND RADICCHIO SALAD

with Ginger-Sesame Dressing

This is a winter salad that works on a combination of pungent, bitter, tart, and sweet tastes. Persimmons are plentiful where I live, and they are available dried starting around Christmas and through the rest of the winter. These dried persimmons are so delicious that people absolutely get addicted to them, so, if you can get your hands on some, do it. However, I know they are not available most places, and it's fine to substitute raisins, diced prunes, diced dried figs, or the like in their place.

2 large bunches fresh watercress
    (6 cups leaves, loosely packed)
2 small heads radicchio (4 cups torn
    leaves, loosely packed)
2 heads Belgian endive
1 fennel bulb

1 large green apple
1 large dried persimmon, or ½ cup
    other dried fruit
Ginger-Sesame Dressing (recipe
    follows)

Break the watercress sprigs off their thick stems and discard the stems. Separate the radicchio leaves and tear them into bite-sized pieces. Wash the greens and spin them dry in a salad spinner or in kitchen towels.

Discard any bruised outer leaves of the endives and slice the endives crosswise. Trim the fennel, quarter it lengthwise, and slice thinly. Cut the apple into wedges, trim out the core, and slice the wedges crosswise. Cut the persimmon, or other dried fruit, into raisin-sized pieces.

Toss everything together in a very large salad bowl, pour the dressing over it, and toss again until all parts of the salad are evenly coated.

Serves 8.

GINGER-SESAME
DRESSING

I'm usually a minimalist, happiest with a touch of great olive oil and a few drops of an excellent vinegar. But in this dressing, 9 ingredients are combined for a refreshing and subtle effect.

about 2 inches fresh ginger root (2 Tbs. minced)	1 Tbs. soy sauce
2 Tbs. fresh-squeezed lemon juice	1 Tbs. rice vinegar
3 Tbs. fresh-squeezed orange juice	1 Tbs. honey
2 Tbs. dark sesame oil	3 Tbs. sesame seeds
	½ cup thinly sliced green onions

Peel the ginger root and cut it in thin slices, then mince it very finely. You need about 2 tablespoons of minced fresh ginger. Combine the ginger with the lemon juice, orange juice, sesame oil, soy sauce, rice vinegar, and honey in the container of a blender. Process until the mixture is well blended and the ginger nearly puréed.

Dip a lettuce leaf into the dressing to taste it. Correct the seasoning with a little salt or more rice vinegar if you like.

Toast the sesame seeds in a pan, stirring them constantly, until they are a uniform caramel color; don't let them get dark brown. Set them aside until you're serving the salad.

Just before serving the salad, add the sliced green onions. Pour the dressing over a very large salad and toss until all the leaves glisten. Sprinkle about a teaspoon of the toasted sesame seeds over each serving.

This makes ⅔ cup dressing,
enough to dress a salad for 8.

TIMBALES OF TAHITIAN SQUASH AND PEARS

If Tahitian squash cannot be found, substitute Kabocha, buttercup, Hubbard, or acorn squash.

1 lb. peeled, cubed Tahitian squash
1 lb. peeled, cubed yams
1 cup water
½ tsp. salt
2 large onions
2½ Tbs. butter
3 medium pears, Anjou or Bartlett
   (ripe but not mushy)

½ cup good white wine
½ cup heavy cream
5 eggs
white pepper to taste
butter and fine dry breadcrumbs for
   the ramekins

garnish: Sweet Red Pepper Purée (page 345)

Combine the squash, yams, water, and salt in a heavy-bottomed saucepan, cover, and simmer gently until the squash and yams are completely tender.

Peel and chop the onions. Cook them slowly in 2 tablespoons of butter, stirring often, until they are caramelized—a uniform, deep golden brown.

Meanwhile, peel and core the pears and cut them into even cubes between ¼ and ½ inch in size. When the onions are soft and light brown, remove them from the pan, add the remaining bit of butter, and sauté the pear cubes in it for a few moments. Then add the wine, cover the pan tightly, and simmer the pears on a very low flame for about 15–20 minutes, until they are tender.

Combine the cooked squash and yams, the onions, and the cream, and purée in a blender or food processor until perfectly smooth. Lightly beat the eggs and whisk them into the vegetable purée. Season to taste with salt and white pepper, then stir in the poached pears.

Prepare 8 timbale molds, ramekins, custard cups, or individual soufflé dishes: butter them thoroughly and coat them with fine dry breadcrumbs. Divide the squash and pear mixture evenly among the ramekins, filling each a little short of the top. Place the ramekins in a baking pan deep enough to hold water at least halfway up the molds, and bake them that way in a preheated 325° oven for about 50 minutes.

Unmold by sliding a thin knife around the edge of the ramekin and tipping it out onto the serving plate. Surround each unmolded timbale with a small ribbon of Sweet Red Pepper Purée and serve warm.

Serves 8.

Rosemary Sorbet (page 345)

WILD MUSHROOM SOUP

approximately 7 cups Mushroom
Stock (recipe follows)
3 oz. dried porcini
2 large yellow onions
2½ Tbs. butter
2 cloves garlic, chopped
salt to taste
1½ lbs. fresh wild mushrooms,
cleaned and sliced; use porcini if

you can get them, morels,
chanterelles, or a combination
3 Tbs. cognac
½ cup good red wine
dash of white pepper
pinch of cayenne
⅓ cup heavy cream

garnish: fresh dill

Make the Mushroom Stock. You can sort through the dried porcini and use any tiny or tough bits for the stock, reserving better pieces for the soup.

Put the dried porcini in a bowl and pour over them 2 or 3 cups of boiling water, enough to cover. Leave them to soak for about 30 minutes, then take them out of the water and rinse each one carefully. Strain the soaking water through a paper filter to get rid of all the sediment and reserve it for the stock.

Peel the onions, quarter them lengthwise, and then slice them. Melt 1½ tablespoons butter in a large non-stick skillet and slowly cook the onions and chopped garlic in it, with a bit of salt, until the onions are golden brown.

Slice the soaked porcini into wide strips, chopping any especially tough parts. Thoroughly clean the fresh wild mushrooms and slice them thinly. If you have morels, just cut them in half lengthwise, leaving the tiny ones whole. You should have about 7 cups of prepared mushrooms.

Add the remaining butter and all the wild mushrooms to the onions in the skillet, turn up the heat, and sauté everything together for a few minutes, stirring. Add the cognac and stir another minute or two, until it is gone.

Add the Mushroom Stock and the soaking liquid from the dried porcini. Simmer everything together for 45 minutes to 1 hour; the flavors should be well developed. Add ½ cup of red wine, simmer a few more minutes, and taste. Finish the seasoning with a little more salt if it's needed, a dash of white pepper, a pinch of cayenne, and the cream.

Serve this exquisite soup steaming hot, in wide soup bowls, with a sprinkle of chopped fresh dill on top. Pass a platter of fresh-baked pierogi for the full experience.

Serves 10–12.

MUSHROOM STOCK

This is a great stock to use in making mushroom soups, and it could also be used for risotto or pilaf.

1 oz. dried porcini pieces, approx.	½ tsp. dried thyme
2 Tbs. olive oil	6 branches parsley
1 onion, chopped	6 branches cilantro
1 clove garlic, chopped	1 tsp. dried sage
1 cup chopped leek greens	1 tsp. salt
¼ lb. fresh mushrooms, sliced	several peppercorns
3 medium carrots, sliced	2½ quarts spring water
2 stalks celery, sliced	

optional: 2–3 Tbs. sherry

If you are making Wild Mushroom Soup, take all 3 ounces of dried porcini for that recipe and sort through them. Reserve the nice, big pieces for the soup, and use only the smallest bits for the stock. With good-quality dried mushrooms, you should be able to reserve about ¾ of them for the soup; it doesn't matter if you have a little less than an ounce for the stock. If you are making the stock for another purpose, use an ounce of dried porcini.

Pour boiling water over the porcini and leave them to soak for a while.

Heat the olive oil in a big skillet and cook the onion and garlic in it over medium heat, stirring occasionally, until the onion is golden brown. Add the leeks, fresh mushrooms, carrots, and celery, and cook everything together for a few minutes. Add the herbs, salt, peppercorns, and water.

Drain the porcini, reserving the water. Wash the mushrooms carefully, getting rid of all the grit. Strain the soaking water through a paper filter. Add both the porcini and the filtered soaking water to the stock pot.

Simmer the stock for about an hour. Add a few tablespoons of sherry toward the end if you like. Strain the stock through a fine mesh sieve, taste it, and correct the seasoning if necessary.

You should have about 6–7 cups of flavorful stock.

CREAM CHEESE PIEROGI

I usually make these once a year, at Christmas, and then I make hundreds, for a big party. When I go to the store with my shopping list in hand, I always feel I should be getting a license and have a 5-day waiting period before taking home that amount of butter and cream cheese. Well, it's an old-fashioned recipe, but I've been using it for years and years, and it's just too good to change.

3 cups flour	1 egg yolk
1 tsp. salt	1 tsp. water
1 cup butter	Potato Filling and/or Cabbage
8 oz. cream cheese	Filling (recipes follow)
¼ cup heavy cream, chilled	

Put 2¾ cups of flour and the salt into the container of a food processor, and add the butter and cream cheese, cut into chunks. Process briefly, until the mixture has an even, mealy texture with no big lumps. Add the chilled cream and process again, until the pastry holds together and forms a ball. Remove the ball of pastry, wrap it, and chill it for at least 30 minutes.

Sprinkle flour over a large board and roll out half the dough until it is an even ⅛ inch thick. With a cookie cutter or a can, cut it out in 2-inch rounds.

Whisk the egg yolk with the water. Place a rounded teaspoon of filling in the center of a pastry round, then brush the edges with the egg-yolk–water mixture, fold it carefully over the filling, and seal. Press the sealed edges together with the tines of a fork, making a pretty, crimped pattern. Pierce the top of the pastry with a fork or a skewer. (When making several kinds of pierogi at once, I create different patterns with the fork tines to identify each type.)

Continue filling and sealing all the pastry rounds, and repeat the procedure with the second half of the pastry. Brush the tops of the pierogi with the remaining egg-yolk–water mixture, and arrange them on lightly buttered baking sheets. Bake the pierogi at 375° for 15–20 minutes, until they are golden brown on top.

These are best eaten warm, just out of the oven, but they are also fine at room temperature and can be prepared several hours ahead of time. I serve them as an accompaniment to Wild Mushroom Soup, a pairing which is almost a meal in itself. They also make a superb finger food to serve with apéritifs or champagne before dinner.

This makes 40–50 pierogi.

POTATO FILLING FOR PIEROGI

This filling is nothing more than seasoned mashed potatoes reduced to the proper thickness, and it is so good.

3 lbs. russet potatoes
5–6 Tbs. buttermilk, or puréed
   cottage cheese
1 Tbs. butter

1 medium onion, finely chopped or
   minced
salt and pepper to taste

Boil the potatoes in their jackets in salted water until they are tender. Drain them, let them cool until you can just handle them, then peel them and cut them into big pieces. You can put them through a ricer if you want to, but it's not strictly necessary. Add the buttermilk or puréed cottage cheese and mash with a potato masher.

Melt the butter in a large sauté pan and cook the minced onion in it, with a dash of salt, until the onion is soft and just turning golden. Add the potatoes to the pan and continue mashing everything together over medium heat as the excess moisture cooks away and the potatoes become thicker. Taste, and add as much salt and pepper as needed.

When the potatoes are thick enough to hold a stiff shape, put them away in a covered bowl to chill for an hour or two before using.

This makes about 2 cups of potato filling, enough for 20–25 pierogi. If you are not making another kind of filling, double this to fill a full recipe of pierogi.

CABBAGE FILLING FOR PIEROGI

1 tsp. olive oil
2½ Tbs. butter
1 large onion, very finely chopped
3½ cups finely shredded cabbage,
    packed (1 large cabbage)

salt
pepper
1 Tbs. cider vinegar
2 hard-boiled eggs
4 Tbs. chopped fresh dill

Heat the oil and butter in a large non-stick sauté pan and cook the onion in it over medium heat, stirring occasionally, until the onion is golden.

Be sure the cabbage is finely shredded or chopped. I like to use the grating attachment on my food processor for this. Blanch the shredded cabbage for a moment in boiling, salted water, then drain it and squeeze out the excess moisture.

Add the cabbage to the onion, along with a teaspoon of salt and some fresh-ground pepper. Cook over medium heat, stirring often, for about 30 minutes. The cabbage should be greatly reduced in volume, and beginning to turn golden brown. Grind on some black pepper, and add the cider vinegar, stirring it in.

Sieve the hard-boiled eggs, or mince them, and stir them into the cabbage, along with the chopped dill. Taste and correct the seasoning with more salt or pepper if needed. It helps to chill the filling before using it, as it becomes stiffer and easier to work with.

This makes about 1½ cups of cabbage filling, enough for 20–25 pierogi. If you are not making another kind of filling, double this to fill a full recipe of pierogi.

PINEAPPLE MERINGUE TORTE

This beautiful dessert is refreshing and light, perfect for a special-occasion meal when you want to end with something festive but not heavy.

for the meringue layers:
1 cup blanched almonds
6 large egg whites
¼ tsp. cream of tartar

1½ cups powdered sugar
½ tsp. almond extract

for the filling:
2 cups crushed pineapple with its juice
½ cup water
¼ cup fresh lime juice

grated zest of 2 limes
¾ cup sugar
4 Tbs. cornstarch
3 egg yolks

garnish: additional powdered sugar

Toast the almonds in a 300° oven for 10–15 minutes, or just until they release their fragrance and begin to turn golden. Do not let them brown. Allow the almonds to cool, then grind them in a food processor.

Line 2 baking sheets with parchment, and draw a 10-inch circle on each sheet.

Beat the egg whites with the cream of tartar until they hold soft peaks, then add the powdered sugar and almond extract, and continue beating them until they hold stiff peaks. Fold in the ground almonds.

Spread the beaten whites evenly within the 2 circles, smoothing the tops carefully with a wide knife or spatula. Bake the meringues in a 300° oven for 45 minutes, then lower the heat to 250° and bake another 30 minutes. The meringues should be dry and pale ivory in color.

Slide the meringues, still on their parchment, carefully onto racks and let them cool completely.

While the meringues bake, prepare the filling. Combine the pineapple and its juice, the water, lime juice, lime zest, sugar, and cornstarch in a medium-sized non-reactive pot and stir until the cornstarch is completely dissolved. Bring the mixture to a boil, lower the heat a little, and stir it as it boils gently for 8–10 minutes, or until it becomes completely translucent and thickens.

Remove the filling from the heat, let it cool for a moment, and whisk in the egg yolks, one at a time. Return it to very low heat and whisk for 5 minutes. Do not let it boil. When it thickens again, remove it from the heat, transfer it to a covered bowl, and allow it to cool completely.

To assemble the meringue, first turn over the meringue layers and gently peel the parchment away. Work carefully, as the meringue layers are now at their most fragile, very dry and easy to crack. Later, they will become softer and slightly chewy in the center.

Place one layer upside-down on a large, lovely platter. Stir up the cooled pineapple filling and spread it evenly over the meringue, swirling it right out to the edge. Place the second layer right side up on top of the filling. Cover the torte with plastic wrap and chill it in the refrigerator for several hours.

Before serving, sift powdered sugar over the top of the torte. Protect the edges of the platter with strips of wax paper, or dust the excess sugar off the edges of the platter with a pastry brush. The torte can be served just like that, simple and elegant, or it can be decorated with berries and mint sprigs, thin twists of lime zest, or edible flowers.

Serves 8–10.

ABOUT VEGETABLE BROTH

Nothing is as useful to have on hand in the kitchen as a supply of good broth, ready to make a soup or a sauce or to greatly enhance rice and grain dishes. There are many recipes for broth and stock. Some are very basic; others develop specific flavors and are therefore limited to certain dishes. They take a little time to make, but are not nearly as much trouble as you might think. In fact, it only takes a few minutes to rinse and slice some vegetables, and once you get used to the idea of making your own broths, it becomes easier and easier.

Now, if you happen to have a nice broth on hand, and if you put up tomatoes in the summer when they're great, you can make a fabulous soup in about 5 minutes. You can make a marvelous risotto. You can serve noodles and a few vegetables in a bowl of broth and have a one-dish meal that's ready almost instantly.

In the past, the only way to have this kind of convenience was to make extra amounts of stock and freeze it in small containers. You could get a perfectly usable chicken broth in a can, but the available vegetable broths were not satisfying. The canned products I tried from health food stores always tasted a little too sweet and carroty for me, and the dissolving cubes and powders were downright nasty.

Now, fortunately, the demand for an acceptable, commercially available vegetable broth has been felt. Good canned vegetable broth is easy to find in the supermarket, and it has become a staple item in my pantry.

Still, home-made is best, and so I think it's good to have a formula for a basic clear vegetable broth, and some variations on the theme. The requirement for a basic broth, which can be used in almost any recipe, is a balance of flavors, neither too sweet nor too bitter, with no single aggressive flavor dominating. It should be delicate, taste nice when sipped from a cup, but lighter if reduced by a third and salted. This kind of neutrality serves most recipes very well. The idea is to support the other flavors in a dish, not to fight with them.

For some dishes, a stronger-flavored broth is needed. If you are making a broth with a specific dish in mind—for example, a mushroom soup or a pea soup—you can make a broth strongly flavored with that element. Clear soups, where the broth is the main thing, are a law unto themselves. Taste and adjust.

It's good to make broth when you're in the kitchen anyway, cooking other things. Then it becomes almost effortless, sort of a calculated by-product. Another way to make life easier is to save those leek tops and chard stems in plastic bags in the crisper, and when they start to add up, set up the stock pot.

After a while, you won't be measuring anything anymore, and you'll see that, once you throw a few vegetables and herbs in the pot with some water, the broth really makes itself.

I have included three recipes here: a very basic broth, a darker broth for which a few vegetables are browned in oil first, and a more complex version of that. But the possible combinations are many. Read through the list of vegetables at the end of the basic recipe, think about what you like, and you will be on the way to devising your own favorite broth.

BASIC LIGHT
VEGETABLE BROTH

5 large carrots (1½ cups sliced)
2 large stalks celery (1½ cups sliced)
2 large onions
1 head garlic
green top of 1 large leek (2–3 cups sliced)
thick peels of 2 small potatoes
1 turnip or rutabaga

1 bay leaf
1 tsp. dried thyme
1 tsp. black peppercorns
4 branches flat-leaf parsley
12 branches cilantro
1½ tsp. salt
12 cups water

Wash all the vegetables thoroughly. Scrape the carrots and peel the onions. Thickly peel the potatoes, reserving the inside for another use. Slice or coarsely chop everything except the head of garlic, which can just be sliced crosswise and put in as is.

Combine all the vegetables, herbs, and seasonings with the water in a large pot. The water should just cover everything when you first put it all together. Bring the water to a boil, lower the heat, and let the broth boil gently for about 45 minutes. All the vegetables should be completely soft, and the flavors fully released into the liquid.

Strain the broth through a colander, then through a fine sieve to remove any sediment or cloudiness. Taste, and correct the salt if needed, but bear in mind that it's best to leave a broth undersalted until you know how you're going to use it.

You should have 7–8 cups of mild-flavored,
amber-colored vegetable broth.

Variations: Many other vegetables can be added to this broth, enriching it and altering its character. Here is a partial list of vegetables I've tried and liked:

chard leaves and stems
kale leaves and stems
mushrooms
fennel
peeled winter squash
parsnips

tomatoes
broccoli stems
green onions
summer squash
celery root

However, it is important to be aware of the individual characteristics of each vegetable, and that some need to be used in moderation.

Chard, kale, and mushrooms all can add an earthy richness to the stock, but none should be allowed to dominate. Mushrooms, especially wild ones, are an excellent addition to stock but have a distinct, woodsy taste, so only add a few unless you want Mushroom Stock.

Fennel, winter squash, and parsnips add sweetness. Fennel has a distinct anise flavor and should be used, but with care.

Tomatoes will add tartness.

Broccoli stems are nicer than you think, but, again, a little goes a long way.

Green onions, summer squash, and celery root are terrific and not overwhelming, so throw some in if you have them on hand.

After you've made a few batches of broth, you will have a very good sense of what does what, and you will develop your own favorite combinations.

DARK VEGETABLE BROTH

The flavor of this broth is enhanced by browning some of the vegetables in a little oil before simmering them in water. Use it when you want a deeper, earthier taste in a soup or stew.

2 large onions
8 cloves garlic
5 large carrots (1½ cups sliced)
2–3 stalks celery (1½ cups sliced)
8 small mushrooms
1 Tbs. olive oil
1 tsp. salt
pinch of cayenne
10 cups water

green top of 1 large leek (2–3 cups
    sliced)
1 turnip
thick peel of 1 large potato
4 branches flat-leaf parsley
12 branches cilantro
1 bay leaf
1 tsp. black peppercorns

Peel and coarsely chop the onions and garlic. Scrape and slice the carrots, and slice the celery and mushrooms. Heat the olive oil in a large sauté pan, and add the onions, garlic, carrots, celery, mushrooms, salt, and cayenne. Stir the vegetables frequently over a medium flame for the next 10–15 minutes, until they are well browned. Don't worry about any dark bits that are sticking to the pan.

Add the water. Thoroughly wash the leek top and slice it and the turnip. Add them to the broth, along with the potato peel, parsley, cilantro, bay leaf, and peppercorns. Bring the water to a boil, then lower the heat and let it boil gently for about 45 minutes. All the vegetables should be completely soft, and the broth dark brown and fragrant.

Strain the broth through a colander, then through a fine sieve to eliminate any sediment. Taste, and correct the salt if needed.

This makes about 6 cups of broth.

ASSERTIVE VEGETABLE BROTH

This is a broth with a more complex, assertive flavor. It has a slightly sweet-tart edge from the addition of fennel and tomatoes, among other things.

2 large onions
8 cloves garlic
5 large carrots (1½ cups sliced)
2–3 large stalks celery (1½ cups sliced)
1 Tbs. olive oil
1½ tsp. salt
pinch of cayenne
12 cups water
green top of 1 large leek
thick peel of 1 large potato

1 turnip or rutabaga
2 parsnips
1 cup chopped fennel stems
2 medium tomatoes
4 branches parsley
12 branches cilantro
⅓ cup brown lentils
1 bay leaf
1 tsp. dried thyme
1 tsp. black peppercorns

Peel and coarsely chop the onions and garlic. Scrape and slice the carrots, and slice the celery. Heat the olive oil in a large sauté pan, and add the onions, garlic, carrots, celery, salt, and cayenne. Stir the vegetables frequently over a medium flame for the next 10–15 minutes, until they are well browned. Don't worry about any dark bits that are sticking to the pan.

Add the water. Thoroughly wash the leek top, scrub the potato, turnip, and parsnips, and rinse the fennel stems, tomatoes, and fresh herbs. Slice the leek top, cut the peel off the potato thickly, and slice or coarsely chop the turnip, parsnips, fennel stems, and tomatoes. Add all the remaining ingredients to the water in the pan, and bring it to a boil. Lower the heat and let the liquid boil gently for about 45 minutes. All the vegetables should be completely soft, and the broth quite dark and aromatic.

Strain the broth through a colander, then through a fine sieve to take out the sediment. Taste, and correct the seasoning if needed.

This makes about 7–8 cups of broth.

MAKING APPLE BUTTER
AND
PUMPKIN BUTTER

Here are two conserves for the winter. Apple Butter and Pumpkin Butter are both so easy to make, and so rewarding for the effort put in, that I recommend them for a family project. There is no tricky part—nothing needs to set up or jell. In both cases, you only have to cook down the apples or the pumpkins, with sugar and spice to your taste, and when it looks thick enough, it's done.

Though they make welcome home-made gifts for the holidays, don't make the mistake of giving them all away.

APPLE
BUTTER

This is what I usually make with my boys before the holidays, and we give away jars and jars of it, wrapped in bright red or green tea towels. Every year it comes out differently, because we use different combinations of apples, but it's always delicious. This year we used a mix of Granny Smiths, Winesaps, Johnny Golds, and Golden Delicious. Use whatever varieties you like, the best available in your area, but be sure to include some of the tart ones.

The amount of sugar and the amounts of spices are also just as flexible as can be, as it's all a matter of taste. The formula given here was actually used once, and faithfully recorded, but will probably never be precisely duplicated.

15 lbs. apples, mixed tart and sweet	¾ tsp. ground cloves
3 cups apple cider	½ tsp. ground nutmeg
¼ cup apple cider vinegar	½ tsp. ground ginger
2¼ cups brown sugar	spring water as needed
2 Tbs. ground cinnamon	

Peel and core the apples, and combine them in a large, heavy-bottomed kettle with the cider and cider vinegar. Simmer, stirring occasionally with a wooden spoon, for a long, long time—maybe hours. The apples will soften, fall apart, turn to mush, start to thicken.

Add most of the sugar and the spices and continue cooking and stirring for at least another ½ hour, adding a little spring water only if the mixture becomes so thick that it could scorch. Taste. Correct the seasoning if you like, adding a bit more sugar, more spices, or a touch of vinegar. Simmer for another little while to blend the flavors before tasting again. When it tastes the way you like it, you're done. This is apple butter, after all, not brain surgery.

You can leave it slightly lumpy, or make it beautifully smooth by running it through a blender in batches. Spoon the hot apple butter into sterile jars, screw on scalded lids, and process the jars in a boiling water bath for at least 20 minutes, or according to the manufacturer's instructions. Remove the jars, allow them to cool, and check the seals.

Processed this way, the apple butter will last as long as any sealed preserve. If you haven't the time for the canning process, you can freeze it in small batches, or simply spoon it into perfectly clean, scalded jars, put on scalded lids, and keep it in the refrigerator for several weeks.

This makes about a dozen 12-oz. jars.

PUMPKIN BUTTER

If you like pumpkin pie, but don't feel quite right about having a slice of it for breakfast every day during October, November, and December, have this on your toast instead. It's fat-free, and has a wonderfully rich flavor. Sometimes we make a big batch of this to pack into pretty jars and give away for Christmas (instead of apple butter), but we always keep half for ourselves.

The secret is to use a good pumpkin. The giant ones that are grown primarily for use as jack-o'-lanterns don't have a very intense flavor. Smaller pumpkins tend to be much better, and I've had great success with a variety called Sweet Mama, as well as with the grayish-white Albinos. Ask for advice at the farmers' market, in the produce department, or from a good gardener, to find out about the best pumpkin available in your area.

9½–10 lbs. pumpkin, weighed
   whole
¾ tsp. salt
4–5 tsp. ground cinnamon
1 tsp. ground ginger, more to taste
½ tsp. ground nutmeg, more to
   taste

½ tsp. ground cloves, more to taste
4–5 Tbs. cider vinegar
2½–3 cups brown sugar

optional: 2 Tbs. molasses

Cut the pumpkin in half, scrape out all the seeds, then put the pumpkin halves cut side down in a lightly oiled baking dish. Bake the pumpkin in the oven at 400° for about an hour, or until it feels soft when poked with a wooden spoon.

Remove from the oven and allow to cool slightly, then turn the pumpkin halves over and scoop the soft flesh out of the rind. Be sure not to get pieces of rind into the mix. You should have 8–10 packed cups of cooked pumpkin.

Combine the pumpkin in a large non-reactive, heavy-bottomed pot with the remaining ingredients. Bring the mixture to a simmer and stir over low heat for 20–30 minutes, as the flavors marry and the excess moisture cooks away. Adjust the amounts of vinegar and sugar by tasting. Pumpkins vary a great deal in flavor and sweetness, so you have to play with this a little.

Purée the mixture in batches in a blender, and taste again; correct the seasoning if necessary and cook the purée down a little more if it feels thin—it should hold a soft shape.

Spoon the hot pumpkin butter into sterile canning jars, screw on new, scalded lids, and process in a boiling water bath for at least 20 minutes, or according to manufacturer's instructions. The pumpkin butter can also be frozen in small batches, or simply kept in tightly covered containers in the refrigerator for several weeks.

This makes about 8–10 cups of thick pumpkin butter.
It develops its best flavor after a few days, and I like it served cold,
spooned onto toast or a muffin.

BISCOTTI

Biscotti are very popular now, and seem to be everywhere, from supermarkets and bakeries to tiny shops and coffee bars. Most of the biscotti I've bought have been delicious, and I have no objection to "store-bought," but if they are not easily available where you live, here is a basic recipe, with several variations. It will give you excellent biscotti for a fraction of the price we pay for the fancy packages.

Having a big jar of crisp, almond-studded biscotti on hand is amazingly nice. They can turn an ordinary dish of ice cream or a plate of berries into a fancy dessert, and a cup of coffee into a treat. They keep well, and they're very low in fat—what more could we want?

ALMOND BISCOTTI

2 Tbs. butter	2 eggs
3–3½ cups flour	2 egg whites
1 tsp. baking powder	1 cup sugar
½ tsp. baking soda	½ tsp. almond extract
¼ tsp. salt	½–1 cup chopped almonds

Melt the butter and let it cool to lukewarm. Sift together 3 cups flour with the baking powder, baking soda, and salt.

Beat the eggs and egg whites until foamy. Add the sugar and continue beating until thick and creamy. Beat in the almond extract, the melted butter, and the chopped almonds.

Stir the sifted flour mixture into the beaten eggs, using a wooden spoon—the dough will become too stiff for a beater.

Take half the dough and turn it out on a well-floured board. Sprinkle more flour on top and shape it into a smooth log about 1½ inches in diameter and about 14–15 inches long. You may have to work in a little extra flour if the dough is too soft to hold a shape—that will depend on the size of the eggs—but don't use any more flour than you need to. You will be able to handle the slightly sticky dough if you just keep it well dredged in flour.

Lift the log carefully onto a large baking sheet that is lined with parchment (or oiled, if you don't have parchment). Form another log with the other half of the dough and place it on the baking sheet, at least 4 inches away from the first one. Pat the logs down gently to flatten them just a little.

Bake the logs at 325° for about 25 minutes, or until they feel firm to the touch. Take them out and let them cool for at least 10–15 minutes. Turn the oven temperature down to 275°.

Using a thin, sharp, serrated knife, cut the logs on a diagonal into ½-inch slices. Arrange the slices upright on 2 baking sheets, with space between them for air circulation, and bake them again at 275° for about 40 minutes. Reverse the positions of the baking sheets midway through the baking time to be sure that all the biscotti bake evenly.

Remove the biscotti from the oven and let them cool completely on wire racks. Makes about 4 dozen biscotti. They keep well if packed in airtight tins or jars once they have completely cooled. I've heard that they keep for 3–4 weeks, but I can never keep mine that long.

Anise Biscotti

Add a tablespoon of whole or slightly crushed anise seed to the beaten egg mixture. You can eliminate the almonds if you want to, or leave them for a nice combination of flavors.

Chocolate-Almond Biscotti

Sift ⅓ cup of unsweetened American process cocoa into the flour mixture.

Gingerbread Biscotti

When sifting the dry ingredients, increase baking powder to 1½ tsp., and add 1½ tsp. of ground ginger, 2 tsp. of cinnamon, and a pinch of cloves.

When beating the eggs, use only 1 whole egg, reduce the sugar to ¾ cup, and add ¼ cup of molasses. Eliminate the almond extract. The chopped almonds are optional.

Chocolate-Dipped Biscotti

Melt some excellent bittersweet chocolate carefully in a heavy-bottomed pan, stirring it over very low heat so that it does not scorch.

Dip biscotti into the chocolate, one by one, and lay them on racks or on wax paper until the chocolate hardens. You can dip them halfway, either lengthwise or vertically, for a nice effect. You can also arrange them on wire racks and drizzle the melted chocolate over them from a spoon, making random patterns or zigzags.

The important thing is to allow the chocolate to cool completely before moving the biscotti. This is a slow process. It can take well over 2 hours. You can speed the process by putting the dipped or drizzled biscotti into the refrigerator, but the chocolate will lose its pretty sheen.

Many Other Variations

Once you've made a few batches of biscotti and have gotten the hang of it, you will do your own variations. You can add finely grated lemon or orange zest to the batter, or finely chopped dried fruit, or use hazelnuts instead of almonds, and so on.

I n d e x

Index entries in *italics* refer to menus.

blackberries:
    Berry Cobbler, 62–3
    Cassis Sorbet, 43–4
    Parfaits of Fruit and Mascarpone, 193
Bocconcini di Parma, 356
Boiled Pinto Beans, 33
Borscht, Raspberry, 20
Bowl, Dinner in a, 261
Bowl of Noodles, A, 255
Boysenberry Sauce, 348
    Warm Chocolate Cakes with Crème Anglaise and, 347–8
bread(s), 261
    Bread Stuffing with Apples and Walnuts, 389–90
    Bruschetta with Caramelized Fennel and Onion, 342
    Buttermilk Scones, 310–11
    Cheddar Cheese Straws, 382–3
    Cheese Toasts, 273
    Easter Baba, 376–7
    Fast Buttermilk Yeast Rolls, 251–2
    Garlic Bread, 60–1
    Garlic Crostini, 67
    Herbed Croutons, 190–1
    Honey-Sweetened Buttermilk Cornbread, 111
    Irish Soda Bread, 268–9
    Jalapeño and Cheese Cornbread, 264–5
    Naan, 213–14
    Oat Bread with Maple Syrup, 308
    Pan Bagnia, 14–15
    Panzanella, 95–6
    Parmesan Cheese Toasts, 58
    Parmesan and Rosemary Focaccia, 243
    Pumpernickel Parmesan Toasts, 21
    Rosemary Focaccia, 338–9

bread(s) *(cont.)*
    Semolina Focaccia with Onion and Garlic, 280
    Simple Focaccia, 189
    Three-Grain Cranberry Bread, 309–10
    Toasted Polenta Slices, 266–7
    Toasts with Grilled Chèvre, 173
    Tomato and Onion Batter Bread, 270–1
    Tomato and Onion Focaccia, 353
    see also sandwich(es)
broccoli:
    Broccoli Soup, 233
    Penne with Oyster Mushrooms and Chinese Broccoli, 257–8
Broth, Vegetable, 410–15
    about, 410–11
    Assertive, 415
    Basic Light, 412–13
    Dark, 414
Brown and Wild Rice Pilaf, 150
Brownies, 120
Brunch, Salad Lunches, and Tea, 277–312
Bruschetta with Caramelized Fennel and Onion, 342
buckwheat:
    Buckwheat Crepes, 137
    Buckwheat Crepes with Onions, Apples, and Cheese, 136
    Buckwheat Crepes with Potato and Mushroom Filling, 184
    Buckwheat Crepes with Onions and Apples, 134–40
    Buckwheat Crepes with Wild Mushrooms, 182–5
Bulgur Pilaf with Fennel, Raisins, and Pine Nuts, 131
buttermilk:
    Buttermilk Coffee Cake, 303
    Buttermilk Scones, 310–11

chile(s) *(cont.)*
Corn Crepes with Goat Cheese
Stuffing in Mole Poblano,
203–4
Cornmeal Griddlecakes with
Sweet Chipotle Sauce,
Nopalitos, Crème Fraîche, and
Pine Nuts, 324–5
Cranberry-Jalapeño Sauce, 138
Green Chile and Mint Chutney,
212–13
guajillo, 79
Guajillo Chile Salsa, 31–2
Hot Chipotle Salsa, 128
jalapeño, 78
Jalapeño and Cheese Cornbread,
264–5
Mole Poblano, 204–5
New Mexican, 79
Ortega Chile Potatoes, 300–1
pasilla, 79
Pasilla Chile Paste, 365
poblano, 78–9
Salsa Cruda, 240
salsas, 80–1
serrano, 79
Simple Chipotle Sauce, 247
Stewed Green Tomatoes with Red
Jalapeños, 386–7
Sweet Chipotle Sauce, 326–7
Tamale Pie, 126–7
see also specific chiles
Chili, Black Bean, 11–12
Chilled Orange Slices in Grand
Marnier and Cognac, 199
Chinese Broccoli, Penne with Oyster
Mushrooms and, 257–8
chipotle chile(s), 79
Cornmeal Griddlecakes with
Sweet Chipotle Sauce,
Nopalitos, Crème Fraîche, and
Pine Nuts, 324–5

chipotle chile(s) *(cont.)*
Hot Chipotle Salsa, 128
Simple Chipotle Sauce, 247
Sweet Chipotle Sauce, 326–7
chocolate:
Brownies, 120
Chocolate-Almond Biscotti, 420
Chocolate Caramel Nut Tart,
224–5
Chocolate and Chile Torte, 364–5
Chocolate-Dipped Biscotti, 421
Chocolate-Dipped Macaroons, 18
Chocolate Spongecake, 222–3
Mole Poblano, 204–5
Warm Chocolate Cakes with
Crème Anglaise and
Boysenberry Sauce, 347–8
White Peach Mousse in
Chocolate Collars with
Raspberry Coulis and Fresh
Berries, 327–8
Chopped Egg and Dill Sandwiches,
309
Chowder, Oyster Mushroom, 250–1
Chunky Tomato Sauce, 231
chutney:
Cranberry, 145
Green Chile and Mint, 212–13
Cilantro Filling, Tamales with
Zucchini and, 84–5
Cinco de Mayo Dinner, 82
Cinnamon Custard Ice Cream,
156–7
Clafouti with Apricots, 281
cobbler:
Berry, 62–3
Wild Mushroom, 179–80
coffee:
Cafe de Olla, 88
Cafe de Olla Sorbet, 129
Coffee Flan, 39
Coffee Granita, 285

Crème Fraîche, and Pine Nuts,
Cornmeal Griddlecakes with
Sweet Chipotle Sauce,
Nopalitos, 324–5
crepes:
Bocconcini di Parma, 356
Buckwheat Crepes, 137
Buckwheat Crepes with Onions,
Apples, and Cheese, 136
Buckwheat Crepes with Potato
and Mushroom Filling, 184
Corn Crepes with Goat Cheese
Stuffing in Mole Poblano,
203–4
Crepes with Swiss Chard,
21–2
Crisp, Apple, 176
Crostini, Garlic, 67
Croutons, Herbed, 190–1
Crumble, Apple and Pear, 252–3
cucumber:
Haricots Verts, Red Potato, and
Cucumber Salad, 287–8
Yogurt with Cucumber, Mint,
Raisins, and Nuts, 211–12
Yogurt-Cucumber Dip, 196
Cumin Rice, Garlic and, 86–7
curly endive:
Salad of Curly Endive, Avocado,
Grapefruit, and Fennel,
202
Watercress and Curly Endive
Salad, 138–9
see also endive
Currants and Almonds, Fragrant
Rice Pilaf with, 210–11
custard:
Cinnamon Custard Ice Cream,
156
Crème Anglaise, 70
Warm Chocolate Cakes with

custard *(cont.)*
Crème Anglaise and
Boysenberry Sauce, 347–8
see also flan

Dark Vegetable Broth, 414
desserts, *see* cake(s); caramel; choco-
late; cookies; crepes; flan; ice
cream; sorbet; *specific fruits*;
tart(s); torte(s)
Dill Sandwiches, Chopped Egg and,
309
Dinner in a Bowl, 261
Dinner Parties for Fall and Winter,
Little, 187–225
Dinner Parties for Spring and
Summer, Little, 65–105
dip:
Roasted Eggplant, 100
Yogurt-Cucumber, 196
Dolmades (Stuffed Vine Leaves),
99–100
dressing:
Ginger-Sesame, 401
Sesame Oil, 110

Early Spring Dinner, An, 4–7
Easter Baba, 376–7
Easter Brunch, 367–78
Easy Tea, An, 306–13
egg(s):
Artichoke Frittata, 15–16
Chard and Parsley Frittata, 336–7
Chopped Egg and Dill
Sandwiches, 309
Green Herb Frittata, 61–2
Huevos Mexicanos, 301
Rice Pilaf Frittata, 151
Sweet Corn Soufflé, 362–3

flan *(cont.)*
  Onion and Thyme Flan, 373–4
  Pumpkin Flan, 181
focaccia:
  Parmesan and Rosemary Focaccia,
    243
  Rosemary Focaccia, 338–9
  Semolina Focaccia with Onion
    and Garlic, 280
  Simple Focaccia, 189
  Tomato and Onion Focaccia,
    353
Fondue, Tomato and Garlic, 363
*Formal Dinner Party for Late
  Summer, A,* 357–66
Four Easy Soup Dinners, 262–71
Fragrant Rice Pilaf with Currants
  and Almonds, 210–11
French Soup and Salad Lunch, A,
  286–90
Fresh Basil Pesto, 319
Fresh Cheese with Basil Pesto,
  318–19
Fresh-Chopped Tomatoes with
  Basil, 335–6
Fresh Corn Tamales, 9–10
Fresh Herb Salad, 148
Fresh Pasta, 49–50
Fresh Peach Ice Cream, 26
Fresh Tomato Risotto, 56
frittata:
  Artichoke, 15–16
  Chard and Parsley, 336–7
  Green Herb, 61–2
  Rice Pilaf, 151
Frittata Supper, A, 59–63
fruit(s):
  Fruit Smoothie, 274
  Parfaits of Fruit and Mascarpone,
    193
  Teddy's Fruit Salad, 302–3

fruit(s) *(cont.)*
  Winter Fruit Compote, 185
  see also specific fruits
Fuji Apples, and Pistachio Nuts,
  Salad of Radicchio, 114

Gala Dinner for Late Spring, A,
  316–29
Galette, Plum and Walnut, 151–2
garbanzo bean(s):
  Hummous, 102
  Stewed Garbanzo Beans and
    Potatoes in Indian Spices,
    209–10
garlic:
  Charred Tomatoes with Garlic
    and Olives, 101
  Garlic Bread, 60–1
  Garlic Crostini, 67
  Garlic and Cumin Rice, 86–7
  Greens and Garlic Soup, 265–6
  Mashed Potatoes with Roasted
    Garlic, 391
  Rigatoni with Garlic, Olives, and
    Raw Tomatoes, 260
  Roasted Beet, Asparagus, and
    Garlic Salad, 173–4
  Roasted Green Beans with Garlic,
    220–1
  Roasted Whole Garlic, 159
  Sautéed Spinach and Garlic,
    384–5
  Semolina Focaccia with Onion
    and Garlic, 280
  Spaghetti with Garlic and Oil,
    123
  Spinach, Green Garlic, and
    Mushroom Pie, 370–1
  Tomato and Garlic Fondue,
    363

ice cream *(cont.)*
    Rosemary Sorbet, 345–6
    Strawberry Ice Cream with Triple
        Sec, 296–7
Indian Dinner, An, 207–15
Indian Spices, Stewed Garbanzo
    Beans and Potatoes in, 209–10
Informal Winter Buffet, An, 216–25
Irish Soda Bread, 268–9

jalapeño chile(s), 78
    Cranberry-Jalapeño Sauce, 138
    Jalapeño and Cheese Cornbread,
        264–5
    Salsa Cruda, 240
    Stewed Green Tomatoes with Red
        Jalapeños, 386–7

Kabocha squash:
    Risotto di Zucca, 6–7
    Roasted Autumn Vegetables,
        149–50
    Roasted Kabocha Squash and
        Green Tomatoes, 197

leek(s);
    Leek and Potato Soup, 267–8
    Polenta with Leeks and
        Gorgonzola Garnished with
        Caramelized Fennel and
        Onions, 38
    Pumpkin, Potato, and Leek Soup,
        110–11
Lemon Cheesecake Ice Cream, 293
lentil(s):
    Guillermina's Lentil Soup, 263–4
    Lentil Salad, 17
    Wheat and Lentil Pilaf with
        Shiitake Mushrooms, 74–5

lima bean(s):
    Lima Bean Purée, 351–2
    Lima Bean Soup, 190
Little Dinner Parties for Fall and
    Winter, 187–225
Little Dinner Parties for Spring and
    Summer, 65–105
Lunches, Salad, a Brunch, and Tea,
    277–312

Macaroons, Chocolate–Dipped, 18
mango:
    Orange and Mango Sorbet, 366
    Sorbet, 12
Maple Syrup, Oat Bread with, 308
Marinated Grilled Eggplant, 337–8
mascarpone:
    Honey-Sweetened, 339
    Parfaits of Fruit and, 193
Mashed Potatoes with Roasted
    Garlic, 391
Mazurek, Gypsy, 378–9
Melon Soup with Mint Cream,
    Cold, 68
Meringue Torte, Pineapple, 408–9
Mexican Dinner, A, 8–12
Mezze for Ten, 97–105
Middle Eastern Pilaf Dinner, A, 71–7
Midsummer Dinner, A, 40–4
Mimosas, 300
mint:
    Cold Melon Soup with Mint
        Cream, 68
    Green Chile and Mint Chutney,
        212–13
    Minted Tomato Salad with Feta
        Cheese, 72
    Spa Salad with Bitter Greens,
        Asparagus, and Mint, 5–6
    Yogurt with Cucumber, Mint,
        Raisins, and Nuts, 211–12

Anna Thomas wrote her first cookbook, *The Vegetarian Epicure*, while she was a film student at UCLA, and followed it a few years later with *The Vegetarian Epicure, Book Two*. When she is not cooking, she writes screenplays and produces films. Her screen credits include *My Family, Mi Familia* and *El Norte*, both of which were nominated for an Academy Award. She lives in Ojai, California, with her husband, Gregory Nava, and their two sons.

A Note on the Type

This book was set in a modern adaptation of a type designed by the first William Caslon (1692–1766). The Caslon face, an artistic, easily read type, has enjoyed over two centuries of popularity in our own country. It is of interest to note that the first copies of the Declaration of Independence and the first paper currency distributed to the citizens of the newborn nation were printed in this typeface.

Composed by North Market Street Graphics,
Lancaster, Pennsylvania
Printed and bound by R. R. Donnelley & Sons,
Harrisonburg, Virginia
Designed by Lynette Cortez Design